# Mosaic 1

# Grammar

4th Edition

**Patricia K. Werner**

**Lou Spaventa**

**With contributions by Lida R. Baker, Mary Curran, and Mary McVey Gill**

# McGraw-Hill/Contemporary

*A Division of The **McGraw-Hill** Companies*

Mosaic 1 Grammar, 4th Edition

Published by McGraw-Hill/Contemporary, a business unit of The McGraw-Hill Companies, Inc., 1221 Avenue of the Americas, New York, NY 10020. Copyright © 2002, 1996, 1990, 1985 by The McGraw-Hill Companies, Inc. All rights reserved. No part of this publication may be reproduced or distributed in any form or by any means, or stored in a database or retrieval system, without the prior written consent of The McGraw-Hill Companies, Inc., including, but not limited to, in any network or other electronic storage or transmission, or broadcast for distance learning.

Some ancillaries, including electronic and print components, may not be available to customers outside the United States.

 This book is printed on recycled, acid-free paper containing 10% postconsumer waste.

5 6 7 8 9 0 QPD/QPD 0 9 8 7 6 5 4

ISBN 0-07-232983-1
ISBN 0-07-118022-2 (ISE)

Editorial director: *Tina B. Carver*
Series editor: *Annie Sullivan*
Developmental editor: *Jennifer Monaghan*
Director of marketing and sales: *Thomas P. Dare*
Project manager: *Joyce M. Berendes*
Production supervisor: *Kara Kudronowicz*
Coordinators of freelance design: *Michelle M. Meerdink/David W. Hash*
Cover image: *© Corbis*
Senior photo research coordinator: *Lori Hancock*
Photo research: *Pam Carley/Sound Reach*
Supplement coordinator: *Genevieve Kelley*
Compositor: *Interactive Composition Corporation*
Typeface: *10.5/12 Times Roman*
Printer: *Quebecor World Dubuque, IA*

The credits section for this book begins on page 445 and is considered an extension of the copyright page.

INTERNATIONAL EDITION ISBN 0-07-118022-2
Copyright © 2002. Exclusive rights by The McGraw-Hill Companies, Inc. for manufacture and export. This book cannot be re-exported from the country to which it is sold by McGraw-Hill. The International Edition is not available in North America.

# Mosaic 1    **Grammar**

## Boost your students' academic success!

*Interactions Mosaic, 4th edition* is the newly revised five-level, four-skill comprehensive ESL/EFL series designed to prepare students for academic content. The themes are integrated across proficiency levels and the levels are articulated across skill strands. The series combines communicative activities with skill-building exercises to boost students' academic success.

*Interactions Mosaic, 4th edition* features

- updated content
- five videos of authentic news broadcasts
- expansion opportunities through the Website
- new audio programs for the listening/speaking and reading books
- an appealing fresh design
- user-friendly instructor's manuals with placement tests and chapter quizzes

**In This Chapter** sections show students the grammar points that will be covered in the chapter.

Chapter 6

Money Matters

**IN THIS CHAPTER**

**Part 1**  Count Versus Noncount Nouns
**Part 2**  Indefinite Adjectives and Pronouns
**Part 3**  The Definite Article
**Part 4**  Units of Measurement

## Introduction

In this chapter, you will study some of the uses of noun clauses, including reported speech and embedded questions. You will also study how to reduce these clauses to phrases. Finally, you will review a variety of clauses and other structures covered in the text.

The following passage was written by the noted anthropologist Margaret Mead many years ago, yet its message holds true today. This passage introduces the chapter theme, "Together on a Small Planet," and raises some of the topics and issues you will cover in the chapter.

### Margaret Mead Speaking on the Future of Humanity

I am optimistic by nature. I am glad that I am alive. I am glad that I am living at this particular, very difficult, very dangerous, and very crucial period in human history. To this extent my viewpoint about the future reflects a personal temperamental bent—something that must always be taken into account. But, of course, unsupported optimism is not enough. 5

I support my optimism with my knowledge of how far mankind has come. Throughout the hundreds of thousands of years that human life has evolved, at first physically and later culturally, human beings have withstood tremendous changes and have adjusted to radically new demands. What we have to realize, I believe, is that human ingenuity, imagination, and faith in life itself have been 10 crucial both in initiating changes and in meeting new demands imposed by change.

As an anthropologist I also have seen how a living generation of men born into a Stone Age culture has moved into a modern world all at once, skipping the many small steps by which mankind as a whole moved from the distant past into 15 the present.

I find these things encouraging. An earlier generation invented the idea of invention. Now we have invented the industrialization of invention—a way of meeting a recognized problem by setting hundreds of trained persons together to work out solutions and, equally important, to work out the means of putting solutions 20 into practice.

This is what made it possible to send men to the moon and to begin the exploration of outer space. This should give us reason to believe also that we can meet the interlocking problems of runaway populations, war, and the pollution of the earth on which we depend for life. None of these problems is 25 insoluble.

What we need is the will to demand solutions and the patience to learn how to carry them out.

Margaret Mea

**Discussing Ideas.** What do you believe about the future of our world? Ar optimistic, as Mead was? Or are you pessimistic? Why?

---

**Introduction** sections introduce both the theme and the grammar points that will be covered in the chapter.

**Discussing Ideas** questions reinforce students' understanding of the topics through comprehension questions and encourage students to express themselves.

---

**PART 5**

## Past Verb Forms: The Past Perfect Tense; The Past Perfect Continuous Tense

### Setting the Context

**Prereading Questions**   All over the world, people have been moving from rural areas into the cities. What effects has this migration had?

### The Urbanization of America

Like much of the world, the United States did not develop large urban centers until this century. Before World War I, the majority of Americans had lived in rural areas or in small towns. In 1900, for example, over 40 percent of the U.S. population lived or worked on farms.

World War I and the Depression of the 1930s changed American life dramatically. By 1930, for example, the farm population had dropped to 30.1 percent. During the Depression, over three-quarters of a million farmers lost their land. As individuals and entire families moved to cities in search of work, urban areas grew tremendously. Today, almost 80 percent of Americans live in metropolitan areas. 10

This migration from rural to urban areas has had a great impact on American society, just as it has in many parts of the world. In general, people in urban areas are more mobile and more independent, families are less stable, and friendships are often short-lived. Although cities may offer greater economic opportunities, they also present many difficulties in maintaining "the ties that bind": close, long- 15 term relationships with family and friends.

---

**Setting the Context** activities introduce key vocabulary and further familiarize students with the chapter theme. Introductory activities include model conversations, readings, class discussions, prediction activities, previewing, and pair interviews.

**Prereading Questions** encourage students to share what they know about the topic before they read.

## A. Indefinite Adjectives and Pronouns with Both Count and Noncount Nouns

Indefinite adjectives such as *some*, *many*, and *little* are used with nouns instead of giving specific amounts. Indefinite pronouns such as *some*, *someone*, *any*, and *anyone* replace nouns. Certain expressions work with both count and noncount nouns: *any*, *some*, *a lot (of)*, *lots (of)*, *plenty (of)*, *no*, and *none*. Compare the following:

|  | Indefinite Adjectives | Indefinite Pronouns |
|---|---|---|
| **Count Nouns** | Do you have **any** dollar bills? | I don't have **any**. |
| | Jack has **some** dollar bills. | Jack has **some**. |
| | Harry has **a lot of** dollar bills. | Harry has **a lot**. |
| | I have **no** dollar bills. | I have **none**. |
| **Noncount Nouns** | Do you have **any** money? | Do you have **any**? |
| | Jack has **some** money. | Jack has **some**. |
| | Harry has **a lot of** money. | Harry has **a lot**. |
| | I have **no** money. | I have **none**. |

Note: In formal English, none is always followed by a singular verb: None of the people has arrived. (formal) None of the people have arrived. (informal)

 **1**  **Rapid Oral Practice.**  In pairs, ask and answer questions using these cues and words such as *some*, *any*, and *a lot (of)*.

**Examples:**  homework tonight
    A:  **Do you have any homework tonight?**
    B:  **Yes, I have some homework.**
    money
    A:  **Do you have some money?**
    B:  **No, I don't have any.**

1. cash
2. checks
3. credit cards
4. interesting news (about . . .)
5. information about good dentists (doctors, therapists, and so on)
6. assignments tonight
7. free time today
8. advice (about . . .)
9. change
10. coins

## B. (A) Few and (Not) Many with Count Nouns

| Examples | Meanings | Notes |
|---|---|---|
| How **many** (dollars) do you have? | | Few, a few, many, and not |
| I have **a few** (dollars). | I have some dollars, but not a lot. | many are used with count nouns. Many can be used |
| I **don't** have **many** dollar bills. | I have only a small number of dollars, probably not enough. | in affirmative statements, but it is more common in questions with how and in |
| I have **few** dollar bills. | I probably don't have enough. | negative statements. |

---

**Grammar explanations and charts** provide clear, easy to understand, and visually appealing grammar presentations.

**Pairwork** activities encourage students to personalize and practice the target language.

**Using What You've Learned** provides students with opportunities to do less structured, more communicative activities.

**Groupwork** activities maximize opportunities for discussion.

**Video news broadcasts** immerse students in authentic language, complete with scaffolding and follow-up activities.

---

### Using What You've Learned

 **4**  Briefly tell or write a short autobiography. Be sure to include any important events from the past and present, and any plans for the future. You may answer some of these questions: When and where were you born? Where did you live while you were growing up? Where did you go to school? What did you study? Have you ever worked? What are you doing now? What special hobbies or interests do you have? What are some of your plans for the future?

If you choose to tell your autobiography, work in small groups and take turns. When one person finishes, the other group members may ask questions if they have any.

If you choose to write, write three paragraphs—one each for past, present, and future events. When you finish, exchange autobiographies with another classmate.

 **5**  In small groups, take turns talking about your own experiences learning a new language or adjusting to life in a new culture. Share some of your stories—funny ones, sad ones, embarrassing ones, happy ones. Later, write your story and, if possible, make a class collection of "memorable moments" you have had.

### Video Activities: An Exchange Student

**Before You Watch.**  Discuss these questions in small groups.

1. What is an exchange student?
2. What problems do you think exchange students might have?

**Watch.**  Check all the correct answers.

1. Where is Adáh from?
    a. the United States    b. Switzerland    c. Turkey

2. Circle the kinds of problems that exchange students and their families sometimes have
    a. money    b. chores
    c. studying    d. cultural/language problems

3. What kind of problem did Adáh have?
    a. Her homestay sister was jealous of her.
    b. She had to share the computer.
    c. She didn't have a good social life.

4. Who was Adáh's best friend?
    a. Jeli    b. Corey    c. her date

5. What happened to Adáh's best friend?
    a. She got sick.    b. She had a car accident.    c. She went home.

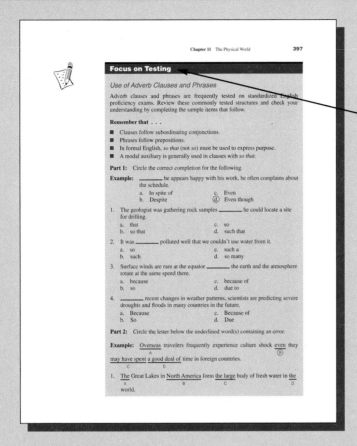

**Focus on Testing** helps students prepare for academic exams and standardized tests, such as the TOEFL.

Don't forget to check out the new *Interactions Mosaic* Website at www.mhcontemporary.com/interactionsmosaic.

- Traditional practice and interactive activities
- Links to student and teacher resources
- Cultural activities
- Focus on Testing
- Activities from the Website are also provided on CD-ROM

# Mosaic 1   Grammar

# Chapter 1

# New Challenges

# Introduction

Chapter 1 is a review chapter. It covers some basic structures and grammatical terms, and it looks at some special challenges involved in learning a new language and adjusting to life in a new culture. While you are reviewing the grammar topics in the chapter, you will have a chance to get to know more about your classmates' ideas and backgrounds.

The following passage introduces the chapter theme, "New Challenges," and raises some of the topics and issues you will cover in the chapter.

---

### Studying a New Language and Culture

Learning to communicate in another language can be very difficult and frustrating at times, but it can also be one of the most rewarding experiences of your life. Being able to communicate in another language will open doors for you to experience a world of new people, places, and ideas. It will offer you a look at cultures from every part of the earth. And if you have the opportunity to live in another   5
culture, the experience will show you many things—above all, about your own culture. It will reveal cultural similarities and differences that you had never noticed in the past. In addition, the experience can also show you a great deal about your own personal beliefs, attitudes, and perceptions. Within a short time in another culture, you will find that you begin to learn a great deal about yourself and your   10
own country and culture.

---

**Getting to Know Your Class**   Learning always involves asking questions. Why not begin by finding out a little about your classmates? Talk with three classmates to gather the information in the following chart. You can write the information in the chart, or you can use a piece of paper.

| Name | Hometown and Native Language | Family | Interests (Sports, Hobbies, etc.) | Something Special |
|---|---|---|---|---|
|  |  |  |  |  |
|  |  |  |  |  |
|  |  |  |  |  |

Use some of these questions and create others.

What's your name?                         What do you like to do . . . ?
Where are you from?                       Which sports . . . ?
What country . . . ?                      What hobbies . . . ?
What language . . . ?                     What's something special about you?
Do you have a big family?                 Do you do anything unusual?
How many . . . ?                          Do you have . . . ?

| **PART 1** | # Review of Basic Sentence Structure |

## Setting the Context

**Prereading Questions**   You are going to read a passage by a student from Switzerland who spent time studying English in the United States. What effects do you think this experience may have had on him?

### How My American Stay Affected Me

When I left Switzerland, my life changed completely. I had not known what I should expect or how I would be affected in education, sophistication, and personality through my stay in the United States. Coming from a small country and not having 5 traveled outside of Europe, I was not exactly what people would call a sophisticated man. Now I believe that I am a little more aware. Not only did I learn about the United States, but I also learned tremendously about other fascinating cultures. 10 Most of all, I learned to understand and to accept other cultures. Living in a new country and learning about new cultures has been, I believe, the most important experience in my life.

Daniel Pfister

**Discussing Ideas.**   Write three things you expected before beginning your English studies. Then choose a partner. Take turns discussing your expectations. Have your experiences been different from your expectations? If so, how?

## A. Parts of Speech

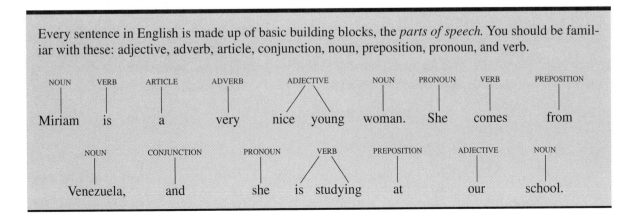

Every sentence in English is made up of basic building blocks, the *parts of speech.* You should be familiar with these: adjective, adverb, article, conjunction, noun, preposition, pronoun, and verb.

| NOUN | VERB | ARTICLE | ADVERB | ADJECTIVE | | NOUN | PRONOUN | VERB | PREPOSITION |
|------|------|---------|--------|-----------|--|------|---------|------|-------------|
| Miriam | is | a | very | nice | young | woman. | She | comes | from |

| | NOUN | CONJUNCTION | PRONOUN | VERB | PREPOSITION | ADJECTIVE | NOUN |
|--|------|-------------|---------|------|-------------|-----------|------|
| | Venezuela, | and | she | is studying | at | our | school. |

## B. Kinds of Sentences

A sentence is a group of words that expresses a complete idea. There are four kinds of sentences. Each includes at least one subject and one verb. The chart gives some examples.

|  | **Examples** | **Notes** |
|---|---|---|
| **Questions** | What is your name?<br>Are you a student? | A question asks for information or for a "yes" or "no." |
| **Statements** | My name is Miriam.<br>That's a beautiful name. | A statement gives information or opinions. |
| **Exclamations** | What a lovely name you have!<br>We won the World Cup! | An exclamation expresses surprise, pleasure, or other emotions. |
| **Commands** | (you) Tell me about yourself.<br>Have a seat, please. | A command tells what to do. The subject "you" is understood. |

**1**  Tell whether these sentences are questions, statements, exclamations, or commands. Identify the part of speech of each italicized word.

                  *noun verb*

**Examples:**  My *name is* Rudi.    *(statement)*

                     *pronoun*

           What's *yours?*    *(question)*

1. *My* name *is* Anton.
2. Tell *me* your *last* name.
3. If *you* really *want* to know, it's Boxrucker.
4. What *an unusual* name you *have!*
5. Are you *from Switzerland?*
6. I've *always* wanted to go *there,* but I've *never had the opportunity.*
7. Switzerland is *a beautiful, mountainous* country *in* the heart *of* Europe.
8. The *capital* is Bern, *and its other* important cities *are* Geneva and Zurich.
9. Are the *Swiss* Alps *an* old *or a relatively* young *mountain range?*
10. How *beautiful they* are!

## C. Subjects

The subject is normally the most important person, place, thing, or idea in the sentence. Subjects can take several forms: nouns, pronouns, phrases, and clauses.

|  | **Examples** | **Notes** |
|---|---|---|
| **Noun or Pronoun** | **Miriam** comes from Venezuela.<br>**She** is from Caracas. | A noun names a person, place, thing, or idea. Pronouns replace nouns. |
| **Phrase** | **Many Venezuelan students** are studying in the United States.<br>**To study in the United States** can be expensive.<br>**Studying in the United States** can be expensive. | A phrase is a group of related words.<br>Infinitive (*to* + simple form) or gerund (*ing* form) phrases can be used as subjects. These and other verb forms are covered in Chapter 7. |
| **Clause** | **How long they stay in the United States** depends on many things. | A clause is a group of related words that includes a subject and a verb. Dependent clauses are covered in Chapters 8 to 12. |

## D. Verbs, Objects, and Complements

Some verbs tell what the subject does. These verbs can be transitive or intransitive. Intransitive verbs do not have objects, but transitive verbs *must* have objects. Other verbs are linking verbs; they connect the subject to the complement. A complement is a noun, pronoun, adjective, phrase, verb form, phrase, or clause that describes the subject. Common linking verbs include *be, appear, become, feel, get* (when it means *become*), *look, seem, smell, sound,* and *taste.* The chart gives some examples.

|  | **Examples** | **Notes** |
|---|---|---|
| **Intransitive Vebs** | Miriam **travels** often. | An intransitive verb is complete without an object. |
| **Transitive Verbs and Objects** | When she travels, she always **buys** souvenirs. | A transitive verb *must* have an object. It is incomplete without one. |
| **Direct Object** | She bought her daughter **a sweater.** | Direct objects answer the questions *who(m)?* or *what?* |
| **Indirect Object** | She bought **her daughter** a sweater. | Indirect objects answer the questions *to/for who(m)?* or *what?* |
| **Linking Verbs and Complements** | Miriam **is** a lawyer.<br>She **seems** happy with her work.<br>It **appears** to be a very interesting job. | Linking verbs are followed by complements: information that describes the subject. Remember that adverbs cannot be used as complements after linking verbs.<br>Example:<br>Correct: *He seems happy.*<br>Incorrect: *He seems happily.* |

**2**   Find the subjects, verbs, objects, and/or complements in the following sentences. Underline each subject once and each verb twice. Circle objects or complements.

**Example:**   Every year, thousands of foreign students begin (university studies) in North America.

1.   Most of these students have studied some English before coming to an English-speaking country.
2.   Many already read and write English fairly well.
3.   A major difficulty for all new students, however, is to understand and speak English.
4.   Making phone calls or understanding directions can be difficult.
5.   Many Americans use a lot of slang.
6.   Each part of the country has variations in vocabulary and pronunciation.
7.   Nevertheless, after the first few weeks, most new students will notice tremendous improvement.
8.   All of a sudden, English becomes a lot clearer and easier!

## E. Pronouns and Possessive Adjectives

| Subject Pronouns | I | you | he | she | it | we | they |
|---|---|---|---|---|---|---|---|
| Object Pronouns | me | you | him | her | it | us | them |
| Possessive Adjectives | my | your | his | her | its | our | their |
| Possessive Pronouns | mine | yours | his | hers | its | ours | theirs |
| Reflexive Pronouns | myself | yourself yourselves | himself | herself | itself | ourselves | themselves |

**3**   Work alone or with a partner. Identify the italicized word or words in each sentence. Each is a pronoun. Tell what kind of pronoun each word is.

**Example:**   Communicating in *your* first language is easier than communicating in a second language.
   **Your** *is a possessive adjective.*

1.   Daniel had a little trouble speaking in *his* second language, English.
2.   After a few months, *he* gained confidence and *his* fluency increased.
3.   *I* wish it had been the same for *me*.
4.   Sometimes *I* ask *myself* if *I* will ever learn a second language well.
5.   Gary started studying Korean a year after *me,* but *his* Korean is much more fluent than *mine*.
6.   When *we* meet, Gary says, "Wow! *Your* language has really improved."
7.   "*My* Korean will never sound like *yours,*" *I* tell *him*.
8.   "Nonsense! People learn at *their* own speed," Gary tells *me*.
9.   "*You* are just better at language than *I* am. Admit *it*."
10.   "Well, neither one of *us* will ever sound like a real Korean. *Our* Korean will sound a lot alike in the end, but *it* will never sound like *theirs*—true Korean."

**4**   Complete the following sentences by using appropriate pronoun forms.

**Example:**   When we communicate, each of ____us____ speaks two distinct languages.

1.   We express _____ with _____ bodies as well as with _____ words.

2.   People's movements often communicate more than _____ words.

3.   Each culture has _____ own body language.

4.   Arabs often move very close when _____ want to communicate.

5.   A Japanese woman will tilt _____ head to the side when _____ is confused or puzzled.

6.   Germans may feel uncomfortable when someone stands or sits close to _____ .

7.   When an American businessperson is doing business, _____ tries to keep eye contact with _____ client.

8.   You can learn more about _____ own body language by observing _____ as _____ talk with others.

## F. Sentence Types

Sentences can be simple, compound, complex, or a combination of compound and complex.

| | Examples | Notes |
|---|---|---|
| **Simple** | Sukariati arrived from Indonesia last week. Sukariati's sister and brother are living here now. Her cousin wanted to come, too, but couldn't. | A simple sentence has at least one subject and one verb. A simple sentence can have a compound subject. A simple sentence can have a compound verb. |
| **Compound** | Sukariati began her classes yesterday, and she likes them a lot. | Compound sentences are sentences joined by a comma and a conjunction: *and, but, for, nor, or, so,* or *yet.* |
| **Complex** | Muljati, who is originally from Jakarta, has lived in the United States for some time. She chose to live in California because she liked the climate. | Complex sentences are sentences joined by connecting words such as *who, that, because, after, while,* and so on. These are covered in Chapters 8 to 12. |

**5**   Label the subject(s) and verb(s) in each of the following sentences. Tell whether the sentences are simple, compound, or complex. If the sentence is compound or complex, circle the connecting word.

**Examples:**

     V    S    V

     Have you met Kunio Takahashi? *simple sentence*

     S    V

     Kunio is one of the most interesting people (whom)

     S    V

     I have met here. *complex sentence*

1. My friend Kunio is from Tokyo, Japan.
2. He has studied English in Canada for a year, and now he hopes to study veterinary science.
3. Because Kunio wants to study both English and veterinary science, he has applied to schools in Canada and Australia.
4. Is he working on an undergraduate or a graduate degree?
5. Kunio already has his bachelor's degree.
6. He will get his master's degree, and then he will begin a doctoral program.
7. What did he study as an undergraduate?
8. I'm not really sure.
9. Why don't you ask him when you see him again?
10. He's so busy enjoying Canadian life that I never see him!

**6**   **Error Analysis.**   Indicate whether the following 12 items are complete or incomplete sentences. If the sentence is incomplete, tell what is missing and add words to correct it.

**Example:**   Learning a new language.

     *Incomplete. It needs a subject and a complete verb.*
     *She is learning a new language.*

     *Or:*   *It needs a verb and a complement.*
     *Learning a new language is challenging.*

1. Is difficult to adjust to a new culture.
2. Learning a new language can be frustrating.
3. Many people confused because of all the new vocabulary.
4. Body language is different from culture to culture.
5. The experience of life in a new country very exciting.
6. Another language will open doors for you.
7. To experience a world of new people, places, and ideas.
8. Cultures from every part of the earth.
9. Think about the similarities and differences across cultures.
10. The experience can show you a great deal.
11. You will learn a lot.
12. You will meet.

## Using What You've Learned

**7** Get into groups and reread the passage "How My American Stay Affected Me" on page 3. Take a few minutes to discuss the ideas and then analyze the passage. Find the subject(s) and verb(s) in each sentence. Then choose one or two sentences and label the parts of speech in each.

**8** Get into groups and read the following passage together. First, discuss the ideas in the passage and your opinions about them. Then, analyze the passage. Find the subject(s) and verb(s) in each sentence. Note whether the sentences are simple, compound, or complex.

---

### New Cultures

Culture hides much more than it reveals. Strangely enough, what it hides, it hides most effectively from its own members. Years of study have convinced me that the real job is not to understand foreign culture but to understand our own. I am also sure that all you ever get from studying foreign culture is a token* understanding. The ultimate reason for such study is to learn more about your own system. The   5
best reason for experiencing foreign ways is to generate a sense of vitality and awareness—an interest in life that can come only when you live through the shock of contrast and difference.

---

Adapted from Edward T. Hall, *The Silent Language*, p. 30

---

**PART 2** # Word Order of Modifiers

## Setting the Context

**Prereading Questions**    In English, word order is important. Is word order important in your first language? How does it differ from English word order? As you read the following passage, think about your first language.

*\*Token* superficial, not in-depth.

---

### Order

The laws of order are those regularities that govern changes in meaning when order changes. "The cat caught the mouse" means something obviously different from "The mouse caught the cat." Order is used differently in different languages and cultures. While order is of major importance on the sentence level in English, this is not the case in some languages.

    Order also has great importance in other parts of cultural systems besides language: order of birth, order of arrival, order in line to get tickets. Order applies to the courses of a meal. Consider what it would be like to start dinner with dessert, then switch to potatoes, hors d'oeuvre,* coffee, salad, and end with meat!

**5**

---

Adapted from Hall, pp. 132–133

**Discussing Ideas.**   Work in pairs or small groups. Take turns comparing your first language to English. Can you give some specific examples of how word order differs?

## A. Adjectives

One or more adjectives can modify a noun. Usually, no more than three or four adjectives are used to describe the same noun. The chart gives examples of the usual order of some descriptive adjectives.

| Number | Quality or Characteristic | Size | Shape | Age | Color | Origin | Noun |
|---|---|---|---|---|---|---|---|
| a | beautiful | | | new | green | Italian | suit |
| three | | big | long | | red | | pencils |
| some | expensive | | | old | | oriental | carpets |
| five | different | small | round | | gold | | rings |

## B. Adverbs

Adverbs modify verbs and adjectives. Many adverbs are formed by adding -*ly* to related adjectives (*quick* → *quickly*). In general, adverbs cannot come between a verb and a direct object.

| | Subject | Verb | Object | Adverb | Adjective (Complement) |
|---|---|---|---|---|---|
| **Modifying Verbs** | Our teacher | speaks | | **slowly.** | |
| | They | answered | the question | **quickly.** | |
| | I | drank | the hot tea | **politely.** | |
| **Modifying Adjectives** | John | is | | **very** | tired. |
| | The test | was | | **extremely** | difficult. |
| | Linda | seems | | **terribly** | unhappy. |

*hors d'oeuvre* (French) appetizers, small snacks before a meal.

Some adverbs are used to express time or frequency. These usually come after the verb *be* or the first auxiliary verb, but before the main verb. In questions, they usually come after the subject. Other expressions come at the beginning or end of sentences. The following chart gives some examples.

| | **Subject and Auxiliary Verb or *Be*** | **Adverb** | **Main Verb (+ Object or Complement)** | **Adverb, Phrase, or Clause** |
|---|---|---|---|---|
| **Adverbs of Time** | Mr. Jones was<br>Dr. Gill will<br>I will | | sick<br>give the test<br>see you | **yesterday.**<br>**today.**<br>**tomorrow.** |
| **Adverbs of Frequency** | We are<br>The train<br>I have<br>Do you | **seldom**<br>**always**<br>**never**<br>**usually** | late<br>leaves<br>been good<br>study English | to class.<br>on time.<br>at math.<br>at home? |

*Note:* See Chapters 2 and 3 for more information on adverbs of frequency and other time expressions.

## C. Adverbials

Adverbials are words or groups of words that act like adverbs—that is, they modify verbs and adjectives. The chart gives some examples. Notice the word order of the different adverbials.

| **Subject** | **Auxiliary Verb** | **Main Verb** | **Indirect Object** | **Direct Object** | **Adverbial of Direction/ Place** | **Adverbial of Manner** | **Adverbial of Frequency/ Time** |
|---|---|---|---|---|---|---|---|
| The men | | ride | | | | on the bus | every day. |
| We | | carried | | our books | to school | in backpacks | this morning. |
| Bob | | brought | me | those shoes | from Italy | | last summer. |
| You | can | go | | | to work | by train | on weekdays. |
| I | couldn't | speak | | Spanish | | fluently | until this year. |

**1**  Add the information in parentheses to the following sentences.

**Example:**  Traveling is an amazing experience. (in foreign countries, always)
*Traveling in foreign countries is always an amazing experience.*

1. Travel can be tiring but rewarding. (very, extremely)
2. You will learn about cultures. (a great deal, foreign)
3. The problem is the language. (most, difficult, often)
4. Travelers who don't speak the language have difficulties. (sometimes, in foreign countries)
5. It is easier if you speak the language. (much, of the country, fluently)
6. If you don't speak the language, however, it is helpful to know some words and phrases. (fluently, extremely, useful)

7. Travel guides to foreign countries have sections that list words and phrases. (usually, special, important)

8. People in foreign countries are happy even if you only try to speak a few words. (usually, very, of their language)

**2** Circle the correct word from each pair to complete the following paragraph. As you make each choice, think about why the other possibility is wrong. The first one is done as an example.

### Distance and Communication

In interpersonal (communicate/(communication)), people in almost every culture
                                        1

recognize four (different/differently) distances: intimate, personal, (society/social),
                          2                                                    3

and public. Intimate distance occurs in a very (close/closely) relationship such as
                                                         4

between a mother and a child. Personal distance lets good friends talk closely but

(comfortable/comfortably). Social distance is used at parties or other gatherings.
         5

Public distance (concerns/concerning) more formal situations such as between a
                          6

teacher and a student.

These (fourth/four) types of distance exist in all countries, but the amount of dis-
              7

tance (usual/usually) depends on the culture. At a party, for example, a Canadian
              8

may sit several feet away from you, while (a/an) Arab may sit very near you.
                                                   9

(Your/Yours) awareness of the other (culture/culture's) use of distance can often help
        10                                           11

you communicate better with (its/it's) people.
                                        12

**3** **Error Analysis.** The following sentences have errors in word order. Find the errors and correct them, as in the example.

**Example:**   Many North Americans speak rapidly English.
            *Correction: Many North Americans speak English rapidly.*

1. It is difficult often to understand Americans.
2. That Italian new student has with English some problems.
3. He went yesterday to a restaurant, but he couldn't understand the waiter.
4. The waiter spoke very rapidly English.
5. The student ate at the restaurant a hamburger.
6. He paid money too much.
7. The waiter realized this and returned immediately the money to the student.
8. Some people always are honest, but other people take frequently advantage of situations like that.

9. Problems with communication interpersonal can from speaking come, but they can come from also differences in body language.

10. The gesture Italian for "Come here" looks exactly almost like the gesture North American for "Good-bye."

**4** Work with a partner. Make complete sentences by putting the following groups of words in correct order. The first word in each sentence is capitalized.

**Example:** important / of / our / Our / part / bodies / an / are / language
*Our bodies are an important part of our language.*

1. expressions / often / Our / people / a / deal / facial / tell / great
2. contact / important / also / Gestures / are / eye / and
3. cultures / use / frequently / some / very / gestures / in / People
4. from / only / them / People / occasionally / North / use / America
5. look / people's / into / some / cultures / People / from / directly / other / eyes
6. Americans / other / not / keep / contact / North / with / constant / do / eye / people

## Using What You've Learned

**5** The following paragraph is incomplete. Add your own descriptive words or phrases.

Visiting a(n) _____ country can be a(n) _____ experience. Sometimes there are _____ problems, especially with _____. People _____ have difficulties because _____. They may feel _____, or they may become _____

_____

_____

**6** Have you had any problems understanding the body language of people from other cultures? Have you misunderstood someone's gestures or facial expressions? Write a short paragraph about your experience. Include as much description as you can. When you finish writing, exchange papers with another student. How were your experiences similar or different?

**7** 1. Test your skill at "reading" body language! With a partner, visit a place where you can observe people. Choose two or more people in a group to watch. Stay far enough away that you cannot hear the people's conversation and try not to let them know you are watching. Notice their physical appearance and body language—their gestures, facial expressions, posture, their physical distance from each other, and so on. What can you guess about the people?

2. Each partner should complete a chart like the on on page 14. (Add more information if you like.) After you have finished, compare your charts. Are your guesses the same?

|  | Person 1 | Person 2 | Person 3 |
|---|---|---|---|
| Male or female |  |  |  |
| Approximate age |  |  |  |
| Occupation |  |  |  |
| Level of education |  |  |  |
| Current mood (sad, happy, angry, and so on) |  |  |  |
| General personality type (talkative, outgoing, quiet, shy, stubborn, modest, conceited, and so on) |  |  |  |
| What is the relationship of this person to the other(s)? |  |  |  |
| Why did you make these guesses? What gave you clues? |  |  |  |

3.   In class, form small groups and talk about your experiences. How many different kinds of body language did you notice? Did people interpret this body language the same way?

**8**   In pairs or small groups, role-play one or more of the following situations. You can also create additional situations if you wish. As you talk, try to give as much description as possible: shape, size, color, height, weight, and so on.

1.   You've just arrived at an international airport in the United States. You have been waiting at the baggage claim for your luggage, but nothing has arrived. Go to the baggage claim counter and ask for help. Describe your luggage and the contents in detail.

2.   You are at an international airport in Canada. You are supposed to meet the sister of your friend and drive her into the city. You can't find anyone who looks like her. Talk to the airline personnel and ask for help. Describe your friend's sister in detail.

3.   You left your jacket at school during orientation, and you are trying to find it. You have gone to the lost and found to ask for help. Describe your jacket in detail.

4.   You bought a car soon after arriving in Australia. You parked it downtown while you were shopping. Your car (and its contents) has been stolen. You have gone to the police for help. Describe your car and all the things that were in it in detail.

 **9** Write two or three sentences. Your sentences don't have to be long, but they should use as many descriptive words as possible. For example, "Late yesterday afternoon, I bought a fascinating new English grammar book." Or "On most weekends, I usually stay up extremely late at night." Give your sentences to your teacher to correct. Then, print each corrected sentence neatly on a piece of paper. Cut each sentence into words or phrases, and put the sentences in an envelope. Finally, work in pairs or groups. Trade "cut up" sentences and then try to reassemble the sentences in correct order.

**PART 3**

# The Principal Parts of Verbs and Verb Tense Formation

## Setting the Context

**Prereading Questions**   What is culture? How much does our culture influence us? Edward Hall says that the most basic and obvious parts of our culture are often the parts that influence us the most. As you read the following passage, try to decide what he means by this. What are some of the most basic parts of your culture? Do they influence you a great deal?

---

### What Is Culture?

Cultures are extraordinarily complex, much more so than TV sets, automobiles, or possibly even human physiology. So how does one go about learning the underlying structure of culture? Looking at any of the basic systems in a culture is a good place to start—business, marriage and the family, social organization—any will do.                                                                                        5

Culture is humanity's medium; there is not one aspect of human life that is not touched and altered by culture. This means personality, how people express themselves (including shows of emotion), the way they drink, how they move, how problems are solved, how their cities are planned and laid out, how transportation systems are organized and function, as well as how economic and government   10 systems are put together and function. However, it is frequently the most obvious and taken-for-granted and therefore the least studied aspects of culture that influence behavior in the deepest and most subtle ways.

---

Adapted from Edward T. Hall, *Beyond Culture,* p. 106

**Discussing Ideas.**   In the first paragraph, Edward Hall gives three examples of basic cultural systems: business, marriage and the family, and social organization. Discuss one of these examples (or one of your own) with another classmate. Compare two cultures in the areas of business, marriage, the family, and so on. What do you think is the biggest difference between these two cultures?

## A. The Principal Parts of Verbs

All tenses and other verb constructions are formed from the five principal parts of the verbs.

| Infinitive | Simple Form | Past Form | Past Participle | Present Participle |
|---|---|---|---|---|
| to walk | walk | walked | walked | walking |
| to play | play | played | played | playing |
| to run | run | ran | run | running |
| to write | write | wrote | written | writing |
| to be | be | was/were | been | being |
| to do | do | did | done | doing |
| to have | have | had | had | having |

The modal auxiliaries—*can, could, may, might, must, ought to, shall, should, will,* and *would*—are not included here because each has only *one* form, the simple form. (See Chapter 4.)

## B. Verb Tense Formation: Regular Verbs

| | Examples | | | Notes |
|---|---|---|---|---|
| **Simple Form** | COMMANDS<br>Stand!<br>Be seated! | SIMPLE PRESENT<br>I walk.<br>She walks. | SIMPLE FUTURE<br>I will walk.<br>She will walk. | The simple form is used to form commands, the simple present tense, and the simple future tense. It is also used with modal auxiliaries. |
| **Past Form** | REGULAR VERBS<br>I walked.<br>She walked. | | | The past form is used for the simple past tense. Regular verbs are the simple form + -ed. |
| **Past Participle** | PRESENT PERFECT<br>I have walked.<br>She has walked. | PAST PERFECT<br>I had walked.<br>She had walked. | FUTURE PERFECT<br>I will have walked.<br>She will have walked. | The past participle is used to form the present, past, and future perfect tenses and all passive voice forms. |
| **Present Participle** | PRESENT CONTINUOUS<br>I am resting.<br>She is resting.<br>We are resting.<br><br>PRESENT PERFECT CONTINUOUS<br>I have been resting.<br>She has been resting. | PAST CONTINUOUS<br>I was resting.<br>She was resting.<br>We were resting.<br><br>PAST PERFECT CONTINUOUS<br>I had been resting.<br>She has been resting. | FUTURE CONTINUOUS<br>I will be resting.<br>She will be resting.<br>We will be resting.<br><br>FUTURE PERFECT CONTINUOUS<br>I will have been resting.<br>She will have been resting. | The present participle is used with the verb *be* to form all continuous tenses. |

*Pronunciation Notes*

The *-s* ending is pronounced three ways, according to the ending of the verb:

| | |
|---|---|
| /iz/ after *-ch, -sh, -s, -x,* and *-z* endings. | *Examples:* teaches, washes, kisses, boxes, buzzes |
| /s/ after voiceless endings: *p, t, k,* or *f.* | *Examples:* stops, hits, looks, laughs |
| /z/ after voiced consonant endings. | *Examples:* calls, listens, plays, sounds, runs |

The *-ed* ending is pronounced three ways, according to the ending of the verb:

| | |
|---|---|
| /id/ after *-d* and *-t* endings. | *Examples:* needed, insisted, waited, wanted |
| /t/ after voiceless endings. | *Examples:* boxed, helped, looked, watched, washed |
| /d/ after voiced endings. | *Examples:* carried, breathed, called, climbed, played, listened |

Spelling note: See Appendix 2 for spelling rules for adding *-s, -ed,* and *-ing.*

**1**  Change the following sentences to the singular. Add *a* or *an* and change pronouns when necessary. Use *his* or *her* instead of *their*. If you do this activity orally, give the spelling of the singular verbs. Notice the different ways the *-s* ending is pronounced.

**Example:**  Children begin to learn about culture at an early age.
*A child begins to learn about culture at an early age.*

1. Children pick up cultural rules quickly.
2. Children rely on their parents.
3. Children watch and imitate their parents.
4. Parents convey a great deal nonverbally, as well as with words.
5. Children also pay attention to their close relatives, such as grandparents, aunts, or uncles.
6. Children learn their society's rules of time, distance, and order.
7. For example, American parents teach children promptness.
8. If children miss the bus, they get to school late.
9. Eventually, the children try to be on time.
10. At first, children usually do things in the same ways as their loved ones.
11. As children grow older, their peer groups become very important to them.
12. Children start to imitate their peers more and more.

**2**  Fill in the blanks with the past tense of the verbs in parentheses to complete the passage. If you do this activity orally, give the spelling of each past tense form. Notice the different ways the *-ed* ending is pronounced.

1. Margaret Mead _studied_ (study) island people in the South Pacific.

2. She first _____ (visit) the isolated Manus tribe in 1928.

3. The Manus _____ (agree) to let her live among them.

4. They _____ (permit) her to record their day-to-day life.

5. The isolation of the Manus tribe _____ (stop) with World War II.

6. The United States government _____ (ship) supplies and soldiers through these islands during World War II.

7. This contact with another culture _____ (affect) every aspect of Manus life.

8. After the arrival of U.S. soldiers, incredible changes _____ (occur) on the islands.

9. Margaret Mead _____ (travel) to the islands again in 1953 and _____ (observe) many changes.

10. She _____ (notice) that the Manus _____ (dress) in Western clothes, _____ (cook) Western food, and _____ (carry) transistor radios.

**3**   Complete the passage by filling in the blanks with the present continuous tense of the verbs in parentheses. If you do this activity orally, give the spelling of each present participle.

1.   Today, social scientists _are studying_ (study) the influence of American television in foreign countries.

2.   Many believe that American television _____ (cause) cultural change.

3.   Stations around the world _____ (carry) American programs, movies, and commercials.

4.   Changes _____ (happen) worldwide because of television.

5.   Some people believe that American TV _____ (create) a world culture.

6.   Through television, people everywhere _____ (get) regular "lessons" in American culture and values.

7.   Some countries _____ (control) the number of American programs on local stations.

8.   Others _____ (begin) to eliminate American shows entirely because they feel the shows _____ (threaten) their own culture.

9.   Few countries _____ (succeed) in eliminating all shows, however.

## C. Verb Tense Formation: Irregular Verbs

Irregular verbs appear often in both spoken and written English. You should know the forms of these verbs *without* consciously thinking about them. The following exercises give you a brief review of some of the more common ones, and Chapters 2 and 3 include more practice.

See Appendix 1 for a complete list of irregular forms.

**4**   Complete the story by filling in the blanks with the past tense of the verbs in parentheses. If you do this activity orally, give the spelling and pronunciation of each verb.

### Adjusting to a New Culture

When I __left__ Brazil to live in the States, I _____ I would probably experience
   1 (leave)                    2 (know)

"culture shock," but I really _____ no idea what culture shock actually _____.
                     3 (have)                                 4 (be)

I _____ through several different stages during my stay, and for a long time I
   5 (go)

_____ that these stages _____ unique to me. Finally, I _____ to discuss my
  6 (feel)              7 (be)                  8 (begin)

feelings with other foreign students, and I _____ that our "stages" _____ along
                              9 (see)                10 (run)

similar lines. At first, we all _____ thrilled about everything "new." Then, problems
                  11 (feel)

_____—with transportation, money, housing, and so on. All of us _____ at that
<br>12 (arise)

point we suddenly _____ exhausted and frustrated—with the language, the peo-
<br>14 (become)

ple, with everything. I almost _____ home! Luckily, I didn't because things _____
<br>15 (go)

better in a short time. Soon, I _____ that I _____ people better. I _____
<br>17 (find)          18 (understand)          19 (grow)

more and more used to my new way of life, and this helped me relax. I _____ a lot
<br>20 (meet)

of nice people, and I _____ some very good friends after that first "crisis." Later
<br>21 (make)

_____ a second crisis, though, and finally real "adjustment." Well, I still haven't
<br>22 (come)

gone back to Brazil. . . .

**5**   Fill in the blanks with the past participles of the verbs in parentheses. If you do this
activity orally, give the spelling and pronunciation of each verb.

### Returning to Your Own Culture

People who have *spent* time in other cultures often talk about "reverse culture
<br>1 (spend)

shock." If you have _____ your country for more than a short tourist trip and then
<br>2 (leave)

have _____ back home, you may have _____ it.
<br>3 (go)                    4 (feel)

What is "reverse culture shock"? Well, imagine the following: you've _____
<br>5 (become)

adjusted to a new culture and you've _____ to enjoy life in it. You've _____ new
<br>6 (grow)                    7 (make)

friends and have _____ a great variety of new experiences. Then it's time to leave,
<br>8 (have)

and you're sad, but you're also very excited about going home. Arriving home is

"wonderful"!—seeing all the friends and relatives you hadn't _____, eating all the
<br>9 (see)

special foods you hadn't _____, reading the newspapers you hadn't _____,
<br>10 (eat)                    11 (read)

hearing music you hadn't _____ in such a long time. But then, after you've _____
<br>12 (hear)                    13 (be)

home for a few weeks, perhaps, things may not seem so "wonderful." You may be-

come critical of your home country; you may not like certain things or ideas. Your city

may have changed, and people may have changed too. Or, perhaps in your eyes,

you've changed and they haven't changed at all.

This is the process of readjustment. It's a difficult period, and many people expe-

rience it after the initial excitement of coming home has _____ off. Fortunately, it

14 (wear)

doesn't usually last as long as adjustment to a new culture does.

## Using What You've Learned

**6**  In small groups, reread the passage "What Is Culture?" on page 15. First, discuss the ideas expressed in the passage and then analyze it. How many of the five different forms of verbs can you find? Underline them. Are all the verb forms used as *verbs?* Or do some function as other parts of speech?

**7**  In groups or as a class, read the following paragraph and discuss the questions after it.

### Each Language Has Its Exceptions

At least 1500 languages are spoken in the world, and some linguists estimate that as many as 8000 languages may exist. Even though most languages seem very different, there are some interesting universal aspects of language. The following cartoon illustrates one: every known language seems to have exceptions to its "rules"!

5

1.  What is wrong in the cartoon?
2.  What exceptions or irregularities exist in your first language? Do there seem to be as many as in English? Why do you think English has so many "special cases"?

**PART 4**      # An Overview of the Tense System

## Setting the Context

**Prereading Questions**   What differences have you noticed between the way people express time in English and in your first language?

---

### Time

Time is a core system of cultural, social, and personal life. In fact, nothing occurs except in some kind of time frame. A complicating factor in intercultural relations is that each culture has its own time frames in which the patterns are unique. This means that to function effectively abroad it is just as necessary to learn the language of time as it is to learn the spoken language.      **5**

---

From Edward T. Hall, *The Dance of Life,* pp. 3–4

**Discussing Ideas.**   Work in pairs or small groups. If possible, find people who have different first languages. Take turns comparing your first language to English with regard to tenses. Does your language have a system of tenses? If so, is it similar to the English system? If not, how does your language express time? Can you give some examples?

## The Tense System

Developing a sense of time in English, as well as a sense of order, is essential to your mastery of the language. The following exercises are designed to give a brief review of the tenses and their time frames *before* you study each tense in more detail.

Note that each tense will be covered in detail in Chapters 2 and 3. The passive voice will be covered in Chapter 5. How the tenses interconnect in complex sentences will be covered in Chapters 8, 11, and 12.

1
Work with a partner. Underline the verbs in the following sentences. Tell the time frame that each expresses (past, present, past to present, or future). In sentences with two verbs, explain the relationship of the verbs by time (earlier, later, at the same time). Then indicate the tense of each.

*past time*              *past to present time*
*(simple past)*            *(present perfect)*

**Example:**   Emilda was born in Switzerland, but she has spent very little of her life there.

1.   While Emilda was growing up, her parents moved frequently.
2.   By the time she was ten, she had already lived in Europe, Africa, and North America.
3.   She would speak French with her father, Italian with her mother, and English at school.
4.   As a result, she speaks three languages fluently.
5.   She's been living in Iowa for the last ten years.
6.   During this time, she has become accustomed to life in the United States, but she misses her family.
7.   She is planning a trip to Europe to visit her parents.
8.   She'll be leaving on September 20.

**2**   The following passage is a story about an Iranian student's first few days in the United States. Complete the story by circling the appropriate verb form from the pair in parentheses. As you make each choice, try to decide why the other possibility is incorrect. The first one is done as an example.

### The Restaurant

Before I ((left)/had left) for the United States, my father (was warning/had warned)
          1                                                    2

me, "Every foreigner (has/is having) problems in a new country." But I (told/was
                        3                                                          4

telling) myself, "Ali, you (will have been/will be) different. You (don't have/won't have)
                           5                                            6

problems in the United States. By the time you (arrive/arrived), you   (will have
                                                  7

learned/will be learning) enough English to understand everyone!" So I (made/have
       8                                                                      9

made) my preparations, and on January 2nd I (flew/had been flying) to Boston.
                                             10

Of course, I (have had/have) many problems since I (arrived/was arriving) in the
              11                                      12

United States. Some of the funniest ones (occurred/occur) during the first few days
                                           13

after my arrival. English (was not/had not been) as easy as I (think/had thought). But
                          14                                   15

I (was making/made) a friend, and I (was having/would have) a good time.
    16                                 17

During those first few days, the most comical experience (was/was being) our
                                                           18

first night out in a Boston restaurant. My friend (spoke/was going to speak) no
                                                    19

English, but I (thought/would think) that I (knew/was knowing) a lot. Before we
               20                            21

(went/have gone) to the restaurant, we (had promised/used to promise) each other
 22                                      23

that we (would speak / spoke) a lot of English. And we (were going to listen / listened)
        24                                                                        25

carefully so that we (learned / would learn) a lot!
                            26

When we (arrived / were arriving) at the restaurant, we (sat / had sat) down, and
                    27                                              28

the waiter (was giving / gave) us menus. While I (was trying / had tried) to read mine,
                29                                    30

my friend (was staring / used to stare) blankly at his. He (understood / understands)
            31                                                    32

nothing! The waiter (came / was going to come) back, and we (ordered / were
                        33                                                    34

ordering). Still staring blankly, my friend (pointed / would point) to the first three items
                                            35

on the menu. The waiter (seemed / was seeming) surprised and (asked / was asking),
                            36                                    37

"(Is / Will . . . be) your friend sure?" I (was answering / answered), "My friend (will be /
    38                                        39                                    40

is sure). I (have / will have) the same." The waiter (was saying / said), "Okay. . . . If you
        41                                                42

(want / are wanting) that, you (have gotten / will get) that. Foreigners . . ." (Imagine /
        43                              44                                                45

To imagine) our surprise when the waiter (came / had come) back with six dishes: two
                                            46

bowls of tomato soup, two bowls of cream of mushroom soup, and two bowls of clam

chowder!

Ali Mohammed Rooz-Behani

**3**   **Error Analysis.**   Many of the following sentences contain errors because the verb
tenses and time expressions do not correspond. Discuss the sentences and suggest possible corrections. Put a check (✓) next to sentences that are correct as they are. The first
one is done as an example.

        *had studied*                      *came*
1.   After Andrea ~~studied~~ in Argentina, she ~~had come~~ to Canada.
2.   She has finished her studies in Argentina in 1996.
3.   Andrea had been buying her ticket before the exchange rates changed.
4.   Andrea said that she was going to stay in Canada for a year.
5.   While she lived in Toronto, she was working on her master's degree.
6.   She has received her degree three months ago.
7.   Since she finished her degree, she travels around the country.
8.   She wants to visit as many places as possible.
9.   She is staying in Montreal since last week.
10.   Next week, she will be leaving for South America.

# Using What You've Learned

**4** Briefly tell or write a short autobiography. Be sure to include any important events from the past and present, and any plans for the future. You may answer some of these questions: When and where were you born? Where did you live while you were growing up? Where did you go to school? What did you study? Have you ever worked? What are you doing now? What special hobbies or interests do you have? What are some of your plans for the future?

If you choose to tell your autobiography, work in small groups and take turns. When one person finishes, the other group members may ask questions if they have any.

If you choose to write, write three paragraphs—one each for past, present, and future events. When you finish, exchange autobiographies with another classmate.

**5** In small groups, take turns talking about your own experiences learning a new language or adjusting to life in a new culture. Share some of your stories—funny ones, sad ones, embarrassing ones, happy ones. Later, write your story and, if possible, make a class collection of "memorable moments" you have had.

## Video Activities: An Exchange Student

**Before You Watch.**    Discuss these questions in small groups.

1.   What is an exchange student?

2.   What problems do you think exchange students might have?

**Watch.**    Check all the correct answers.

1.   Where is Adáh from?

    a. the United States        b. Switzerland        c. Turkey

2.   Circle the kinds of problems that exchange students and their families sometimes have

    a. money            b. chores

    c. studying          d. cultural/language problems

3.   What kind of problem did Adáh have?

    a. Her homestay sister was jealous of her.

    b. She had to share the computer.

    c. She didn't have a good social life.

4.   Who was Adáh's best friend?

    a. Jeli           b. Corey           c. her date

5.   What happened to Adáh's best friend?

    a. She got sick.      b. She had a car accident.      c. She went home.

**Watch Again.**   Compare answers in small groups.

1.   How old is Adáh? _____

2.   What are the initials of the exchange student organization?

   a. EVS              b. AFS                   c. ALS

3.   Look at Adáh's report card and answer these questions.

   a. What languages is she studying?
   b. What science class is she taking?
   c. What is her average grade?

4.   What percentage of exchange students go home early or change families?

   a. 2%             b. 12%                 c. 20%

5.   Look at the chart that Adáh made of her "highs and lows." In which month did she feel the best?

   a. August            b. September              c. October

**After You Watch.**   Complete the paragraph with the correct form of the verbs in parentheses.

Adáh _____ (be) an exchange student from Turkey. She _____ (live) with an American family in California. Adah _____ (be) in the United States since last August. She _____ (go) to an American school and _____ (take) regular classes. This semester she _____ (study) calculus, English, French, American history, and physics. She _____ (do) very well in all her classes. Adáh also _____ (have) a great social life. She _____ (have) many American friends. She _____ (be) also friends with other exchange students.

# Chapter 2

# Looking at Learning

# Introduction

Chapter 2 reviews uses of auxiliary verbs—*be, do,* and *have*—and covers the present tenses—the simple present, present continuous, present perfect continuous, and present perfect. More information on the present perfect tense is given in Chapter 3, and modal auxiliaries are covered in Chapter 4. Much of this chapter is review, and you may not need to study everything in detail.

The following passage introduces the chapter theme, "Looking at Learning," along with information and issues you will cover in the chapter.

### The Diversity of Education in the United States

While you are studying English, you are probably thinking about other educational possibilities, for now or for later. If you are currently living in the United States or planning to go, you will find an incredible variety of alternatives for study.

In terms of higher education, over 3200 colleges and universities with four-year programs operate in the United States. They employ more than 650,000 teachers and administrators and teach about 14 million students, over 400,000 of whom come from outside the United States. These colleges and universities range in size from 500 students to more than 50,000 students at one campus. Some charge over $28,000 annual tuition, while others charge as little as $450 per year.    5

If you're thinking about a shorter program, there are around 1300 community colleges that offer degree programs in the United States. Community colleges are different in three ways: they offer two-year (not four-year) degrees only; they normally have both academic and vocational/technical programs; and they are relatively inexpensive. The average tuition nationwide is around $600.    10

Even the most academically oriented people enjoy other pursuits, however, and the educational system recognizes this. Over 5000 other centers exist, including language or technical institutes, business programs, and so on. So if you've always wanted to study Italian, auto mechanics, bowling, watercolor painting, or windsurfing, there's a school for you. Many cities and towns have programs in adult education, and most universities offer "extension" programs that involve a very wide variety of courses for credit or for enjoyment.    15

    20

**Discussing Ideas.**   How does the education system in the United States compare with the one in another country you are familiar with? Can and do adults return to school at different times? Are part-time programs available? Is it possible to take a variety of classes for enjoyment or personal enrichment?

**PART 1**

# Auxiliary Verbs

## Setting the Context

**Prereading Questions**   Are you planning to do further academic work in English? If so, you probably have many thoughts on your mind. Have you asked yourself some of the questions in the following passage?

## Studying at a North American College or University

"What is the college system like? Is the Canadian system the same as the U.S. system? I hope I'm not going to have many problems in adjusting. What is the system for grading? I don't understand it. What kind of exams are given? Is it difficult to graduate?"

"Will I be able to understand my professors? There'll be a lot of homework, won't there? Should I buy a tape recorder to tape classes?"  **5**

"Have I applied to enough schools? I've sent in everything—transcripts, test scores, letters of recommendation; why haven't I heard anything yet? There isn't much time."

"What kind of English test scores do I need to get into academic courses? Do  **10** I have to take other entrance exams? All colleges give their own English placement tests, don't they?"

"When should I take the TOEFL test? How long does it take to get the scores?"

"How much will my education cost? Can I get any financial aid?"  **15**

**Discussing Ideas.**   Can you answer any of the questions in the preceding passage? What other questions, issues, or problems have occurred to you?

**Culture Note**

*The TOEFL test (Test of English as a Foreign Language) is very commonly used throughout the United States and Canada as a measure of English proficiency. Most major colleges and universities require certain test scores as part of the admission process. For more information on the TOEFL and other tests given by Educational Testing Service (TOEIC, GMAT, LSAT, etc.), check www.ets.org.*

## A. Statements, Yes/No Questions, and Short Responses

| With *Do* | | |
|---|---|---|
| **Examples** | | **Notes** |
| **Affirmative Statements** | **Negative Statements** | The simple present and past tenses use forms of *do* in questions, negatives, short responses, and tag questions. The verb *have* follows the same patterns when it is a main verb in these tenses. See Appendix 4 for more examples. |
| We study a lot. | They don't study a lot. | |
| Maria has a lot to do. | He doesn't have a lot to do. | |
| **Yes/No Questions** | **Possible Responses** | |
| Do you study a lot? | Yes, I do.      No, I don't | |
| Does she have a lot to do? | Yes, she does.    No, she doesn't. | |

| With *Be*, *Have*, and Modal Auxiliaries | | |
|---|---|---|
| **Examples** | | **Notes** |
| **Affirmative Statements** | **Negative Statements** | Sentences with continuous and perfect tenses, modal auxiliaries, and the verb *be* as a main verb all follow the same pattern for formation of questions, negatives, short responses, and tag questions. See Appendix 4 for more examples. |
| We are studying. | They aren't studying now. | |
| Maria can help. | Ming can't help. | |
| Tomas has left. | Ali hasn't left. | |
| **Yes/No Questions** | **Possible Responses** | |
| Are you studying now? | Yes, I am.   No, I'm not. | |
| Can Leah help? | Yes, she can.   No, she can't. | |
| Has Alfred left? | Yes, he has.   No, he hasn't. | |

**1**   **Review.**   Many English speakers use incomplete questions in conversation. Form complete questions from the following by adding auxiliary verbs and subjects.

**Examples:**   Working hard?
*Are you working hard?*
Study until late last night?
*Did you study until late last night?*
Gotten any sleep?
*Have you gotten any sleep?*

1. Doing okay today?
2. Get any sleep last night?
3. Work late last night?
4. Have a lot of homework today?
5. Writing a paper for history class now?
6. Need some ideas for your paper?
7. Finished writing it?
8. Already entered it on the computer?
9. Printed it yet?
10. Want me to proofread it?
11. Have to hand it in today?
12. Going to campus soon?
13. Your roommate already leave?
14. Your roommate say when she was coming back with the car?
15. Want a ride?
16. Ready to leave now?

**2**   **Review.**   Working in pairs, make short conversations using the information in parentheses in Nos. 1–5. After you have completed this the first time, change roles or work with a new partner to practice it again.

**Example:** A: I saw Tomoko last night.

<u>*Have you seen her recently?*</u> (see her / recently)

B: No, <u>*I haven't. Is she still studying biology?*</u> (still / study biology)

A: No, <u>*she isn't. She's studying botany now.*</u> (botany)

B: <u>*Do you have her phone number? I'd like to call her.*</u> (phone number / call)

A: Sorry, I don't.

1. A: I ran into Professor Sommer yesterday.

_____ (see him / recently)

B: No, _____ (still / teaching beginning German)

A: No, _____ (German literature)

B: _____ (schedule / make an appointment with him)

A: Sorry, _____

2. A: I saw Brenda the other day.

_____ (run into her / recently)

B: No, _____ (still / study accounting)

A: No, _____ (finance)

B: _____ (e-mail address / send her a message)

A: Sorry, _____

3. A: I got a card from your old roommate yesterday.

_____ (hear from him [her] / recently)

B: No, _____ (still / go to the University of Massachusetts)

A: No, _____ (Boston College)

B: _____ (address / write)

A: Sorry, _____

4. A: I had lunch with Tony last week.

_____ (talk to him / recently)

B: No, _____ (still / take classes at the community college)

A: No, _____ (work at a bank)

B: _____ (phone number / call)

A: Sorry, _____

5. A: I saw Miki this morning.

_____ (call her / recently)

B: No, _____ (still / write textbooks)

A: No, _____ (novels)

B: _____ (address / visit)

A: Sorry, _____

## B. Information Questions

Information questions ask *when? where? why? how? how often?* and so on. As in yes / no questions, an auxiliary verb normally precedes the subject in information questions. See Appendix 4 for more examples.

| Question Word | Auxiliary Verb + Negative | Subject |
|---|---|---|
| **When** | do | you have class? |
| | did | you have class last semester? |
| **Where** | will | you take classes? |
| | are | you going to take classes? |
| | have | you taken classes? |
| | had | you taken classes before enrolling here? |
| **Why** | are | you late? |
| | weren't | you on time yesterday? |

*Common Question Words*

| | |
|---|---|
| **how** | . . . asks about manner |
| **how . . . like** | . . . asks for an opinion |
| **how** + adjective or adverb | |
| **how cold** (fast, old, and so on) | |
| **how far** | . . . asks about distance |
| **how long** | . . . asks about length of time |
| **how many** | . . . asks about quantity (count nouns) |
| **how much** | . . . asks about quantity (noncount nouns) |
| **how often** | . . . asks about frequency |
| **what** | . . . asks about things |
| **what . . . be (look) like** | . . . asks for a description* |
| **what** + noun | . . . asks for specific details |
| **what** color (country, kind of, size, and so on) | |
| **what time** | . . . asks for a specific time |
| **when** | . . . asks about time (specific or general) |
| **where** | . . . asks about place |
| **which** + noun | . . . asks about a specific person, place, and so on |
| **which** book (city, one, person, and so on) | |
| **who(m)** | . . . asks about people |
| **whose** | . . . asks about ownership or possession |
| **why** | . . . asks for reasons |
| **why . . . not** | . . . gives suggestions |

*Note: What does he look like? asks for a physical description. What is he like? asks about qualities or characteristics (*nice, fun, serious,* and so on).

**3**   Complete the following questions by adding appropriate question words or phrases.

**Example:**   ____Why____ are you leaving?
Because I have to study.

1. _____ did you leave home this morning?

   At 8:30.

2. _____ did you get to school today?

   By bus.

3. _____ did you take?

   The express bus.

4. _____ are you going later?

   To the library.

5. _____ don't you study at home?

   Because it's too noisy.

6. _____ roommates do you have?

   Three.

7. _____ do your roommates make noise?

   Almost every night.

8. _____ do you live with?

   Two Americans and one international student.

9. _____ do you pay for rent?

   $300 a month.

10. _____ is your apartment like?

    It's large but it's old.

11. _____ is it to campus from there?

    Three blocks.

12. _____ does it take to get there?

    About fifteen minutes.

**Culture Note**

*A roommate is someone who shares a dormitory (dorm) room or an apartment with you. Generally, roommates share expenses, like rent and utilities such as electricity and gas. Sharing housing is very common among young people in the United States, and most universities are surrounded by relatively low-cost student dormitories and apartments.*

## C. Information Questions about Subjects: Who, Whose, Which, *and* What

In some information questions, the question word replaces part or all of the subject. Auxiliary verbs are *not* used, and the order of the subject and verb does *not* change.

| | **Examples** | **Notes** |
|---|---|---|
| **Question** | **Who** teaches that class? | *Who* is used only with people. It normally takes a singular verb, even if the answer is plural. |
| **Response** | Dr. Johnson. | |
| **Question** | **Who** teaches that class? | |
| **Response** | Dr. Johnson and two teaching assistants. | |
| **Question** | **Whose** class has a lot of reading? | *Whose* replaces a possessive noun or pronoun. |
| **Response** | Dr. Johnson's class. | |
| **Question** | **Which** art class has the most work? **Which** (one) has the most work? | *Which* can be used with or without a noun. It normally refers to one or more people, places, or things familiar to the speaker. |
| **Response** | Art 210. | |
| **Question** | **What** makes the class so difficult? | *What* is generally more informal than *which,* and it usually refers to one or more people, places, or things unfamiliar to the speaker. |
| **Response** | The amount of homework. | |

**4**    Complete the following questions by using *who, what, which,* or *whose.*

**Example:**    <u>Who</u> is your roommate this semester?
         I have three. Miki, Mary, and Anni. One is from Canada, one is from Spain, and one is from Poland.

1.    _____ is the Canadian?

     Mary is.

2.    _____ roommate is from Spain?

     Anni is.

3.    _____ is the most difficult thing about roommates from different countries?

     The problems with language. We speak four different ones.

4.    _____ accent gives you the most difficulty?

     Miki's accent. It's very strong.

5.    _____ roommate brought that great CD player?

     Anni did.

6.    _____ kinds of music do you listen to?

     Miki likes rock music, but Anni likes Latin jazz and salsa.

7.    _____ buys the most CDs?

     Miki does.

8.    _____ CD is your favorite?

     Right now, I like the Shania Twain CD a lot. But last week, it was Carlos Santana.

9.    _____ mother came to visit last week?

     Miki's mother, Bakka.

10. _____ did Bakka say about the rock music?

She doesn't like it. She likes classical music better.

**5**  **Rapid Oral Practice.**  First, make short questions for the following answers. Some answers can have more than one question. Then, work in pairs. Take turns asking and answering the questions.

**Example:**  A:  *When?*  B:  At 3:00.

1.  A:  _____  B:  On Monday.

2.  A:  _____  B:  At the library.

3.  A:  _____  B:  Ann and Mary.

4.  A:  _____  B:  For two semesters.

5.  A:  _____  B:  Mary's.

6.  A:  _____  B:  Three times a week.

7.  A:  _____  B:  10:00.

8.  A:  _____  B:  The red one.

9.  A:  _____  B:  Four hours.

10.  A:  _____  B:  Fifty miles per hour.

11.  A:  _____  B:  Because I want to.

12.  A:  _____  B:  Size 12.

13.  A:  _____  B:  That one.

14.  A:  _____  B:  Twenty-two years old.

15.  A:  _____  B:  English class.

**6**  First, create information questions for the answers on the following page. Have your teacher check your questions if necessary. Then, in pairs, alternate asking the questions and giving these answers.

**Example:**   Q:   *How often do you study at the library?*

A:   I usually study there once or twice a week.

1.  Q:   _____

A:   In the evening, from about 7:00 to 9:00.

2.  Q:   _____

A:   I walk.

3.  Q:   _____

A:   Because it's quieter than my apartment.

4.  Q:   Oh, you have an apartment. _____

A:   About five blocks from here.

5.  Q:   I'm looking for an apartment too. _____

A:   Well, our apartment rents for $800 a month.

6.  Q:   Eight hundred dollars a month? _____

A:   I have three roommates right now. Two of my roommates, Miki and Anni, are here now.

7.  Q:   _____

A:   She's the one with brown hair and a red dress.

8.  Q:   _____

A:   She usually rides her bike.

9.  Q:   _____

A:   My other roommate is tall and slim.

10.  Q:   _____

A:   Oh, it's *my* watch beeping. Sorry. . . .

11.  Q:   _____

A:   It's almost 9:00 o'clock.

12.  Q:   _____

A:   I set my alarm because it's so quiet here at the library that I sometimes fall asleep!

## D. Negative Yes/No Questions

Negative *yes/no* questions often show a speaker's expectations or beliefs. A negative question can mean the speaker hopes for a *yes* answer but realizes a *no* answer is also possible. If the speaker is sure of a *no* answer, he or she can ask a negative question to show anger or surprise. Note that contractions must be used in negative questions.

| Examples | |
|---|---|
| **Asking for Information** | TEACHER:   "You look confused. **Didn't you study?**" |
| | STUDENT:   "Yes, I did, but I didn't understand the homework." |
| **Showing Surprise or Anger** | TEACHER:   "This paper has a lot of misspelled words! **Didn't you use your dictionary to check the spellings?**" |
| | STUDENT:   "No, I didn't. I'm sorry." |

**7**  First change the following questions to negative questions. Then work in pairs and take turns asking and answering the questions. As you practice, vary the tone of your voice. Ask some of the questions to get information, and ask other questions to show surprise or anger.

**Example:**   Are you going to the library?
   A:   (surprised) Aren't you going to the library?
   B:   Well, no, I'm not. I'm too tired.

1.   Are you going to study tonight?
2.   Are your roommates going to study tonight?
3.   Did you buy your books?
4.   Did Miki buy her books?
5.   Have you finished your work?
6.   Has Anni finished her work?
7.   Are you reviewing for the quiz?
8.   Are your friends reviewing for the test?
9.   Have you turned in your assignment?
10.   Can you go with us to the party?
11.   Can your roommates go with us?
12.   Can Miki go with us?

**8**  In pairs, take turns making requests and responding to them. Using the example as a model, respond with appropriate negative questions.

**Example:**   A:   Could I borrow your lab manual? (you / buy one)
   B:   Didn't you buy one?

1.   Could I borrow your notes from the lecture? (you / go to class)
2.   Could I borrow your dictionary? (you / have one)
3.   How can I get in touch with Dr. Mills? (her phone number / be in the directory)
4.   Could you lend me some money? I'm broke. (your check / arrive)
5.   Let's go to a movie tonight. (you / need to study)
6.   I don't feel like studying. (you / be worried about your grades)
7.   My roommate went skiing last weekend. (he or she / study for the test)
8.   My friends didn't take the midterm exam in Math. (they / be worried about that)

**9** First, use the following statements to make negative questions with *why*. Then, work in pairs, taking turns asking and answering the questions.

**Example:**   I'm not going to study.

          A:   Why aren't you going to study?

          B:   I'm not going to study because I've got a headache.

1. I didn't go to class today.
2. I haven't finished my homework.
3. I don't like rock music.
4. My cousins can't come to visit this weekend.
5. We aren't going to go to the party.
6. My roommate didn't pay the rent.
7. I didn't return your books to the library.
8. We won't be able to go to your apartment tonight.
9. You shouldn't buy that car.
10. We don't want to practice more questions!

**10** **Error Analysis.**   Many of the following sentences contain errors in formal, written English. Circle each error and correct it, or indicate that the sentence contains no errors.

**Example:**   Why (he didn't come) to the party?

        *Correction: Why didn't he come to the party?*

        Why didn't they come to the party? (*Correct*)

1. Do I haves to do all the homework for tomorrow?
2. Does he has the right directions to get here?
3. Which sweater did she buy?
4. Who did call you?
5. Where he is studying now?
6. Why you don't come to visit us more often?
7. Whose car are you driving?
8. Whose dictionary you are using?
9. Who told you that story?
10. Did not she mail the package?
11. Where you have classes?
12. Whose book this is?
13. Where you got this?
14. Did not you study economics?
15. How long time does it take you to get to school?

**11** **Review.**   Complete the following conversation using appropriate forms of the verbs *be, do,* and *have*. Use negative forms and contractions and add pronouns when necessary. The first two are done as examples.

*Toshio:* Excuse Me, Jim. <u>  *Am*  </u> I interrupting you? <u>  *Do*  </u> you have a few
                                  1                        2

minutes?

*Jim:* Sure, _____ _____. I was just about to take a break. What _____ the
          3      4                                                    5
problem?

*Toshio:* I _____ understand this paragraph. I've looked up all the new words, but I
            6
still _____ understand the ideas. What _____ the paragraph mean to you?
       7                                   8

*Jim:* Let me see the passage. . . . Why _____ you write all those notes? Oh, they're
                                          9
definitions, right? You looked up a lot of words! How long _____ it take you to read
                                                            10
this? _____ it boring to read using a dictionary all the time? Sometimes it _____
       11                                                                      12
better to guess the meanings of words. A dictionary _____ always help.
                                                     13

*Toshio:* I know. My English teacher tells me not to use the dictionary all the time. I

guess I have a bad habit. When I read, I stop at every new word. By the end, I _____
                                                                               14
remember any of the ideas.

*Jim:* _____ you gone through this paragraph without stopping?
        15

*Toshio:* No, I _____.
                 16

*Jim:* Let's do it together. Then, we'll go back and look at the details.

## Using What You've Learned

 **12**  Silently read the following description of good readers. As you read, observe yourself
and think about your own reading style. Perhaps you haven't thought about this before,
but it will help you to know more about how you read. Think about the passage. Do
you use any of the techniques mentioned in it? Do you read the same way in your first
language and in English?

After reading and thinking about your own style, get into small groups. Take the
most important ideas from the passage and write a short questionnaire about reading
skills to give to your classmates. Use yes/no questions. Exchange questionnaires with
another group. While you are completing the questionnaire, share ideas on how to
improve both your reading speed and comprehension in English.

### A Good Reader

A good reader reads fast and understands most of what he or she reads.
Although each person is different, most good readers share six characteristics.

1.  Most good readers read a great deal. They make time for reading and spend
    two full hours, three to four days a week, reading.
2.  Fast readers look for the main ideas in their reading. They don't waste time
    and effort on unimportant details.

3.  Good readers practice comprehension by reading more and more difficult material.

4.  Fast readers plan their time for reading. Like students with assignments, good readers give themselves time limits, saying, "I want to finish this book by tomorrow. How much time can I spend?"

5.  Good readers set goals. (To set a goal, they may read for fifteen minutes for quick understanding, then count the number of pages read and multiply by four. This gives them a number of pages to try to read each hour.) Steadily, they increase these goals.

6.  Fast readers concentrate. They do not let outside distractions or daydreams interfere with their reading.

 **13** Read the following cartoon "Real Life Adventures." What is happening in it? Can you understand the general idea even though none of the questions in the cartoon is complete? After reading the cartoon, work in pairs. Write a dialogue for the cartoon using complete questions and statements instead of the shortened forms.

---

PART 2     # The Simple Present and Present Continuous Tenses

## Setting the Context

**Prereading Questions**   It's Toshio's first week at a new school, and he is lost. He stops to ask for help. What questions do you think he will ask?

### Getting Around

*Toshio:* Excuse me. Could you help me, please? I'm new here and I don't know my way around campus. I'm looking for the undergraduate library.

*Connie:* Sure! It's not too far from here. In fact, I'm going that direction in a few minutes. Do you mind waiting a little while? I need to speak to a professor, and she normally stops at her office around this time.

*Toshio:* Thanks, take your time. I appreciate your helping me.

*Connie:* So, you're new here. Where're you from?

*Toshio:* I'm from Kobe, Japan. I'm studying English, and I'm taking two undergraduate courses this semester.

*Connie:* Are there many Japanese students here? I hardly ever meet international students. I'm majoring in philosophy, and international students rarely take classes in the department. In general, international students choose business or science majors, right?

*Toshio:* Like me, for example. I'm doing work in computer science.

*Connie:* Oh, here's Dr. Johnson. I'll be right back. . . .

**Discussing Ideas.**   Have you had any interesting, funny, or not-so-funny experiences learning your way around a new place? Share some of them with your classmates.

**Culture Note**

*In the United States and Canada, the entire area where a university is located is called "the campus." In many places, the campus is simply a group of buildings. In other places, the campus is like a large park, with a great deal of open space, trees, gardens, and even lakes.*

## A. The Simple Present Tense

The simple present tense often refers to actions or situations that do not change frequently. It is used to describe habits or routines, to express opinions, or to make general statements of fact. The simple present can also be used to refer to the future.

| Uses | Examples | Notes |
|------|----------|-------|
| **Facts** | Alan and Lu **are** professors at the university.<br>Alan **works** in the physics department.<br>Lu **teaches** music. | Time expressions frequently used with this tense include *often, every day, from time to time.* Questions with *when . . .?* and *how often . . .?* are also common with this tense. See the following pages for more information on time expressions and their placement in sentences. |
| **Routines** | Lu **has** classes every day.<br>Alan **doesn't have** classes on Tuesdays or Thursdays. | |
| **Opinions** | **Do** they **enjoy** their work?<br>Lu **enjoys** her classes very much.<br>Alan **doesn't like** to teach. | |
| **Reference to the Future** | Next year, Alan **has** a sabbatical.<br>He **doesn't teach** next year. | |

*Note:* See Appendix 2 for spelling rules for verbs ending in *-s.*

**1**  **Review.**   Give the *he* or *she* form (third person singular) of the following verbs in the present tense. Then list them according to the way the *-s* ending sounds in each: *s* (walks), *z* (runs), or *ez* (watches).

1.  carry
2.  establish
3.  reply
4.  watch
5.  go
6.  employ
7.  laugh
8.  bet
9.  worry
10.  box
11.  fly
12.  do
13.  collect
14.  argue
15.  stay

**2**  Form complete sentences from the following cues. Use the simple present tense and pay attention to the spelling and pronunciation of the *-s* endings.

**Examples:**  be an exchange student
*Toshio is an exchange student.*
live in a dormitory
*He lives in a dormitory.*

1.  be Japanese
2.  come from Kobe, Japan
3.  have an American roommate
4.  enjoy several hobbies
5.  like music and cooking
6.  do a lot of sports, like tennis, golf, and swimming
7.  watch a lot of TV
8.  stay out late sometimes
9.  not like American food very much
10.  not go to the cafeteria very often

11. go to movies once or twice a week
12. study at the library now and then
13. play tennis almost every day
14. not be a very good student
15. miss his family

 **3** Now tell about yourself. Answer the following in complete sentences using the simple present tense. Then, in pairs, take turns asking each other these questions.

1. What are three facts about yourself?
2. What are three things that you like (to do)?
3. What are two things that you don't like (to do)?
4. What are three things that you do every day?
5. What are two things that you do not do every day?

**4** Look at this picture and think about working in a laboratory. Every day, thousands of students do research in laboratories. They work with professors and participate in many types of scientific work. What does a researcher do? Make statements about working in a lab from the following cues, and then add three original sentences. Use *a researcher, a student, he,* or *she* in your statements.

**Example:** work with new ideas
*A researcher works with new ideas.*

1. experiment with new ideas
2. try alternatives
3. follow instructions from a professor
4. use a microscope or other equipment
5. calculate statistics
6. work with chemicals
7. observe specimens
8. watch for changes

9.   record findings
10.   research information
11.   enter data
12.   use computers

## B. Adverbs of Frequency and Other Time Expressions

Expressions such as the following are frequently used with the simple present tense. Many of these expressions also appear with verbs in the present and past perfect tenses.

| Adverbs of Frequency | | Other Time Expressions |
|---|---|---|
| always | . . . 100 percent . . . | without fail |
| almost always | | as a rule |
| usually, normally, typically | | on a regular basis |
| commonly, generally | | by and large |
| often, frequently | | in general |
| sometimes | | at times, from time to time |
| occasionally | | on occasion |
| seldom | | (every) now and then |
| rarely | | (every) now and again |
| hardly ever | | once in a (great) while |
| almost never | | |
| never | . . . 0 percent . . . | |

## Placement of Adverbs of Frequency

Adverbs of frequency and several other one-word adverbs can be placed before the main verb in a sentence. They usually follow auxiliary verbs and *be* used as a main verb. *Ever,* meaning "at any time," is often used in questions and negatives. Longer time expressions are normally placed at the beginning or the end of a sentence.

| | Examples |
|---|---|
| **In Statements with One Verb** | We **usually** go to the university on Mondays. |
| | My roommate **almost always** finishes early. |
| | I **seldom** finish my work before 6:00. |
| **In Statements with Auxiliary Verbs and *Be* as the Main Verb** | Our classes are **generally** interesting. |
| | I don't **always** enjoy them, however. |
| | We have **occasionally** skipped classes. |
| **In Questions** | Are you **ever** late for class? |
| | Do you **usually** get to class on time? |
| **Longer Expressions with Verbs in All Tenses** | **As a rule,** we get to the university early. |
| | I'm late **every now and then.** |

**5**  Quickly reread the conversation "Getting Around" on page 41. Underline all the time expressions and explain their placement.

**Example:**   In fact, I'm going that direction <u>in a few minutes.</u>
*Longer time expressions usually come at the beginning or the end of the sentence.*

**6**  In pairs, take turns asking and answering these questions. Then add a few original questions. Give complete answers.

1.  What is something that you always do in the morning?
2.  What is something that you never eat for breakfast?
3.  What is something that you seldom wear?
4.  Who is someone that you occasionally write to?
5.  Who is someone that you hardly ever see now?
6.  How often do you watch TV or listen to the radio?
7.  How often do you call your friends or family on the telephone?
8.  How often do you use a computer? Do you have e-mail? How often do you e-mail your friends or family?
9.  How often do you go out at night?
10.  How often do you go out on weekends? What do you do? When and where do you do that?

**7**  Complete the following passage with the simple present forms of the verbs in parentheses. Add time expressions when indicated. Note that there are no blanks for the time expressions: you will have to decide on their placement. Then, in groups or as a class, compare your answers. Some sentences will have more than one possible answer. The first one is done as an example.

1.  In many countries around the world, young people _<u>almost always stay</u>_ at home
    1 (stay / almost always)

    until they get married. Universities _____ dormitories, and students
    2 (not provide / in general)

    _____ their own apartments. In the United States and Canada,
    3 (have / rarely)

    however, young people _____ away from home after high school.
    4 (move / frequently)

    Most universities _____ housing facilities, and most college towns
    5 (offer / by and large)

    _____ a variety of rooms, apartments, and houses for rent.
    6 (have / typically)

2.  In many countries, there _____ a great deal of "distance" between
    1 (be / normally)

    teachers and students. Students _____ teachers by their first names,
    2 (call / never)

    for example, or _____ personal problems with them. In the United
    3 (discuss)

    States and Canada, on the other hand, teachers _____ quite open and
    4 (be / sometimes)

    friendly. They _____ students to be informal with them.
    5 (encourage / often)

3. In many parts of the world, students _____ to interrupt their studies.
1 (not choose / as a rule)

They _____ without breaks because it _____ easy to
2 (continue)             3 (be / seldom)

reenter a university after leaving for a semester or two. In contrast, students in the

United States and Canada _____ time off to travel, to work, or to make
4 (take / frequently)

decisions about their lives.

## C. The Present Continuous Tense

The present continuous tense describes actions or situations in progress at the moment of speaking. This includes activities that are happening right now and current activities of a general nature. In some cases, it can also refer to the future. As a rule, the present continuous tense is used for activities that are temporary rather than permanent.

| Uses | Examples | Notes |
|---|---|---|
| **Activities at the Moment of Speaking** | Sandy **is studying** in the other room right now.<br>Jim **is working** on the computer.<br>**I'm proofreading** the report. | Time expressions frequently used with this tense include *now, at the moment, still, today, nowadays, these days,* and expressions with *this (this morning, this week, this year).* |
| **Current Activities** | Sandy **is majoring** in economics.<br>She **isn't taking** many courses this semester. | |
| **Reference to the Future** | Sandy **isn't taking** classes next semester.<br>**Is** she **going** to Europe instead? | |

*Note:* See Appendix 2 for spelling rules for the *-ing* ending.

**8** **Review.** Add *-ing* to the following verbs, making any necessary spelling changes.

1. study
2. occur
3. travel
4. insist
5. write
6. open
7. plan
8. happen
9. begin
10. change
11. swim
12. heat

**9** Make complete sentences from the following cues. Use the present continuous tense and pay attention to the spelling of the *-ing* endings. Then look at the picture and make five more sentences about Toshio.

**Examples:** not study right now
*Toshio's not studying right now.*
play tennis again
*He's playing tennis again.*

1. have fun in the United States
2. get a lot of exercise this semester
3. play tennis tonight and tomorrow night

4.   not study very much
5.   not do very well in school
6.   fail one course
7.   enjoy himself
8.   plan to study more next week

 **10**   Now tell about yourself. Answer the following in complete sentences using the present continuous tense. Then, in pairs, take turns asking each other these questions.

1.   What are three things that you are doing right now?
2.   What are two things that you are not doing now?
3.   What are two things that you are doing this quarter (semester)?
4.   What are three things that you are not doing this quarter (semester)?

## D. Verbs Not Normally Used in the Continuous Tenses

The following verbs are seldom used in the continuous tenses, *except* in certain idiomatic uses or in descriptions of a definite action.

| Verbs of Feeling or Thought | | Examples | Notes |
|---|---|---|---|
| appreciate | mind | He **doesn't understand** the problem. | These verbs are rarely used in a continuous tense; the verbs with an asterisk (*), however, sometimes appear in the present perfect continuous tense. The verbs *think* and *consider* occasionally appear in the present continuous tense, also. |
| be | miss | We **need** to talk about it. | |
| believe | need | I **think** that is a good idea. | |
| consider* | prefer | We **prefer** to talk later. | |
| dislike | recognize | | |
| hate | remember | | |
| know | think* | *Compare:* | |
| like | understand | We **have been considering** another possibility. | |
| love | want* | | |
| mean* | | I **am thinking** about several other possibilities now. | |

| Verbs of Perception | | Examples | Notes |
|---|---|---|---|
| appear | seem | This apple **looks** good. | These verbs sometimes appear in a continuous tense in the description of a specific action or in certain idioms. |
| hear* | smell | It **tastes** delicious. | |
| look | sound | | |
| see* | taste | *Compare:* | |
| | | I **am looking** at the apple now. | |
| | | I **am tasting** the apple now. | |

**11**  Complete the following passage with simple present or present continuous forms of the verbs in parentheses.

### Computers and Education

Computers _____are causing_____ a new revolution on university campuses today. At this
                   1 (cause)

moment, students throughout North America _____ term papers on
                                                    2 (edit)

computers. They _____ statistics. They _____ reports. They
                     3 (calculate)                     4 (write)

_____ new products—all on personal computers.
    5 (design)

   Today's computer revolution _____ a major force on campus. In fact,
                                      6 (be)

students who _____ computers _____ that they _____
                 7 (not own)                8 (feel / often)              9 (be)

at a disadvantage. In many cases, they _____ to borrow one or pay for
                                             10 (have)

time at a computer center. Personal computers _____ very common, and
                                                      11 (be)

throughout North America certain colleges and universities _____ stu-
                                                                 12 (require / now)

dents to buy their own.

   Some educators _____ today's emphasis on computers. They _____
                       13 (not like)                                      14 (recognize)

the importance of computer literacy, but they _____ in doing everything by
                                                    15 (not believe)

computer. Most students _____ the computer, however. As psychology
                              16 (prefer)

student Kevin McFarley says, "Right now, I _____ a project for a statistics
                                                 17 (complete)

class. I _____ calculating statistics manually. Without the computer,
             18 (not mind)

though, this project would take weeks to finish. At this moment, the computer

_____ some calculations that would take me two weeks to figure. How can
    19 (do)

a human being compete with that?!"

**Culture Note**

*In primary and
secondary education
alone, over 70 percent
of U.S. schools now
have Internet access.
The number of students
per computer is fewer
than eight, down from
twenty students per one
computer in 1990.*

**12**  The following is an interview about computers, distance learning, and English. The interviewee is Emily Lites, an expert in these areas. Complete the interview with present forms of the verbs in parentheses. In some cases, more than one form may be appropriate. Discuss any difference in meaning in these cases.

*Interviewer:* What __does__ the term distance learning __mean__ and how __is__ it __changing__
                       (do)                                1 (mean)              2 (change)

the way people study?

Emily Lites, M.A., is a well-known English teacher, writer, and innovator. She recently won International TESOL's Award for Excellence in the Development of Materials, and she founded American Business English Internet School in 1997. She can be contacted at www.bizenglish.com.

*Ms. Lites:* Distance learning _____ a hot topic
3 (be)
today. The term _____ learning from a different
4 (mean)
location than the instructor—any location where a
student _____ Internet access. Distance learning
5 (have)
started decades ago with classes by snail (regular)
mail, but today the choices _____ much wider
6 (be)
and _____ a great variety of multimedia applica-
7 (include)
tions: sound, text, images, video, audio cassettes, CD-ROMs, and so forth together

with the World Wide Web. The advantage of working anytime, anywhere is very

appealing.

*Interviewer:* What kinds of courses _____ people _____ over the Internet these
8 (take)

days?

*Ms. Lites:* Here again there _____ a lot of choices. You'll find everything. For
9 (be)

example, some people _____ full MBA and Ph.D. degrees on the Internet while
10 (earn)

others _____ just one course for personal enjoyment. Another area that _____ in-
11 (do)                                                                          12 (become)

creasingly important _____ professional training. Today, many thousands of people
13 (be)

_____ courses to improve their computer skills or language skills online.
14 (take)

*Interviewer:* _____ online classes _____ more than other classes, in general?
15 (cost)

*Ms. Lites:* With some of the major universities, a course _____ a bit less or about the
16 (cost)

same as a face-to-face course. But the student _____ because he or she _____
17 (save/still)                                    18 (not need)

to move to a different city or country, pay for housing, or buy as many books and

supplies. Professional training courses _____ in price from free or low-cost to thou-
19 (range)

sands of dollars. In most cases, you _____ what you _____ for; in other
20 (get)                              21 (pay)

words, a free course _____ a good, comprehensive plan of studies.
22 (not provide/always)

*Interviewer:* You _____ a language school, correct? How many students
23 (own)

_____ you _____ this semester?
24                    (teach)

*Ms. Lites:* Correct . . . That's right. My business partner and I own American

Business English Internet School. Our courses _____ for two-month periods,
25 (run)

and we _____ with business professionals from every corner of the
26 (work/currently)

world—from Argentina to the Ivory Coast, from Brazil to Japan, Turkey, and Ukraine,

for example. Because we _____ in real time with people from all over the world,
27 (work)

a great deal of cross-cultural learning _____ place, and this _____ global
28 (take)                          29 (benefit)

businesspeople tremendously.

*Interviewer:* _____ you _____ giving classes over the Net?
30 (like)

*Ms. Lites:* I _____ it very much. It _____ a great pleasure, and it can be
31 (like)                   32 (be)

very, very rewarding. In one sense, we _____ more closely with people than in
33 (work)

a traditional face-to-face setting because we _____ distracted by other things or
34 (not be)

people. And, we _____ many technologies to interact with participants at a very
35 (use)

detailed level. The student _____ a very intensive learning situation.
36 (have)

*Interviewer:* Do you think that more people will be learning online in the future?

*Ms. Lites:* Yes, definitely! I _____ huge projections for the next few years. Right
37 (see)

now the market _____ . As ABC News _____, "Although e-education
38 (explode)                       39 (report)

_____ in its infancy, investments _____ in, according to
40 (be/still)                              41 (pour)

Eduventures.com, a Boston-based education-industry research firm." E-education in-

vestments represented U.S. $198 million in 1998, U.S. $981 million in 1999, and U.S.

$640 million for the first quarter of 2000. The biggest factor in this growth

_____ the convenience: no one _____ to go anywhere at any particular
42 (be/probably)                        43 (have)

time.

Distance learning _____ best for people who _____ highly
          44 (work)                                    45 (feel)

motivated and independent. These people _____ tremendous gains in their stud-
                                         46 (make)

ies. To try a self-evaluation quiz from the Illinois Online Network to decide if online

learning   is   right   for   you,   go   to   http://illinois.online.uillinois.edu/

model/StudentProfile.htm.

*Interviewer:* Thanks so much for your time, Emily. This has been very informative!

## Using What You've Learned

**13**  Learn more about your classmates, teachers, or friends. Find two or three people who
speak English, in or outside your class, and ask some of these questions.

1.  What are your parents like? What were your grandparents like? What's your
    boyfriend or girlfriend like?
2.  What was your last house / apartment like? What is your house / apartment like?
    What is your home town like?
3.  What do you do on weekends? On weekdays? On holidays?
4.  How do you like the city or town where you live? How do you like your classes?
5.  How do you spend your time? Do you study a lot? Do you get out and do things?

**14**  Read Activity 6 on page 45 again. In pairs or small groups, discuss the differences in
your personal habits based on the questions in the activity. For example, what kinds of
things do you do every morning? Think about your life today compared to two
years ago.

---

**PART 3**

# The Present Perfect Continuous and Present Perfect Tenses

## Setting the Context

**Prereading Questions**   At many schools, student advisors get together with international students periodically to see "how things are going" and to help answer questions
or solve problems the international students may have. The following is one of a series
of brief orientation talks for international students.  What kinds of information do you
think will be included?

---

### Exams

"Good morning, everyone. It's nice to see you again. Well . . . uh, let me get started. Up to now, we've been dealing with lots of basic needs—registering, finding housing, buying books, and so on. But you've all lived here for a while now and you've begun to learn about 'the system,' so it's time to talk about some upcoming realities—exams.      **5**

"Many of your instructors have been giving quizzes since classes started. Quizzes are much shorter and simpler than exams, right? You can expect two major exams in most of your courses: a mid-term and a final exam.

"The two most common types of exams are objective tests and essay tests. Objective tests have traditionally been true/false or multiple choice. Individual   **10** instructors may use other types of questions, though. Essay tests involve writing paragraphs or short essays about a topic. In some cases, your instructors may tell you the topics in advance, or if you're lucky, they might give you a choice of topics to write about.

"Any questions so far? Not yet? Well then, let's take a look at some sample   **15** exams. . . ."

---

**Discussing Ideas.**   What is the difference between quizzes and exams? What kinds of exams are common in U.S. and Canadian universities? Have you taken exams in any academic classes?

## A. The Present Perfect Continuous Tense

The present perfect continuous tense describes actions or situations that developed in the past and have continued to the moment of speaking. This tense often implies that the action or situation will continue in the future. Without time expressions, the present perfect continuous refers to a general activity that began in the past and has continued to the present. With time expressions such as the following, this tense stresses the duration of an activity.

|  | **Examples** | **Notes** |
|---|---|---|
| **Actions and Situations that Began in the Past and Have Continued to the Present** | How long **have** you **been studying** English?<br><br>I've **been studying** English for six years.<br><br>My brother **has** also **been taking** English since he was in high school.<br><br>Lately, he **has been complaining** about his classes. | Time expressions frequently used with this tense include *for* + period of time, *since* + beginning time, *all morning* (*day, week,* and so on), *lately, so far, to date, up to now, until now.* Questions with *how long . . .?* are often used with this tense. |

*Note*: See Appendix 2 for spelling rules for the *-ing* ending. See page 47 for a list of verbs not normally used in the continuous tenses.

**1**  In pairs, ask and answer questions based on the following cues, using the example as a model.

**Example:**  computer / interesting / learn to program in BASIC

    A:  How has your computer class been going? What have you been doing in it?

    B:  It's an interesting class. During the last few days we've been learning to program in BASIC.

1. psychology / interesting / do experiments with rats
2. economics / confusing / study World Bank policies
3. German / hard / memorize irregular verbs
4. physics / interesting / learn about Isaac Newton
5. botany / enjoyable / plan a field trip
6. statistics / boring / calculate probabilities
7. Chinese history / informative / read about the Cultural Revolution
8. grammar / fascinating / review verb tenses

**2**  In pairs, take turns asking questions and responding to them. Using the following cues and the example as a model, form questions with *How long . . . ?* and answers with *for* or *since.* You may give long or short answers.

    **Example:**  work on that report / early this morning

        A:  You look tired! How long have you been working on that report?

        B:  Too long! I've been working on it since early this morning.

1. study / 6:30 A.M.
2. research that term paper / three days
3. do homework / midnight
4. practice your presentation / early this morning
5. memorize German verbs / more than two hours

6.  prepare that report / late last night
7.  calculate those statistics / dinnertime
8.  review English grammar / over six hours!

 **3**  In pairs, take turns asking questions and responding to them. Form logical questions using *How long . . . ?*

**Example:**   A:   You're still in school!

*How long have you been working on your degree?*

B:   I've been working on my master's degree for about three years.

1.  A:   I didn't know that you were a jogger.

_____?

B:   Well, I've been running about three years. I run two miles each day.

2.  A:   I didn't know that you moved.

_____?

B:   We've been living in Cambridge for two months.

3.  A:   It's still raining! What a shame. I come to Boston, and the weather is terrible.

_____?

B:   For almost a week.

4.  A:   I didn't know that you could play the guitar.

_____?

B:   A long time. Since I was in elementary school.

5.  A:   Did you know that Alfonso is an expert in karate? He has his black belt.
    B:   You're kidding! I never would have guessed.

_____?

6.  A:   Did you know that I'm writing a book? I'm almost finished with it.
    B:   Really? That's great!

_____?


## B. The Present Perfect Tense

In some cases, the present perfect tense can also describe actions or situations that developed in the past and that have continued up until the moment of speaking. It implies that the action or situation will continue in the future. A time expression, such as those following, is used to give this meaning with verbs such as *begin, expect, hope, live, study, teach, wait,* and *work.* In addition, this use of the present perfect tense occurs frequently with verbs not normally used in the continuous tenses.

Note that, in other cases, the present perfect tense usually refers to actions or situations that occurred at an unspecified time in the past. Chapter 3 covers that use of the present perfect tense.

|  | **Examples** | **Notes** |
|---|---|---|
| **With *For, Since,* and Other Time Expressions** | We**'ve worked** hard for several weeks. | Time expressions that give this meaning of the present perfect tense include *for, since, so far, till now, to date, up to now.* |
|  | I**'ve studied** a lot since the beginning of the semester. |  |
|  | Our teacher **hasn't taught** here for very long. |  |
| **With Verbs Not Normally Used in the Continuous Tenses** | We **haven't understood** everything in class. | Remember that the following nonaction verbs are occasionally used in the present perfect continuous: *consider, mean, think, want.* See page 47. |
|  | The class **has seemed** difficult. |  |
|  | The homework **has been** complicated. |  |

*Note:* See Appendix 1 for a list of irregular past participles and Appendix 2 for spelling rules for the *–ed* endings.

**4**   Quickly reread the passage "Exams" on page 52. Then answer the following questions.

1.   What tenses are used in lines 1–4? What time frames are expressed? What time expressions are used?

2.   What tense is used in the first sentence of the second paragraph? What is the time frame? What time expression is used? Compare this time expression to the one in line 3. How are the expressions different in terms of meaning and structure?

**5**   Answer the following questions in your own words. Use *for, since,* or other time expressions in your answers.

1.   How long have you been in this country?

2.   How long have you lived in this city?

3.   How long have you studied English?

4.   Have you understood everything in your classes so far?

5.   Up to now, which class has seemed the most difficult?

**6**   Complete the following with present perfect or present perfect continuous forms of the verbs in parentheses. Use contractions when possible. Mark all cases where both forms are possible and try to explain any difference in meaning between the two tenses. The first one has been done as an example.

---

**From:**          Emily Church
**Date:**          10/20/00
**To:**            Susan Weir
**Cc:**
**Subject:**       Hi from school!

Dear Susan:

I *'ve meant or 've been meaning* to write you for weeks, but I _____ much time!
       1 (mean)                                                    2 (not have)

My classes _____ much more difficult this semester, and I _____
                3 (seem)                                                             4 (be / not)

able to do anything but study. I _____ dropping one course, but so far I
                                    5 (consider)

_____ which one. To be honest, I _____ all my classes up to now,
   6 (not decide)                              7 (enjoy / really)

and I _____ all the work. It's funny . . . until now, I _____ science
        8 (not mind)                                              9 (hate / always)

courses, but this semester I _____ to change my mind. Physics class
                                  10 (begin)

_____ my best. We _____ Newtonian physics for the past few weeks
   11 (be)                      12 (study)

and I _____ so many interesting things. Of course, I _____ every-
        13 (learn)                                                14 (not understand)

thing, but my teaching assistant _____ me extra help. I _____ that a
                                      15 (give)                      16 (appreciate)

lot. Perhaps that's why my attitude about science _____. Along other lines,
                                                        17 (change)

everything _____ fine here. How _____ you _____? How
               18 (be)                      19 (do)               20

_____ things _____? I _____ of you a lot. Please give my
   21 (go)                22              23 (think)

best to everyone.

Love to all! XOXOXO

**7**   Complete the following passage with simple present, present continuous, present perfect, or present perfect continuous forms of the verbs in parentheses. In some cases,
more than one answer is possible. Add adverbs when indicated. Pay attention to their
position in the sentence.

### International Students in the United States

For over two hundred years, the United States _has been_ a center of study for inter-
                                                  1 (be)

national students. Since World War II, however, the international student population

_____ substantially, and today between 400,000 and 450,000 inter-
   2 (grow)

national students _____ U.S. universities. Recently, the growth rate
                      3 (attend)

_____ to slow, however.
   4 (begin)

The Far East _____ the greatest numbers of students in the United
                  5 (have)

States, and China _____ the list with over 70,000. Malaysia and Korea to-
                      6 (lead / usually)

gether _____ around 75,000 students annually.
          7 (send)

Who _____ these students? In general, over 70 percent _____
        8 (be)                                                        9 (be)

males, and around 80 percent _____ single. Over two-thirds of these
                                  10 (be)

students _____ for their education through personal or family funds. Less
<br>11 (pay)

than one-third _____ scholarships or sponsorship from companies or orga-
<br>12 (receive)

nizations.

What _____ these students _____ ? In terms of majors, busi-
<br>13 (study / usually)

ness _____ the largest numbers—about 20 percent of the total international
<br>14 (attract)

student population. This _____ a new trend, however. Twenty years ago, en-
<br>15 (be)

gineering was the most popular subject among international students, but since 1984,

enrollment _____ somewhat. Now, engineering students _____
<br>16 (decline)                                                        17 (make)

up only about 17 percent of the total international student population. In contrast,

enrollment in business and management courses _____ since 1969.
<br>18 (increase)

## Using What You've Learned

**8**   Visit your student advisor, your local library, or search the Internet to get information
on a school or university that interests you. On the Internet, you can use "college
search" or "university search" on a variety of search engines. You can find out about
academic studies, or you can look into other types of programs such as vocational/
technical, adult education, or university extension programs. The school can be located
in your own area or in another part of the country.

Using the information you gather, prepare a brief report for your classmates. Be
sure to include the following information:

Admissions requirements
Tuition and other costs
Starting dates and length of program
Description of course(s) or major(s)

# Video Activities: High-Tech Jobs and Low-Tech People

**Before You Watch.**   Discuss these questions in small groups.

1.   Which two of these are high-tech jobs?

    a.  telephone repairperson        b.  computer programmer
    c.  television camera operator     d.  biochemist

2.   What subjects do people usually study in order to get high-tech jobs?

    a.  liberal arts                 b.  engineering
    c.  mathematics               d.  social sciences

**Watch.**   Check all the correct answers.

1.   What is surprising about Mark Riley's work?

    a.  He enjoys programming computers.
    b.  He doesn't have a college degree.
    c.  Programming computers used to be his hobby.

2.   What problem do high-tech companies have?

    a.  not enough work
    b.  not enough high-paying jobs
    c.  not enough qualified job applicants

3.   What kind of people did high-tech companies used to look for?

    a.  college graduates
    b.  liberal arts graduates
    c.  engineering graduates

4.   According to an official at Play Inc., what kind of people are high-tech companies looking for now?

    a.  healthy    b.  smart    c.  loyal    d.  creative    e.  driven

**Watch Again.**   Compare answers in small groups.

1.   What companies are mentioned in the video?

    a.  Play Inc.         b.  Manpower        c.  Go High Tech

2.   Which company helps people find jobs? _____

3.   Complete the quotations:

    a.  A job has to offer more than _____.

    b.  It's not so important to Play whether or not you have a

    _____. It's more important that you want

    _____.

**After You Watch.**   Make *wh* questions about the underlined information.

1. Companies have been changing <u>their hiring practices</u>.

2. <u>Many high tech companies</u> are hiring workers who need training.

3. They have started hiring <u>people with liberal arts degrees</u>.

4. They train workers <u>after they hire them</u>.

5. <u>Most employers</u> are happy with their new employees.

# Introduction to Focus on Testing

Testing is a major feature of academic life. Two basic types of tests exist: subjective and objective. Subjective questions can have a variety of answers, but objective questions have only one correct answer. You may be familiar with objective American English proficiency tests such as the TOEFL and the TOEIC, or British tests such as the University of Cambridge Tests. Throughout this book, you will have short practice exams. In each, you will find reminders about common problems or hints on how to answer. Use these practice exams to help you find structures or ideas you don't understand well or need to study more.

## Focus on Testing

### Types of Standardized Tests

Following are examples of some of the types of questions asked on objective tests. Later, in Chapters 3 to 12, you will have short practice exams that are similar to the TOEFL and the TOEIC.

**True/False:**   Write *T* for true statements and *F* for false statements.

1. __*T*__ The simple present tense is used to express facts, opinions, and habits.
2. _____ The present prefect tense is used with actions at a specific time in the past.
3. _____ The present perfect continuous tense is almost always used with nonaction verbs like *understand* and *seem*.

**Correct/Incorrect:**   Write *C* for correct statements and *I* for incorrect statements.

4. __*I*__ John is appearing to be angry.
5. _____ This is unusual because he generally seems quite happily.
6. _____ I think John feels upset today.

**Cloze:**   Complete the following by adding the correct word(s).

7.   How _____*many*_____ people did you invite to the party?

8.   _____ book is that on the table? It's Mary's.

9.   _____ time did the class begin?

**Multiple Choice:**   Circle the correct completion for the following.

10.   We _____ your help.
   a.   appreciate really
   b.   are really appreciating
   c.   really are appreciating
   (d.)  really appreciate

11.   She _____ here since she was eight years old.
   a.   lives
   b.   has living
   c.   has lived
   d.   has live

12.   Alex _____ up at 6:45 every morning.
   a.   is getting
   b.   has been get
   c.   get
   d.   gets

**Error Analysis:**   Circle the letter below the word(s) containing an error.

13.   Since the mid-1980s, the number of international students <u>who</u>
                                                                                              A

are <u>studying</u> engineering <u>has</u> <u>been declined</u> somewhat.
         B                                       C              (D)

14.   In many countries, young people do not buy <u>generally</u> their own
                                                                                A

apartments because the cost of housing is high and <u>because</u> parents <u>prefer</u>
                                                                                          B                                C

their children <u>to stay</u> at home.
                             D

15.   Margaret Mead began <u>first</u> <u>her</u> studies of people from <u>different</u> islands in
                                              A         B                                              C

<u>the</u> South Pacific in 1928.
   D

# Chapter 3

# Relationships

# Introduction

This chapter covers the past and future tenses and gives you more information on the present perfect tense. It also covers the expressions *used to, would,* and *was/were going to.* Some of this chapter will be a review for you, and you may not need to study everything in detail.

The following passage introduces the chapter theme, "Relationships," and raises some of the topics and issues you will cover in the chapter.

### Families

Exactly what is a family? Until about 40 years ago, the traditional American family consisted of a working husband, a wife at home, and two or more children. Responsibilities were clearly divided in the American nuclear family. While the husband was earning a living, the wife was caring for the home and raising the children. Of course, there were exceptions, but this concept of the family was the general rule until the 1960s.     5

Since the 1960s, however, the family has become more diverse, fragile, and changeable. Americans have accepted differing concepts of families, including single-parent, blended, two-paycheck, interracial, childless, and commuter families.     10

Some critics believe that the American family has suffered greatly because of all the changes in society. According to these critics, the family had been much stronger before it began to struggle with issues such as divorce, working mothers, gay couples, and unmarried relationships. Today's strongest critics feel that the traditional nuclear family will become rare in the 21st century.     15

Nationwide, however, most Americans believe that the family is going to survive. In fact, almost all major surveys in recent years have found that the American family is as strong as it has ever been. For most Americans, the family continues to provide their deepest source of satisfaction and meaning in life. Thus, although today's family is different from what it used to be, it seems to be thriving.     20

**Discussing Ideas.**   Think about a culture you know.  Do you think there is a "typical" family in this culture?

---

**PART 1**

# Past Verb Forms: The Simple Past Tense; The Past Continuous Tense

## Setting the Context

**Prereading Questions**   What made you the way you are? Some people believe your position in your family is a major factor. Do you agree?

### Where Do You Fit?

Are you the oldest or youngest child? Are you in the middle or an only child? Many psychologists believe that your position in your family helped to shape you and your relationship to others. As a newborn, you quickly developed a relationship with your parents and later, while you were growing, you formed relationships with your siblings. According to psychologists, your birth order affected how your parents and your brothers and sisters reacted to you and treated you. That is, you and they behaved in certain ways depending on your position in the family. All of this strongly influenced your development, and in turn, influences you as an adult: what you think about yourself now and how you react to and treat others.

**Discussing Ideas.**   Think about your own family. Do you believe your birth order affected you and your brothers and sisters? In what ways?

## A. The Simple Past Tense

The simple past tense describes actions or situations that began and ended in the past.

| Uses | Examples | Notes |
|------|----------|-------|
| **Past Actions** | Martin **grew** up in the country. Later, he **lived** in a small town. When **did** he **move** to the city? He **bought** a farm two years ago. | Time expressions frequently used with this tense include *ago (two weeks ago, a month ago today, in the past, in 1995, in March).* Sequence expressions are also used: *first, then, later, finally.* These often begin or end sentences. Adverbs of frequency normally come before the verb. |
| **Past Situations or Conditions** | He **didn't like** life in a large city. He always **preferred** the country. | |

*Note:* See Appendix 1 for a list of irregular verbs and Appendix 2 for a variety of spelling rules.

## Spelling Rules for *-ed* Endings

1.  If the simple form of a verb ends in *-y* after a consonant, change the *-y* to *i* and add *-ed*.

    **Examples:**   try / tried    carry / carried    knit / knitted

2.  If the simple form of a one-syllable verb ends in one consonant after a vowel, double the last consonant (except *x*) and add *-ed*.

    **Examples:**   plan / planned    stop / stopped

    **Note:**   The letters *w* and *y* at the end of words are vowels, not consonants.

    **Examples:**   row / rowed    play / played

3.  If the simple form of a verb ends in an accented (stressed) syllable, follow the preceding rule for one final consonant after one vowel.

    **Examples:**   permit / permitted    prefer / preferred

4.  If the simple form of a verb ends in *-e*, add only *-d*.

    **Examples:**   tie / tied    change / changed

5.  Add *-ed* to the simple form of all other regular verbs.

    **Examples:**   want / wanted    ask / asked    belong / belonged

---

### Pronunciation Notes

The *-ed* ending is pronounced three ways, according to the ending of the verb:

- ■ */id/* after *-d* and *-t* endings.

    **Examples:**  existed, knitted, needed, wanted

- ■ */t/* after voiceless endings.

    **Examples:**  cooked, helped, talked, washed, watched

- ■ */d/* after voiced endings.

    **Examples:**  argued, danced, listened, lived, played, sewed

---

**1**   Quickly reread the passage "Where Do You Fit?" on pages 62–63. Underline all the regular verbs in the simple past tense. Then group the verbs here according to the pronunciation of the *-ed* ending.

| /t/ | /d/ | /id/ |
|---|---|---|
| _helped_ | _____ | _____ |
| _____ | _____ | _____ |
| _____ | _____ | _____ |

**2**   **Review.**   Add *-ed* to the following verbs, making any necessary spelling changes. Pronounce the past forms aloud, emphasizing the various pronunciations of the *-ed* ending. List them according to pronunciation: */t/ (washed)*, */d/ (changed)*, */id/ (waited)*.

| | | | |
|---|---|---|---|
| 1.  need | 5.  travel | 9.  permit | 13.  cry |
| 2.  study | 6.  paint | 10.  wrap | 14.  play |
| 3.  insist | 7.  hope | 11.  occur | 15.  clean |
| 4.  rob | 8.  agree | 12.  stop | 16.  worry |

**3**   Complete the passage with the simple past form of the verbs in parentheses. Include adverbs when indicated, and pay careful attention to spelling. The first one is done as an example.

### The First Born

Lily __was__ Bob and Dorothy's first child. When Dorothy _____ pregnant, the
  1 (be)                                                                          2 (become)

couple immediately _____ to prepare for the baby. They _____
                          3 (begin)                                            4 (go)

shopping for baby furniture and _____ toys and playthings. Dorothy
                                        5 (buy)

_____ little clothes and blankets. And when Baby Lily _____ into the
  6 (make)                                                              7 (come / finally)

world, the happy parents _____ in love with their precious child. They
                                8 (fall)

_____ pictures of Baby Lily's first smile, step, and birthday party. At bedtime,
9 (take)

they _____ and _____ her and _____ her little stories and
10 (sit)          11 (hold)          12 (tell)

_____ her books and _____ her lullabies. They _____ up in
13 (read)          14 (sing)          15 (wake)

an instant if they _____ her cry during the night. They _____ letters
16 (hear)          17 (write)

and _____ cards to friends and relatives detailing every little thing Lily
18 (send)

_____. In fact, her parents _____ Lily their complete attention. That
19 (do)          20 (give)

is, until her sister, Cathy, _____ born two years later. . . .
21 (be)

**4**    Complete the passage with the simple past form of the verbs in parentheses. Include adverbs when indicated, and pay careful attention to spelling. The first one is done as an example.

## Youngest Children

Jane _was_ the youngest of Dorothy and Bob's children. Because of her special posi-
1 (be)

tion as the "baby of the family," Jane _____ lots of attention. Her mother
2 (get/always)

_____ her often, her father _____ her on his lap, and her brothers
3 (carry)          4 (hold)

and sisters _____ turns watching her. All the neighborhood children
5 (take)

_____ with her and _____ her games and songs and stories. Every-
6 (play)          7 (teach)

one _____ her.
8 (spoil)

As parents, Dorothy and Bob _____ more relaxed and experienced by
9 (be)

that time, so they _____ so much about every sniffle and whimper. Because
10 (not worry)

of this, Jane _____ up in a freer, more easy-going environment with fewer
11 (grow)

rules. Jane's parents _____ her to do many things at a younger age, but at the
12 (permit)

same time, they _____ as much help from her. This _____ problems
13 (not demand)          14 (cause/often)

between Jane and her siblings. "When I _____ her age, I _____ the
15 (be)          16 (clean)

house, I _____ the dishes, I _____ the floor, I _____ the
17 (wash)          18 (sweep)          19 (scrub)

bathtub, and I _____ clothes." These _____ common complaints in
20 (iron)          21 (be)

their household.

Jane _____ all the characteristics of youngest children. She _____
       22 (develop)                                                23 (become)

an optimist and _____ good things from life. She _____ rules
                  24 (expect)                            25 (think / frequently)

_____ for other people, though—not for her. Sometimes, she _____
    26 (be)                                                          27 (doubt)

her own intellect and _____ to other people for help or advice. Of all the sib-
                       28 (go)

lings, Jane _____ the most lighthearted and playful.
            29 (be)

**5**   Complete the passage with the simple past form of the verb in parentheses. Include ad-
       verbs where indicated, and pay careful attention to spelling and pronunciation. The
       first one is done as an example.

### Twins

Mary and Daisy _____*were*_____ (be) born only moments apart. The twin girls
                        1

_____ (show) both great similarities and great differences from the moment of
      2

birth. Mary and Daisy _____ (weigh) about the same at birth. They
                              3

_____ (eat) about the same amount, and they _____ (have) similar
      4                                                    5

sleep patterns, and they_____ (cry) at about the same time. But that's where
                              6

many of the similarities _____ (end). As babies, Mary _____ (want / al-
                                7                                    8

ways) attention, but Daisy _____ (enjoy) sitting or lying quietly. Mary
                                   9

_____ (need) to move a lot and play, but Daisy _____ (prefer) to be
      10                                                     11

held. Mary _____ (insist) on being active. Daisy _____ (seem /
                  12                                            13

usually) happiest in quiet times. At birth, Mary and Daisy _____ (share) many
<sub>14</sub>

characteristics, but the two girls _____ (develop) very different personalities.
<sub>15</sub>

**6** Complete the passage with the simple past form of the verb in parentheses. Include adverbs where indicated, and pay careful attention to spelling and pronunciation. The first one is done as an example.

## International Adoptive Children

Camila _*was*_ (be) found when she _____ (be) about two-and-a-half years old.
<sub>1</sub> <sub>2</sub>

Colombian soldiers _____ (find) her alone in an area of guerilla fighting, para-
<sub>3</sub>

military activity, and drug trading. She _____ (have) pneumonia and numerous
<sub>4</sub>

other infections, and she _____ (be/almost) dead. The soldiers _____
<sub>5</sub> <sub>6</sub>

(take) her to a public hospital, and there, she _____ (get/slowly) better. Camila
<sub>7</sub>

_____ (spend) many weeks in the hospital, and from there, she _____
<sub>8</sub> <sub>9</sub>

(go/first) to a public orphanage. A government agency _____ (locate) a fos-
<sub>10</sub>

ter home for her, and Camila _____ (move) there for about six months.
<sub>11</sub>

During Camila's stay with the foster family, the government agency _____
<sub>12</sub>

(try) hard to learn about her family. The agency _____ (broadcast) pictures of
<sub>13</sub>

Camila on local TV, and it _____ (put) posters with her picture all around the
<sub>14</sub>

area. No one _____ (come) forward to get Camila, though, so finally, the
<sub>15</sub>

agency _____ (offer) her for adoption. Dozens of international families were
<sub>16</sub>

waiting for children like Camila. They _____ (want) to adopt a child to love
<sub>17</sub>

**Culture Note**

*Adoption is common in the United States. Most adoptive children come from within the United States, but around 5 percent are foreign-born. Today, there are over 6 million adopted people in the United States.*

and care for. So many families _____ (be/not) able to have children of their
                                              18
own, but they _____ (hope) to create families with adoptive children.
                          19

     Camila _____ (get) her third set of parents and her new family a few years
                      20
ago. At the same time, other children orphaned in Colombia _____ (gain) new
                                                                             21
families. Families from all over the world _____ (open) their houses and their
                                                          22
hearts. Children with no parents, with nothing, _____ (find) a place to live, grow,
                                                           23
and love—in places as diverse as Spain, the Faroe Islands, Australia, and France.

     Today, these children, and many others around the world like them, have a future.

     Perhaps they would have survived, and survived well, in their home surroundings. But

disease, civil war, and other catastrophes _____ (face) them then. Today, with
                                                          24
their adoptive families, they have the opportunity to grow and shine.

## B. The Past Continuous Tense

The past continuous tense describes actions in progress in the recent past (a few moments before the moment of speaking) or at a specific time in the past. It is often used to describe or "set" a scene.

| Uses | Examples | Notes |
|---|---|---|
| **Events in the Recent Past** | Mary, we **were** just **looking** for you.<br>Oh! You startled me! I **was taking** a short nap. | The following time expressions are frequently used with this tense: *a few minutes (moments) ago, at that time, then, just, still.* |
| **Events at a Specific Time in the Past** | A year ago now, we **were living** in Boston.<br>At that time, I **was still working** at the bank, and my wife **was taking** classes. | |
| **Description of a Scene** | It was a beautiful summer evening. We **were** all **sitting** and **talking** on the front porch. Dad **was playing** the guitar, the boys **were singing,** and I **was watching** the stars. | |

*Note:* See page 47 for a list of verbs not normally used in the continuous tenses. See Appendix 2 for spelling rules for verbs with *-ing* endings.

**7**  Use the past continuous tense to answer the following questions in complete sentences.

1.  What were you doing two hours ago?
2.  Where were you living a year ago?
3.  What were you doing when you decided to come to this school?
4.  What were you thinking about a moment ago?
5.  What was your classmate, _____, doing a few minutes ago?

6. What were you doing the day before yesterday?
7. What was your teacher doing at this time yesterday?
8. What were you studying two weeks ago?

**8** These passages describe scenes from the past. Complete them with the past continuous forms of the verbs in parentheses. Pay attention to the spelling of the *-ing* endings. The first one is done as an example.

1. I have a special memory of Christmas when I was five years old. My aunts, uncles,

   and cousins _were visiting_ us. I _____ my beautiful new red dress. We
            1 (visit)            2 (wear)

   _____ around the Christmas tree, and everyone _____ Christmas pre-
   3 (sit)                      4 (open)

   sents. I _____ one big present near the corner of the room. Then my mother
        5 (look at)

   took me over to that present. It was for me! It was the most beautiful dollhouse I

   had ever seen!

2. I have a special childhood memory of a summer night when I was seven or eight.

   My mom and dad and my sisters _____ on the front porch. The sun
                              1 (sit)

   _____, and the sky _____ red and golden. My sisters _____ on the
   2 (set)        3 (become)               4 (swing)

   porch swing, and my mother _____ in her rocking chair. Our dog _____
                 5 (rock)                  6 (lie)

   on the steps. My father _____ his guitar and _____. Everyone
             7 (play)          8 (sing)

   _____ to him. He loved to sing, and he had a wonderful voice. I felt so happy
   9 (listen)

   and peaceful and secure. That night is one of my best memories.

## C. When *and* While

*When* and *while* are frequently used to connect two past actions. Chapter 8 includes more information on these connecting words.

| | **Examples** | **Notes** |
|---|---|---|
| **While** | He was watching TV **while** I was doing the dishes. | *While* may connect two past continuous actions that were occurring at the same time. |
| **When *or* While** | John was talking to the man at the door **when** his mother phoned.<br><br>**While** John was talking to the man at the door, his mother phoned. | *When* or *while* may connect a simple past and past continuous action—*while* + the action in progress or *when* + the action that interrupted it. |
| **When** | **When** the doorbell rang, John answered it. | *When* may connect two simple past actions; *when* comes before the action that happened first. |

**9** Complete the passages with the simple past or past continuous forms of the verbs in parentheses. The first one is done as an example.

This morning everything went wrong at the Peterson household.

1. I ___*wanted*___ to get up early this morning, but I _____ to set the alarm.
          1 (want)                                       2 (forget)

   So I _____. When I _____ up, my brother _____ a long
        3 (oversleep)           4 (get)                     5 (take)

   shower. So I _____ to wait for a long time. While I _____ my bike
                 6 (have)                       7 (ride)

   to school, I _____ a flat tire. I _____ my first class, and I _____
         8 (get)            9 (miss)                10 (be)

   late for my second class. It _____ a good morning.
                       11 (not be)

2. I _____ up very early this morning and _____ the house while
       1 (wake)                           2 (leave)

   everyone else _____. I _____ the bus at 6:45 in order to get to work
         3 (sleep / still)     4 (catch)

early. I _____ the newspaper on the bus, and I _____
       5 (read)                                6 (not pay)

attention to the traffic when suddenly a car _____ a red
                                        7 (run)

light and _____ the bus on my side. When the car
           8 (hit)

_____ into us, I _____ off my seat, _____
9 (crash)           10 (fall)                11 (cut)

my head, and _____ my arm. What a day!
            12 (break)

**10** Using the simple past and past continuous tenses with *when* and *while,* tell a story using the following information.

    **Example:**   This morning everything went wrong for Dave Peterson too.

*At 8:30 A.M., Dave woke up late and took a two-minute shower. While he was getting out of the shower, . . .*

| | |
|---|---|
| 8:35 A.M. | wakes up late |
| 8:36–8:38 A.M. | takes a shower |
| 8:39 A.M. | gets out of the shower |
| 8:39 A.M. | falls on the floor |
| 8:39–8:40 A.M. | shaves |
| 8:40 A.M. | cuts his face |
| 8:40 A.M. | throws the razor on the floor |
| 8:41–8:42 A.M. | gets dressed |
| 8:42 A.M. | tears a hole in his shirt |
| 8:43 A.M. | finds a new shirt |
| 8:44 A.M. | makes coffee |
| 8:45 A.M. | pours the coffee |
| 8:45 A.M. | spills coffee on his shirt |
| 8:46–8:47 A.M. | looks for another clean shirt |
| 8:47 A.M. | hears the doorbell |
| 8:47 A.M. | runs to the door, but no one is there |
| 8:48 A.M. | loses his temper |
| 8:48 A.M. | goes back to the bedroom |
| 8:50 A.M. | lies down and goes back to sleep |

## Using What You've Learned

**11** Do you have a memory of a particular time in your childhood when you disobeyed your parents? What was the rule that you broke? Why did you do it? What happened to you? Use these questions to help you tell about that time.

    1.  How old were you?

    2.  Where were you living?

    3.  What did you do?

4. Why was this against your parents' rules?
5. How angry were your parents?
6. How did you feel?
7. Did you get punished? What was your punishment?
8. Did you ever break that rule again?
9. How do you feel about it now?
10. Would you do it again if you were a child?

**12** "The Family Circus" is a daily cartoon. Billy is the oldest child in the family. He has a bad habit of going places *indirectly*. Follow his path, telling step by step where he went and what he did. Use the simple past tense. Add articles and other words as needed.

**Example:**   *Billy got off the school bus. He got into a soccer game.*

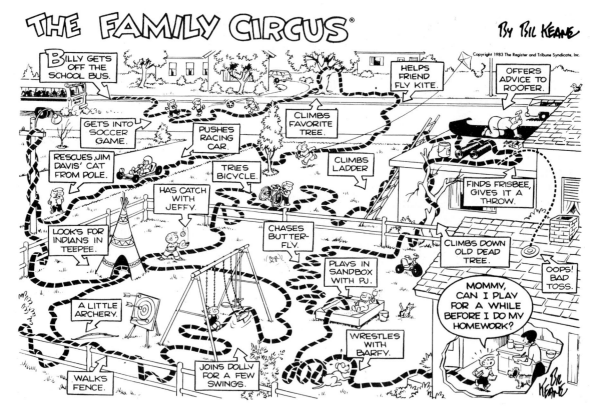

**13** The passage "Where Do You Fit?" on pages 62–63 discusses birth order. Edward Hall's passage on page 10 in Chapter 1 also mentions that order of birth can be an important aspect of culture. Take some time to give your own perspectives on birth order.

First, get into groups according to birth order—that is, all students who are the oldest should work together, students who are the youngest together, only children together, and middle children together. If you are a twin or a triplet, move from group to group!

In your groups, take turns discussing what it was like to grow up as the oldest, youngest, second, and so on. Do you believe your order of birth is an important factor in your development? In your culture in general?

| PART 2 | # The Present Perfect Tense with Unspecified Past Time |

## Setting the Context

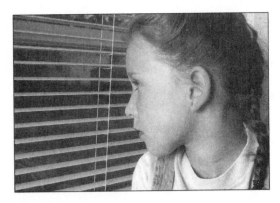

**Prereading Questions**    These days, some school-age children come home to empty houses after school because both of their parents (or sole parent) are working. Do you know any children who do this?

### Taking Care of Herself

Alicia Owens is eight years old. For the past two years, she has come home to an empty house. Her mother and her father work all day from 9 to 5. Alicia returns home from school by 3 o'clock. Alicia's mother, Laurie, calls her from work at 3:15. Alicia has already made herself a cup of cocoa and is sitting in front of the TV set when her mother calls. She asks if everything is all right. Alicia always says, "Yes,   **5** Mom."

     Alicia is not allowed to invite her friends to her house when her parents are not home. Sometimes she receives invitations to play at a classmate's home after school. However, she cannot accept them unless either her mother or father knows where she is. As a result, Alicia has spent a lot of afternoons alone in her   **10** house, usually watching TV or playing on the computer. By the time her parents arrive, she has also finished her homework, and she has set the table for dinner. Sometimes she has even done laundry and started preparing dinner. All by herself.

     When Alicia was born, her mother took maternity leave and stayed at home.   **15** But when Alicia was six months old, her mother brought her to the home of a child-care worker who took care of the very young. When Alicia was two and a half, she began attending preschool. Although Alicia is just eight years old, she has attended school for nearly six years. In that time, she has learned to take care of herself. She can dress herself, make herself snacks, get in and out of her house,   **20** answer the phone, and take messages.

**Discussing Ideas.**    In your culture, at what age, generally, do children begin staying home alone? Who takes care of the children if the parents are working or away?

## A. The Present Perfect Tense

Chapter 2 included information on use of the present perfect tense in a past-to-present time frame. It has a more common use, however. The present perfect tense frequently refers to an event that happened (or did not happen) at an unknown or unspecified time in the past. It also refers to *repeated* past actions. *No specific time* is given with these statements. When a specific past time is used, the verb is in the past tense.

| Uses | Examples | Notes |
|---|---|---|
| **Events at Unspecified Times in the Past** | **Have** you ever **gone** to Austria? <br> I **haven't** ever **been** there. <br> I**'ve visited** Germany, though. <br> *Compare:* I **went** there last year. | Time expressions frequently used with this meaning of the present perfect include *already, ever, recently, still, yet, (how) many times,* and so on. |
| **Repeated Actions at Unspecified Times in the Past** | How many times **have** you **visited** your sister? <br> I**'ve been** there five times. <br> We**'ve called** her twice this month. <br> *Compare:* We **called** her last week. | |

*Note:* See Appendix 1 for a list of irregular past participles and Appendix 2 for spelling rules for the *-ed* ending of regular past participles.

**1**  Reread the passage "Taking Care of Herself" on page 73. Underline the verbs in simple past and present perfect and circle time expressions.

**2**  Read the following pairs of sentences. In each pair, one sentence has a past meaning (a completed action) and one has a past-to-present meaning (still in progress). Write past (P) or past-to-present (P-T-P) for each.

**Example:**   _P_ A. I've been in New York.
        _P-T-P_ B. I've been in New York since Friday.

1.  _____ A. I've lived in Boston.

    _____ B. I've lived in Boston for ten years.

2.  _____ A. We've been making some changes.

    _____ B. We've made some changes.

3.  _____ A. She's worked in that law firm since June.

    _____ B. She's worked in that law firm.

4.  _____ A. I've studied for the test.

    _____ B. I've been studying for the test.

5.  _____ A. Ling has been playing soccer on Fridays.

    _____ B. Ling has played soccer.

6.  _____ A. Our family has visited Paris.

    _____ B. Our family has been visiting Paris every summer for the past ten years.

7. _____ A. They've been trying to call Billie.

_____ B. They've tried to call Billie.

8. _____ A. Bruce hasn't spoken to Deb.

_____ B. Bruce hasn't been speaking to Deb.

9. _____ A. Gabriel has taught algebra.

_____ B. Gabriel has taught algebra since 1988.

10. _____ A. Judy's read that book.

B. Judy's been reading that book.

## B. Already, (Not) ever, Just, Never, Recently, Still, and (Not) yet

These adverbs are frequently used with the present perfect tense.

|  | **Examples** | **Notes** |
|---|---|---|
| **Questions** | Have you **ever** read that book? | *Ever* must come before the past participle. |
|  | Have you **already** read the book?<br>Have you read it **already?** | *Already* can be used before the past participle or at the end of the sentence. |
|  | Have you read it **yet?** | *Yet* is generally used at the end of the sentence. |
| **Affirmative Statements** | I've **already** read it.<br>I've **just** read it. | *Already* and *just* come before the past participle. |
|  | I've read it **recently.**<br>I've **recently** read it. | *Recently* can come at the end of the sentence or before the past participle. It is sometimes used to begin the sentence. |
| **Negative Statements** | I have **never** read it. | *Never* generally comes before the past participle. |
|  | I have**n't ever** read it. | *Not ever* must come before the past participle. |
|  | I **still** haven't read it. | *Still* must come before *have* or *has*. |
|  | I haven't read it **yet.** | *Yet* is generally used at the end of the sentence. |

**3** Go around the class in a chain, asking and answering questions about the following.

**Examples:**   meet a movie star

A:   *Have you ever met a movie star?*

B:   *Yes, I have. I met Cameron Diaz once! She gave me her autograph.*

be on the Concorde

B:   *Have you ever been on the Concorde?*

C:   *No I haven't. In fact, I've never even seen it.*

1. be in a hurricane (earthquake, or other natural disaster)
2. lose your wallet
3. buy a car
4. have an accident
5. get a speeding ticket
6. have a flat tire
7. read a novel in English

8. be on television
9. design a Website
10. fall asleep in a class
11. play chess
12. find a buried treasure
13. fly a small plane
14. ride a camel
15. take the TOEFL test

**4**  In pairs, take turns making statements and responses. Complete each conversation by adding a sentence that uses *already*. Change nouns to pronouns when appropriate.

**Example:**   A:   Don't start the washing machine! I haven't put all my clothes in yet.

   B:   *Sorry! I've already started it.*

1. Don't put the broom away. I haven't swept the floor yet.
   Sorry! . . .
2. Don't walk in the kitchen. The floor hasn't dried yet.
   Sorry! . . .
3. Don't wax the floor. I haven't washed it yet.
   Sorry! . . .
4. Don't mail those bills! I haven't signed the checks yet.
   Sorry! . . .
5. Don't throw the newspaper away! Your father hasn't read it yet.
   Sorry! . . .
6. Don't start painting the walls. I haven't washed them yet.
   Sorry! . . .
7. Don't turn off the computer! I haven't checked my e-mail yet.
   Sorry! . . .
8. Don't go food shopping yet! I haven't told you what I need.
   Sorry! . . .

**5**  Complete the passage with the present perfect form of the verbs in parentheses. Use *still . . . not* or *not . . . yet* when indicated.

### Procrastinators

My friend Larry is always procrastinating. For example, he _____ in his apartment
                                                                    1 (live)

for a year now, but he _____ any furniture. He _____ to study at the university
                          2 (not buy / still)                      3 (want)

for a long time, but he _____. His hair _____ so long he can barely see, but
                          4 (not register / yet)         5 (grow)

he _____ it cut. He _____ books he borrowed from me for over three months,
      6 (not get / still)         7 (keep)

and he _____ them. I _____ several messages for him on his answering
            8 (not return / still)       9 (leave)

machine, and he _____ me back. I know what he will say when I finally talk to
                    10 (not call / yet)

him. "Tomorrow, I'll do it tomorrow." Those are his favorite words.

## Using What You've Learned

**6** Play a game of "Find Someone Who Has  . . ." This is a two-part game.

Step 1:  First, on a piece of paper, write three things that you have done: "I've climbed a mountain," "I've been to India," and so on. Do not show this to your classmates. Your teacher will collect the papers and make a list to distribute another day.

Step 2:   Your teacher will distribute the list. Walk around the room and ask your classmates, "Have you  . . . ?" When you find the person who has done that, ask him or her to sign the paper. The first student who gets signatures for each item wins the game.

**7** Are you a procrastinator? Have you written to your friends or family lately? Have you been to the language lab? Have you done your laundry yet? You still haven't paid your rent? List five things that you planned to do during the past month but still haven't done. Then, in small groups, compare your lists. How many of you are true procrastinators?

**PART 3**

# The Simple Future Tense; *Be Going To;* Present Tenses with Future Meaning; The Future Continuous Tense; The Future Perfect and Future Perfect Continuous Tenses

## Setting the Context

**Prereading Questions**   What will families be like in the future? What kind of families will our children and our children's children have?

---

### Family Life in the 21st Century

What are photos of a family gathering in 2050 going to look like? Will families in urban areas across the world grow smaller? Will the very poor in rural areas continue to have large numbers of children? Will there be mostly older people in such a photo? Probably. Why? Because people are living longer and staying healthier, and people in economically rich societies are having fewer children. For example, **5** in the United States in 1980, people over 65 made up only 11.3 percent of the total population. In 2050, people over 65 will make up over 22 percent of the total population. Furthermore, in the 1950s, the average family had 4.8 children, while in the 1980s, it had 1.3 children. How many children will be in an American family photograph in the year 2050? Will all the faces smiling at the digital camera be se- **10** nior citizens?

---

**Discussing Ideas.**   Do you think that the trend toward an older population is also happening in other countries that you are familiar with?  Why or why not?

## A. The Simple Future Tense

The simple future tense expresses intentions, and it can be used to express requests, promises, offers, and predictions.

| Uses | Examples | Notes |
|---|---|---|
| **Intentions** | I'll **try** to be home early tonight. | Time expressions such as the following are often used with future forms: *this afternoon (evening), tonight, later, in a while, in the future, in September, in 2050*, and so on. |
| **Offers and Promises** | I'll **help** you with the housework in a little while. Thanks. Then I **will make** you a special dinner! | |
| **Predictions** | With your help, we'll **finish** by 10:00. | |
| **Requests** | **Will** you **promise** to help? | |

**1**   The following are predictions researchers have made about the future in the United States. Add *will* to form complete sentences. Then discuss whether these predictions may be true for other countries also.

**Example:**   American divorce rates / remain high
          *American divorce rates will remain high.*

1.   Fifty percent of marriages / end in court
2.   A majority of people / marry more than once during their lives
3.   Some couples / get divorced and remarried three or four times
4.   More and more marriages / be interracial or intercultural
5.   Different concepts of the family / exist
6.   The traditional nuclear family / not be the most common type of family in the United States
7.   In general, couples / have fewer children
8.   People / change jobs and careers several times during their lifetime
9.   Universities / be filled with "aging" students

10. Many people / earn four or five different college degrees
11. People / keep in touch with their families by electronic communication in place of face to face communication
12. Material prosperity / not bring happiness

## B. Other Forms Used for the Future: Be Going To, Present Tenses with Future Meaning

|  | **Examples** | **Notes** |
|---|---|---|
| ***be going to*** | I'm **going to be** home no later than 7:00.<br><br>What **are** we **going to have** for dinner? | *Going to* is often used to express specific future plans or intentions. It is used frequently in conversation and is often pronounced *gonna* or *gunna*. In some cases, *will* and *going to* are interchangeable, but *will* is preferred in formal English. |
| **Present Continuous** | I **am serving** dinner at 7:30.<br>The guests **are coming** around 7:00. | Both the present continuous and the simple present can be used to express future time. Normally a time expression or the context indicates that the action or situation is in the future. Verbs of movement such as *go, come, arrive*, and *leave* are often used in present tenses, even when they have future meanings. |
| **Simple Present** | Dinner **is** at 7:30.<br>We **leave** for the movie at 9:00. | |

**2** In pairs, take turns asking and answering the following questions.

1. Will you see your family (boyfriend, girlfriend, best friend) soon?
2. When are you going to call them (him, her) next?
3. Will the call be long distance?
4. Will it be expensive?
5. When are you going to write your next letter (or e-mail) to your family or a good friend?
6. Are you e-mailing someone after class?
7. What will you write about?
8. Is anyone coming to visit you soon?
9. When will the guests arrive?
10. What are you planning to do with them?

**3** Complete the passage with future forms of the verbs in parentheses. The first one is done as an example.

### Work Life and Home Life

Technology has already changed the world of work, and in the near future improve-

ments such as video conferencing and faster Internet access *are going to make* it
<br>                                    1 (make)

even easier for people to work from their homes. In general, people _____ less tied
                                                                    2 (be)

to an office. Work _____ a more international focus and _____ round-the-clock
                   3 (have)                                4 (need)

attention. Therefore, it _____ even more difficult to separate work and home life.
                        5 (become)

   Changes in the nature of work combined with changes in the workforce _____
                                                                        6 (bring)

about major changes in company policies. Because women now constitute nearly half

of the workforce, corporations have already become more dependent on female

workers. Because of this, opportunities for females to advance _____, and com-
                                                               7 (increase)

pany policies _____ more "family friendly."
             8 (become)

   In the future, gender inequality _____. With more and more women in
                                    9 (disappear / hopefully)

fields once dominated by men, the gap between male and female wages _____.
                                                                    10 (close)

When this happens, power balances _____ not only at the office, but also in the
                                  11 (change)

home. When both sexes have equivalent jobs and paychecks, it _____ the
                                                             12 (not be / always)

woman who works "the second shift" of housework after hours or who stays home

when a child is sick. In addition, women _____ child custody in a divorce as
                                         13 (not receive)

often as they do now.

## C. The Future Continuous Tense

The future continuous tense normally refers to actions that will be in progress, often at
a specified time, in the future.

| Uses | Examples | Notes |
|------|----------|-------|
| **Actions in Progress in the Future** | Can you imagine! At this time tomorrow we'll **be landing** in London!<br>Yes, but at the same time next week, we'll **be flying** home. | These time expressions are often used with the future continuous tense: *at this time next week* (*month,* and so on), *at that time* (*at 3:00,* and so on), *the day after tomorrow, a week* (*year*) *from today.* |

*Note:* See page 47 for a list of verbs not normally used in the continuous tenses. See Appendix 2 for spelling rules
for verbs with *-ing* endings.

**4**   The future continuous tense often gives a friendlier and more conversational feeling
than the simple future does. Change the following sentences to the future continuous.

**Example:**   I'll see you.
             *I'll be seeing you.*

1. We'll see you later this evening.
2. Will you go to the party tomorrow night?
3. They'll arrive in town the day after tomorrow.
4. I'll call you soon.
5. Deb will fax me the forms shortly.
6. He won't come home for dinner tonight.
7. When will we have our next exam?
8. Will Kim join us for dinner?
9. Judy will write us soon.
10. Brad will get his test results soon.
11. Kerri will meet us at the lecture hall.
12. Terry will let us know when he can leave.
13. They will wait for us outside the theater.
14. I'll look for you at the game.
15. When will you get together with Bill?

**5** Complete the following in your own words, using the future continuous. Give as many sentences as you can for each.

**Example:** Right now I am sitting in class. At this time tomorrow . . .
*I'll be studying at the library. I'll be working on . . .*

1. Right now I am living . . . (with my parents / in an apartment).
   A month from now . . .
2. This session I am going to . . . (name of school). Next session . . .
3. This session I am taking English. Next session . . .
4. Right now I am studying grammar. At this time tomorrow . . .
5. Today I'm wearing . . . Tomorrow . . .
6. Tonight I'm . . . Tomorrow night . . .
7. This year I'm . . . Next year . . .
8. These days I'm . . . but soon . . .

**6** In pairs, take turns asking and answering the following questions. Give as much information as you can for each answer.

**Example:** What will you be doing the day after tomorrow?
*I will probably be studying for a test. I'll be reviewing my notes for chemistry, and I'll . . .*

1. What will you be doing at this time tomorrow?
2. What will you be doing at this time on Saturday?
3. What will you be studying a month from now?
4. Will you still be going to school six months from now?
5. Will you be working a year from now?
6. Where will you be living a year from now?
7. Who will you be living with a year from now?
8. Will you be using English a year from now?

## D. The Future Perfect and Future Perfect Continuous Tenses

These tenses refer to situations or actions that will have occurred *before* another event or time in the future. They appear in written English, but they are not used often in spoken English.

|  | **Examples** | **Notes** |
|---|---|---|
| **Future Perfect** | By the end of this trip, we **will have traveled** over ten thousand miles. | Time expressions used with these tenses include *before, when, by the time . . . , by* + date or time. |
| **Future Perfect Continuous** | When you arrive, you **will have been flying** for more than 22 hours. | |

*Note:* See page 47 for a list of verbs not normally used in the continuous tenses. See Appendix 1 for a list of irregular past participles and Appendix 2 for spelling rules for the *-ed* and *-ing* endings.

**7**   Change the following sentences to the future perfect tense. When possible, use *even, more,* or *even more* (for emphasis) in your new sentences.

**Example:**   The role of women has changed greatly.
*By 2030, the role of women will have changed even more.*
Many women have gone back to school.
*By 2030, even more women will have gone back to school.*

1.   Families have become smaller.
2.   Many couples have chosen to have children later in life.
3.   The cost of living has increased.
4.   Raising children has gotten more expensive.
5.   The cost of a college education has grown higher.
6.   Children have spent much time alone while their parents are working.
7.   Many men have begun to do housework.
8.   Many women have gone back to school.
9.   Many women have started to work outside the home.
10.  Two-income families have become common.
11.  Many men and women have changed careers several times.
12.  Distance education has provided many people with a way to study at home.
13.  Many universities have started to offer degree programs with flexible schedules.
14.  The Internet has provided many new ways of studying and learning.
15.  Many companies have offered job retraining as new areas are created.

## Using What You've Learned

**8**   In pairs or small groups, role-play the following scenes.

1.   Imagine you are talking to your boyfriend or girlfriend.
   a.   Make him or her an offer.
   b.   Make him or her a promise.
   c.   Make a prediction.

2.   Imagine you are talking to your father or mother.
     a.   Make him or her a promise.
     b.   Make a request of him or her.

3.   Imagine you are talking to your teenage son or daughter.
     a.   Make a request of him or her.
     b.   Make a prediction.

4.   Imagine you are talking to an investor in your new company.
     a.   Tell him/her your plans for your company's expansion.
     b.   Tell him/her why he/she will make a lot of money by investing in your company.

5.   Imagine you are the leader of a new nation. You are giving a televised speech to your citizens.
     a.   Make three positive promises about the future.
     b.   Make three negative promises about the future.

**9**  What do you think life will be like in the 21st century? What do you hope you will be doing? Where will you be living? Will you have gotten married? Will you have children? Grandchildren? Will you still be in the same career?

    Use this timeline to make notes about your ideal future. Write your ideas above the time you expect them to come true.

| now | in 10 years | in 20 years | in 30 years |
|---|---|---|---|

    Then, in small groups, discuss your plans and dreams using the timeline you have made. Be sure to consider changes that will be occurring in the world around you—politically, economically, and technologically. After you have finished, you may want to choose one member of the group to give a brief summary of your discussion to the class.

---

**PART 4**

# Past Verb Forms: The Habitual Past; The Future in the Past

## Setting the Context

**Prereading Questions**  The following passage is a childhood story from a great storyteller, Al Monom. As you go through it, think about your childhood. Was there a storyteller in your family? Was storytelling an important part of family gatherings?

### The Old Days

My Pa used to play the violin. Us children* would gather around the potbelly stove in the kitchen during those long, freezing-cold winter nights in Wisconsin, and we would be glued to the sounds of that old violin. My Pa made that violin sing.

    That violin gave us our best entertainment because my Pa used to play for dances around the county. We would get so excited when he told us that we were going to go to a dance. About one Saturday night a month, he

5

---

*us children   colloquial for "we children."

would hitch the horses, pack the entire family into the wagon, and take us off to     **10**
the dance. Now that was real excitement!

I still have that violin. It has got to be at least 150 years old now. I've played it
on and off through the years, and others have picked it from time to time. But
nobody has made it sing the way Pa used to.

Al Monom, age 87, Middleton, Wisconsin

**Discussing Ideas.**   Al Monom grew up a long time ago, and his childhood was very
different from childhood today. Think about children growing up now. For a child, how
is life different today from what it used to be 50, 60, or 70 years ago?

## A. The Habitual Past: Would and Used To

Both *would* + simple form and *used to* + simple form are used to describe actions in
the past that were repeated on a regular basis. For situations and continuous actions in
the past, however, only *used to* is possible; *would* cannot be used. *Used to* can also
refer to actions or situations in the past that no longer exist.

| Uses | Examples |
|---|---|
| **Repeated Actions in the Past** | When I was a child, my family **would travel** in the West every summer. <br> We **used to visit** the Teton Mountains every year. |
| **Continuous Actions or Situations in the Past** | My father **used to live** near the mountains. (not: *would live*) <br> He **used to work** as a forest ranger. (not: *would work*) |
| **Past Actions or Situations that No Longer Exist** | Campsites **used to be** free; now you have to pay to camp. (not: *would be*) |

*Note:* Do not confuse the constructions *used to* + simple form and *be used to* + gerund, which means "be
accustomed to." Compare: *I used to get up early. (I don't anymore.) I am used to getting up early. (I frequently get
up early and it doesn't bother me.)*

**1**   Underline all uses of *would* and *used to* in the passage "The Old Days" on pages
83–84. Then substitute simple past verbs in each case. Does the meaning change?

**2**   Using *would* in a sentence can give a nostalgic, almost poetic, feeling to the words.
Add *would* to these sentences, making any necessary changes. Then discuss the differences in meaning between the original and the new sentences.

**Example:**   My grandfather often spent hours reading.
    *My grandfather would often spend hours reading.*

1.   On Sundays, my grandfather often sat in his old oak rocking chair.
2.   He smoked his pipe.
3.   He read for hours and hours.

4. Sometimes he stopped reading for a while.
5. He took out his old mandolin.
6. He played songs for us.
7. He sang lovely melodies to us.
8. He held us on his lap in the big old rocking chair.

**3** Using *would* or *used to,* change the following sentences from the simple past tense to the habitual past. Note any cases where *would* cannot be used.

**Example:** We lived in a small town.
*We used to live in a small town. (Would cannot be used.)*

1. Our family had a television, but we seldom watched it.
2. We always found other ways to pass the time.
3. All of the children in the neighborhood were friends.
4. In the summer, we always played games, rode our bicycles, and went swimming.
5. All of us liked to swim.
6. In autumn, we always made big piles of leaves to jump in.
7. In winter, we skated and skied all the time.
8. We built snow slides through the backyards and went down them on sleds every day after school.
9. Finally springtime came after months of winter.
10. We waited for summer to arrive again.

## B. The Future in the Past: Was/Were Going To

*Was/were going to* + verb is used to describe past intentions. In many cases, the action was not completed.

| Uses | Examples |
|---|---|
| **Past Intentions (Action Completed)** | I said I **was going to get** an "A" in English, and I did.<br>Last summer, our family **was going to visit** friends in Colorado. We did. |
| **Past Intentions (Action Not Completed)** | Last summer, we **were going to visit** friends in Colorado, but we didn't have enough time. |

**4**    In pairs, use the following cues to ask and answer questions.

**Example:**    clean your room

A:    *Have you cleaned your room yet?*

B:    *I was going to clean it a while ago, but I didn't have time.*

Or:    *I said I was going to clean it a while ago, and I did.*

1.    make your bed
2.    sweep the floor
3.    take the garbage out
4.    pick your clothes up

5.    do the laundry
6.    iron your shirts
7.    straighten your room up
8.    do your homework

**5**    Make sentences using *was/were going to*. Use the following cues and add ideas of your own.

**Example:**    Ann / make a cake / no sugar
*Ann was going to make a cake, but she didn't have any sugar.*

1.    the man / use the pay phone / no coins
2.    you / tell me a story / forget
3.    her friends / visit her new apartment / get lost
4.    the children / eat ice cream / melt
5.    Bob / ride his bicycle / flat tire
6.    Jose / play tennis / start raining
7.    Dorothy / study in the library / too noisy
8.    Craig and Gus / go swimming / too cold

## Using What You've Learned

**6**    Imagine these people's lives. All have experienced major life changes. In pairs or small groups, create stories about each. Make original sentences with *used to* and *would* to compare their lives in the past with their lives today.

**Example:**    a couple with a new baby

*Before their baby arrived, John and Susan used to do lots of things. They used to go to the movies often, but now it's more difficult because they need to get a babysitter. And, they would often go out for dinner, but they don't have as much money as they used to, so they eat at home a lot. Above all, they used to be able to sleep all night. Now they wake up every three hours.*

1. a person who suddenly becomes famous
2. newlyweds
3. a freshman (first year student) at a university
4. a foreigner in a strange country
5. a newly elected president
6. a person beginning his or her first job
7. children of recently divorced parents
8. a person who wins the lottery

**7** Your childhood may have been very different from those of your classmates. In small groups, choose a certain time period and take turns describing it in detail. You may want to tell about school vacations, or your first year in high school, or weekends when you were seven or eight years old. To get started, try to think of some of the funniest, most interesting, most awkward, or most memorable periods of your childhood. Then, after you have shared your story, write a short composition about it. As a class, you may want to put together a collection of childhood memories.

**Examples:**  *When we were children, our family used to go to the mountains for a month every summer. Our vacations were always in the mountains because my dad used to do a lot of climbing. On those vacations, we'd usually camp for most of the time. I'd share a tent with my two brothers. . . .*

*When I was a freshman in high school, I started going to dances. Our school used to have dances every Saturday night. They were terrible! All the boys would stand along one side of the room and all the girls along the other side. For the first hour or so, no one would dance. The girls would giggle and the boys would push and shove each other. . . .*

**8** What did you learn about yourself in Activity 7 on page 77? Are you a procrastinator or not? Use your list from Activity 7 or make a new list of the important things you wanted to do during the past month. Then note whether or not you did each. If you did not, give a sentence explaining why not. If you wish, make a chart like the one that follows.

| Planned To Do | Done | Still Haven't Done | Why Not |
|---|---|---|---|
| write my brother | | X | I was going to write a long letter telling about my life, but I got too busy. |
| balance my checkbook | | | |
| organize my apartment | | | |
| | | | |
| | | | |

## PART 5

# Past Verb Forms: The Past Perfect Tense; The Past Perfect Continuous Tense

## Setting the Context

**Prereading Questions**   All over the world, people have been moving from rural areas into the cities. What effects has this migration had?

### The Urbanization of America

Like much of the world, the United States did not develop large urban centers until this century. Before World War I, the majority of Americans had lived in rural areas or in small towns. In 1900, for example, over 40 percent of the U.S. population lived or worked on farms.

World War I and the Depression of the 1930s changed American life dra-     5
matically. By 1930, for example, the farm population had dropped to 30.1 percent. During the Depression, over three-quarters of a million farmers lost their land. As individuals and entire families moved to cities in search of work, urban areas grew tremendously. Today, almost 80 percent of Americans live in metropolitan areas.     10

This migration from rural to urban areas has had a great impact on American society, just as it has in many parts of the world. In general, people in urban areas are more mobile and more independent, families are less stable, and friendships are often short-lived. Although cities may offer greater economic opportunities, they also present many difficulties in maintaining "the ties that bind": close, long-     15
term relationships with family and friends.

**Discussing Ideas.**   Is this pattern of rural-to-urban migration true in other countries you are familiar with? Why do people leave their rural homes? How does the move to a city affect them, their families, and their friends?

## A. The Past Perfect Tense

The past perfect tense refers to an activity or situation completed *before* another event or time in the past. This tense may be used in a simple sentence, but it normally contrasts with the simple past in a compound or complex sentence.

|  | **Examples** | **Notes** |
|---|---|---|
| **Simple Sentences** | Until 1932, the O'Keefes **had lived** on a farm. By the end of 1932, they **had** already **lost** their farm and moved to the city. | Time expressions such as *already, barely, just, no sooner, rarely, recently, still, yet, ever, never,* or connecting words such as *after, before, by, by the time (that), until, when* are often used with the past perfect. Chapter 8 includes more information on uses of this tense with connecting words and complex sentences. |
| **Complex Sentences** | Before the Depression began, the O'Keefes **had been** prosperous farmers. The children **had** just **begun** school when their parents lost the farm. | |

*Note:* See Appendix 1 for a list of irregular past participles and Appendix 2 for spelling rules for the *-ed* ending.

## The Simple Past Versus the Past Perfect Tense

Although the past perfect tense is often preferable in formal English, the simple past is frequently used instead of the past perfect in conversation. The meaning of the sentence must be clear, however. For example, in sentences with *when,* the time difference in the two tenses can change the meaning of the sentence. Compare:

|  | **Examples** |
|---|---|
| **Simple Past + Simple Past** | It **began** to rain **when I went** out. (The rain began at that time.) |
| **Past Perfect + Simple Past** | It **had begun** to rain **when I went** out. (The rain had begun earlier.) |

**1**  This activity tells the story of an immigrant family in the United States. Using *by* and the past perfect tense, form complete sentences from the cues that follow.

**Example:**   1848 / John and Mary O'Keefe / leave Ireland

*By 1848, John and Mary O'Keefe had left Ireland.*

1.  1850 / the O'Keefes / start a farm in Wisconsin
2.  1852 / they / build a house
3.  1853 / they / clear several acres of land
4.  1854 / the O'Keefes and other families / construct a church and a school
5.  1880s / the O'Keefes / raise a family of ten children
6.  1885 / their son John / marry Catherine
7.  1890 / Catherine / give birth to a daughter, Amanda
8.  1910 / Amanda / get married to Ed
9.  1920 / they / have a beautiful baby girl
10. 1950 / their daughter / begin her own family

**2**  Complete the following sentences by using either the simple past or the past perfect tense of the verbs in parentheses, as in the example.

**Example:**   Before changing lifestyles ___*began*___ (begin) to separate modern families, several generations of the same family ___*had often lived*___ (live / often) together.

1.  Until the automobile, the Depression, and the world wars _____ (bring) changes in U.S. society, American lifestyles _____ (remain) constant for a century.

2.  American society _____ (begin / already) to change when World War II _____ (break out).

3.  After rural families _____ (move) to the cities in search of work, they _____ (create) new lives there instead of returning to their farms.

4.  Women _____ (work / rarely) outside the home before World War II _____ (produce) a labor shortage.

5.  After women _____ (experience) the world of work, many _____ (find) it difficult to return to their traditional roles.

6.  By the time that World War II _____ (come) to an end, the American way of life _____ (change) tremendously.

## B. The Past Perfect Continuous Tense

The past perfect continuous tense, like the past perfect tense, is used to contrast an earlier and a later time in the past. It may be used instead of the past perfect tense to emphasize the continuous nature of the earlier activity. The past perfect continuous tense is seldom used in conversation but does appear in written English.

| | **Examples** | **Notes** |
|---|---|---|
| **Simple Sentences** | Before the Depression, the O'Keefes **had been making** a decent living. Until the Depression, they **had been planning** to buy a larger farm. | The following time expressions are commonly used with the past perfect continuous: *after, already, before, by, by the time (that), until*, and *for* + a period of time. Chapter 8 includes more information on this tense in complex sentences. |
| **Complex Sentence** | Before they lost their farm, the O'Keefes **had been making** a good living. | |

*Note:* See page 47 for a list of verbs not normally used in the continuous tenses. See Appendix 2 for spelling rules for the *-ing* ending.

**3**　Using *by the time that* and *already,* combine the following pairs of sentences. Be sure to change verb tenses when necessary.

**Example:**　Women fought to get the vote for years.
　　　　　　　The 19th Amendment was ratified in 1920.
　　　　　　　*Women had already been fighting to get the vote for years by the time that the 19th Amendment was ratified in 1920.*

1. Serious economic problems affected world trade for several years.
   The stock market crashed in 1929.
2. Farmers struggled to maintain their farms for several years.
   The drought of 1935–36 began.
3. Blacks and other minorities tried for years to receive equality under the law.
   Congress passed the Civil Rights Act in 1964.
4. Martin Luther King, Jr. worked for civil rights for more than a decade.
   He received the Nobel Peace Prize in 1964.
5. The Soviet Union experimented with spacecraft for several years.
   The United States began its space program.
6. Young Americans explored ways of working and helping abroad.
   John F. Kennedy established the Peace Corps in 1961.

**4**   **Review.**   Complete the following passage with appropriate past forms of the verbs in parentheses. In some cases, more than one choice may be possible. Be prepared to discuss your choices. The first two are done as examples.

## Immigrant Families and the Great Depression

It _____was_____ 6:45 in the morning, and Katherine Nuss _____was going_____ out into the gray
    1 (be)                                      2 (go)

morning light. She _____ around the corner to the streetcar stop and
                       3 (walk)

_____ the journey to the great houses of High Street. The wages _____
  4 (begin)                                                5 (be)

low—$2 for a 12- or 13-hour day. Some nights it _____ nearly nine o'clock by the
                                                6 (be)

time she _____ from the trolley to her own home at 1020 West Mulberry Street.
          7 (trudge)

Nevertheless, the work _____ money. While she _____ floors, _____
                   8 (mean)                    9 (scrub)         10 (wash)

windows, _____ woodwork, and _____ meals for the rich families of
             11 (polish)                12 (cook)

Springfield, she _____ her children and _____ the family together.
              13 (support)            14 (keep)

In 1933, the economic situation _____ worse in her town, as in the rest of the
                           15 (get)

nation. At that time, America _____ close to the bottom of the Great Depression.
                   16 (come)

Her husband _____ disabled, and they _____ many children to feed. So,
            17 (be)                18 (have)

Katherine Nuss _____ back to work. Once again, she _____ houses, the
          19 (go)                      20 (clean)

same thing she _____ as a teenage immigrant fresh off the boat from Europe.
                    21 (do)

She _____ house for the wealthy families on the hill in order to keep her own
      22 (clean)

family together.

Both she and her husband _____ the preciousness of family because of
                              23 (know)

their own hard experiences. Many years before, as children, both _____ their
                                                                      24 (lose)

own parents because of death or immigration to America. Both, as adults, _____
                                                                              25 (place)

family as one of the highest values of life.

Katherine _____ a little girl in Austria-Hungary when her mother
              26 (be)

_____. Her father _____ her with relatives and
      27 (die)                        28 (leave)

_____ for America. Like millions of other immigrants, he _____
      29 (sail)                                                              30 (look)

for his future in the New World.

Katherine _____ 14 years old when her father _____ for her. She
              31 (be)                                      32 (send)

_____ at Ellis Island, New York, in 1910—alone, frightened, and unable to speak
  33 (arrive)

a word of English. All she _____ _____ a slip of paper with her father's
                              34 (have)   35 (be)

home address in Cincinnati.

**Culture Note**

*Ellis Island, in New York Harbor, was the first federal immigration center in the United States. The center was opened on January 1, 1892 to receive and process the documents of new immigrants. Between 1892 and 1924, over 12 million new Americans passed through Ellis Island. As many as 5000 people per day were processed there.*

**5**   **Review.**   Complete the passage with appropriate forms of the verbs in parentheses. Add adverbs when indicated. The first one is done as an example.

### Family Responsibilities

Household chores *are usually* boring. All of us in the Peterson household
                    1 (be / usually)

_____ busy schedules, so we _____ to share the chores. Our plan
  2 (have)                            3 (try)

_____ out though! For example, our sons, Dan and Ed, _____ the din-
4 (work / seldom)                                              5 (do / usually)

ner dishes, but tonight they _____ for exams. So guess who _____ the
                                6 (study)                            7 (wash)

dishes tonight? Me! Our daughter, Sue, _____ care of the laundry, but she
                                          8 (take / normally)

_____ friends out of town. So guess who _____ the laundry this week?
  9 (visit)                                        10 (do)

Me! My husband and I _____ cooking, as a rule, but he _____ with one of
               11 (alternate)                                              12 (meet)

his most important clients this evening. So guess who _____ dinner again? Me!
                                                              13 (make)

I _____ doing all these chores, and, in fact, I _____ housework.
     14 (not mind)                                                 15 (like / even)

Time _____ my problem, however. I _____ 35 hours a week, and I
     16 (be / always)                           17 (work)

_____ to stay late at my job. I _____ that the family schedules _____
18 (have / often)                        19 (understand)                              20 (change)

and that "someone" _____ to keep up the house. But I _____ to
                    21 (need)                                      22 (seem / almost always)

be the "someone." It _____ easy to have two full-time jobs!
                     23 (not be)

**6**   **Review.**   The opening passage of this chapter is repeated below. First, complete the
passage with appropriate forms of the verbs in parentheses. Then, look back at page 62
and compare your choices with the original. The first one is done as an example.

### Families

Exactly what ___*is*___ a family? Until about 40 years ago, the traditional American
              1 (be)

family _____ of a working husband, a wife at home, and two or more children.
        2 (consist)

Responsibilities _____ clearly divided in the American nuclear family. While the
                 3 (be)

husband _____ a living, the wife _____ for the home and _____
        4 (earn)                          5 (care)                              6 (raise)

the children. Of course, there were exceptions, but this concept of the family

_____ the general rule until the 1960s.
     7 (be)

Since the 1960s, however, the family _____ more diverse, fragile, and
                                      8 (become)

changeable. Americans _____ differing concepts of families, including single-
                      9 (accept)

parent, blended, two-paycheck, interracial, childless, and commuter families.

Some critics believe that the American family _____ greatly because of all
                                              10 (suffer)

the changes in society. According to these critics, the family _____ much
                                                              11 (be)

stronger before it _____ to struggle with issues such as divorce, working
                   12 (begin)

mothers, gay couples, and unmarried relationships. Today's strongest critics

_____ that the traditional nuclear family will become rare in the 21st
     13 (feel)

century.

Nationwide, however, most Americans _____ that the family _____.
14 (believe)                                    15 (survive)

In fact, almost all major surveys in recent years _____ that the American family
16 (find)

is as strong as it has ever been. For most Americans, the family _____ to pro-
17 (continue)

vide their deepest source of satisfaction and meaning in life. Thus, although today's

family _____ different from what it _____, it seems to be thriving.
18 (be)                                   19 (be)

## Using What You've Learned

**7** The 20th century was a period of tremendous change worldwide: in work and careers, family life, education, medical care, transportation, eating habits, shopping, and entertainment, to name only a few areas. Choose one area of change as the topic for a short composition. First, describe the situation 25, 50, 75, or 100 years ago. Then, describe the situation today, making comparisons between the past and present. Finally, use your composition as the basis for a three-minute presentation to the class.

**Example:** *Until the age of television, most Italian families had spent their evenings together. They would talk, read, sing, or tell stories. . . .*

**8** Every culture has favorite folk stories. Many of these teach us lessons about life. Can you remember a folk story that you particularly liked as a child? In small groups, share some stories. You may want to write these stories and make a short collection of folktales from around the world.

## Video Activities: True Love

**Before You Watch.** Work in small groups. Number these reasons why couples (dating or married) end their relationships from 1 (most common) to 5 (least common).

_____ a. money problems

_____ b. different priorities

_____ c. lack of communication

_____ d. the romance is gone

_____ e. problems with family or friends

**Watch.** Circle the correct answers.

1. What is Dr. Mary Quinn's job?

   a. a medical doctor        b. a teacher        c. a couple's counselor

2. According to the reporter, what does love *not* require?

    a. bonding       b. time       c. loyalty       d. communication

3. What products can help couples improve their communication skills?

    a. books       b. movies       c. music       d. games

4. The woman from the dating service says that after people find a partner, they often get _____.

    a. married       b. lazy       c. discouraged

5. Dr. Quinn says that _____ can help keep couples close.

    a. commitment       b. marriage       c. traditions

**Watch Again.**   Compare answers in small groups.

1. Check Dr. Quinn's four tips for improving communication.

    _____ a. Ask questions.

    _____ b. Choose your words carefully.

    _____ c. Listen closely.

    _____ d. Pick a good time to talk.

    _____ e. Put things in terms of yourself.

    _____ f. Make statements about your needs.

2. The woman with the red hair says that if your partner isn't thoughtful, you should _____.

    a. be more thoughtful

    b. leave him / her

    c. tell him / her how you feel

3. Match the phrases with their meanings.

    1. split up               a. good feeling

    2. kick back            b. end a relationship

    3. a high                c. get lazy

**After You Watch.**   Complete this conversation between a couple's counselor and a married couple.

*Dr. Fields:* What _____ (seem) to be the problem?

*Rosa:* I _____ (be) not sure. We _____ (keep) arguing. In fact, we never _____ (talk) anymore. We just _____ (argue).

*Daniel:* That _____ (be) because you _____ (be) always angry. I _____ (come) home from work. I _____ (be) tired and she _____ (want) to talk.

*Rosa:* Of course I _____ (want) to talk. I _____ (be) home with the baby all day. I _____ (need) some adult conversation. But you just _____ (give) me one word answers. I _____ (ask), "How _____ (be) your day?" and you _____ (say), "Fine."

*Dr. Fields:* Rosa I _____ (understand) how you feel. However, I _____ (find) that statements often _____ (work) better than questions. _____ (try) saying, "I'd really like to hear about your day." I _____ (think) you'll find that you'll get a better response.

## Focus on Testing

### *Use of Verbs*

Verb forms and tenses are frequently tested on standardized English proficiency exams. Review these commonly tested structures and check your understanding by completing the following sample items.

**Remember that** . . .

■ All tenses should be formed correctly, and the tense should be appropriate for the time frame(s) of the sentence.

■ Verbs of feeling, perception, and possession are not generally used in continuous tenses. Also, many of these verbs are linking verbs; adverbs cannot be used as complements after linking verbs.

■ A singular verb is used with a singular subject, and plural verbs are used with plural subjects.

**Part 1:** Circle the correct completion for the following.

**Example:** John _____ quite ill in the past few days.

     a. had became        c. has became
     b. had become      (d.) has become

1. Most major surveys in recent years _____ that Americans are satisfied with their family life.
     a. have find          c. has found
     b. find              d. have found

2. The Jacksons seem _____ with their decision to move.
     a. please          c. happily
     b. happy          d. pleasant

3. When Mary was younger, she _____ tennis much more than now.
     a. used to like     c. was liking
     b. would like      d. like

4.  By 1924, over 12 million new Americans _____ the United States through Ellis Island.

    a.  had been entering           c.  had entered
    b.  have entered                d.  had been entered

**Part 2:**   Circle the letter below the word(s) containing an error.

**Example:**   An individual <u>may feel</u> <u>frustratedly</u> if she has difficulties in speaking
                    A            B           Ⓒ

          the language <u>where she is living</u>.
                              D

1.  <u>Long before</u> the Prime Minister <u>left</u> for Canada, she <u>had discussing</u> the
        A                                  B                    C

    issue <u>in depth</u> with the entire cabinet.
              D

2.  <u>By the time that</u> the report <u>is finished</u>, the committee <u>will have spending</u>
            A                      B                          C

    over two months <u>working</u> on it.
                        D

3.  <u>Since</u> the Depression <u>of the 1930s</u>, the farm population in the United States
        A              B

    <u>have dropped</u> from around 30 percent <u>to less than</u> 4 percent.
          C                                      D

4.  Soon after <u>the</u> Sweeneys <u>had arrived</u> in America, they <u>had started</u> <u>farming</u> in
                  A                B                        C          D

    central Wisconsin.

# Chapter 4

# Health and Leisure

# Introduction

In this chapter you will study the forms and functions of the modal auxiliaries, as well as some structures related to them in usage. This chapter emphasizes the present forms, active voice. In Chapter 5, you will study the passive forms. In Chapter 10, you will review these and study the past forms in more detail.

The following passage introduces the chapter theme, "Health and Leisure," and raises some of the topics and issues you will cover in the chapter.

**Culture Note**

*Medical care is very expensive in the United States. Many Americans have health insurance paid for by an employer, or they buy insurance for themselves. However, information in the last U.S. Census pointed out that over 40 million people in the United States do not have any medical insurance.*

### How Healthy Are You?

Good health is not something you are able to buy at the drugstore, and you can't depend on getting it back with a quick visit to the doctor when you're sick, either. Keeping yourself healthy has to be your own responsibility. Mistreating your system by keeping bad habits, neglecting symptoms of illness, and ignoring common health rules can counteract the best medical care.   5

Nowadays, health specialists promote the idea of wellness for everybody. Wellness means achieving the best possible health within the limits of your body. One person may need many fewer calories than another, depending on metabolism. Some people might prefer a lot of easier exercise to more strenuous exercise. While one person enjoys playing 72 holes of golf a week, another would   10
rather play three sweaty, competitive games of tennis.

Understanding the needs of your own body is the key. Everyone runs the risk of accidents, and no one can be sure of avoiding chronic disease. Nevertheless, poor diet, stress, a bad working environment, and carelessness can ruin good health. By changing your habits or the conditions surrounding you, you can lower   15
the risk or reduce the damage of disease.

**Discussing Ideas.**   Have you noticed any major differences between health care issues in North America and other countries you are familiar with?

---

| PART 1 |
|---|

# Modal Auxiliaries and Related Structures of Ability and Expectation

## Setting the Context

**Prereading Questions**   What is *physical fitness?* Can you describe a physically fit person?

**Are You Physically Fit?**

Check off your answers to the following questions.

| | Yes | No |
|---|---|---|
| Can you go through a busy day and feel good the next morning? | | |
| Are you able to lift one half of your body weight? | | |
| Can you bend and twist easily in all directions? | | |
| Can you walk a mile in 15 minutes? | | |
| Do you maintain your weight? | | |

After checking off your answers to the questions in the preceding chart, decide whether you are physically fit or you have to get into better shape.

## A. Introduction to Modal Auxiliaries

A modal has only one form for all persons of the verb, but it can have several meanings and time frames, depending on the context in which it is used. A complete list of the modals discussed in this chapter appears in Appendix 5; the list also includes related structures (structures often used in place of modal auxiliaries).

| | Examples | Negative Contractions | |
|---|---|---|---|
| **Statements** | He **should get** more exercise. | can't | shouldn't |
| **Questions** | **Would** you **like** to go jogging? | couldn't | won't |
| **Negatives** | I **can't play** tennis today. | mustn't | wouldn't |

## B. Expressing Present and Past Ability

With *can, could,* and *be able to,* affirmative and negative statements and questions all give the meaning of ability. In rapid speech, *can* is weakly stressed (*kin*). *Can't* is stressed more strongly.

| Modals | Examples |
|---|---|
| **Present Ability**<br>**can (cannot)**<br>**(not) be able to** } + **simple form** | John **can** run five miles, but I **can't (cannot).**<br>How many miles **are** you **able** to run? |
| **Past Ability**<br>**could (not)**<br>**(not) be able to** } + **simple form** | He **couldn't** run as fast as she **could.**<br>I **wasn't able to** run because of the rain. |

**1**   It is often difficult to distinguish *can* and *can't* in rapid conversation. Of course, there is a tremendous difference in meaning! As your teacher rapidly reads the following sentences, circle *can* or *can't* according to what you hear.

*Hint:* **Can** has little stress, and **can't** is more clearly pronounced.

1. I (can / can't) swim a mile.
2. John (can / can't) run a mile.
3. I (can / can't) walk a mile.
4. She (can / can't) ski very well.
5. He (can / can't) jog ten miles.
6. They (can / can't) skate very well.
7. I (can / can't) ride a bike.
8. I (can / can't) hear the difference between the two words!
9. He said he (can / can't) come.
10. I'm sure she said she (can / can't).

**2**   With a partner, take turns making statements. Choose one sentence in each pair, but don't tell which sentence you are choosing. Your partner should add a statement.

**Example:**   a.   I can surf.      Partner A:   *I can't surf.*
             b.   I can't surf.     Partner B:   *But I can.* or *I can't either.*

1. a. I can swim.
   b. I can't swim.
2. a. I can roller-blade.
   b. I can't roller-blade.
3. a. I can play the guitar.
   b. I can't play the guitar.
4. a. I can speak Japanese.
   b. I can't speak Japanese.
5. a. He can ride a bike.
   b. He can't ride a bike.

6. a. She can touch her toes.
   b. She can't touch her toes.
7. a. He can do a cartwheel.
   b. He can't do a cartwheel.
8. a. She can work tonight.
   b. She can't work tonight.
9. a. They can play piano.
   b. They can't play piano.
10. a. They can make pizza.
    b. They can't make pizza.

**3** Your teacher will make a list of all the things that students in your class can do. Copy the list into the following chart. Then check the box that reflects your ability in this activity. Here are some suggestions for a list of your abilities: using a computer, rollerblading or doing other sports, playing musical instruments, speaking different languages, and so on.

| Activity | Can Do Well | Can Do Fairly Well | Can't Do Very Well | Can't Do at All |
|---|---|---|---|---|
| 1. *use a computer* | | | | |
| 2. | | | | |
| 3. | | | | |
| 4. | | | | |
| 5. | | | | |
| 6. | | | | |
| 7. | | | | |
| 8. | | | | |
| 9. | | | | |
| 10. | | | | |
| 11. | | | | |
| 12. | | | | |

Then with a partner, take turns making statements and asking questions about the chart.

**Example:** A: I can use a computer very well. Can you?

B: I can too.

**4** Look at the chart you made for Activity 3. Compare your ability in each activity between the present and the past. What can you do now? What could you do when you were younger? Discuss your present and past abilities with a partner, using the following patterns:

*When I was younger, I could (couldn't) . . .*

*Now that I'm older, I can . . .*

> *I still can't . . .*

> *I can't . . . anymore.*

**Example:** *When I was younger, I couldn't use a computer, but now I use a computer every day!*

**5** The chart below gives you the approximate calories you burn in sports and other activities. Use the information to form at least six sentences with *can*. Note that you must use the *-ing* form of a verb after *by*.

**Example:**    *You (A person) can burn over 300 calories by walking briskly for an hour.*

**Culture Note**

*In the United States fitness centers have become so popular that there are special gyms and fitness programs for toddlers and infants under one year of age. Naturally, they are accompanied by their moms or dads.*

---

## How Many Calories Can You Burn?

Food produces energy. One ounce of fat gives 267 calories of energy. A pound of fat is equivalent to 4272 calories.

| CALORIES BURNED PER HOUR | ACTIVITY |
|---|---|
| 72–84 | sitting and talking |
| 120–150 | walking at a slow pace |
| 240–300 | doing housework (cleaning, mopping, scrubbing) |
| 300–360 | walking briskly; playing doubles tennis; playing Ping-Pong (table tennis) |
| 350–420 | bicycling; ice- or roller-skating |
| 420–480 | playing singles tennis |
| 480–600 | downhill skiing; jogging |
| 600–650 | running (5.5 mph); bicycling (13 mph) |
| over 660 | running (6 or more mph); handball; squash; swimming (depends on stroke and style—excellent overall conditioner) |

---

## C. Expressing Expectation

*Should* and *ought to* have two different meanings. One meaning is *will probably*. The other meaning of advice is covered later in this chapter. With both meanings, *should* is more commonly used.

| Modals | Examples | Notes |
|---|---|---|
| **should (not) +** simple form | He **should arrive** very soon. **Shouldn't** she **arrive** soon? This **shouldn't take** long to do. | Negative questions with *should* are often used for emphasis. In rapid speech, *ought to* sounds like /otta/. |
| **ought (not) to +** simple form | We **ought to be** finished soon. | |

**6** Take turns reading the following statements and creating new statements. The first student reads the statement from the text. The second student forms a sentence with *should*, and the third student uses *ought to* for the same sentence. As an alternative, write your new versions of the original statement, one with *should* and one with *ought to*.

**Example:**   We expect the doctor to arrive at any minute.

      A:   We expect the doctor to arrive at any minute.

B:   The doctor should arrive at any minute.

C:   The doctor ought to arrive at any minute.

1.   The doctor expects the exam to take only a few minutes.
2.   She doesn't expect there to be any problems.
3.   She expects to have plenty of time to answer questions.
4.   The doctor expects your exam to be normal.
5.   She doesn't expect you to need another checkup for at least a year.
6.   You can expect your bill to arrive within a week.
7.   We expect the insurance to cover most of your bill.
8.   We don't expect to have any problems with your coverage.
9.   The company doesn't expect insurance premiums to go up until next year.
10.  The company expects premiums to increase within 18 months.

**7**   Complete each little story using one of the modal forms studied in this section: *be able to, can, could,* or *should.*

**Before**

1.   Before I began exercising at Ernie's Exercise Emporium, I _wasn't able to lose_ (not lose) weight, and I _____ (not find) any clothes that fit me well.

**After**

2.   Now that my muscles are so big, I _____ (not find) anything to wear. Well, my instructor said that I _____ (to find) some clothes at "Miki's Muscle Shop for High Powered Females." They _____ (have) something that fits me!

**Before**

3.   Before I began exercising at Ernie's Exercise Emporium, I _____ (not run), I _____ (not jog). I _____ (not walk), I _____ (not sit / even) without getting tired. I _____ (not do) anything!

**After**

4.   Now I _____ (not do / still) anything! But the doctor says that I _____ (to leave) the hospital soon.

## Using What You've Learned

**8**  In recent years, Americans have become more concerned about their health. In fact, for many people, fitness has become almost an obsession. In large cities and small towns alike, people jog regularly, join sports teams, and go to health clubs to work out.

What is the attitude toward fitness in a culture(s) you are familiar with? Have attitudes changed in recent years? Are there differences for males and females? Discuss these questions in a small group. As an alternative, you can write a brief essay giving your own experiences and opinions, or you can interview another person.

**PART 2**  # Modal Auxiliaries of Request, Permission, and Preference

## Setting the Context

**Prereading Questions**   Ticket agencies often sell tickets for many different kinds of entertainment events from circuses to rock concerts. What kinds of entertainment do you enjoy? Where do you buy tickets?

**At the Ticket Window**

**Discussing Ideas.** Look at the picture. What do you think the young woman likes to do with her leisure time? How about the older woman? Why is she at the ticket counter?

## A. Requesting Action

One form of request involves asking someone to do something. The following modal auxiliaries are often used in these requests.

| Modals | Examples | Notes |
|---|---|---|
| **Would you mind . . . ? + gerund (verb + *ing*)** | **Would** you **mind** call**ing** the theater for the movie schedule?<br><br>**Would** you **mind** not go**ing** to the matinee? | *Would you mind* . . . is always followed by a gerund. A negative response means "I will." Informal answers are often affirmative, however. |
| **Would you . . . ?**<br>**Could you . . . ?**<br>**Can you . . . ?**<br>**Will you . . . ?** } + simple form | **Would you** call the theater for the movie schedule?<br><br>**Could you** call the Granada Theater?<br><br>**Can you** get us two tickets to the concert?<br><br>**Will you** find us three seats together up front? | *Please* is often added to any request. *Could* and *would* are appropriate in most circumstances.<br><br>*Can* is informal, and it is used among friends.<br><br>*Will* is somewhat rude in tone. It is used in urgent situations or among friends. |

### Pronunciation Note

In rapid speech *can, could, will,* and *would* are seldom pronounced clearly. Listen carefully as your teacher reads the following words:

| Normal Speech | Rapid Speech | Normal Speech | Rapid Speech |
|---|---|---|---|
| Can you . . . ? | /kenya/ | Will you . . . ? | /willya/ |
| Can he . . . ? | /keni/ | Will he . . . ? | /willi/ |
| Could you . . . ? | /kudja/ | Would you . . . ? | /wudja/ |
| Could he . . . ? | /kuddi/ | Would he . . . ? | /wuddi/ |

**1** Your teacher will read the following requests, but *not* in the order listed. Listen carefully and write down the form that you hear.

1. Could you help?
2. Could he help?
3. Would you help?
4. Wouldn't he help?
5. Can't you help?
6. Couldn't you help?
7. Can you help?
8. Wouldn't you help?

**2** In a situation where polite requests haven't worked, we often use more direct language. Imagine that you are teaching a friend how to make polite requests. Your friend has overheard a conversation in a theater that went something like the following.

*Man in Back:* Remove your hat! I told you I can't see through it.
*Man with Hat:* Don't talk to me that way!
*Man in Back:* Take it off now!
*Man with Hat:* Don't give me orders!
*Man in Back:* Move to another section!
*Man with Hat:* Move? You move!
*Man in Back:* Go!
*Man with Hat:* Hold my hat, darling. I'm going to teach this guy a lesson.

Change the commands in the conversation above to polite requests for action by using *could, would,* or *would you mind.*

**Example:**   Remove your hat! *Would you mind removing your hat?*

## B. Requesting Permission

Another form of request involves asking permission. The following modal auxiliaries are often used in these requests.

| Modals | Examples | Notes |
|---|---|---|
| **Would you mind if I . . . ? + past form** | **Would you mind if I didn't go** to the game today? I'm tired. | *Would you mind if I . . .* is always followed by the past tense of a second verb. It is polite and very formal. A negative response means "It's all right." |
| **May I . . . ?** **Could I . . . ?** **Can I . . . ?** } + **simple form** | **May I** help you? **Could I** talk with the manager, please? **Can I** see the fall schedule of games? | *May* is formal. It is most often used in service situations. *May* and *could* are preferred in polite speech. *Can* is very informal, but it is often used in conversation. |

**3**  In pairs, take turns making and responding to requests for permission. Complete the following conversations by using *may, could,* or *can.* (Remember that *can* is informal and may not be appropriate for all situations.)

**Example:**  (see the manager)

I'm sorry, but . . .

A:  **May (Could) I see the manager?**

B:  **I'm sorry, but she's not available at the moment.**

**1.** (change my table)

Yes, of course . . .

**2.** (speak with the manager)

I'm sorry, but . . .

**3.** (have the check now)

Certainly . . .

**4.** (pay by check)

Yes, if . . .

**5.** (borrow your menu)

Sure . . .

**6.** (use the telephone)

Sorry, but . . .

**4**  In pairs, complete the following conversations asking for permission or for action. Use *can, could, may, would, would you mind . . . ,* or *would you mind if . . .* in your requests. Use each form at least once.

**Example:**  A.  *Can you give me a six o'clock reservation?*

B.  Of course. What name shall I put it under?

1.  A: _____

B:  No, I wouldn't. I forgot to take it off. Sorry.

2.  A: _____

B:  No problem! We can have lunch together next week.

3.  A: _____

B:  Sure, I could. Where would you like to eat?

4.  A: _____

B:  Of course I wouldn't mind. Would you like me to order?

5.  A: _____

B:  No, not at all. Smoking is permitted in this area of the restaurant.

6.  A: _____

B:  Sure, I am not using them anyway.

7.  A: _____

B:  No, I wouldn't. I'd be happy if you joined me.

8.  A: _____

B:  Thank you, but I only need one ticket.

**5.**  Make a chain around the class. Turn to the person next to you (your "neighbor") and make a request. Before you make your request, tell the class "who" you are addressing. Then make your request, and your neighbor will respond. Your neighbor then asks his or her neighbor, and so on, continuing the chain. After each, the class should decide if the form of the request was appropriate or not (for example, was the request polite enough? too polite?). Add other situations if necessary.

**Example:**   A:   (*to my grandfather*) **Grandpa, would you please let me use your car?**

B:   **Why of course! Would you like the Rolls Royce or the Mercedes?**

B:   (*to a stranger*) **Excuse me, sir. Could I . . . ?**

1.   You would like to borrow your sister's (brother's, roommate's, father's, aunt's, grandfather's) car.
2.   You need to use a telephone. Ask a stranger (your teacher, your friend, the school administrator, your roommate) for change for the pay phone.
3.   You would like to use your sister's (brother's, roommate's, cousin's) favorite sweater (jacket, coat) for a special night out. Ask to borrow it from him or her.
4.   You would like your roommate (brother, sister, friend, cousin) to lend you a bicycle. Ask him or her to lend it to you for a couple of days.
5.   You need to talk with your advisor. Ask the assistant for an appointment.
6.   You need to make a dentist appointment. Ask the receptionist for an appointment.
7.   You need to get a prescription filled in a drug store. Ask the pharmacist (the cashier) to help you.
8.   You don't have enough money for the rent and you desperately need to borrow $100. Ask your mother (father, roommate, best friend, boyfriend, girlfriend, classmate) to lend (or give) you the money.

## C. Expressing Preference

| Modals | | Examples | Notes |
|---|---|---|---|
| I would (not) like . . .<br>Would you like . . . ?<br>Wouldn't you like . . . ? | + infinitive or noun | I **would like** a window seat.<br>No, I **would like (prefer)** to sit in the middle section.<br>**Would you like** to see the new play?<br>**Wouldn't you like (prefer)** to see the new play? | Affirmative and negative statements and questions with *would like (prefer)* may express desires or preferences. *Would like (prefer)* is followed by either a noun or an infinitive. |
| I would rather (not) . . .<br>Would you rather (not) . . . ?<br>Wouldn't you rather . . . ? | + simple form | **I'd rather not** go in the afternoon.<br>**Would you rather** go in the morning or the afternoon?<br>**Wouldn't** you **rather** go in the morning? | Affirmative and negative statements and questions with *would like* express preferences or choices. The contracted form (*I'd*, etc.) is almost always used in conversational English. |

**6**   Imagine that you have unlimited time and money. What would you like to do? Choose from the following list and add your own ideas. *Note:* for emphasis, you can say *I would really like to . . .* or *I would love to . . . .* Make at least eight sentences.

**Example:**   travel around the world
> *I would like (love) to travel around the world.*

1.   spend a month at a health spa
2.   hire my own private chef
3.   move to Paris
4.   run a marathon
5.   get a Ph.D
6.   compete in the Olympics
7.   buy a yacht
8.   study art
9.   learn yoga
10.   take the TOEFL five times
11.   play a musical instrument well
12.   study a lot more English grammar

**7**   Look at the list in Activity 6. Choose five things you wouldn't like to do. Then give an alternative for each.

**Example:**   travel around the world
> *I wouldn't like to travel around the world. I'd rather stay here and study grammar.*

Or:
> *I'd rather not travel around the world. I'd much rather stay here and study grammar.*

**8**   **Review.**   Add appropriate words or phrases to complete the following conversation. The first two are done as examples.

*Ticket Agent:* Good afternoon. Total Ticket Sales. <u>Would</u> you <u>mind</u> holding for a minute?
1        2
(click) Hello. Thank you for holding. _____
3
_____ help you?
4
*Estela:* Hello. I _____ _____ to purchase
5        6
two tickets for the Saturday night MegaLoud concert.

*Ticket Agent:* MegaLoud is sold out for Saturday evening. _____ you _____
<sub>7</sub>                    <sub>8</sub>
tickets to their Sunday concert?

*Estela:* No. I'd _____ see them on Saturday evening. Are you sure I _____ get
<sub>9</sub>                                                    <sub>10</sub>
tickets for that performance?

*Ticket Agent:* There is a standby list, and of course you could come to the theater on the
night of the performance to check for returned tickets. Would _____ _____ to go
<sub>11</sub>      <sub>12</sub>
on the list or come to the theater?

*Estela:* I _____ _____ not go to the theater if there's a chance I can't see the
<sub>13</sub>   <sub>14</sub>
concert. _____ you just put me on the standby list and call me if there's a ticket
<sub>15</sub>
available?

*Ticket Agent:* I _____ put your name down right now. You're the first on the list.
<sub>16</sub>

*Estela:* Thanks. Let's hope there're two tickets available.

## Using What You've Learned

**9**  Have you been to a play or out to dinner recently? Will you go soon? In pairs, practice making telephone calls to purchase tickets or make reservations by phone for:

1.  three front row seats to the local production of *Godspell* on Thursday evening
2.  a reservation for a party of four at *Le Spigot,* a trendy and hard-to-get-a-reservation-for French nouvelle cuisine restaurant for Saturday at 7 P.M.
3.  your choice

**10**  Have you been to the doctor or dentist recently? Will you see one soon? In pairs, practice making telephone calls to arrange appointments. Role-play making appointments by phone for the following:

1.  a routine medical checkup
2.  getting your teeth cleaned
3.  an emergency dental or doctor's appointment

**11**  Work in pairs and role-play the following situations. Make the characters male or female, depending on each pair. As you role-play, think about how polite you should be when you make your requests.

1. You are in a movie theater watching an excellent new movie. The person next to you is a man (or woman) around 60 years old. He (She) keeps talking during the film. Ask him (or her) to be quiet.

2. You are waiting in line to buy tickets for a concert. Two people come to talk to the person in front of you and enter the line in front of you. Ask them to go to the back of the line.

3. This is your first time in a small neighborhood restaurant and bar where people seem friendly and most know each other. Someone nearby is smoking. Ask the person not to smoke.

4. You are at home and it is 1:30 A.M. Your neighbors are young, and many are college students. They often make noise, and tonight they are making a lot of noise. You have an important exam tomorrow, and you want to be able to sleep. Ask them to be quiet.

 **12** Work with a partner. Imagine that you have a friend visiting from out of town. Your friend is a good friend but very hard to please. He or she is very particular about what to do. Make at least five good suggestions of things to do. They may include suggestions on movies, restaurants, trips, classes, concerts, and so forth. Your "finicky" friend will respond.

**Example:**   A:   Let's go out and see New York at night. Would you like to hear some jazz in Greenwich Village?

   B:   **Jazz is boring. I'd rather stay here and do crossword puzzles.**

   A:   **Well, would you like to . . . ?**

---

**PART 3**   # Modal Auxiliaries and Related Structures of Need and Advice

---

## Setting the Context

**Prereading Questions**   What is the Red Cross? Have you ever visited or needed the services of the Red Cross?

---

### Medical Emergencies

Everyone ought to know the basic steps to follow in case of a medical emergency. If you don't, you should contact your local Red Cross. The Red Cross gives guidelines and offers short courses on what to do in emergency situations.

---

**Discussing Ideas.**   Do you know what to do in a medical emergency? What are some of the basic steps to follow? If you don't know, the following pages will give you at least the basic information.

## A. Expressing Present Need or Lack of Need

| Modals and Related Structures | Examples | Notes |
|---|---|---|
| **Present Need**<br><br>**must (not)**<br>**have to** } + **simple form** | You **must** get a doctor to look at that cut on your hand.<br><br>John **has to** go for a physical exam, so he can't play tennis today.<br><br>You **must not** forget to go to the dentist for your checkup. | In affirmative statement and questions, *must* and *have to* have similar meanings. Both mean "need to."<br><br>In rapid speech, *have to* and *has to* sound like *hafta* and *hasta.*<br><br>*Must not* expresses a strong need not to do something. |
| **Present Lack of Need**<br><br>**don't (doesn't)** } + **simple**<br>**have to** } **form** | I **don't have to** see the doctor because my fever went away. | In negative statements, *do/does not have to* refers to something that is *not* necessary to do. Its meaning is very different from *must not.* |

**1**   Change these commands to statements using *must / must not.*

**Example:**   Don't use electrical appliances in the water!
*You must not use electrical appliances in the water.*

1. Call a doctor right away!
2. Get an ambulance immediately!
3. Don't move!
4. Don't touch that!
5. Turn off the electricity!
6. Find someone to help!
7. Don't drink that!
8. Give me some bandages!

**2**   Read the following guidelines for emergencies. Then complete the sentences below with *must not* or *don't / doesn't have to.*

---

The American Red Cross gives these guidelines to follow in emergency situations.

1. If necessary, rescue the victim as quickly and carefully as possible.
2. Call for medical help immediately.
3. Check to see if the victim is breathing, and give him or her artificial respiration if necessary.
4. Control severe bleeding.
5. If you suspect poisoning, immediately give a conscious victim water or milk to dilute[†] the poison. If you suspect a chemical poison, don't let the victim vomit. If the victim is unconscious or having convulsions,[‡] however, do not give any fluids.
6. In an accident, do **not** move the victim unless absolutely necessary.
7. Always check for injuries **before** moving the victim, if possible.

---

[†]*dilute*   make thinner or weaker
[‡]*convulsions*   violent muscle contractions

---

**Example:**   If the victim has a neck injury, you *must not* move him or her.

1. If you _____ make an emergency rescue, do not move the victim.

2. You _____ move a person with a neck or back injury unless absolutely necessary.

3. If your victim has swallowed a poison and is unconscious, you _____ give him or her anything to drink.

4. If your victim has swallowed a chemical poison, you _____ try to make her vomit.

5. You _____ try different remedies with a poison victim if you are not sure of the poison.

6. You _____ study first aid, but it may be helpful someday.

7. A person who knows first aid _____ call a doctor about every small accident.

8. In a true emergency, you _____ wait. Call a doctor immediately.

**3**   Read the following medicine label. Then rephrase the instructions to tell what the user *must* or *must not* do. Make at least five statements.

**Example:**   *You must not use this medicine if the printed seal is not intact.*

USE ONLY IF PRINTED SEAL UNDER CAP IS INTACT.

Adult Dose: Use only as directed by your physician.

WARNINGS: Do not give this medicine to children under age 12. Keep this and all drugs out of the reach of children. In case of an overdose, contact a physician or a poison control center immediately. Do not use this product if you are pregnant or nursing a baby. Do not use this product while operating a vehicle or machinery. Consult your physician before using this product if you have any of the following conditions: heart problems, high blood pressure, asthma.

**4**   An important part of first aid is knowing what is serious and what is not—what we must do versus what we don't have to do immediately. Use *must, must not,* or *don't/doesn't have to* to complete each set of sentences.

**Examples:**   a.   This is very serious. We _must_ hurry!
                 b.   This is not very serious. We _don't have to_ rush.
                 c.   This is very serious. We _must not_ wait any longer.

1. a.   I _____ see a doctor because I'm feeling much better.

   b.   I really _____ see a doctor because I've been feeling worse every day.

   c.   I _____ wait any longer. I need to see a doctor because I'm very sick.

2. a.   This accident is not very serious. We _____ call for an ambulance.

   b.   This accident has caused serious injuries. We _____ call for an ambulance.

   c.   This accident is serious. We _____ wait a moment longer.

3. a.   There is no emergency. We _____ hurry with the victim.

   b.   There is an emergency. We _____ delay!

   c.   There is an emergency. We _____ get help for the victim immediately.

4. a. That car is going to explode. We _____ move the victim right away.

   b. That car is about to explode. We _____ wait. We need to rescue the victim.

   c. That car is not in danger. We _____ rescue the victim immediately.

5. a. The situation is under control and everything will be OK. We _____ worry.

   b. The situation is serious, and everyone is nervous, but we _____ panic.

   c. This situation is very serious, but we all _____ remain calm.

## B. Expressing Past Need or Lack of Need

*Had to* and *didn't have to* are used to talk about past needs. Note that *must* does not have this meaning in the past.

| Modals | Examples | Notes |
|---|---|---|
| **Past Need**<br>**had to + simple form** | I **had to** see a doctor for my sore throat.<br>**Did** you **have to** buy antibiotics for your sore throat? | In affirmative statements and questions, *had to* implies that the action was completed. |
| **Past Lack of Need**<br>**didn't have to + simple form** | I **didn't have to** take antibiotics because I had the flu.<br>We **didn't have to** have medical exams. We had them last term. | In negative statements, *did not have to* refers to something that was not necessary to do. |

**5** Imagine that you took a first aid class and practiced what to do in an emergency—a fire in an apartment. Tell what you *had to do* and *didn't have to do* by changing these commands to past tense statements.

**Example:** Rescue the victims quickly and carefully.

*We had to rescue the victims.*

1.  Call the fire department fast!
2.  Get a doctor!
3.  Check the victims carefully!
4.  Don't worry about the cat! It already jumped out the window.
5.  Give the child artificial respiration!
6.  Don't worry about the dog! It wasn't inside.
7.  Check the man for injuries!
8.  Control the man's bleeding!

**6**  In pairs, take turns making the following statements and responding to them. Make suggestions from the phrases in parentheses or invent your own suggestions. Use *had better, ought to,* and *should.*

**Example:**   A:   My knee has been swollen and sore since I played tennis.
                    (go to an orthopedist)

              B:   *You'd better go to an orthopedist.*

1.  I've had a headache for several days. (call the doctor)
2.  I've had a toothache since last week. (see a dentist)
3.  I can't see well at night anymore. (have your eyes checked)
4.  I can't get rid of this cold. (stay in bed for a few days)
5.  None of my clothes fit anymore. (go on a diet)
6.  I'm not doing well in my classes. (study more)
7.  I don't understand the next assignment. (talk to the teacher about it)
8.  I have a problem with my visa. (check on it right away)

**7** Test your understanding and your memory! Without looking back, write T (true) or F (false) next to the following statements. After you have finished, look back at Activity 2 on page 115 and check your answers.

1. _____ You should always call for help immediately.

2. _____ You should check to make sure the victim is breathing.

3. _____ If the victim is breathing, you ought to try artificial respiration.

4. _____ If you believe that the victim has swallowed a poison, you should give the person water or milk to dilute it.

5. _____ You shouldn't try to give liquids to someone who is unconscious.

6. _____ You should always check for injuries before you try to move a victim.

7. _____ The last thing you ought to do is call for medical help.

## D. Expressing Advice About the Past (Not Taken)

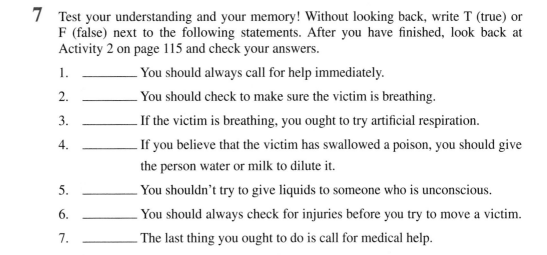

| Modals | Examples | Notes |
|---|---|---|
| **should (not) have** ⎫<br>**ought (not) to have** ⎬ + **past participle** | You **should have** seen a doctor.<br>**Should I have** gone to the nurse's office for a flu shot?<br>We **ought to have** known that we'd catch colds in this rainy, chilly weather. | In affirmative and negative statements questions, *should have* and *ought to have* give advice on past actions or situations. *Ought to have* is seldom used in questions, however. Both imply that the subject did not complete the action or take the advice. In rapid speech, these sound like /shudda/ and /ottuv/. |

**8** Change the following from commands to affirmative or negative statements by using *should, ought to, had better, have to,* or *must.*

**Example:** If someone feels faint:

Have the person lie flat with his head low.

Or: Make the person lower his head between his knees and breathe deeply.

*If someone feels faint, you should have him lie flat. You must keep his head low. You should make him breathe deeply.*

1. If someone gets cut seriously:
   Try to stop the bleeding at once.
   Use a clean bandage to cover the wound.
   Do not remove the bandage when the bleeding stops.
   Try to raise the wound up high.

2. If you suspect a broken bone:
   Don't let the victim bend the surrounding joints (knee, ankle, elbow, and so on).
   Give first aid for shock.
   Don't touch an open wound.

Cover the wound gently.

3. If you suspect a head injury:

Keep the person quiet.

If possible, do not move him or her.

Loosen the clothing around his or her neck.

Do not give the person any stimulants (coffee, and so on).

4. If someone is choking:

Hit the person's back, between the shoulder blades, with the heel of your hand as quickly and forcefully as possible.

Or:

Press against the upper stomach or lower chest several times quickly (the Heimlich maneuver).

5. If someone gets burned (first- or second-degree burns):

Apply cold water until the pain goes away.

Dry the burned area very gently.

Cover the burn with a bandage to protect it, if necessary.

Do not break any blisters or remove any skin.

**9**

**Culture Note**

*The American Cancer Society encourages a healthy lifestyle. It suggests seven CHOICES: Cut out tobacco. Hold the fat. Opt for high-fiber fruits, vegetables, and grains. Intake of alcohol: only in moderation. Call your doctor for regular checkups. Exercise every day. Safeguard your skin from the sun.*

In rapid conversation, it is often difficult to distinguish present and perfect modals. As your teacher reads the following sentences, circle the modal form (present or perfect) that you hear.

1. They (should come / should have come).
2. He (ought to set / ought to have set) a specific time.
3. She (should become / should have become) a doctor.
4. She (ought to quit / ought to have quit) her job.
5. It (should cost / should have cost) less.
6. We (shouldn't let / shouldn't have let) that happen.
7. He (ought to run / ought to have run) more often.
8. We (shouldn't shut / shouldn't have shut) all the windows.
9. That (shouldn't hurt / shouldn't have hurt) very much.
10. I (should buy / should have bought) some cough drops.

**10**

In pairs, respond to the following sentences with a statement using either *should have* or *ought to have*.

**Example:**   Jack studied first aid last semester.

*I should have studied it too, but I didn't.*

1. Veronica went to the dentist last week.
2. Centa gave blood at the Red Cross.
3. Midori took a first aid class last quarter.

4. Ted checked his blood pressure this morning.
5. Futoshi had a checkup yesterday.
6. Nancy took Vitamin C this morning for her cold.
7. Carlos spent several hours reading his health insurance policy.
8. Ali studied for his anatomy exam last night.

**11** Veronica was the first to arrive at a car accident. She tried to help, but she panicked and did everything wrong. Use the information from Activity 2, page 115, and Activity 8, page 119, to help you tell what she *should (not)/ought (not) to have done.*

**Example:**   A young girl had a burn from an accident. Veronica washed the burn with hot water.

*Veronica shouldn't have washed the burn with hot water.*

*She should have applied cold water until the pain stopped.*

1. One man started to faint. Veronica made him stand up quickly.
2. A woman had a head injury. Veronica had the woman walk around and drink several cups of coffee.
3. A boy had serious cuts. Veronica let the boy bleed for a few minutes. Then she covered the wound with a newspaper.
4. Another man had a broken arm. Veronica moved his elbow and shoulder to check them.

## Using What You've Learned

**12** Think about the information on first aid that is given in this section. Then work in pairs or small groups and try to give "common sense" answers to the following questions.

**Example:**   If someone feels faint, why should you make the person lower his or her head and breathe deeply?

*The person needs more oxygen going to his or her brain. Lowering his or her head will send more blood to the brain.*

1. Should you try to move anyone who has had an accident? Why or why not?
2. Why should you check for injuries before moving a victim?
3. When should you move a victim? Try to give an example.
4. If someone has a serious cut, why should you raise the wound up high?
5. If someone is choking, where and why should you hit the person?
6. If someone has swallowed a chemical poison such as a cleaning fluid, why shouldn't you make the person try to vomit?

**13** Around the world, many remedies exist for common problems and ailments. In small groups, share some of your own remedies for the following. Try to use *ought to, should,* and *have to* when possible as you discuss your cures.

| | | |
|---|---|---|
| 1. indigestion | 5. insomnia | 9. heartburn |
| 2. hiccups | 6. a cold | 10. a cramp in your leg |
| 3. a rash | 7. a toothache | 11. stress |
| 4. a headache | 8. a stomachache | 12. carsickness or airsickness |

**14**   Have you ever broken a tooth? Cut yourself with a kitchen knife? Broken an arm or leg while participating in a sport? Had a car accident? These are times when we commonly use or need first aid.

Write about a time when you used first aid or when you needed first aid. What happened? Was it an emergency? What did you do? Did someone help you or did you help someone? Write a short essay explaining your experience.

**15**   Think about all the advice that people have given you about maintaining good health. Perhaps someone told you to take a cold shower every day. Or maybe your doctor recommended that you take a multivitamin when you were a child to grow strong. Some people think that wearing a copper bracelet improves your health. Think about one piece of good advice someone gave you concerning your health. Write about it. Then think of advice that someone gave you about maintaining good health that didn't work at all. Write about it.

**16**   Suppose that someone you know who is younger than you (a brother or sister, for example) is going to a faraway country where the customs, food, health conditions, and style of life are completely different from what you know. What advice would you give that person about staying healthy and free from illness? Discuss your ideas in small groups.

---

### PART 4

# Modal Auxiliaries of Possibility and Probability

---

## Setting the Context

**Prereading Questions**   Have you ever been snowboarding?  If you have, write a sentence or two telling what it is like to snowboard.  If you haven't, imagine what it must be like.

---

#### Snowboarding

*Announcer:* "Here we are at the U.S. Snowboarding Open at Stratton Mountain in the state of Vermont. Our first competitor is Jim Smiley. Jim is only 16 years old. He may be the youngest snowboarder in the competition. Jim is coming over the first hill, and he   **5** looks good. He might be the fastest snowboarder so far. Look out! Jim just *wiped out on that mogul. He might have hurt himself too. No, it looks like he's okay. Yes, Jim Smiley is smiling at the crowd and waving.   **10**

"Phew! That could have been a dangerous fall!"

---

*wiped out on that mogul = crashed and fell on a bump in the hill

 **Discussing Ideas.** Work with a classmate. Can you tell each other anything about snowboarding, surfing, skiing, or windsurfing? What is common to all four of these outdoor sports? What is different about them?

## A. Expressing Present and Past Possibility

| Modals | Examples | Notes |
|---|---|---|
| **Present Possibility**<br><br>**may (not)**<br>**might (not)** } + **simple form**<br>**could (not** | He **may** be the youngest competitor.<br>He **might** win if he keeps going this fast.<br>He **might not** finish the race if he continues to go so fast.<br>**Could** he have a chance to win? | In affirmative and negative statements, *may (have)*, *might (have)*, and *could (have)* all express possibility. All mean "possibly" or "perhaps." *May* is not used with questions with this meaning. In rapid speech, *may have* is pronounced /mayuv/, *might have* is pronounced /mituv/, and *could have* is pronounced /cudduv/. |
| **Past Possibility**<br><br>**may (not) have**<br>**might (not) have** } + **past participle**<br>**could (not) have** | Jim **may have** fallen over a bump in the hill.<br>He **might have** hurt himself.<br>He **couldn't have** hurt himself very badly. He's getting up. | |

 **1** The modals *may, might,* and *could* are often used to suggest possibilities. Negative questions beginning *Why don't you* or *Why don't we* are also used to make suggestions. In groups of three, practice negative questions and modals of possibility by making short conversations from the following cues.

**Example:**    want to learn to snowboard
        take lessons
        have a talent for it
        A: **I've been wanting to learn to snowboard.**
        B: **Why don't you take lessons?**
        C: **You might have a talent for it.**

1.  wonder about my future
    go to an astrologer
    tell you what will happen

2.  think about becoming an astronaut
    write to NASA*
    find out how to apply

---

*NASA The U.S. National Aeronautic and Space Administration

3. read about sky diving
   try it
   find it very exciting

4. watch sky divers near my home
   take some lessons
   become a sky diver yourself

5. argue with my friend who doesn't believe in UFOs
   rent a copy of *Close Encounters of the Third Kind*
   become convinced after he watches the movie

6. hope to take a ride in a hot air balloon
   go to the annual balloon race in New Mexico
   find someone to take you up

7. learn how to hang glide
   teach me
   find the courage to try it with you as my teacher

8. research the first airplanes
   tour the Air and Space Museum in Washington, D.C.
   learn a great deal about old planes there

**2**  Rephrase the following statements to use *may, might,* or *could have.*

**Example:**   Mary thinks she hurt herself when she went windsurfing.

*Mary may (might) have hurt herself when she went windsurfing.*

1. Bob thinks he lost his surfboard at the beach.
2. I think his brother borrowed it.
3. Joan thinks Patrick was stranded on his board out in the water.
4. She thinks the wind stopped blowing.
5. Peter thinks they went windsurfing last week.
6. I think they went boogie boarding.
7. Bob thinks Alan hurt his head.
8. He thinks Alan got hit by somebody's board.
9. Michael thinks someone stole his windsurfing sail.
10. We think a friend found it and took it home.

**3** You are at the seashore with your friend. There are lots of people in the water and on the shore. There are also fish and marine mammals. You and your friend are looking out to sea. You are trying to identify the figures that you see moving about in and on the water. Use *may, might* or *could (have)* to guess what you are looking at.

**Example:** There's something flying right over the water. It has a large bill.
*It might be a pelican.*

1. There's something inside that seashell. It's moving. It has claws.
2. It looks like there's a person standing on a board with a sail.
3. Something just jumped out of the water and back in. It was really big.
4. I see a black pipe just above the surface of the water. I also see rubber fins.
5. Those two swimmers out there have wet suits and some tanks on their backs. They have spears too.
6. There's a girl paddling out to that wave on her surfboard.
7. There were two surfers before that wave crashed. Now I only see one.
8. There are a lot of birds around that boat.
9. Some people seem to be digging in the sand.
10. That swimmer out there is holding onto the buoy.

## B. Expressing Present and Past Probability

| Modals | Examples | Notes |
|---|---|---|
| **Present Probability**<br>**must (not) + simple form** | You **must** like board games if you like Monopoly.<br>You **must** be holding a Get Out of Jail Free card.<br>You **must not** be worried about landing in jail. | In affirmative and negative statements, *must* and *must have* express probability. Both mean "probably." *Must* is not used is this meaning. In rapid speech, *must have* is pronounced /mustuv/. |
| **Past Probability**<br>**must (not) have + past participle** | You **must have** been happy to win the game.<br>You **must have** been holding more than one Get Out of Jail Free card.<br>You **must not have** worried about landing in jail. | |

**4**   In pairs, take turns making statements and responses. Use *must* with the cues in parentheses to form your responses.

**Example:**   I am the chess champion of my school. (be pretty good)
*You must be pretty good.*

1.   I hear music coming out of Katie's room. (be listening to her new CD)
2.   Fred likes poker and Monopoly. (like games of chance)
3.   The kids put away the jigsaw puzzle. (finish it)
4.   Dad didn't complete the crossword puzzle. (give up)
5.   I see the card table is out and Mom's made her favorite dip. (be ready to play cards with her friends)
6.   Johnny's name is at the top of the list on *Street Fighter.* (get the highest score)
7.   The chessboard still has the pieces on it. (Bill and Bob . . . finish their match)
8.   How strange! Mark is listening to the radio. (the television . . . be broken)
9.   Lou had a big grin on his face when he got home from the poker game. (win)
10.   Mike got a new computer game, but he returned it to the store today. (like it)

**5**   In emotional situations, we often use *must feel* + adjective in a response to empathize with someone—to show that we understand. In pairs, take turns making statements with *must feel* + adjective. Choose appropriate adjectives for your responses. Use these words and statements, or create your own.

| Positive Emotions | Negative Emotions | |
|---|---|---|
| ecstatic | angry | nervous |
| excited | awful | sad |
| happy | bored | scared |
| pleased | depressed | stressed |
| proud | exhausted | terrible |
| thrilled | frightened | upset |
| | frustrated | |

**Example:**   A:   I just won a Monopoly tournament! I'm the champ!
            B:   *You must feel ecstatic!*

1.   I just found out that I need to have a tooth pulled.
2.   I just broke my surfboard on a rock. It was brand new.
3.   I stayed up all night playing poker.
4.   I just got some bad news from home.
5.   I got a job teaching windsurfing.
6.   I'm taking a scuba diving course beginning this weekend.
7.   I just won a trophy in a surfing contest.
8.   I was supposed to go up in a hot air balloon, but the weather is too bad to fly.

**6**   In pairs, take turns making the following statements with *must have felt* + adjective.

**Example:**   A:   I won six straight games of Monopoly from my brother. I'd never done that before!

　　　　　　B:   *You must have felt great (good).*

1.   I fell off my surfboard and cut my leg on some coral.
2.   I think I discovered a new star last night when I looked through my telescope.
3.   I saw a whale breaching* yesterday morning.
4.   I lost control of my windsurfer and started heading out to sea.
5.   I am going on a long distance trip in a hot air balloon.
6.   I lost every game of Monopoly that I played with my sister.

**7**   Reread the opening passage "How Healthy Are You?" on page 100. Then do the following:

1.   Underline all the modal auxiliaries in the passage. What form of the verb follows each modal?
2.   Find the verb in line 1. What form follows the expression *are able?* Can you substitute a modal auxiliary and keep the same basic meaning? Do you need to make any changes?
3.   Find the verb in line 3. What form follows the verb *has?* Can you substitute a modal auxiliary and keep the same basic meaning? Do you need to make any changes?
4.   Look at these pairs of sentences. Can you explain any differences in meaning?

| | |
|---|---|
| a.   That person may need fewer calories per day. | That person needs fewer calories per day. |
| b.   Some people might prefer strenuous exercise. | Some people prefer strenuous exercise. |
| c.   Another person would rather play golf. | Another person plays golf. |
| d.   You can lower the risk by exercising. | You lower the risk by exercising. |

## Using What You've Learned

**8**   Look around the room. Is anyone absent from class? Does anyone look particularly excited or happy? Does anyone look worried? Does anyone look as if he or she is not feeling well? Try to guess why.

**Example:**   Jorge is not here.

　　　　　　*He may be sick.*

　　　　　　*He might have gone away for a long weekend.*

　　　　　　*He must not have done his homework!*

---

*breaching*   leaping out of the water

## Focus on Testing

### Use of Modal Auxiliaries

Modal auxiliaries are frequently tested on standardized English proficiency exams. Review these commonly tested structures and check your understanding by completing the sample items below.

**Remember that . . .**

■  Modal auxiliaries are followed by the simple form of a verb.

■  Perfect modal auxiliaries use modal + *have* + past participle.

**Part 1:**  Circle the correct completion for the following sentences.

**Example:**  John _____ sick; he didn't go to class yesterday.

      a.  may              c.  must

      b.  may have being    (d.)  must have been

1. A person who is physically fit _____ the same weight.
   a. should be able stay
   b. should to be able stay
   c. should being able to stay
   d. should be able to stay

2. Syrup of ipecac _____ the best known antidote to most poisons.
   a. maybe
   b. may to be
   c. may be
   d. may being

3. If an accident victim is dizzy and cannot move an arm or leg, she _____ a head injury.
   a. could be have
   b. could have
   c. could be had
   d. could had had

4. There _____ no wind because that windsurfer isn't moving.
   a. must have been
   b. could have been
   c. must be
   d. can't be

**Part 2:**  Circle the letter below the underlined word(s) containing an error.

**Example:**  An individual <u>may to feel</u> frustrated if she has <u>difficulties</u> in <u>speaking</u>

                         (A)                              B         C

      the language of the country <u>where she is living</u>.

                                      D

1. She would <u>much</u> rather <u>to exercise</u> moderately <u>than</u> <u>strenuously</u>.
             A            B              C    D

2. A person <u>may had had</u> a heart attack <u>if he or she</u> has <u>chest pain</u> and
             A                      B          C

   <u>breathing</u> difficulties.
       D

3. Most people <u>who eat</u> a healthy diet should <u>be able get</u> all the calcium
               A                          B

   <u>they need</u> from their normal <u>food intake</u>.
       C                    D

4.  Jim <u>may feel</u> a little nervous because this <u>might have be</u> the first
          A                                                    B
    <u>snowboarding competition</u> that he <u>will enter</u> this year.
                  C                              D

---

## PART 5  Review: Chapters 1 to 4

**1  Review.**  The following story is about the origin of one of America's most famous board games, Monopoly. Choose the form of the verb in parentheses that best completes the story.

**Monopoly**

Monopoly (is / was) a game manufactured by Parker Brothers. Each player (buy / buys)
     1

and (sell / sells) real estate. Charles Darrow (invents / invented) the game in 1933. At
   3                     4

the time, he (is / was) an unemployed engineer. He (has / had) lost his job at the begin-
       5                   6

ning of the Depression, a prolonged period of economic hardship in the United States

that (occurs / occurred) at the end of the 1920s and (continues / continued) into the
     7                             8

1930s. Darrow (is / was) out of work for three years. During those years, he
         9

(walks / walked) dogs and he (fixes / fixed) electric irons in order to make money. He
  10            11

(keep / kept) himself busy by trying to invent things.
  12

    First, Darrow (tries / tried) to create better bridge score pads, and then he
         13

(makes / made) jigsaw puzzles. Unfortunately, no one (is / was) interested in Darrow's
  14                          15

inventions. Finally, Darrow (begins / began) dreaming about the time before the
<sub>16</sub>

Depression. At that time, he and his wife often (go / went) on vacations. He
<sub>17</sub>

(remembers / remembered) one visit especially. It (is / was) their visit to Atlantic City,
<sub>18</sub>                                                    <sub>19</sub>

New Jersey. He (draws / drew) maps of the streets of Atlantic City. Pretty soon he
<sub>20</sub>

(has developed / had developed) his game.
<sub>21</sub>

Darrow and his wife (begin / began) to spend every evening playing the new
<sub>22</sub>

game. In the game, they (buy / bought), (rent / rented), (develop / developed), and
<sub>23</sub>                      <sub>24</sub>                      <sub>25</sub>

(sell / sold) real estate. They (play / played) the game with large amounts of money,
<sub>26</sub>                                  <sub>27</sub>

which (aren't / weren't) real. At a time when there (is / was) no television and people
<sub>28</sub>                                                    <sub>29</sub>

(cannot / could not) afford to go out to the movies, the game (is / was) their entertain-
<sub>30</sub>                                                    <sub>31</sub>

ment. Soon their friends (begin / began) to stop by to play the game. They
<sub>32</sub>

(ask / asked) Darrow for their own sets of the game. Pretty soon, Darrow
<sub>33</sub>

(cannot / could not) make enough sets by hand, so he (goes / went) to Parker Brothers
<sub>34</sub>                                              <sub>35</sub>

with his game. At first, Parker Brothers (reject / rejected) Monopoly. However, Darrow
<sub>36</sub>

(doesn't / didn't) get discouraged. Finally, Parker Brothers (make / made) Darrow an
<sub>37</sub>                                                    <sub>38</sub>

offer, and the rest (is / was) history. Monopoly (is / was) the most popular game in the
<sub>39</sub>                          <sub>40</sub>

world today. Versions of the game (are / were) produced in 15 languages.
<sub>41</sub>

**Culture Note**

*Board games are still popular, but now many of these games are also available in CD-ROM versions and online. Next time you are surfing the Internet, you can look for the latest information on Monopoly or your favorite board game.*

---

**2**   **Review.**   Complete this passage about windsurfing by choosing the verb form in parentheses that best tells the story.

### Ride the Wind

Windsurfing (must / had to) be the hottest, coolest, smoothest, and fastest way that
<sub>1</sub>

you (can / could) sail across the water. "It (is / was) really thrilling," (says / said) one
<sub>2</sub>                          <sub>3</sub>                          <sub>4</sub>

windsurfer. "When I (catch / caught) the wind, I (fly / have flown) across the water. I
<sub>5</sub>                          <sub>6</sub>

(want / wanted) to keep going. I never (have wanted / want) to stop. I often
<sub>7</sub>                                  <sub>8</sub>

(became / become) so excited that I (don't / didn't) pay attention to how far away I
9                                    10

(am / was) from the shore."
11

    To windsurf, you (don't / didn't) need to live close to the ocean. You (can / might)
                              12                                    13

windsurf on a lake or even on a pond. If you (decide / decided) to try windsurfing,
                                       14

remember one thing: you (are / were) sure to fall into the water lots of times. You
                                  15

(can / could) plan on getting very wet your first day. However, even if you (do / did) fall
16                                                17

a lot on your first day, you (can / are able to) expect to do better the next time.
                                18

    To windsurf, you (need / needed) to know how to keep your balance and change
                                19

your position on the board. You (might / might have) learn in as little as three to six
                                    20

hours. You (will / would) begin to feel your body move with the board. People who
                        21

(windsurf / windsurfed) agree that if you (know / knew) how to ride a bike, you
             22                                    23

(can / could) learn to windsurf. When you (learn / learned), try to pick a hot day for your
24                                    25

first day or rent a wetsuit because you (will / would) definitely get wet.
                                  26

**3**   **Review.**   Requesting Action: For each case below, ask the person responsible to do something. Use *can you, could you, will you, would you,* or *would you mind*.

      **Example:**   You are beginning to eat your soup in a restaurant. You taste it and it tastes cold. Ask the waiter to heat it up for you.

               *Would you mind heating this soup up for me?*

1.   You have just finished your meal at a restaurant and you want the parking valet to get your car for you.
2.   You are having trouble carrying your windsurfer onto the beach. You ask a swimmer who is near you.
3.   You have just landed on Park Place in a game of Monopoly. You are paying for a hotel. You want the player next to you to put a hotel on Park Place because you can't reach it from your seat.
4.   Your friend is watching a balloonist through his binoculars. You are very interested in getting a look too. You ask your friend.
5.   You are about to show a film on the night sky. To do so you need to turn off the lights in the room. You are near the front of the room. The lights are near the back. There is a woman sitting near them.
6.   You are trying to ride a wave on your surfboard. The surfer near you is too close to you.

**4**   **Review.**   Complete this story by using *would, used to,* or by leaving the space blank.

### At the Beach

When we were little, my parents <u>used to/would</u> take us to the beach at Coney Island.
1

We usually went on Sunday after church. My mother _____ pack lunches for all of
2

us. At that time, my father _____ have an orchestra and he _____ come home
3                                    4

late on Saturday, so sometimes we went with my uncle, and my father _____ meet
5

us there later. In the middle of summer, the sand at Coney Island beach _____ was
6

very hot. We _____ get there early to be next to the ocean. However, that meant that
7

it _____ take longer to get to the cool wooden boardwalk from our blanket. So, our
8

feet often _____ felt as if they were on fire by the time we _____ got to the board-
9                                              10

walk. However, the boardwalk _____ meant food: a hotdog, a potato knish, an extra
11

large ice cream cone, a cold soda. Today, when I _____ look back on those Sun-
12

days at the beach, it _____ seems like I _____ remember the food as much as
13                        14

I _____ do the cool ocean water.
15

Note: This paragraph uses "would" and "used to" many times in order for you to practice the
structures. In a standard written paragraph, however, these expressions might be used only once
or twice each.

# Video Activities: Bottled Water

**Before You Watch.**   Answer and discuss these questions in small groups.

1.   Where do you get your drinking water?

   a. from a store      b. from the city water supply      c. from a well

2.   Which kind of water is better in these ways? Write T for tap water or B for bottled water.

   _____ a.  price

   _____ b.  safety

   _____ c.  taste

   _____ d.  convenience

**Watch.**   Check the correct answers.

1.   The NRDC is probably a _____.

   a.  water bottling company
   b.  consumer group
   c.  doctors' organization

2.   The NRDC study found that _____.

   a.  tap water is often the same as bottled water
   b.  tap water contains harmful chemicals
   c.  bottled water is safer than tap water

3.   Sonia Scribner (the owner of *The Water Lady*) believes that consumers should _____.

   a.  go right to the source      b.  buy bottled water      c.  drink tap water

4.   The NDRC thinks that it's time for _____.

   a.  the public to drink bottled water
   b.  the government to make tap water safer
   c.  people to realize that bottled water is not always better

**Watch Again.**   Compare answers in small groups.

1.   What did the NRDC find in water?

   a.  lead            b.  mercury            c.  bacteria            d.  arsenic

2.   Complete the statements with the numbers.

   | 4 | 1/3 | 1,000 | 103 | 25 |
   | --- | --- | --- | --- | --- |

   a.  The public spent _____ billion dollars on bottled water in 1997.

   b.  The NRDC tested _____ kinds of bottled water.

c. Some bottled water is _____ times as expensive as tap water.

d. The NRDC found that _____ % of bottled water is tap water.

e. _____ of the water tested was the same quality as tap water.

**After You Watch.**   Complete the sentences with modals from the box below.

| would | rather | should | must |
|-------|--------|--------|------|
| ought to | can | could | might |

1. Many people believe that they _____ drink bottled water.

2. They think that because it's more expensive than tap water, it _____ be better.

3. However, tests show that you _____ be drinking water that is unsafe.

4. _____ you _____ drink safe tap water or pay money for possibly harmful bottled water?

5. The NRDC recommends drinking tap water. That way you _____ be safe and save money too.

## Focus on Testing

*Review of Problem Areas: Chapters 1 to 4*

A variety of problem areas are included in this test. Check your understanding by completing the sample items below.

**Part 1:**   Circle the correct completion for the following.

**Example:**   John seems _____ with his work.

    a.   happily            c.   contentment
    b.   happy             d.   contentedly

1. The new research park being developed here _____ to a consortium of investors.

    a.   is belonging          c.   is belong
    b.   belonging            d.   belongs

2. Would they mind _____ late?

    a.   if I come            c.   if I came
    b.   to come             d.   to coming

3. Dust devils spin like tornados but _____ more than two or three hundred feet in the air.

    a.   rarely reaches       c.   reach rarely
    b.   reaches rarely      d.   rarely reach

4.  Vitamins C and E _____ help to deter cataracts from developing.
    - a. may
    - b. may be
    - c. must be
    - d. must

5.  Using a different order of words can _____ of a sentence.
    - a. change often the meaning
    - b. change the meaning often
    - c. to change often the meaning
    - d. often change the meaning

6.  We _____ home because there are no waves to surf here today.
    - a. should have stayed
    - b. could stay
    - c. must stay
    - d. may have stayed

7.  When the sea is rough, you _____ take more precautions in the water.
    - a. have to
    - b. must to
    - c. have
    - d. had to

8.  Before Carole met her husband, she _____ she would be single all her life.
    - a. has thought
    - b. would think
    - c. thinks
    - d. had thought

**Part 2:**   Circle the letter below the underlined word(s) containing an error.

**Example:**   An individual <u>may feel</u> frustrated if she <u>have</u> difficulties in <u>speaking</u>
                                       A                              Ⓑ                          C
the language of the country where she <u>is living</u>.
                                                              D

1.  <u>Physically fit</u> people <u>should be</u> able <u>stay</u> the <u>same weight</u> over a period of
          A                            B                  C              D
    several years.

2.  Before the Second World War <u>had ended</u>, the number of people in the
         <u>A</u>                                      B
    United States <u>working</u> in agriculture <u>had dropped</u> substantially.
                          C                                      D

3.  Doctors <u>has discovered</u> that <u>chronic pain</u> <u>can have</u> a <u>strong</u> psychological
                       A                            B                C              D
    component.

4.  Coal and oil were formed <u>when</u> plants <u>become</u> buried in <u>marshes</u> or swamps
                                          A                  B                      C
    and then <u>decayed</u>.
                   D

5.  Although <u>traveling</u> in a foreign country <u>is usually</u> very interesting and
                      A                                        B
    exciting, it <u>can often be</u> tiring <u>extremely</u>.
                         C                        D

6.  Wendy <u>couldn't have call</u> when she <u>said</u> she did because I was at home
                 A                              B
    <u>working</u> and I <u>would've heard</u> the phone ring.
         C                    D

7.  Mary <u>would liking</u> to hear from you if you <u>have</u> the time <u>to write</u> <u>her</u>.
              A                                        B              C        D

8.  I <u>had been</u> asleep <u>when</u> the robbers <u>broke</u> into the house and <u>take</u> all the
         A              B                    C                        D
    jewelry.

# Chapter 5

# High Tech, Low Tech

# Introduction

In this chapter you will study the forms and uses of verbs in the passive voice. You will notice that the time frame of a passive verb may be the same as that of an active verb, but the focus of the passive sentence is quite different. As you study the chapter, pay careful attention to the focus of the passive constructions.

The following passage introduces the chapter theme, "High Tech, Low Tech," and raises some of the topics and issues you will cover in the chapter.

### Old and New Technology

Old inventions are not necessarily eliminated by new ones. After all, people did not stop riding bicycles after the car was invented. Thus, older inventions may be replaced, but they seldom disappear because new roles are created for them. Some of the best examples of this are from the field of long-distance communication.                                                                                    5

Until the 19th century, communication had been limited by distance and time. Then came a series of amazing inventions that extended the range of human communication. Each of these inventions was expected to replace existing technology. For example, when the telephone was invented in 1876, it was feared that letters would become obsolete. When television was introduced in the 1940s,    10 many people predicted the "death" of radio. And as television became more popular, people worried that it would lead to the "death" of books and reading.

But it is clear that these predictions were wrong. The older technologies— letters, books, and the radio—have not disappeared. Instead, their roles have been changed by the appearance of new technology. Television, together with the   15 automobile, has provided a new role for the radio. Both television and the radio have created new roles for the newspaper. And all of these have affected the book.

The technology of the 21st century is progressing rapidly. With the availability and affordability of the personal computer, more and more households   20 are wired to the World Wide Web on the Internet. This puts the individual in instantaneous contact with other computer users anywhere in the world. Information on the World Wide Web has proliferated to the point where much of what once was in libraries and archives can now be found on the Internet. Thus communication has become at once global and personal. Commercial enterprises   25 that use the Internet are now among the fastest growing businesses in the world. E-commerce, business via the Internet, has begun to make its influence felt in the new century.

At the same time, the inventions of one and two centuries before still play important roles in the daily life of millions of people all over the world. The telephone   30 and the television, in their new forms, such as the cell phone and the watchman, are still with us, and, oh yes, that most ancient technology, the book, is still with us too.

**Discussing Ideas.**    Can you think of examples of new inventions that have made old inventions obsolete? Can you think of  products or systems that may become obsolete due to new inventions? For example, will e-mail completely replace regular mail?

| **PART 1** | # The Passive Voice with Simple Tenses |
|---|---|

## Setting the Context

**Prereading Questions**   What do you know about early forms of long-distance communication? How did people communicate with each other from far away?

### The Telephone: Past, Present, and Future

During most of human history, even the most important news was difficult to deliver. Then, in the 1800s, the telephone was invented. At first people were suspicious of the new technology, but today millions of phone calls are made daily by people all over the world. Some offices 5 already have "videophones"—telephones connected to video screens that allow callers to see one another as they speak. In the future, videophones will be installed in every home and office, just as ordinary telephones are today. 10

**Discussing Ideas.**   What would your life be like today without telephones? What will your life be like in a world of "videophones"?

## A. Introduction to the Passive Voice

Most transitive verbs (verbs that take an object) can be used in both the active voice and the passive voice. A form of the verb *be* is always used in passive sentences. It is singular or plural to agree with the subject, and it also tells the tense of the passive construction. You will notice that the time frame of a passive verb may be the same as that of an active verb, but the focus of the sentence is different.

|  | **Examples** | **Focus** |
|---|---|---|
| **Active** | *subject          verb        direct object*<br>Alexander Graham Bell **invented** the telephone. | *Alexander Graham Bell* |
| **Passive** | *agent*<br>The telephone **was invented** by Alexander Graham Bell. | *the telephone* |
| **Active** | *subject        verb   direct object*<br>Millions of people **use** the Internet every day. | *millions of people* |
| **Passive** | *agent*<br>The Internet **is used** by millions of people every day. | *the Internet* |

**1**   Which of the following sentences are in the active voice and which are in the passive voice? Label each. Then label the subject (S), verb (V), object (O), and / or agent (A) in each sentence. Finally, tell the primary focus of each sentence.

**Example:**

$$\overset{S}{} \quad \overset{V}{} \quad \overset{A}{}$$

*Passive* The first fax machine was manufactured by Muirhead, Ltd., of England. *Focus: the first fax machine*

$$\overset{S}{} \quad \overset{V}{} \quad \overset{O}{}$$

*Active* Muirhead, Ltd., of England manufactured the first fax machine. *Focus: Muirhead, Ltd.*

1. _____ The telephone was invented by Alexander Graham Bell in 1876.

2. _____ Intel Corporation created the first microprocessor for computers in 1971.

3. _____ The Walkman was developed by Sony Corporation in 1979.

4. _____ Bank credit cards were first introduced by Bank of America in 1958.

5. _____ Willis Carrier of the United States invented air conditioning in 1911.

6. _____ Mattel Toy Co. created the Barbie doll in 1958.

7. _____ Penicillin was discovered by Sir Alexander Fleming in 1928.

8. _____ Warner Brothers introduced movies with sound in 1927.

9. _____ The phonograph was invented by Thomas Edison in 1877.

10. _____ Microsoft created the Windows Operating System.

11. _____ Chocolate in the form that we eat today was first produced by Rodophe Lindt of Switzerland in 1880.

12. _____ The American Express Company invented travelers' checks in 1891.

## B. The Passive Voice with Simple Tenses

The passive voice of verbs in simple tenses is formed in this way: *(will) be (am, is, are, was, were)* + past participle (+ *by* + agent). Adverbs of frequency usually come after the first auxiliary verb. The passive forms have the same general meanings and time frames as verbs in the active voice.

| | | Examples | Focus |
|---|---|---|---|
| **Simple Past** | **Active** | A computer company **installed** a new computer network in our office. | a computer company |
| | **Passive** | A new computer network **was installed** in our office (by a computer company). | a new computer network |
| **Simple Present** | **Active** | Computer companies **install** new computer networks every day. | computer companies |
| | **Passive** | New computer networks **are installed** (by computer companies) every day. | new computer networks |
| **Simple Future** | **Active** | A computer company **will install** a new computer network next week. | a computer company |
| | **Passive** | A new computer network **will be installed** (by a computer company) next week. | a new computer network |

**2** Underline all uses of the passive voice in the passage "The Telephone: Past, Present, and Future" on page 139. Give the tense of each.

**3** Complete the following by using the past, present, or future tense of the verbs in parentheses. Use the passive voice.

**Example:** Until the latter part of the 20th century, most day-to-day information <u>was stored</u> in a card filing system.

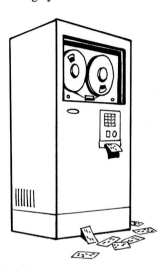

1. The first generation of computers _____ (invent) in the early 1940s.

2. Today the computer _____ (take) for granted by much of the world.

**Culture Note**

*The Internet is a giant network of computers. It began as an experimental four-computer network established by the U.S. Department of Defense so that researchers could communicate with each other. By 1971, this network linked over two dozen sites, including Harvard and MIT. By 1974, there were over 200 sites. Today, it is estimated that use of the Internet doubles each day.*

3. Between 1980 and 2000, millions of personal computers _____ (sell) to consumers.

4. Computers _____ (use) by over 500 million people throughout the world.

5. Today, almost the entire world _____ (connect) by the Internet.

6. In many offices, computers _____ (connect) to each other in a network.

7. Messages _____ (received) via e-mail.

8. Written documents _____ (transmit) by computer and then printed out on printers.

9. In the future, even faster computers _____ (invent).

## C. The Passive Voice in Sentences with Indirect Objects

In active voice sentences with both a direct and an indirect object, either object may become the subject of the corresponding passive sentence.

|  | **Active** | **Passive** |
|---|---|---|
| **Direct Object** | The United States gave **the patent** for the telephone to Bell. | **The patent** for the telephone was given to Bell by the United States. |
| **Indirect Object** | The United States gave **Bell** the patent for the telephone. | **Bell** was given the patent for the telephone by the United States. |

**4** Sit in groups of three students. Student A should read the active voice sentences that follow. Students B and C should change them to the passive voice. Follow the example.

**Example:** A: **The school secretary gave Sam an important message.**
B: **Sam was given an important message by the school secretary.**
C: **An important message was given to Sam by the school secretary.**

1. The phone company sent me information about new types of phone service.
2. Mrs. Jones will give the results of the test to the students within the next week.
3. The salesman showed Mr. Sanchez some computer software.
4. Every year, a rich businesswoman gives our town $100,000 to spend on the schools.
5. The judges awarded Joseph first prize in the essay contest.
6. My father lent me that beautiful sports car.

**5** The following sentences are in the active voice. Some of the sentences have objects, but others, with linking verbs, do not. Decide which sentences can be changed to the passive voice. Label the subject (S), verb (V), and object (O) in each sentence. Then change the sentence to the passive voice. In sentences with a direct and an indirect object, give both possibilities.

**Example:**
$$\overset{S}{\text{Philipp Reis}} \overset{V}{\text{was}} \text{ a German inventor. } \underline{\textit{cannot be changed}}$$
$$\overset{S}{\text{Reis}} \overset{V}{\text{designed}} \text{ an } \overset{O}{\text{early telephone}} \text{ around 1861. } \underline{\textit{can be changed}}$$
<u>*An early telephone was designed by Reis around 1861.*</u>

1. We learn in school that Alexander Graham Bell invented the telephone.
2. The true story is more dramatic, however.
3. In 1876, two inventors completed patent applications on the same day.
4. One was a schoolteacher named Alexander Graham Bell.
5. The other was a professional inventor named Elisha Gray.
6. Gray and Bell did not work together.
7. The two inventors developed very similar telephones.
8. Gray finished first.
9. However, the U.S. patent office received Bell's application two hours before Gray's.
10. Thus, the patent office gave the official patent to Alexander Graham Bell.
11. Elisha Gray took Bell to court.
12. Gray sued Bell for the rights to the talking machine.
13. Bell won in court.
14. To this day, the whole world gives credit to Bell for inventing the telephone.

**6** Marc, Sharon, and Annette McLean are planning a surprise party for their parents' anniversary Friday evening. Today is Thursday. The following list shows which tasks the children completed before today. (These tasks are indicated by a ✓.) Other tasks will be done as indicated. Use the information in the list to write ten additional passive sentences in the past and future tenses.

**Example:**   *The invitations were ordered by Marc two months ago.*
  *The turkey will be cooked by Annette on Friday afternoon.*

| **Marc** | **Sharon** | **Annette** |
|---|---|---|
| ✓ order invitations— 2 months ago | ✓ pick up invitations from printer—1 month ago | ✓ address and mail invitations—3 weeks ago |
| buy flowers—Friday afternoon | bake the cake— Wednesday night | cook the turkey— Friday afternoon |
| set the table—Friday afternoon | ✓ buy champagne— Tuesday | ✓ buy decorations—last week |
| clean the house— Friday morning | clean the house— Friday morning | put up the decorations— Friday afternoon |

## D. By + *Agent*

*By* + noun (or pronoun) can be used in passive sentences to tell who or what performed the action of the verb. However, most passive sentences in English do not contain these phrases. Use *by* + agent only if the phrase gives the following information.

|  | **Examples** | **Notes** |
|---|---|---|
| **Information Necessary to the Meaning of the Sentence** | The majority of overseas phone calls are transmitted **by satellite.** | *By* + agent must be used if the sentence is meaningless without it. |
| **A Name or Idea that Is Important in the Context** | The telephone was invented by **Alexander Graham Bell.**<br><br>Telephones are made ~~by people~~ in factories. | Proper names are often included because they give specific information. Other nouns and pronouns are often omitted. |
| **New or Unusual Information** | Today most overseas calls are transmitted **by satellite.**<br><br>The calls are beamed ~~by satellite~~ from one country to another. | *By* + agent is generally included if the phrase introduces new or unusual information.<br><br>After the agent is understood, the phrase is usually omitted to avoid repetition. |

**7**  In a "team" or "group" effort, the final result or product is more important than the effort of each individual. In speaking and in writing, passive sentences are often used to focus on the product or result. Passive sentences without *by* + agent give even more emphasis to *what was done,* not *who did it.* Look at your sentences from Activity 6 again. Rewrite each sentence, but this time, omit *by* + agent. Compare each set of sentences, and notice the difference in emphasis.

**Example:**  order invitations—two months ago

> *The invitations were ordered by Marc two months ago.*
> *The invitations were ordered two months ago.*
> *(The second sentence puts more emphasis on the action.)*

**8**  Read the following passive voice sentences below and underline the phrase with *by* in each sentence. Then decide whether each *by* + agent is necessary to the meaning of the sentence. Tell which phrases you would omit and why.

**Examples:**  Sentence 1  *Do not omit the phrase because it tells who started the company.*

Sentence 2  *The phrase can be omitted. It is obvious that the companies were created by people.*

1. Federal Express, the first overnight package delivery company, was started <u>by Frederick Smith</u> in 1973.
2. Similar companies were created <u>by people</u> in the years that followed.
3. Before Federal Express was created by Smith, packages were always shipped by air freight companies on regular commercial airlines.
4. In those days, fast delivery of packages was never guaranteed by anybody.
5. Commercial airline flights were often delayed by bad weather or equipment problems.

6. Packages were sometimes lost by the airlines.

7. Sometimes packages were delivered by the air freight companies weeks after the mailing date.

8. At Federal Express, overnight delivery is guaranteed by the company.

9. Federal Express planes and trucks are used by the company in order to guarantee service.

10. Currently, over two million packages are delivered worldwide by Federal Express each day.

**9** One very common use of the passive voice is in the description of processes. The following paragraph describes a process. Rewrite it, changing sentences from the active voice to the passive whenever possible. Use *by* + agent only if it is important to the meaning of the passive sentence.

---

### The Work of an Urban Bomb Squad

Bomb squads are an unfortunate necessity in many cities these days. These squads are special police units. Their function is to respond to bomb threats, locate a bomb if there is one, and remove it safely from the premises. As soon as the bomb squad arrives at the scene of a bomb threat, several things happen. First, the bomb squad evacuates the building. Then, the bomb squad searches     5
the building. If the members of the squad find a bomb, they remove it from the building. They take the bomb outside, and they place it inside a specially designed van. Once the bomb is inside the van, the bomb squad explodes it. The bomb squad allows the occupants of the building to go back inside only after the squad has determined that it is safe.     10

---

 **10** Working in pairs, take turns asking and answering questions using the following cues. Add words as needed to form correct sentences. Use the passive voice in your answers whenever possible.

**Example:**   car / steal

    A:  **What happened to your car?**
    B:  **It was stolen.**

1. goldfish / die
2. brother / transfer to New York
3. photocopier in your office / break down
4. house / paint
5. cat / disappear two weeks ago
6. children / go inside to eat lunch
7. grandmother's house / destroy in a fire
8. newspaper / not deliver today
9. the receptionist / promote to office manager
10. baseball game / cancel

## E. Verbs Commonly Used in the Passive Voice

These verbs are frequently used in the passive voice. A variety of prepositions can follow them: *by* is also used depending on the context.

| Verbs | | Examples |
|---|---|---|
| be based on | be located in (at, on) | The movie **was based on** the novel. |
| be connected to | be made of (from) | Wash your hands! You **are covered with** dirt! |
| be covered with | be made up of | |
| be filled with (by) | be related to | He **was known for** his honesty. |
| be formed of (from, by) | be used for (as, with) | He **was known as** a very honest person. |
| be known for (as) | be used to + *verb* | |
| be known to + *verb* | | The class **is made up of** students from many places. |
| be involved in (with) | | She **is related to** the president. |

*Note:* See Chapter 7 for information on verbs of emotion in passive constructions *(He's interested in sports. I'm bored with this book).*

**11**  Complete the following sentences by adding appropriate forms of the verbs in parentheses. Use past, present, or future tenses. Then add appropriate prepositions in the spaces provided. Include adverbs when indicated.

**Example:**  Today, magazines and newspapers ___*are filled*___ (fill) ___*with*___ stories about the Internet.

1.  Electronic mail, which _____ (know / commonly) _____ e-mail, is the fastest growing means of communication in the world.

2.  Today, millions of people from all seven continents _____ (connect) _____ each other through the Internet.

3.  Today's Internet _____ (base) _____ a network built for researchers in the United States during the 1970s.

4.  The original network of the 1970s _____ (use) _____ communicating about research projects at different universities.

5.  At that time, most of the research projects _____ (relate) _____ the defense industry.

6.  Today, the Internet _____ (make / actually) _____ hundreds of regional computer networks.

7.  Today, networks _____ (locate) _____ in over 60 countries.

## F. Anticipatory It *and the Passive Voice*

The passive voice is often used with *it* to avoid mentioning the agent or source. *By* + agent is rarely used with these constructions. *It* is often used with the passive form of verbs such as *believe, confirm, deny, estimate, fear, hope, mention, report, say,* and *think.*

|         | **Examples** | **Notes** |
|---------|--------------|-----------|
| **Active** | **People said,** "The earth is flat." | Past expressions like *it was believed* often indicate that these ideas have changed. *That* is added when a direct quote is changed to reported speech. In reported speech, verbs often shift to past tenses. See Chapter 12 for more information on reported speech. |
| **Passive** | **It was said,** "The earth is flat." **It was said** that the earth **was flat.** | |

**12**   As we learn more about our world, many of our beliefs change. Expressions such as *it was believed, felt, thought,* or *said that* . . . are used to indicate past beliefs that have changed. In these cases, *would* and *was/were going to* express "the future in the past."

Rephrase the following quotations to include these expressions:

| | |
|---|---|
| It was believed that . . . | It was feared that . . . |
| It was said that . . . | It was thought that . . . |
| It was felt that . . . | It was hoped that . . . |

*Note:* remember to use past forms in the *that* clause.

**Examples:**   "The telephone is going to change people's lives."
*It was feared that the telephone was going to change people's lives.*
"People won't write letters anymore."
*It was believed that people wouldn't write letters anymore.*

1. "People will forget how to read."
2. "Parents will not be able to supervise their children's conversations."
3. "Telephones are going to eliminate the postal service."
4. "Paper companies will go out of business."
5. "People are going to gossip more."
6. "People are not going to have any privacy."
7. "People won't send telegraphs anymore."
8. "Letters will become obsolete."

**13**   First read the following passage for meaning. Then complete the passage with either active or passive forms (simple present or past tenses) of the verbs in parentheses. The first two are done as examples.

### The Impact of the Telephone

Many new inventions ___are used___ every day, but the telephone ___became___ an everyday
        1 (use)                      2 (become)

item faster than almost any other invention in history. In May 1877, six telephones

_____ in commercial use. In November 1877, there _____ 3000, and by 1881,
   3 (be)                                    4 (be)

133,000. Today, people everywhere _____ by the telephone, although most of us
                                        5 (affect)

_____ it without really thinking about it. In the beginning, however, many people
 6 (use)

**Culture Note**

*The radio had existed almost 40 years before it began being used regularly by 50 million people. The TV had existed over 12 years before it reached 50 million viewers. After 16 years in existence, the personal computer was being used by 50 million people. In contrast, within only four years of the Internet's being opened to the public, 50 million people were connected.*

_____ the telephone. It _____ by some that
7 (fear)                              8 (believe)

the telephone _____ evil, and laws _____ by a
9 (be)                                    10 (suggest)

few to prohibit telephones in bedrooms in order to

prevent secret conversations. (Telephones would

allow private romantic conversations, and this would

corrupt people, especially young girls!) But, these

ideas and fears _____ as the demand for
11 (overcome)

telephones grew.

At first in the United States, young boys _____ to operate the telephone
12 (employ)

switchboards, but because of their bad language and tricks many of them _____
13 (lose)

their jobs. Soon, in September 1878, Emma M. Nutt _____ as the first woman tele-
14 (hire)

phone operator. In France, women _____ from the beginning. This was in part
15 (employ)

because all boys and young men _____ to serve in the army. More important,
16 (require)

the female voice _____ much clearer over early telephone lines.
17 (sound)

In the late 1800s, the telephone, together with the typewriter, _____ thou-
18 (bring)

sands of women to work in offices. New fashions _____ to suit the needs of female
19 (create)

workers, and "appropriate" clothing for work _____. The shirtwaist dress
20 (introduce / soon)

and the blouse _____ for women "going to business." The telephone, obviously,
21 (design)

_____ begin the social revolution that _____ today.
22 (help)                                     23 (continue)

Today, the telephone _____ so much a part of our lives that we _____
24 (be)                                                              25 (not notice)

it unless it _____ out of order. In fact, with hundreds of millions of telephones
26 (be)

worldwide , no other invention _____ so much.
27 (use)

**Culture Note**

*Cellular (cell) phones
are increasing in
popularity daily in the
United States as well as
around the world. As a
result, several states in
the United States have
passed laws prohibiting
drivers from using cell
phones while driving
because of rising
accident rates for cell
phone users.*

## Using What You've Learned

14   Have you ever played quiz games like $10,000 Pyramid or Trivial Pursuit? These are
question-and-answer games based on categories of information. To play a classroom
version, first choose several (five or six) categories: music, art, inventions, buildings,

discoveries, and so forth. Then separate into two teams, and make at least five questions for each category. For example, "Who invented the sewing machine?" or "Name the composer(s) of 'Hey Jude.'" Don't let the members of the other team hear you; they will be asked these questions. After you have completed your questions, give them to your teacher. Play the game by choosing categories and questions. Your teacher will ask each team the questions; a different member must answer each time. You may play until you reach a certain score or until all the questions have been asked. You may also add special rules such as "An answer must be grammatically correct to score points," or "Five bonus points are given for a correct answer using the passive voice."

| **PART 2** | # The Passive Voice with Perfect Tenses |

## Setting the Context

**Prereading Questions**    What are *gadgets?* Can you give any synonyms—words that have the same meaning?

---

### Gadgets, Gadgets, and More Gadgets!

In the past 50 years, our way of life has been revolutionized by gadgets of all types: television sets and VCRs, microwave ovens and garage door openers, cordless phones and laptop computers, just to name a few. Until the 1940s or 1950s, however, most of these common household items had not even been dreamed of!

---

COMMITTED reprinted by permission of United Feature Syndicate, Inc.

**Discussing Ideas.**   Can you name other common gadgets that did not exist 15 or 20 years ago? What new gadgets do you think will be created soon?

## The Passive Voice with Perfect Tenses

The passive voice of verbs in perfect tenses is formed in this way: *have (has, have, had)* + *been* + past participle (+ *by* + agent). Adverbs of frequency usually come after the auxiliary *have*.

| | | Examples | Focus |
|---|---|---|---|
| **Present Perfect** | **Active** | New technology **has revolutionized** the communications industry. | new technology |
| | **Passive** | The communications industry **has been revolutionized** by new technology. | the communications industry |
| **Past Perfect** | **Active** | Before the 1950s, researchers **had not yet developed** high-quality audio and video equipment. | researchers |
| | **Passive** | Before the 1950s, high-quality audio and video equipment **had not yet been developed.** | high-quality audio and video equipment |

**1**   The following list shows "old" inventions and the newer inventions that have replaced them. Form sentences using the present perfect tense, passive voice. If possible, add information to make the sentences interesting.

**Example:**   typewriters / word processors

> *In many offices and homes, typewriters have been replaced by word processors.*

1.   shoelaces and zippers / Velcro
2.   records and turntables / CDs and CD players
3.   brooms / vacuum cleaners
4.   electric fans / central air conditioners
5.   conventional ovens / microwave ovens
6.   telephone operators / pagers and voice-mail systems
7.   eyeglasses / contact lenses
8.   orchestras / music synthesizers
9.   home-movie cameras / camcorders*
10.   letters / e-mail
11.   TV movies / videos and DVDs

**2**   Imagine that you work in a recording studio and you are going to videotape a TV commercial. In pairs, go over your final checklist before you begin recording. Ask questions using the present perfect tense of the passive voice. Give short answers using the past participle, as in the example.

---

*\*camcorders*   video camera-recorder combinations

**Example:**   call the actors
      A:  **Have the actors been called?**
      B:  **Called!**

**1.** test the microphones
**2.** check the lights
**3.** clean the camera lenses
**4.** focus the camera

**5.** test the loudspeakers
**6.** adjust the sound
**7.** load the film
**8.** close the doors

**3**  First underline the object in each sentence. Then change the sentences from the active to the passive voice. Omit the agent unless it is important to the meaning of the sentence.

**Example:**   In just 40 years, companies have introduced <u>an amazing selection of audio and video equipment</u>: color television, transistor radios, cassette players, video recorders, compact discs, and DVDs.

*In just 40 years, an amazing selection of audio and video equipment has been introduced: color television, transistor radios, cassette players, video recorders, compact discs, and DVDs.*

1. In the past 40 years, researchers have revolutionized audio and video technology.
2. By the mid-1950s, Ampex Corporation had introduced the first modern video recorder.
3. The television industry has used the Ampex system since that time.
4. By the late 1950s, companies had introduced the first stereo record.
5. Since 1960, researchers have developed high-quality sound systems.
6. By the late 1980s, scientists had developed compact discs and lightweight camcorders.
7. In recent years, MCA, RCA, and several European companies have designed and produced videodisc systems.
8. Apple Computer has created a computer program that will program your VCR for you if you don't know how!

**4**  Use simple or perfect forms of the verbs in parentheses to complete the following passage. Choose between active and passive forms. The first one is done as an example.

### Those Amazing Machines!
### (Also Known as Microelectronic Devices*)

In recent years, we <u>*have grown*</u> very dependent on machines of all kinds—in business,
                        1 (grow)

in industry, and in our own homes. Nowadays the average person _____
                                                                   2 (surround)

---

*Microelectronics deals with electric currents in small components such as transistors and microchips. Microelectronic devices are found everywhere today.

every day by hundreds of devices that _____ microelectronic technology.
3 (use)

For example, this technology _____ in microwave ovens and digital clocks.
4 (employ)

In just half a century, microelectronic technology _____ it possible to pro-
5 (make)

duce practical devices for everyday life. High-speed cameras with automatic focusing

_____. Compact disc players _____. Remote control devices
6 (create)                                    7 (develop)

_____ for televisions and video recorders and for telephone answering ma-
8 (produce)

chines. Fifty years ago, none of these devices _____ because microelectronic
9 (exist)

technology _____.
10 (not invent / yet)

All microelectronic devices _____ with similar types of components,
11 (construct)

which are smaller, cheaper, and more reliable than components of the past. This ex-

plains why some devices, such as VCRs, answering machines, and especially home

computers, _____ much less now than they did when they first _____
12 (cost)                                                                      13 (appear)

on the market. It also explains why the average home today _____ more than
14 (contain)

30 machines and electronic devices!

## Using What You've Learned

**5** Make a list of all the gadgets that are mentioned in this section. Put a check mark next
to each device that you own or have owned and count the number of check marks.
Then talk with your classmates to see which student has the largest number of these
gadgets.

Next, make a list of gadgets that you have in your home but that were not mentioned in these activities. Again, compare with your classmates to see who has the
largest number of gadgets.

Finally, choose *one* gadget that you absolutely could not live without and prepare
a short presentation about it. Include the following:

When was the item invented?

By whom was it invented?

How is it made?

How is it used today?

How was it used in the past or what was used instead of it?

How has this item been modified or changed in recent years?

# PART 3 The Passive Voice with Continuous Tenses

## Setting the Context

**Prereading Questions** When were the first cars developed? Since then, what other major breakthroughs in transportation have occurred?

### The Future of Transportation

Amazing changes are taking place in all the methods of transportation that we use every day. It was only about 100 years ago that gasoline-powered cars were being developed. Today, prototypes of electric cars are being tested by large automakers such as Ford and Honda. Planes are being designed that will travel from New York to Tokyo in 2 1/2 hours. And trains that travel as fast as 300 miles    5 per hour are being built in several countries.

**Discussing Ideas.** Name all the types of transportation that you have used in your lifetime. Can you give the normal speed for each of these today? Does your list include any high-speed transportation? Which? How fast could you travel on this?

## The Passive Voice with Continuous Tenses

The passive voice of verbs in the present and past continuous tenses is formed in this way: *be (am, is, are, was, were)* + *being* + past participle (+ *by* + agent). Adverbs of frequency generally come after the first auxiliary verb.

|  |  |  | Examples | Focus |
|---|---|---|---|---|
| **Present Continuous** | **Active** | | Many cities **are using** computers to help regulate traffic. | many cities |
| | **Passive** | | Computers **are being used** in many cities to help regulate traffic. | computers |
| **Past Continuous** | **Active** | | Ten years ago, cities **were using** traffic officers to regulate traffic. | cities |
| | **Passive** | | Ten years ago, traffic **was being regulated** by traffic officers. | traffic |

*Note:* The future continuous tense (*will be* + verb + *ing*) and the present and past perfect continuous tense (*have, has,* or *had been* + verb + *ing*) are not used in the passive voice.

**1**  Working in pairs, take turns asking questions and forming answers using the present continuous tense, passive voice. Make up some other examples.

**Example:**  A:   Why are you wearing your black suit?

B:   (brown suit / cleaned) *My brown suit is being cleaned.*

| **A** | **B** |
|---|---|
| 1. Why is the traffic so slow today? | Main Street / repaired |
| 2. Why don't you practice piano today? | piano / tuned |
| 3. Why is your office closed? | new computer system / installed |
| 4. Why can't we go into the cafeteria? | floor / washed |
| 5. Why are they staying in a hotel? | their house / painted |
| 6. What is happening to that bus? | it / towed away |
| 7. Where is your new suit? | it / altered |
| 8. Why are you taking the bus to school today? | my car / repaired |

**2**  With the same partner or a new partner, repeat Activity 1. This time, change the questions and answers to past time.

**Example:**  A:   **Why was the traffic so slow today?**
              B:   **Main Street was being repaired.**

**3**  In pairs, change the following sentences from the present continuous, active voice to the past continuous, passive voice.

**Example:**  A:   Today computers are typing letters. (secretaries)

B:   *Fifty years ago, letters were being typed by secretaries.*

1. Today computers and pilots are navigating planes. (only human pilots)
2. Today private package delivery services are delivering packages. (only the U.S. Postal Service)
3. Today computers are controlling traffic signals. (traffic officers)

4.   Computers are running automobile assembly lines. (assembly line foremen)
5.   Today computers are controlling switches in train tracks. (human switch operators)
6.   Today Japan is making most of the world's motorcycles. (the United States)
7.   Today several countries are operating high-speed trains. (only Japan)
8.   Today many countries are exporting cars. (only a few countries)

**4**   The following sentences give some information about the history of the automobile. Change the sentences to the passive voice. Omit *by* + agent if it is not necessary to the meaning of the sentence.

**Example:**   In 1890, people were already driving gasoline-powered cars in France.
*In 1890, gasoline-powered cars were already being driven in France.*

1.   By 1929, American automakers were producing approximately five million cars a year.
2.   In 1950, the United States was manufacturing two-thirds of the world's motor vehicles.
3.   By 1960, manufacturers were introducing compact cars because of competition from Europe.
4.   By the 1970s, competition from Japan was threatening the U.S. auto industry.
5.   By 1980, the United States was producing only one-fifth of the world's cars.
6.   Today, foreign manufacturers are actually making many so-called "American" cars.
7.   These days, automakers are finding ways to make automobile engines more fuel-efficient.
8.   Several big automakers are building and testing electric cars.
9.   They are testing alternative fuels such as methanol.
10.  People are also building new mass-transport systems.

**5**   Complete the following passage with either active or passive forms (simple, perfect, or continuous tenses) of the verbs in parentheses. Include adverbs when indicated. In some cases there may be more than one correct answer. The first one is done as an example.

### Developments in Transportation

Amazing developments *are currently taking* place in transportation technology. Some
                      1 (take / currently)

technological changes _____ and others _____. In the
                              2 (implement / already)                3 (implement / soon)

21st century, the major forms of transportation that _____ in the 20th century—
                                                         4 (use)

cars, trains, and planes—will still be popular, but they _____ in significant
                                                           5 (modify)

ways. Here are three examples of work that _____ now to improve our
6 (do)

familiar methods of transportation:

**Electric and Hybrid Cars.** Air pollution is a serious problem in many large cities, and

most of this pollution _____ by exhaust from automobiles. In California, a law
7 (cause)

_____ stating that by 1998, 2 percent of the cars sold there had to be electric.
8 (pass)

This percentage had to go up to 5 percent by 2001 and 10 percent by 2003. Conse-

quently, automakers worldwide _____ hard to create a cheap, efficient, and
9 (work)

attractive electric car. Small electric hybrid cars _____ by Japanese au-
10 (introduce/already)

tomakers Honda and Toyota. Other hybrid vehicles _____ by U.S. and
11 (develop/currently)

European manufacturers.

**Trains.** The Maglev (Magnetic Levitation System) is a futuristic-

looking, high-speed magnetic train that originally _____ in
12 (develop)

Japan. The train is capable of covering the 340 miles from Tokyo to

Osaka in about one hour. Test lines _____, and it _____
13 (build)           14 (project)

that within a few years these high-speed trains _____ through-
15 (operate)

out Japan. In the United States, Acela, a high-speed train from Wash-

ington to Boston, _____ in late 2000. Other high-speed train
16 (inaugurate)

projects _____ around the U.S., and several, including lines in
17 (study)

Pennsylvania, _____ during the next few years. Southern
18 (open/hopefully)

California officials anticipate Maglev service _____ in place within the next two
19 (be)

decades to accommodate the expected increase in the population by 22 million

people.

## Using What You've Learned

6   The time is the year 2025. The place is an airport in New York, where, in about one
    hour, the new "hyperspace" plane will be taking off on its first regularly scheduled
    flight to Tokyo. Imagine that you are a radio news reporter at the scene on this history-
    making day. Your assignment is to describe to your listeners the activities that are
    taking place during these last moments before takeoff. Try to provide as many details

as possible concerning the activities of the following:

the passengers    the ground crew

the plane          the luggage and cargo

the flight crew

Write your description. Use the present continuous tense, active or passive voice. Then role-play your description for the class.

**7**  Write a brief composition about changes that are occurring in your work or field of study. Try to include information on research that is currently being done, new technology that is being introduced, and other changes that are being implemented.

Use your composition as the basis for a presentation for the entire class or for a small group discussion. If you work in groups, you may want to separate according to general areas of interest—for example, those who are interested in business, those who are involved in the sciences, and so on. If you prepare a presentation, you might include drawings, diagrams, or other visual aids to help in explaining.

**PART 4**

# The Passive Voice with Modal Auxiliaries

## Setting the Context

**Prereading Questions**   What do you know about the first computers? When were they built? What were they used for?

**Culture Note**

*Banking has also changed dramatically with computer technology. Many people no longer go into a bank. ATM cards, banking by phone, and banking via the Internet have drastically reduced traditional business at the teller's window, and e-banks are becoming more and more common. For many transactions, cash and credit cards may soon be replaced by a new form: e-money.*

**BIZARRO**                     By DAN PIRARO

### Computers in Our Lives

It was only a little over 50 years ago that the first computer, Mark I, was developed for military use. Since then computers have come to play a vital role in almost every aspect of our lives. Today, phone calls can be directed by computers; cars can be assembled by computerized robots; messages, files, photographs, and

music can be sent over the Internet; children may be taught with the help of   **5**
computers; and much more. Computers can even be used to arrange people's
romantic relationships!

**Discussing Ideas.**   What other current uses of computers can you think of? What
possible future uses of computers can you suggest?

## The Passive Voice with Modal Auxiliaries

The passive voice of modal auxiliaries is formed in this way:  modal (*can, could, may, might, must, ought to, shall, should, will, would*) + *be* + past participle (+ *by* + agent).

|         | Examples | Focus |
|---------|----------|-------|
| **Active** | Today we **can use** personal computer to write letters. | we |
| **Passive** | Today computers **can be used** to write personal letters. | computers |
| **Active** | Writers **may use** computers to help them do research. | writers |
| **Passive** | Computers **may be used** by writers to help them do research. | computers |
| **Active** | A doctor **might use** a computer to get the latest information about a drug. | a doctor |
| **Passive** | A computer **might be used** by a doctor to get the latest information about a drug. | a computer |

**1**   In the following sentences, change the verbs from the active voice to the passive voice whenever possible. Omit the agent unless it is important to the meaning of the sentence.

**Example:**   Nowadays we may find robots in hundreds of different industries.
*Nowadays robots may be found in hundreds of different industries.*

1.  We can define a robot as an "intelligent" machine.
2.  Robots can copy the functioning of a human being in one way or another.
3.  One early robot, "Planobot," was simply a mechanical arm that people could tilt or rotate.
4.  Nowadays, people can design robots to do many jobs that would be dangerous or boring for humans.
5.  For example, robots might replace human workers in dangerous areas such as nuclear power plants or coal mines.
6.  In hospitals, people can program "nursing" robots to lift patients, wash them, and put them back in bed.
7.  In the future, we might use robots for such complex tasks as making beds and preparing a steak dinner.
8.  Though some robots are able to "say" a limited number of words, people cannot yet program robots to think like people.
9.  In the future, however, people will use artificial intelligence to create robots that are more humanlike.
10. Wouldn't it be wonderful if people could design computers to perform all kinds of unpleasant tasks—such as homework?

**2**  Complete the following with the active or passive forms of the modals and verbs in parentheses. The first one is done as an example.

### Hero

How would you like to have your own personal robot "servant"? Although not quite as advanced as the robots portrayed in Hollywood movies, some household robots are now available. One of them, named HERO, _can be programmed_ to perform a
1 (can / program)
number of useful tasks around the house. HERO _____ lights on and off.
2 (can / turn)
He _____ packages. Amazingly, he _____ to teach languages!
3 (also / can / carry)                                4 (can / even / use)

Personal robots of the future will be more sophisticated. They _____ as
5 (will / design)
complete entertainment centers, with the ability to sing, dance, even tell jokes!

Moreover, all the electronic equipment in the house—television, radio, phone, computer, and so on—_____ by these robots. Imagine: Someday, our dinners
6 (will / regulate)
_____, our dishes _____, our laundry _____, and our cars _____
7 (may / cook)          8 (may / wash)          9 (may / fold)          10 (may / repair)
—all by our own personal robots! For the time being, however, all of those chores
_____ by humans.
11 (must / still / perform)

**3**   The following passage is written entirely in the active voice. It contains sentences that could be improved by using the passive voice. Rewrite the selection, using sentences in the passive voice when appropriate. Omit the agent if it is not necessary to the meaning of the sentence.

---

### Computerized Robots

Never temperamental, always on time, always efficient, Epistle reads the mail each morning, chooses the most important letters, and marks the most important parts long before the boss arrives. Epistle is not an ordinary secretary. Epistle is a robot.

IBM developed Epistle a number of years ago. Today people are designing        5
computerized robots that are even more sophisticated than Epistle to think and reason like the human brain. These machines will use artificial intelligence to perform their functions.

Artificial intelligence has already begun to affect the lives of millions. People are building both robots and computers that can do amazingly humanlike work.    10
For example, in many U.S. hospitals, computers can diagnose diseases with at least 85 percent accuracy. In England, scientists have developed a "bionic nose" that can distinguish subtle differences in smell. They can use the nose in the food and wine industries to check freshness and quality.

Until recently, we could program robots to perform only routine tasks. In the    15
near future, computers utilizing artificial intelligence may give robots full mobility, vision, hearing, speech, and the "sense" to make logical decisions.

---

**4**   **Review.**   Complete the following passage by using either the active or passive voice of the verbs in parentheses. Use any of the tenses and modals covered in this chapter. The first one is done as an example.

### The History of Computers

In 1944, the first general-purpose computer, Mark I, _was put_ into operation. It was
                                                    1 (put)

very slow and very large. In fact, all the early computers  were extremely large, and

several floors of a building _____ to house them.
                            2 (need)

By the end of the 1950s, computers _____ to use transistors. Transistors
                                    3 (develop)

_____ computers smaller, less expensive, more powerful, and more reliable. Today
4 (make)

these _____ as second-generation computers.
      5 (know)

Third-generation computers, which _____ in the 1960s, _____ chips to store
                                   6 (develop)              7 (use)

the memory of the computer. These computers  were still very large, however. But by

the 1970s, when the silicon chip _____, computers _____ truly small and
                                  8 (develop)          9 (become)

affordable. Computers with these silicon chips _____ fourth-generation computers.

10 (call)

Fifth-generation technology is still in its infancy, yet promises refined voice recognition,

parallel processing and, at this point, who knows what else.

**5**   **Review.**   Complete the following passage by using either the active or passive voice of the verbs and modals in parentheses. Use any of the tenses and modals covered in this chapter. The first one is done as an example.

## Developments in Telecommunications

During most of human history, communication _was limited_ by time and distance. In

1 (limit)

the past 200 years, however, revolutionary changes in communication _____. In

2 (occur)

the 19th century, the telegraph and telephone _____. Radio, television, and

3 (invent)

computers _____ in the early and 20th century. Since then, these inventions

4 (develop)

_____ the way people live and work.

5 (change / completely)

Today all these communications devices _____ together. This new wave of

6 (can / link)

technology _____ "telecommunications"—the use of television, radio, tele-

7 (call)

phones, and computers to communicate across distance and time. In the early 1990s,

telephones, computers, and video screens _____, allowing offices to have

8 (may / connect)

"videoconferences" in which participants could see and talk to each other and in

which computer files _____. By the year 2000, people with home computers,

9 (can / share)

laptops and portable computers _____ to electronic mail services and libraries

10 (connect)

around the world so that they could communicate and access information from home,

on airplanes, or just about anywhere. According to the Gartner Report (October 2000),

personal computers _____ in 61.7 percent of all U.S. households. Because of

11 (can / find)

technology, people living in one part of the world now _____ almost instantly

12 (can / inform)

about events occurring thousands of miles away.

According to *U.S. News and World Report,* the 1990s _____ "as a period

13 (view)

when American businesses, large and small, _____ fundamentally. The

14 (transform)

widespread adoption of information technologies was a major reason." Now, in the

21st century *everyone,* not just businesspeople in the United States, _____ by

15 (affect)

developments in telecommunications.

**6** **Review.** Reread the opening passage "Old and New Technology" on page 138. Then, individually or in pairs, do the following:

1. Underline the subject and verb of the first sentence. Is the verb in the active or passive voice? Can you rephrase the sentence to begin with *new inventions?*
2. Underline the subjects and verbs in the second sentence. Unlike the first sentence, the second sentence does not have a phrase with *by.* Can you add one? Why do you think the phrase with *by* was not used?
3. Underline all the other passive voice verbs in the passage. Tell whether they refer to past, present, or future time. Then tell the agent for each. If the agent is not included in the passive construction, tell who or what you think the agent is.

## Using What You've Learned

**7** Think of the tremendous changes that computers have brought in recent years. For example, look at the tasks that follow. All of these can now be done electronically. In the past, however, they had to be done manually.

In pairs or small groups, discuss the changes in these tasks and add others that you can think of. Then choose one or two that you are particularly familiar with. Prepare a brief report for your classmates, telling how the process was done in the past and how it is done today. If possible, include changes that may occur in the near future too. Use the passive voice whenever possible in your report.

**Example:** *Until the last 25 years or so, letters could only be handwritten or typed. And they could only be sent by regular mail or by someone who was traveling to a certain place. Today they can be mailed or sent by express mail and delivered overnight to almost any part of the globe. They can be faxed, or sent electronically almost instantly.*

banking
compose music
design cars
diagnose illnesses
draw three-dimensional objects
figure taxes
investing in stocks
keep household records (balance checkbooks, pay bills, and so on)
mix paint
obtain information from libraries
purchase tickets (for airlines, concerts, sports events, and so on)
sort mail
teach children
write and send letters

# Video Activities: Internet Publishing

**Before You Watch.**

1.   Match the words with their meanings.

    1. online        a. part of a story usually published in chronological order

    2. download    b. on the Internet

    3. installment   c. to move information from the Internet to your computer

2.   Do you use the Internet? What do you use it for?

**Watch.**   Circle the correct answers.

1.   What kinds of things does William Bass download onto his computer?

    a. music        b. research       c. sports articles     d. pictures

2.   What is true about Stephen King's book, *The Plant?*

    a. It was published online.      c. It was published in parts.

    b. It was free.               d. It was a bestseller.

3.   According to William Bass, the best thing about books online is that they're _____.

    a. cheap        b. convenient    c. easy to read

4.   What did Stephen King threaten to do if not enough people paid for his book?

    a. charge more for the rest of the book

    b. not write another book online

    c. not finish the rest of the book

5.   Gillian McCombs says that electronic books will _____.

    a. help sell regular books

    b. let authors make more money

    c. never replace paper and ink books

**Watch Again.**   Compare answers in small groups.

1.   How much did Stephen King charge for *The Plant?* _____

2.   What was the minimum percentage of paid downloads Stephen King would accept?

    a. 25%        b. 75%       c. 95%

3.   The male publishing expert says that Stephen King's book will _____.

    a. be the death of paper and ink books

    b. not change the publishing industry

    c. not be a success

**After You Watch.**   Complete the sentences with the passive or active form of the verb in parentheses.

1.   Online books can _____ (download) onto your computer

2.   Stephen King recently _____ (publish) a book online.

3.   Each consumer _____ (charge) $1 for King's book.

4.   Unfortunately, not enough people _____ (pay) for the book.

5.   In the fall of 2000, it _____ (announce) that no more installments _____ (publish).

## Focus on Testing

### Use of the Passive Voice

Verbs in the passive voice are frequently tested on standardized English proficiency exams. Review these commonly tested structures and check your understanding by completing the following sample items.

**Remember that . . .**

■   The passive is formed in this way: (modal auxiliary) + *be* + past participle.

■   The verb *be* is singular or plural depending on the subject of the passive sentence.

■   The verb *be* gives the appropriate tense and time frame for the sentence.

**Part 1:**   Circle the correct completion for the following.

**Example:**   John _____ never complaining about his work.
      a.   be known for
      b.   is know for
      (c.)  is known for
      d.   was know for

1.   Nowadays the majority of overseas telephone calls _____ by satellite.
    a.   transmit
    b.   transmitting
    c.   are transmitted
    d.   are transmitting

2.   Their house _____ three times since they bought it 20 years ago.
    a.   has been redecorated
    b.   had been redecorated
    c.   has been redecorating
    d.   has redecorated

3. Before turning on the switch, make sure the machine _____.
   a. plugs in
   b. is plugged in
   c. has plugged in
   d. be plugged in

4. Whenever you access information from the Internet, it must _____ carefully; not all information comes from reliable sources.
   a. evaluate
   b. be evaluated
   c. have been evaluated
   d. been evaluated

**Part 2:** Circle the letter below the underlined word(s) containing an error.

**Example:** Difficulties with <u>culture</u> shock <u>are</u> often <u>relate</u> to an individual's
                         A            B         ⓒ
ability to speak the language of the country <u>where she is living</u>.
                                                       D

1. The top floor of the parking structure <u>collapsed</u> during the earthquake and
                                         A
   <u>could</u> not <u>used</u> for the next <u>six months</u>.
     B        C               D

2. A plane is currently <u>been</u> designed <u>that</u> will <u>allow for</u> travel between New
                           A            B        C
   York and Tokyo in approximately <u>two-and-a-half</u> hours.
                                    D

3. Everyone <u>was relieved</u> to hear that the child who <u>had been missing</u> for three
                A                                B
   days <u>were found</u> <u>unharmed</u>.
        C       B

4. Experts <u>predict</u> that by 2020, the population of southern California
           A
   will have <u>growing</u> from <u>16 million to 22 million people</u>, thus <u>creating</u>
           B                C                D
   increasingly greater demands on transportation systems.

# Chapter 6

# Money Matters

# Introduction

In this chapter, you will study many uses of nouns, pronouns, articles, and adjectives. As you study, try to understand the differences between types of nouns in English. This will help you with singular and plural forms as well as the various words and expressions used with nouns.

The following passage introduces the chapter theme, "Money Matters," and raises some of the topics and issues you will cover in the chapter.

### The Global Economy

Of all the sciences, only two are subjects that have a direct and noticeable effect on our lives every day. One is meteorology, the study of weather. Heat, cold, sun, and rain affect us in many ways—in the kind of clothing we wear, for example, and the types of activities we do outdoors. Economics is the other science that affects the daily life of all of us. Each time we spend money, or it is spent on us, we are    **5** contributing to the economic life of our country, and in fact, of the world.

Most people have a basic understanding of the weather, but how many people feel comfortable with the subject of economics? Often, economics seems to be a mysterious subject. Newspapers and television use terminology that can resemble a foreign language. They speak of *the gross national product, the balance of pay-*   **10** *ments, the cost of living, interest, productivity, stocks and bonds,* and so forth.

In some ways, economics is like an enormous jigsaw puzzle. Each piece is basic, but the pieces interconnect, one to another, in a large picture. To look at the whole picture, you must begin piece by piece. Knowledge of the individual pieces and their interconnection will help you understand the global picture.    **15**

**Discussing Ideas.**   According to the passage, which sciences affect us every day? Why? Can you give some examples of economic activities in your daily life? What are other economic terms you have heard? Can you explain them?

---

**PART 1**

# Count Versus Noncount Nouns

## Setting the Context

**Prereading Questions**   What does *wealth* mean? Can you give some examples of wealth?

### What Is Wealth to You?

■  To some people, wealth may mean ownership of businesses, houses, cars, stereos, and jewels.

■  To others, wealth may mean control of resources, such as oil, gold, silver, or natural gas.

■  To the philosophical, wealth may be intangible. It can be found in honesty,    **5** love, courage, and trust.

■  To much of the world, however, wealth is having enough food: bread, rice, fish, meat, and fruit.

**Discussing Ideas.**   How would you describe a *wealthy* person?

## A. Introduction to Count and Noncount Nouns

A noun can name a person, a place, an object, an activity, an idea or emotion, or a quantity. A noun may be concrete (physical or tangible) or abstract (nonphysical or intangible). Both abstract and concrete nouns can be classified into two types: count nouns and noncount nouns.

| Count Nouns | | |
|---|---|---|
| | **Examples** | **Notes** |
| **Singular** | I have a **friend.**<br>My **friend** owns a **car.** | Count nouns are nouns that can be counted (*apples, oranges,* and so on). They have both singular and plural forms. Most count nouns are concrete, but some can be abstract. |
| **Plural** | **Friends** are very important.<br>New **cars** are expensive. | |

| Noncount Nouns | | |
|---|---|---|
| | **Examples** | **Notes** |
| **Mass Concrete Nouns** | **Air** and **water** are necessary for life.<br>We need to buy **coffee, rice,** and **sugar.** | Noncount nouns are usually mass concrete nouns (*food, water,* and so on) or abstract nouns (*wealth, happiness,* and so on) that we don't count. Noncount nouns are singular, even though some end in *-s* (*economics, mathematics, news, physics*). |
| **Abstract Nouns** | **Honesty** is the best policy.<br>We need more **information.**<br>We're concerned about your **health.**<br>Have you studied **economics** or **physics?** | |

**1**   Quickly reread "What Is Wealth to You?" on page 168 and then do the following:

1.  Underline all the nouns.
2.  Group the nouns in the chart that follows.
3.  Make a list of any nouns that are confusing to you and discuss these as a class. For example, are there nouns that can go in more than one category?

| Count Nouns | | Noncount Nouns | |
|---|---|---|---|
| **Singular** | **Plural** | **Concrete (Tangible)** | **Abstract (Intangible)** |
|  | *people* |  |  |
|  |  |  |  |
|  |  |  |  |
|  |  |  |  |

## B. Groups of Count and Noncount Nouns

Certain patterns exist with count and noncount nouns. For example, noncount nouns often refer to categories or groups, while specific items in these groups are often count nouns. Some groups of words are usually noncount, such as food items and weather terms. Other nouns may be count or noncount, depending on the meaning. Compare the following:

| Noncount | Count | Noncount | Count |
|---|---|---|---|
| advice | hints<br>ideas<br>suggestions | information, news | articles<br>magazines<br>newspapers |
| equipment | machines<br>supplies<br>tools | money | cents<br>dollars<br>quarters |
| friendship, love | feelings<br>friends<br>relatives | nature | animals<br>forests<br>mountains<br>oceans |
| furniture | chairs<br>lamps<br>tables | time | days<br>hours<br>minutes |
| homework | assignments<br>essays<br>pages | traffic, transportation | buses<br>cars<br>trains |

| Common Noncount Food Items | | | Common Noncount Weather Items | | |
|---|---|---|---|---|---|
| bread | fruit | rice | air | water | |
| butter | meat | sugar | rain | weather | |
| coffee | milk | tea | snow | wind | |

| Nouns That Can Be Both Count and Noncount | | |
|---|---|---|
| **Noncount** | I studied **business** in college. | *business* = an idea or activity |
| **Count** | We have **a business** in Florida. | *a business* = a store or firm |
| **Noncount** | We had **chicken** for dinner. | *chicken* = a type of food |
| **Count** | My uncle has **a chicken.** | *a chicken* = a bird |
| **Noncount** | I have **time** to go there now. | *time* = an unspecified period of minutes, hours, and so on. |
| **Count** | I have gone there many **times.** | *times* = occasions |
| **Noncount** | That window needs new **glass.** | *glass* = a transparent material |
| **Count** | Would you like **a glass** of water? | *a glass* = a container to drink from |
| | I need new **glasses.** | *glasses* = a device to help people see better |
| **Noncount** | **Statistics** is an important area in the study of economics. | *Statistics* = area of study |
| **Count** | What are the current population **statistics** for your country? | *Statistics* = measurements of variations |

**2** In each pair of sentences, the same noun acts as a count and a noncount noun. Identify count (C) and noncount (N) nouns.

**Example:** __N__ We're having fish for dinner tonight.
__C__ My uncle caught three fish this morning.

1. _____ What time is it?

   _____ We had a wonderful time on Saturday.

2. _____ Is a tomato a fruit or a vegetable?

   _____ Fruit is good for you.

3. _____ My friend eats salad every day.

   _____ Would you like a salad?

4. _____ My brother is majoring in business.

   _____ We hope to start a small flower business.

5. _____ Do you like fish?

   _____ My aunt caught four fish last night.

6. _____ Lucy bought some new wine glasses.

   _____ Glass can be recycled fairly easily.

7. _____ We're having turkey on Thanksgiving.

   _____ He's never seen a live turkey.

8. _____ Jane bought some Colombian coffee.

   _____ Could we have two coffees, please?

9. _____ Work is a central part of many people's lives.

_____ We bought several works of art at the auction.

10. _____ Living abroad can be a wonderful experience.

_____ How much work experience do you have?

**3** **Error Analysis.**  Many of the following sentences have errors in their use of singular and plural with nouns. Find and correct the errors.

*glasses*

**Example:**  Do you know where my (glass) are? I can't see without them.

1. How many time have you been to New York?
2. We need more informations about that.
3. Do you have any advice for me?
4. The office manager recently purchased some new equipments.
5. We have a lot of homeworks to do for Monday.
6. There are several new student here from Taiwan.
7. I brought ten dollar with me.
8. He has some very nice furniture in his new apartment.
9. I have three assignment for tomorrow.
10. Traffic is very heavy today.

**4** Working in pairs, separate these nouns into groups. Make a chart like the following one to help you. *Note:* Many of the following terms appear throughout the chapter; check their meanings if you do not know them.

| | | | |
|---|---|---|---|
| ✓ advice | employment | market | salary |
| ✓ automobile | gasoline | money | supply |
| ✓ belief | gold | news | time |
| ✓ business | honesty | oil | traffic |
| capitalism | inflation | price | wealth |
| company | interest | product | weather |
| consumer | investment | productivity | work |
| economics | machine | profit | |
| employee | machinery | resource | |

| Count | | Noncount* | Meaning of Nouns That Are |
|---|---|---|---|
| **Singular** | **Plural** | | **Both Count and Noncount** |
| *automobile* | *automobiles* | *advice* (abstract) | *business—C = store or company* |
| *belief* | *beliefs* | *business* | *business—N = activity or idea* |
| *business* | *businesses* | (abstract) | |

*You might try to separate your list of noncount nouns into abstract and mass nouns.

## C. Singular and Plural Forms: Subject/Verb Agreement

Some count nouns can be collective; they refer to a group as *one* unit. Collective nouns can be singular or plural, but in American English, they are generally singular. Other nouns are always plural. For all nouns, words or phrases that come between the subject and verb do not usually affect the use of singular or plural.

|  | **Singular** | **Plural** |
|---|---|---|
| **Count Nouns** | A **friend is** someone who cares about you. | **Friends are** people who care about you. |
| **Noncount Nouns** | **Friendship is** very important to me. |  |

| | **Nouns** | | **Examples** |
|---|---|---|---|
| **Common Collective Nouns (generally singular)** | army<br>assembly<br>audience<br>class<br>committee<br>congregation<br>congress<br>couple<br>crew | faculty<br>family<br>government<br>group<br>public<br>senate<br>series<br>staff<br>team | **The audience was** eager for the show to begin.<br>**The public is** upset about the issue.<br>**The senate is** going to vote tomorrow.<br>**The staff was** in agreement about the changes. |
| **Nouns with No Singular Form (always plural)** | binoculars<br>clothes<br>glasses<br>pajamas<br>pants<br>pliers<br>police | premises<br>shears<br>shorts<br>slacks<br>scissors<br>tongs<br>tweezers | **Your pants are** in the laundry.<br>**Those pliers were** expensive.<br>**The scissors are** in that drawer.<br>Where **are the tweezers?** |

**5** In these sentences, choose the correct form (singular or plural) of the verb in parentheses.

**Example:** News from home ((is)/ are) very important to me.

1. Finance (is / are) one of five major area studies in business.
2. The class (is / are) preparing a report on international finance.
3. Economics (is / are) a difficult subject for many people.
4. Economists often (helps / help) shape government policies.
5. The economic theories of John Maynard Keynes (has / have) shaped the policies of many governments.
6. The government (has / have) changed economic policies several times.

7.  The advice from the accountants (was / were) very valuable.
8.  Congress (has / have) voted not to raise taxes.
9.  The staff (has / have) written a full report on the issue.
10. The police (is / are) on the way here.
11. The information that we were given about the new machines (was / were) useful.
12. The new equipment (has / have) worked very well.

## D. Indefinite Articles: A and An

*A* or *an* is used before a singular count noun. The indefinite article may mean *one,* or it may mean an unspecified person or thing.

|   | Examples | Notes |
|---|---|---|
| **a** | I bought **a** banana. <br> I bought **a** house. <br> **A** European man lives next door. | *A* is used before a singular count noun that begins with a consonant sound. |
| **an** | I wasted **an** egg. <br> I wasted **an** hour. | *An* is used before a singular count noun that begins with a vowel sound. |

*Note: A* or *an* is never used with a noun that functions as a noncount noun.

**6**  **Rapid Oral Practice.**   The following nouns are all singular. Some are count and some are noncount. Form complete sentences by using *We have* or *We don't have.* Use *a* or *an* with count nouns and nothing with noncount nouns.

**Examples:**   imported car
         *We have an imported car.*
         delicious food in . . .
         *We have delicious food in Italy.*

1.  computer
2.  heavy traffic in . . .
3.  problem with traffic in . . .
4.  income tax in . . .
5.  high (low) unemployment in . . .
6.  high (low) gas prices in . . .
7.  information for you
8.  time for . . .
9.  news for you
10. hot (cold) weather during . . .
11. suggestion for you
12. advice for you
13. high (low) inflation in . . .
14. high (low) inflation rate in . . .
15. a lot of air (water) pollution in . . .

## E. Unspecified or Unidentified Count and Noncount Nouns

Both count and noncount nouns may be used to refer to unspecified or unidentified people, things, and so forth. In this case, a singular count noun is preceded by *a* or *an,* but plural count nouns and noncount nouns are used without articles.

|  | **Examples** | **Notes** |
|---|---|---|
| **Count Nouns** <br> **Singular** | A house can be expensive. | *a house* = one house or any house in general <br> *Remember:* Either an article or an adjective *must* be used with a singular count noun. |
| **Plural** | Houses are getting more expensive. | *houses* = all houses in general <br> *Remember:* Articles are not used with unspecified or unidentified plural count nouns. |
| **Noncount Nouns** | Love is wonderful. <br> Time is money. <br> Health is better than wealth. | *Remember:* Articles are not used with unspecified noncount nouns. Noncount nouns always take singular verbs. |

**7** What does wealth mean to you? What do you value and why? From the following list, choose three or four items that are important to you. Put them in order (first, second, and so on). Make count nouns plural and use *are*.

**Example:**  I think . . . is / are (very) important because . . .

*First, I think good health is important because without health, we have nothing. Second, I think . . .*

| | | |
|---|---|---|
| accurate information | good health | love |
| clean air | good neighbors | money in the bank |
| courage | good public education | peace in the world |
| elegant clothes | health insurance | reliable transportation |
| expensive car | homework | respect |
| free time | honesty | safe housing |
| good advice from family and friends | jewelry | |
| | large family | |

**8** Our societies suffer from many negative issues. From the following list, choose three or four issues that you think are very bad for the physical and mental health of a society. Put them in order, beginning with the worst. Make count nouns plural and use *are*.

**Example:**  I think . . . is / are (very) bad because . . .

*First, I think little respect for laws is bad because without laws, people do anything they want. Second, I think . . .*

| | | |
|---|---|---|
| air pollution | drug abuse | little respect for laws |
| alchohol abuse | drug trafficking | poor education |
| censorship of the news | high interest rates | poor health care |
| computer crime | high unemployment | poor system of justice |
| corruption | lack of good, low-cost housing | violent crime |
| crowded schools | | water pollution |

**9** The following statements include noncount nouns and singular and plural count nouns. Complete each statement by using *a* or *an,* or use *X* to indicate that no article is necessary.

**Examples:**    I've always been interested in _X_ economics.

                I've never taken _an_ economics class.

1. _____ economics is concerned with two basic groups: _____ consumers and _____ suppliers.

2. _____ economists study the interrelationship between the two groups.

3. For example, _____ economist might study the way _____ supplier creates _____ market for _____ new product.

4. _____ economics also deals with the interrelationship between _____ larger groups, including _____ regions and _____ countries.

5. As we all know, _____ change in the economy of _____ country such as Japan can affect _____ people all over the world.

6. Economists study how events in _____ region can affect _____ markets and _____ prices in other regions.

7. For example, _____ weather in California can affect the price of _____ fruit in Massachusetts.

8. Today, _____ important issue involves _____ "new economy" companies and _____ "old economy" companies.

9. _____ "old economy" company is one that makes _____ traditional goods, like _____ cars or _____ furniture or _____ steel, or handles _____ services, like _____ health care, _____ banking, or _____ legal issues.

10. _____ "new economy" company may be _____ Internet-based goods or service company with no "brick and mortar"* store or office, or it may produce _____ computer hardware or software.

**Culture Note**

*Today, over half of Americans have investments in a stock market, though the majority of accounts are under $5000. The two primary stock markets in the United States (and the world) are the New York Stock Exchange and the NASDAQ (National Association of Securities Dealers Automated Quotation), where many of the "new economy" stocks are traded.*

**10** The following definitions of economic terms include both count and noncount nouns. Complete the definitions by using *a* or *an,* or use *X* to indicate that no article is necessary.

**Example:**    The *balance of* _X_ *payments* is the difference between the amount of _X_ money that leaves _a_ country and the amount that comes in through _X_ imports, _X_ exports, _X_ investments, and so on.

---

*brick and mortar*    idiom to describe traditional business locations, actual offices, or factories physically built at one location, for example, a WalMart store or a Chrysler assembly plant, as opposed to a company working solely from a laptop computer with a modem.

1. _____ *black market* is the illegal sale of _____ products.

2. *Capital* is _____ money or _____ assets such as _____ gold or _____ buildings that can be used to make _____ investments.

3. _____ *depression* is _____ very severe drop in economic activity. _____ high unemployment and _____ low production usually occur during _____ depression.

4. The *gross national product (GNP)* is the total value of _____ goods and _____ services produced in _____ country during _____ specified period of _____ time (usually a year).

5. The *money supply* is the total amount of _____ money in circulation.

6. _____ *productivity* is the total national output of _____ goods and _____ services divided by the number of _____ workers.

**11** The following sentences make generalizations about large companies. Change the nouns or noun phrases in italics from plural to singular or from singular to plural. Add or omit *a* or *an* and make other changes in verbs and pronouns. (Note that in this activity, *multinational* and *multinational corporation* have the same meaning.)

**Example:** *Multinational corporations* are *companies* that operate in more than one country.

*A multinational corporation is a company that operates in more than one country.*

1. *Multinationals,* such as IBM or Pepsi, may operate in over 100 countries.
2. Because of their size, *multinational corporations* can often make *products* at *lower costs* than *local industries* can.
3. *Multinationals* can also make *countries* dependent on them.
4. *A multinational corporation* may import *a raw material* from *a foreign country.*
5. *A multinational* may make *a product* in one country and export it to another country.
6. Today *a country* may require *a company* to build *an assembly plant* in *an area* where *a product* will be sold.
7. Building *a factory* in *a foreign country* can still benefit *a multinational.*
8. It eliminates *a major expense* in transportation.

## Using What You've Learned

**12** A *generalization* is a general statement that expresses an idea or an opinion about people, things, ideas, and so on. It often gives a general rule or conclusion based on limited or insufficient information. For example, consider these statements. Are they always true?

1. French people drink wine.
2. Japanese people always have dark hair.
3. American men are tall.
4. Latin Americans are fantastic dancers.

Note that these generalizations use nouns without articles. This is one of the most common ways to make generalizations. As a class or in small groups, think of some of other generalizations.

 13  Form teams of two or more students each. Take turns giving noncount noun categories for each of the following groups of count nouns. The team with the highest number of correct answers wins. Your teacher or a classmate can be the judge of correct answers. A classmate can also be the timekeeper. Set a ten- or fifteen-second limit for answering. Then try to add new items of your own.

**Example:**   movies and plays
*entertainment*

1.   taxis and subways
2.   dimes and nickels
3.   beds and dressers
4.   newspapers and magazines
5.   compositions and reading assignments
6.   snowstorms and thunderstorms
7.   minutes and seconds
8.   paintings and sculptures
9.   records, tapes, and CDs
10.  earrings and necklaces

 14  Proverbs are wise sayings that have endured over time. Some proverbs deal with how we manage money—are we wise or foolish with our resources? In groups, read the proverbs and compare them to proverbs in your first languages. Can you explain the meaning of each?

1.   A penny saved is a penny earned.
2.   An ounce of prevention is worth a pound of cure.
3.   A fool and his money are soon parted.
4.   A bird in the hand is worth two in the bush.

## PART 2    Indefinite Adjectives and Pronouns

### Setting the Context

**Prereading Questions**   Is economics a mystery to you? The following observation gives you one man's explanation of economics in very simple terms.

### Economics in My Life
For many people, economics is a mystery, but I deal with it every day. Economics is just a complicated way of explaining why I make only a little money and why another guy makes a lot of money.

**Discussing Ideas.**   Can you give your own very simple definition of economics?

## A. Indefinite Adjectives and Pronouns with Both Count and Noncount Nouns

Indefinite adjectives such as *some, many,* and *little* are used with nouns instead of giving specific amounts. Indefinite pronouns such as *some, someone, any,* and *anyone* replace nouns. Certain expressions work with both count and noncount nouns: *any, some, a lot (of), lots (of), plenty (of), no,* and *none.* Compare the following:

|  | **Indefinite Adjectives** | **Indefinite Pronouns** |
|---|---|---|
| **Count Nouns** | Do you have **any** dollar bills?<br>Jack has **some** dollar bills.<br>Harry has **a lot of** dollar bills.<br>I have **no** dollar bills. | I don't have **any.**<br>Jack has **some.**<br>Harry has **a lot.**<br>I have **none.** |
| **Noncount Nouns** | Do you have **any** money?<br>Jack has **some** money.<br>Harry has **a lot of** money.<br>I have **no** money. | Do you have **any?**<br>Jack has **some.**<br>Harry has **a lot.**<br>I have **none.** |

*Note:* In formal English, *none* is always followed by a singular verb: *None of the people has arrived.* (formal) *None of the people have arrived.* (informal)

**1**  **Rapid Oral Practice.**   In pairs, ask and answer questions using these cues and words such as *some, any,* and *a lot (of).*

**Examples:**   homework tonight
   A:   **Do you have any homework tonight?**
   B:   **Yes, I have some homework.**
   money
   A:   **Do you have some money?**
   B:   **No, I don't have any.**

1.  cash
2.  checks
3.  credit cards
4.  interesting news (about . . .)
5.  information about good dentists (doctors, therapists, and so on)
6.  assignments tonight
7.  free time today
8.  advice (about . . .)
9.  change
10. coins

## B. (A) Few *and* (Not) Many *with Count Nouns*

| **Examples** | **Meanings** | **Notes** |
|---|---|---|
| How **many** (dollars) do you have?<br>I have **a few** (dollars). | I have some dollars, but not a lot. | *Few, a few, many,* and *not many* are used with count nouns. *Many* can be used in affirmative statements, but it is more common in questions with *how* and in negative statements. |
| I **don't** have **many** dollar bills. | I have only a small number of dollars, probably not enough. |  |
| I have **few** dollar bills. | I probably don't have enough. |  |

## C. (A) Little *and* (Not) Much *with Noncount Nouns*

| Examples | Meanings | Notes |
|---|---|---|
| How **much** (money) do you have?<br>I have **a little** (money).<br><br>I **don't have much** money.<br><br><br>I have **little** money. | I have some money, but not a lot.<br>I have only a small amount of money, probably not enough.<br>I probably don't have enough. | *A little, little, much,* and *not much* are used with noncount nouns. *Much* can be used in affirmative statements, but it is more common in questions with *how* and in negative statements. |

*Note:* Other expressions such as *numerous, several, a number of,* and *a couple (of)* can be used with plural count nouns. Expressions such as *a good deal of, a great deal of,* and *a large (small) amount of* can be used with noncount nouns.

**2**  *Few* and *little* mean "not many (much)," but *a few* and *a little* mean "some." Indicate the differences in meaning in the following sentences by using + ("some") or − ("not many or not much").

**Examples:**   ⁺ There are a few good restaurants in town.

⁻ There are few good restaurants in town.

1. _____ We have little homework for the weekend.

2. _____ We have a little homework for the weekend.

3. _____ I have a little advice for you.

4. _____ I have a few ideas for you.

5. _____ He has little information on that.

6. _____ There is little traffic today.

7. _____ Do you have a little time?

8. _____ We have a few pages to read for tomorrow.

9. _____ She has a few friends here.

10. _____ She has few friends here.

11. _____ I've got a little money with me.

12. _____ I've got a few dollars with me.

**3**  **Rapid Oral Practice.**   With a partner, take turns making statements and responses modeling the examples that follow. Make count nouns plural and use *a little, little, not much, a few, few,* or *not many.*

**Examples:**   money with me
        A:  **I have a little money with me. How about you?**
        B:  **I don't have much money this week.**

> dollar with me
>
> A: **I have a few dollars with me. How about you?**
>
> B: **I have a few dollars too.**

1. free time today
2. furniture in my house (apartment)
3. friend from . . .
4. problem with . . .
5. extra energy
6. homework tonight
7. news from home
8. assignment this week
9. change
10. food at home

## D. *Modifiers with* A Lot Of, A Little, A Few, Little, *and* Few

*A lot of, a little, a few, little,* and *few* occur frequently in conversation. They are often used with other modifiers. The most common are *quite, just, only, very,* and *too.*

| *Quite* with *A Lot (Of)* and *A Few* | | |
|---|---|---|
| **Count Nouns** | **Noncount Nouns** | **Meaning** |
| She has **quite a few** assignments. | She has **quite a lot of** homework. | a large number or amount |

| *Just* and *Only* with *A Few* and *A Little* | | |
|---|---|---|
| **Count Nouns** | **Noncount Nouns** | **Meaning** |
| She has **just a few** assignments. | She has **just a little** homework. | a moderate number or amount |
| She has **only a few** assignments. | She has **only a little** homework. | a small number or amount |

| *Very* and *Too* with *Few* and *Little* | | |
|---|---|---|
| **Count Nouns** | **Noncount Nouns** | **Meaning** |
| She has **very few** assignments. | She has **very little** homework. | a very small number or amount |
| She has **too few** assignments. | She has **too little** homework. | not enough |

*Note: Too* can also be used with *many* and *much* to mean "more than enough." Compare the following:

> That teacher gives *too many* assignments.
>
> That teacher gives *too much* homework.

**4**   Choose the correct form of the word(s) in parentheses.

**Example:**   Changes are occurring in the economies of ((many) / much) countries around the world.

1. Since the end of the 1980s, tremendous changes have occurred in (many / much) parts of the world.
2. (Few / Little) countries have escaped the major political changes that began in the 1980s.
3. When countries change their political systems, (many / much) other changes also occur.
4. Major economic changes have occurred in more than (a few / a little) countries in the world.
5. With economic changes have come (a number of / a great deal of) social dilemmas.
6. Countries that used to have (very few / very little) difficulty with unemployment and crime are now dealing with serious problems.
7. In controlled economies, often there wasn't (many / much) unemployment or (many / much) crime.
8. In free market economies, there can be (quite a few / quite a little) social problems that hadn't existed before.

**5**   In pairs, ask and answer questions about your hometown or home country. Use the examples and the following cues, changing any count nouns to plural.

Give your own opinions and offer any additional information you know about the subject. If your country has experienced major changes in recent years, talk about both the past and the present.

Questions:   Is there much (any) . . . ?
             Are there many (any) . . . ?
Answers:     There is quite a lot (some, just a little, and so on) . . .
             There are quite a few (only a few, too few, and so on) . . .

**Examples:**   oil
                A:   **Is there much oil in your country?**
                B:   **Unfortunately, there isn't much oil in my country.**
                taxi
                A:   **Are there many taxis in Buenos Aires?**
                B:   **There are quite a few—maybe thousands!**

1. tax
2. poverty
3. crime
4. discrimination
5. air and water pollution
6. high-tech industries
7. farm
8. factory
9. unemployment
10. beautiful scenery
11. English language schools
12. corruption

## E. More Indefinite Pronouns

| Pronouns | | Examples | Notes |
|---|---|---|---|
| everyone    someone<br>everybody    somebody<br>everything    something | | **Formal**<br>**Everyone has his or her** own problems from time to time.<br>**Everyone has his** own problems at times. | Indefinite pronouns are singular. They are always used with singular verbs. In formal English, singular pronouns are used to refer to them. |
| anyone    no one<br>anybody    nobody<br>anything    nothing | | **Informal**<br>**Everyone has their** own problems at times. | In informal English, plural pronouns are often used. |
| Each<br><br>All<br>None | | **Each person was** counted.<br><br>**All were** counted.<br>**None was** missing. (formal)<br>**None were** missing. (informal) | *Each* + noun is always singular.<br>*All* is always plural.<br>*None* generally uses a singular verb in formal English, but a plural verb is sometimes considered correct. |

*Note: Each* + noun is always singular. *All* is always plural. *None* generally uses a singular verb in formal English, but a plural verb is sometimes considered correct.

**6** Choose the form of the word(s) in parentheses that is correct in formal, written English.

**Example:** No one (want / (wants)) to be in a bad economic situation.

1. In today's changing economies, anyone with a good job (is / are) very fortunate.
2. Everyone (worry / worries) about losing (her / their) money.
3. In some parts of the world, you can only get a good job if you know people who (is / are) in a position of power.
4. Every company (has / have) (its / their) own employment policies.
5. Some companies allow everyone to give (his or her / their) ideas.
6. In some companies, all workers can contribute (his or her / their) ideas.
7. Nobody (is / are) surprised when people complain.
8. Anybody can bring (his or her / their) complaints to meetings.
9. None of the workers (was / were) at the meeting last night.
10. No one (was / were) available to give (his / their) opinion.

**7** Reread the sentences in Activity 6. Indicate any sentences that have an informal, conversational alternative.

**Example:** Everyone (worry / worries) about losing (her / their) money.

*Everyone worries about losing their money.—Informal*

## F. One, Another, The Other, Others, The Others

These pronouns and adjectives are often used to list more than one item. The choice depends on how many items are in the group and whether the speaker is referring to the entire group. Compare the following:

We have *two* problems. *One* is lack of money. *The other* is lack of time.

We have *several* problems. One is lack of money. *Others* are lack of time and transportation.

We have *four* problems. *One* is lack of money. *Another* is lack of time. *The others* are lack of transportation and equipment.

|  | **Adjective** | **Pronoun** | **Meaning** |
|---|---|---|---|
| **Singular** | one problem<br>another problem<br>the other problem | one<br>another<br>the other | <br>an additional problem<br>the second of two or the last of a group |
| **Plural** | some problems<br>other problems<br>the other problems | some<br>others<br>the others | <br>additional problems<br>the last of a group |

**8**   Complete the following sentences by using a form of *other (another, other, others, the other, the others)*. The first one is done as an example.

1.   There are five major areas of business. One is accounting, and _another_ is data processing. _____ are finance, management, and marketing.

2.   Accounting is sometimes divided into two branches. One is public accounting and _____ is private accounting.

3.   Marketing experts are responsible for promoting and selling a product. This involves many things, beginning with product design and development. _____ aspects of marketing include packaging, pricing, and advertising.

4.   Financial experts can be divided into three major groups. Financial analysts form one group. _____ groups are bankers and stockbrokers.

5.   Although they may make different products, most factories are organized in a similar way. Two areas of factory organization are purchasing and inventory control. _____ areas include control of production and of distribution.

**9**   Complete the following sentences by using *one* or a form of *other (another, other, others, the other, the others)*.

1.   For investments, people often deposit their money in a financial institution. Several types of financial institutions exist in the United States. The most common are commercial banks. _Other_ common types are credit unions and savings and loans.

2.  Commercial banks generally handle business customers. They offer many services such as checking and savings accounts. _____ services include short- and long-term loans and certificates of deposit.

3.  Credit unions and savings and loans also offer certificates of deposit (CDs). CDs usually offer higher interest rates than regular savings accounts, and they usually have at least two requirements. _____ is to deposit a minimum amount of money ($500, $2500, and so on). _____ is to agree to leave your money on deposit for a minimum amount of time (six months, two years, and so on).

4.  _____ common form of investing is putting money in the stock market. There are two common ways of participating in the stock market. _____ is to buy individual stocks. _____ is to by shares in a mutual fund, which is a pool of money from many people to buy shares in many different companies.

5.  Several major stock markets exist in the United States, including two very famous markets. _____ is the New York Stock Exchange and _____ is the NASDAQ. In addition to these two markets, _____ in the United States and abroad include currency markets, commodities markets, and futures markets.

6.  _____ ways of investing your money include buying bonds, precious metals, or collectibles such as art or cars. _____ way to buy bonds is to purchase them from the U.S. government (savings bonds). _____ types of bonds include state and local government bonds for education, energy, and so on. _____ common precious metal to buy is gold. _____ most common precious metals to buy are silver and platinum. Collectibles include many types of valuable things. Art is perhaps the most common. You can buy artworks directly from an artist. _____ way of finding art is through an art dealer. Or you can visit an auction and try to find pieces you want to collect.

**Culture Note**

*The NASDAQ (National Association of Securities Dealers Automated Quotation) began in 1971 as the world's first electronic stock market. Today, it is the second largest stock market in the world. One of its primary goals has been to bring innovative new companies to the market. In 1999, it listed 89 percent of all IPOs (initial public offerings) in the United States. Many of these "start-ups" were "dot coms," purely Internet-based companies, but the largest percentage of 1999 IPOs were from manufacturing firms. The NASDAQ is home to many small start-ups, but it is also the financial home of such economic giants as Intel and Microsoft.*

**10** **Review.** Choose the form of the word(s) in parentheses that is correct in formal, written English.

### The Organization of a Business

In ((all)/any) economic systems today, most businesses plan their organization carefully. (Another/(One)) common organizational system is the division of labor.
 1                                             2

*Division of labor* means all of the workers (is/are) specialized. Each worker has
 3

(his or her/their) own particular duties to perform. Each duty (is/are) one part of the
 4                                                                5

whole operation. A good example of the division of labor is an assembly line in an

automobile factory. (One/Other) worker may install a door while (another/others) is
<br>               6                                     7

installing the hood. (The other/The others) add lights, windshield wipers, and so on.
<br>                                   8

Normally, the workers don't move. Everyone (stay/stays) in one place, and a conveyor
<br>                                     9

belt moves the product to (him or her/them).
<br>                        10

    The division of labor permits mass production, but it does have (any/some)
<br>                                                            11

disadvantages. For one thing, (few/little) people know or understand all
<br>                                   12

(aspect/aspects) of an operation. In addition, mass production may be efficient, but
<br>               13

(many/much) workers complain that they get (few/little) job satisfaction from working
<br>       14                                          15

on one small duty, day after day. To them, there is (many/much) more satisfaction in
<br>                                         16

doing a job from start to finish.

**11**   **Error Analysis.**   Many of the following sentences have errors in indefinite pronouns and adjectives. Find and correct the mistakes. Use formal, written English.

   **Example:**    Motor City is a town with many automobile factories. *Correct*

                           *many*
<br>                How ~~much~~ factories are there in Motor City?

1.   I've worked at Mass Production Motors for a few years.
2.   We have a lot problems in this factory.
3.   The workers are paid very few money.
4.   We don't get no job satisfaction here.
5.   There are too much unhappy workers in this factory.
6.   Only a little people are happy with their jobs.
7.   Last year there weren't much strikes, but this year we're going to have plenty of.
8.   So far we haven't had much success in changing things.
9.   The management has tried to make some changes, but it's had very little success.
10.   Many of workers are against the changes.
11.   Everyone has his own opinion about the situation.
12.   One person thinks things are getting better, but other person thinks they're getting worse.

## Using What You've Learned

**12** This cartoon was published on April 14, one day before Americans must file their income tax returns. People try hard to find ways of reducing the amount of taxes they must pay. These ways of reducing taxes are called *loopholes.*

Read the cartoon. Then work in pairs and rewrite the dialogue. Make complete questions for the first two frames. For the second two frames, try to put the ideas in your own words. Then compare your new dialogue with those of your classmates.

**cathy®**        **by Cathy Guisewite**

CATHY © 1995 Cathy Guisewite. Reprinted with permission of Universal Press Syndicate. All rights reserved.

**13** Think about the ideas that you discussed in Activity 5, page 182. Write a short composition about an important economic or social issue in your country today. It may be poverty, air pollution, or crime, for example. In your first draft, explain the issue as you see it in more general terms. Later you might want to revise your composition to include specific examples. If your country has experienced significant changes in recent years, you can write a general comparison of the past and present.

## PART 3    The Definite Article

### Setting the Context

**Prereading Questions** What are *natural resources?* Give some examples of resources you are familiar with.

---
#### World Resources: Where Are They?
Some of the world's most important resources are coal, iron ore, petroleum, copper, gold, silver, and diamonds. Many deposits are concentrated in small areas, such as the petroleum deposits off the coast of Venezuela and in the deserts around the Persian Gulf.    5

---

**Discussing Ideas.** Think of an area of the world that you know well. What are this area's most important natural resources?

## A. Introduction to the Definite Article

The definite article—*the*—can be used with both count and noncount nouns when the noun is specifically identified or its identity is already clearly understood. Many times, the particular context determines if *the* should be used or not, but in certain cases, such as with place names and locations, specific rules exist about when to use and not to use *the*.

## B. The *with Count Nouns*

| | Examples | Notes |
|---|---|---|
| **Nonspecific (Without *the*)** | **Singular**<br>Today a **company** may earn over $1 billion annually.<br>**Plural**<br>Today **companies** may earn over $1 billion annually. | *The* is not used with nonspecific nouns. |
| **Specific (With *the*)** | Today, **the companies** that earn over $1 billion annually are primarily oil companies. | *The* is used before a singular or plural count noun when that noun is specifically identified or its identity is already understood. |
| **Unique Nouns** | Many of the largest companies **in the world** are oil companies. Oil companies control most of **the earth's** known oil reserves. | *The* is used with names of people, places, and so on that are considered to be one of a kind. These include *the earth, the world, the moon, the sun, the universe, the president,* and *the pope*.<br>Exception: *on earth* |
| **Repeated Nouns** | He works for **an oil company. The company** has sent him to work in many different parts of the country. He enjoys working for **the company,** but he is tired of traveling. | After a noun has been mentioned once, *the* is used with later references to that noun. |
| **Identifying Phrases** | **The majority of companies** with billion dollar incomes are oil companies. | Phrases that come immediately after a noun often identify it, so *the* is used. *The + noun + of* is a frequent combination. |
| **Identifying Clauses** | Today, **the companies that earn over $1 billion** are primarily oil companies. | Like phrases, clauses may identify or specify *which* person, place, or thing. |
| **Superlatives and Ordinal Numbers** | The company with **the highest income** is Exxon. | *The* is normally used with superlatives (*the most, the least*) and ordinal numbers (*the first*). |

**1**  The following sentences include both specific and nonspecific count nouns. Complete them by using *the,* or use *X* to indicate that no article is necessary.

**Example:**  ___X___ natural resources are important to all countries.

1.  _____ most important resources in England are tin and iron ore.

2. _____ raw materials are used to make _____ products.

3. _____ raw materials that are used to make _____ cars include iron ore, rubber, and petroleum.

4. _____ petroleum deposits are located in many parts of the world.

5. _____ petroleum deposits in the Amazon will be difficult to extract.

6. _____ mines can be _____ very dangerous places to work.

7. _____ mines near Bogotá, Colombia, produce large quantities of salt.

8. _____ coal mines in West Virginia have caused many deaths.

## C. The *with Noncount Nouns*

Articles are not generally used with noncount nouns. However, noncount nouns, like count nouns, may be preceded by *the* when the noun is *specifically identified.*

| | **Examples** | **Notes** |
|---|---|---|
| **Nonspecific (Without *the*)** | **Gold** is a precious metal. | No articles are used with unspecified nouns. |
| **Specific (With *the*)** | **The gold in jewelry** is mixed with other metals. **The gold that is used in jewelry** is mixed with other metals. South Africa produces **the most gold** in the world. | *The* is used with a noncount noun when the noun is identified by a phrase or clause. *The* is usually used with superlatives. |

**2** The following sentences include both specific and nonspecific noncount nouns. Complete them by using *the,* or use *X* to indicate that no article is necessary.

**Example:** _X_ silver is valuable.

1. Most of _____ silver in the United States is used to make photographic and X-ray film.

2. _____ iron ore is used to make _____ steel.

3. _____ iron ore from eastern Canada is high in quality.

4. Japan produces some of _____ best steel in the world today.

5. _____ oil from Saudi Arabia is lighter in weight than _____ oil from Venezuela.

6. _____ oil is the most important single factor in the world's economy.

7. _____ gold is perhaps _____ most highly treasured metal.

8. Since 1910, one-third of _____ gold in the world has been mined in South Africa.

## D. The *with Proper Nouns*

*The* has specific uses with proper nouns, especially with geographical locations. Because proper nouns identify specific places, *the* is often used. There are few exceptions to the rules. Study the information in Appendix 3 and use it for reference.

**3**   **Rapid Oral Practice.**   Use *the* or *X* with the following phrases.

**Examples:**   _the_ Hawaiian Islands
_X_ Hawaii

1. _____ Great Lakes
2. _____ Lake Superior
3. _____ America
4. _____ United States
5. _____ Golden Gate Bridge
6. _____ equator
7. _____ Saudi Arabia
8. _____ 1995
9. _____ 1990s
10. _____ Philippine Islands

11. _____ Museum of Modern Art
12. _____ Rocky Mountains
13. _____ earth
14. _____ Canada
15. _____ president
16. _____ President Kennedy
17. _____ University of California
18. _____ Harvard University
19. _____ eighteenth of March
20. _____ Japanese (people)

**4**   Complete the following sentences by using *the,* or use *X* to indicate that no article is necessary. The first one is done as an example.

1. The world's major source of diamonds is __X__ southern Africa. _____ Star of _____ Africa, the world's largest cut diamond, was found there. Today _____ Star of _____ Africa is one of _____ British crown jewels kept in _____ Tower of _____ London.

2. The world's finest emeralds are mined in _____ Andes Mountains in _____ Colombia, _____ South America. The most important mine is located near _____ town of _____ Muzo on _____ Minero River.

3. The world's largest rock crystal, 1000 pounds, was found in _____ Burma. A piece of this rock crystal is displayed at _____ National Museum in _____ Washington, D.C.

4. The largest known pearl was found in _____ Philippine Islands in _____ 1930s. It weighed 14 pounds, 1 ounce. The largest known black pearl was found near _____ Fiji in _____ 1984.

5. _____ world's largest gold mine is in _____ South Africa. _____ South Africa supplies 60 percent to 70 percent of _____ gold in _____ world. _____ largest uranium field in _____ world is also located in _____ South Africa.

**5**   Make complete sentences from the following cues. Add *of, from,* and *in* and be sure to include *the* when necessary.

**Example:**   large gold deposits / exist / Andes Mountains / South America

*Large gold deposits exist in the Andes Mountains in South America.*

1. oil / be a valuable resource
2. oil / Saudi Arabia / be lightweight and high in quality
3. copper / South America / be easy to mine
4. copper / be important for the communications industry
5. silver / United States / be primarily found / Rocky Mountains
6. silver / be used to make photographic film
7. 40 percent / silver / United States / be used for photography
8. diamonds / be / precious gems
9. large diamond mines / exist / Ural Mountains / Russia
10. 25 percent / diamonds / world / be found / West Africa

**6**   Complete the passage by using *the* or *X* (to indicate that no article is necessary). The first one is done as an example.

### Mineral Resources

_____X_____ minerals are abundant in _____ nature. _____ earth is made up of
   1                          2           3

_____ minerals, and even _____ most valuable minerals are found in _____
   4                     5                      6

common rocks everywhere. Nevertheless, many of _____ minerals near _____
                                         7                8

earth's surface exist in _____ small amounts. As a result, they cannot be mined
                             9

economically. Only _____ big deposits can be mined at a reasonable cost.
                  10

_____ biggest deposits of _____ minerals are distributed unequally around
    11                12

_____ world. Some minerals, like _____ iron in _____ Mesabi Mountains in
   13                      14          15

_____ Michigan, are almost gone. Others, like _____ copper, cobalt, and
   16                             17

_____ petroleum, are located under _____ Atlantic and _____ Pacific Oceans
   18                     19               20

and _____ Persian Gulf.
    21

We have already taken many of _____ mineral deposits that were easy to mine.
                                   22

Today _____ companies have to look harder and deeper to find _____ minerals,
       23                                     24

and _____ cost of _____ minerals reflects this. Unless _____ exploration
    25        26                           27

and _____ technology keep up with our use of _____ resources, _____ cost
         28                                                              29                          30

of _____ minerals will increase dramatically.
       31

**7**  Complete the following by adding *the* or *X* (to indicate that no article is necessary).

### Where Minerals are Located

Some of _____ earth's most valuable resources are found in only a few countries.
                1

For example, _____ South Africa and countries in _____ former Soviet Union
                    2                                                   3

produce one-third to one-half of many vital resources. They are _____ world's
                                                                                              4

largest producers of _____ manganese, _____ chrome, _____ platinum, and
                              5                             6                          7

_____ gold. _____ Australia is another country that contains major resources. It
       8                  9

has large deposits of _____ oil, _____ gas, _____ iron ore, and _____ coal.
                             10                11                     12                          13

In fact, _____ Japan gets almost one-half of its iron ore (which is used to make
                14

_____ steel) and _____ large quantities of _____ coal from _____
       15                      16                                    17                         18

Australia. _____ Canada, too, has _____ large mineral deposits. _____ oil
                   19                            20                                          21

and _____ natural gas deposits in _____ Canada are some of _____ biggest
          22                                   23                                       24

in the world.

**8**  Reread the opening passage "The Global Economy" on page 168. Then do the
following:

1.  Look at the last paragraph of the passage, and underline the nouns. Which are
    singular and which are plural? Which are count nouns and which are noncount?
2.  Look at the word(s) that come before each noun. Which nouns are preceded by
    articles (*a, an,* or *the*)? Which are preceded by adjectives? Which nouns stand
    alone?
3.  Look at the second and third sentences in the last paragraph. Can you explain why
    *a* is used with *picture* in the second sentence, but *the* is used in the third sentence?
4.  Look at the phrase *the study of weather* in the first paragraph. The pattern *the* +
    noun + *of* + noun is common in English. Underline all other examples of this
    pattern in the passage.
5.  Does *economics* take a singular or a plural verb? Can you think of other examples
    of singular nouns that end in *-s*?

## Using What You've Learned

**9**   Are you interested in knowing more about gold? petroleum? diamonds? a certain kind of wood—mahogany, teak, ebony? a certain kind of rock—marble, slate, granite? As a group, pair, or individual project, choose one resource that you would like to learn more about and briefly research it at a library or on the Internet. Gather information on where this resource is found today, how it is extracted, and how it is used. Use your research as the basis for a short composition. Finally, share your information with the rest of the class in a three- to five-minute presentation.

**PART 4**   # Units of Measurement

## Setting the Context

**Prereading Questions**   Can you think of some factors that influence what types of foods people eat in different parts of the world? Read the following passage and identify three factors.

### Diet and the Demand for Food

The demand for different food products depends on three factors: the number of people in the area, their standard of living, and their cultural attitudes. The first two factors are obvious. The third, cultural attitudes, often depends on diet habits and religion. Take attitudes toward diet in the United States, for example. Changes in preferences and prices have had an interesting effect on consumption in   **5** America. In 1940, Americans consumed 19.4 pounds of butter and margarine per person, and most of it was butter. Now they eat less than 16 pounds, most of it margarine. Fruit consumption per person has dropped from 158 pounds to 100 pounds per year. Before World War II, Americans averaged 155 pounds of wheat flour a year; now they average about 120. On the other hand, Americans   **10** are eating more chicken, turkey, and vegetables.

**Discussing Ideas.** According to the passage, how are American eating habits changing? Have your eating habits changed in the last ten years? How?

## Units of Measurement

Units of measurement are commonly used in this pattern: number or percent + unit + *of* + name of item. Note that *of* is not used with *dozen* or *half dozen,* however.

| Units of Measurement | Items |
|---|---|
| bar | hand soap, candy |
| bottle | liquids such as juice, soda, and water |
| box | solids such as cereal and crackers |
| bunch | items that grow together—such as bananas, celery, or grapes—and items that are tied together, such as flowers. In informal English, *a bunch* is often used to mean "a lot." |
| can | liquids and solids such as soda and vegetables |
| carton | eggs; milk, ice cream, and other dairy products |
| dozen, half dozen | eggs; cookies, rolls, and other items bought in quantities of six or twelve |
| gallon, quart, pint, ounce | most liquids and ice cream |
| head | lettuce, cabbage, cauliflower |
| jar | jam, mayonnaise, and other items that are spread with a knife |
| loaf | bread |
| piece, slice | most solids, such as bread, cake, cheese, and meat |
| pound, ounce | cheese, butter, fruit, meat, poultry, and other solids |
| roll | paper towels, toilet paper |
| six-(twelve-) pack | soda |
| tube | toothpaste, creams, and ointment |

**1**   Complete the following grocery lists by adding appropriate units of measurement. Be sure to use *of* when necessary. The first one is done as an example.

2 _pounds of_ ground beef    1 _____ grapes

1 _____ butter    2 _____ crackers

1 _____ milk    1 _____ mayonnaise

1 _____ lettuce    1 _____ toothpaste

3 _____ cereal    1 _____ wine

2 _____ paper towels    1 _____ ice cream

1 _____ jam    3 _____ bread

1 _____ eggs    1 _____ celery

1 _____ soda    2 _____ cheese

**2**  Using the following list of equivalents, convert the amounts from metric to British units. You may give approximate (rounded-off) equivalents.

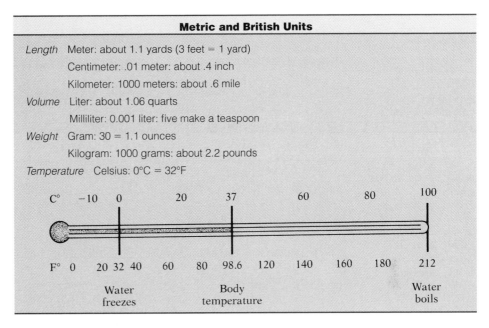

**Metric and British Units**

*Length*  Meter: about 1.1 yards (3 feet = 1 yard)

Centimeter: .01 meter: about .4 inch

Kilometer: 1000 meters: about .6 mile

*Volume*  Liter: about 1.06 quarts

Milliliter: 0.001 liter: five make a teaspoon

*Weight*  Gram: 30 = 1.1 ounces

Kilogram: 1000 grams: about 2.2 pounds

*Temperature*  Celsius: 0°C = 32°F

**Example:**  four liters of milk

*Four liters of milk are approximately equal to one gallon of milk.*

**1.**  one liter of milk
**2.**  three meters of fabric
**3.**  thirty-two liters of gas
**4.**  ten centimeters of tape
**5.**  three kilograms of cheese
**6.**  a meter of rope
**7.**  ten milliliters of sugar
**8.**  twenty degrees Celsius

**3**  Use the list of equivalents above again. This time convert the following amounts from British to metric units. You may give approximate (rounded-off) equivalents.

**Example:**  four gallons of gas

*Four gallons of gas is approximately equal to sixteen liters of gas.*

1.  two pounds of cheese
2.  one quart of milk
3.  five pounds of chicken
4.  two yards of fabric
5.  one teaspoon of salt
6.  ten feet of rope
7.  three inches of string
8.  three teaspoons of sugar

**4**  **Review.**  Complete the next passage by using *a, an,* or *the,* or by using *X* to indicate that no article is necessary. Explain any cases where you feel more than one choice may be appropriate. The first two have been done as examples.

**Culture Note**

*The United States commonly uses the U.S. Customary Measurement System (feet, inches, gallons, quarts, and so on). This system was inherited from, but is now different from, the British Imperial System. Beginning in 1866, the United States passed laws to officially adopt the International (metric) System, but the metric system did not become commonly used. Again in 1964, 1975, and 1988, the United States took official steps to make the metric system the preferred system in the United States. Today, many products are labeled with both measurements, but most Americans still use the "customary" system in their daily lives.*

### The Green Revolution

In 1910, __X__ farmers represented 33 percent of __the__ U.S. workforce, and it took
     1                                     2

more than _____ hour of _____ work to produce _____ bushel of _____
              3             4                 5             6

corn. By 1980, two minutes of _____ work produced _____ same amount, and
                                   7                    8

_____ farm employment had fallen to about three percent. In 1950, _____ very
   9                                                     10

good dairy cow could produce 1200 gallons of _____ milk per year. By 1990,
                                          11

_____ dairy cows were averaging over 2500 gallons _____ year, and some prize
 12                                            13

cows had even reached 6000 gallons. During _____ 1990s, _____ milk produc-
                                      14           15

tion increased by about 20 percent.

These are only two examples of _____ dramatic changes that have occurred
                                        16

in _____ agriculture. Through _____ advances in _____ science and
   17                       18                   19

_____ technology, _____ modern agriculture has become one of _____
 20                 21                             22

greatest success stories of this century.

Yet despite the "green revolution," _____ hunger plagues _____ earth.
                                    23                    24

According to _____ World Bank, over 800 million people are malnourished—so
               25

poorly fed that they are unable to lead _____ normal, active lives—and,
                                         26

unfortunately, _____ number of _____ malnourished people will continue to rise
        27                 28

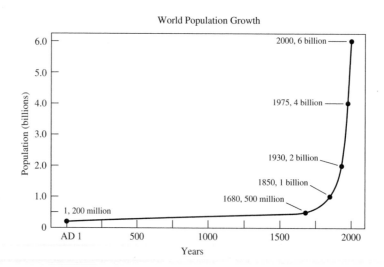

World Population Growth

as _____ 85 million babies are born each year. We need _____ annual food
     29                                          30

increase equal to _____ Canada's total yearly grain harvest just to keep up
               31

with _____ growth in _____ population worldwide.
    32              33

**5**   **Review.**   Complete the following passage by using *a, an, the,* or *X* (to indicate that no article is necessary). Explain any cases where you feel more than one choice may be appropriate.

### Changing Eating Habits

_____ population growth is not _____ only problem that we face in terms of
  1                               2

_____ world food supply. _____ changes in _____ eating habits are also
  3                      4              5

causing _____ problems.
       6

As _____ countries become richer, they consume more meat. _____ meat
      7                                     8

production normally uses more resources in _____ land, _____ water, and
                              9            10

_____ work. When _____ farmland is poor, raising _____ cows is efficient, but
  11            12                   13

when _____ farmland is rich, raising _____ crops gives much more food.
     14                 15

_____ wheat, _____ rice, or _____ other crops grown for _____ direct
  16        17       18             19

human consumption produce much more human food per acre. _____ reason for
                                        20

this is that _____ cow uses up to 90 percent of _____ energy from grain to
        21                        22

convert it to meat.

Today, about one-third of _____ world's grain production is fed to _____
                       23                    24

livestock (cows, pigs, and so on). This amount of grain is enough to supply _____
                                        25

human energy needs of _____ China and _____ India.
          26              27

## Using What You've Learned

**6**   How well do you know grocery prices? Check your budgeting ability. First, make a list of at least ten items that you need to buy. Your list should include food and household items. Use specific units of measurement in your list, and write down what you believe each item costs. Then work with a partner. Do not let your partner see your estimated prices. Your partner should write down estimates for your list, while you write down estimates for your partner's list. Finally, during the next two or three days, go to a grocery store and check the prices. Report back to the class on how accurate you were. You can use the following chart to help you.

| Item | Estimated Cost 1 Name: | Estimated Cost 2 Name: | Store Price |
|------|------------------------|------------------------|-------------|
|      |                        |                        |             |
|      |                        |                        |             |
|      |                        |                        |             |

# Video Activities: Welfare Payments

**Before You Watch.**   Discuss these questions in small groups.

1.  What kinds of problems do you think that the Department of Social Services (DSS) takes care of?

    a.  health          b.  poverty          c.  traffic          d.  tax

2.  A grand jury listens to evidence and decides _____.

    a.  if a person is guilty or innocent
    b.  on appropriate punishment for a criminal
    c.  whether a crime has been committed

3.  What kind of crime is *graft*?

**Watch.**   Circle the correct answers.

1.  What was the grand jury's decision about DSS?

    a.  They weren't giving poor families enough help.
    b.  They often gave money to people that shouldn't get it.
    c.  They needed a new director.

2.  The grand jury felt that DSS's slogan *should* be, "When in doubt, _____ it out."

    a.  check          b.  give          c.  put

3.  What does the DSS's slogan in Question #2 mean?

    a.  If you aren't sure about whether to give people money or not, get more information.
    b.  If you don't know who should get help, ask your supervisor.
    c.  If you have facts about a case, tell the people in charge.

4.  What is Jake Jacobson's job?
    a.  a lawyer for DSS          b.  a client of DSS          c.  director of DSS

5.  The grand jury _____ Jacobson.
    a.  praised          b.  criticized          c.  fired

**Watch Again.**   Complete the statements using the numbers.

| | | | |
|---|---|---|---|
| 20–30 | 7 | 20 | 60 |

1.   DSS gives out $_____ million in overpayments a year.

2.   The county board of supervisors will have _____ days to study the report.

3.   The grand jury said that nothing had changed at DSS for the past _____ years.

4.   The report said that _____ % of the DSS payments were fraudulent.

**After You Watch.**   Read the sentences and find the errors with count and noncount nouns and *a* and *the*. Rewrite the sentences correctly. The number in parentheses shows the number of errors in each sentence.

1.   When a family has a money problems, they can ask DSS for the help.  (2)

2.   The grand jury heard a lot of evidences against the worker at DSS.  (2)

3.   The grand jury found that DSS sometimes gives helps to people who don't deserve them.  (2)

4.   They also found a lot of grafts and corruption.  (1)

## Focus on Testing

### *Use of Articles and Singular and Plural Forms*

Singular and plural forms of nouns and verbs are frequently tested on standardized English proficiency exams. Review these commonly tested structures and check your understanding by completing the following sample items.

**Remember that . . .**

■   A singular subject uses a singular verb. Plural subjects use plural verbs. Generally, words that come between the subject and verb do not affect the use of singular or plural forms.

■   A noncount noun always takes a singular verb.

■   A singular count noun must be preceded by an article or adjective.  Plural count nouns do not have to be preceded by an article or adjective.

■   A collective noun (*committee, staff,* and so on) generally takes a singular verb. Many indefinite pronouns and adjectives are singular.

**Part 1:**   Circle the correct completion for the following.

**Example:**   John _____ happy with his classes.

       a.   seem
       b.   is seem
       c.   seeming
       (d.)  seems

1. Physics _____ the study of matter, energy, force, and motion.
   a. is being
   b. are
   c. is
   d. have been

2. The economic theorist who has perhaps most influenced government policy making in the last 60 years _____ John Maynard Keynes.
   a. is
   b. are
   c. have been
   d. has being

3. Homesickness _____ a problem for students studying far from their homes.
   a. have often been
   b. has often been
   c. has been often
   d. has often being

4. The two largest stock exchanges in the United States _____ the New York and the NASDAQ exchanges.
   a. is
   b. are
   c. has been
   d. had been

**Part 2:**   Circle the letter below the underlined word(s) containing an error.

**Example:**   Anyone can <u>feel frustrated</u> if <u>they have</u> <u>difficulties</u> in speaking
                                    A              Ⓑ              C
        <u>a foreign</u> language.
                         D

1. The committee <u>has</u> been discussing the issue of how <u>each</u> member should
                      A                                              B
   <u>officially</u> register <u>their</u> opinion on a particular matter.
        C                     D

2. In recent years, unemployment <u>have</u> grown <u>considerably</u> among <u>certain</u>
                                       A                  B                   C
   segments of the population, especially <u>those</u> in urban areas.
                                                D

3. Almost everyone who <u>lives</u> on earth is in <u>one</u> way or <u>another</u> affected by <u>the</u>
                            A                        B            C                      D
   global economics.

4. Securities <u>are</u> the <u>economic</u> term for written evidence of a <u>person's</u>
                    A          B                                              C
   ownership or creditorship, such as <u>bonds</u> and stock certificates.
                                           D

# Chapter 7

# Remarkable Individuals

# Introduction

In this chapter you will study the use of gerunds and infinitives, including how they can function as nouns, which verbs they often follow, and how the use of one or the other can change the meaning of a sentence. You will also look at a few uses of other verb forms: simple, present participle, and past participle forms.

You will meet a number of remarkable individuals from different fields. The following passage introduces the chapter theme, "Remarkable Individuals," and raises some of the topics and issues you will cover in the chapter.

---

### What Makes a Remarkable Individual?

In our fast-paced world, we are constantly taking in information about people. Yet, sometimes we confuse what it means to be well-known with what it means to be a remarkable individual. We do not lack people of quality and achievement to admire. However, the media overwhelm us with so much information that we have trouble understanding what genuine accomplishment is.                                               5

We meet people every day. Some of them make little impression on us. But some of them make us think about our own lives because of the quality of their lives. By representing living models of what it means to be fully human, remarkable individuals present us with the gift of self-reflection and self-examination. Could I do what she did? Can I continue on in the face of adversity the way he    10 did? Is one great and good thing worth the work of my lifetime? Remarkable individuals enable us to see what is possible in one life.

---

**Discussing Ideas.**    According to the passage, what sometimes makes it hard to identify a remarkable individual? What are some ways in which remarkable individuals make us think about our own lives? What is their gift to others?

---

**PART 1**

# Introduction to Gerunds and Infinitives

---

## Setting the Context

**Prereading Questions**   What does having *a second job* mean to you? Notice how this term is used in the following passage about Jimmy Carter, a former president of the United States.

---

### A Second Job

For some people, retiring after years of hard work is a lifetime goal. However, former U.S. President Jimmy Carter did not retire after serving four years as the President of the United States. Instead he created a "second job" for himself as an ambassador for world peace, intervening in global conflicts to bring two opposing sides together. He also worked for Habitat for Humanity, a volunteer agency involved in building homes for the poor. 5

Former U.S. President Jimmy Carter building homes for the poor.

**Discussing Ideas.** Do you know of any remarkable leaders like Carter who had a second job after their time in office? Do you think retiring from work completely is a good idea? Does working prolong your life?

## A. Forms and Functions of Gerunds

| | Examples | Notes |
|---|---|---|
| **Noun Object of a Verb** | I enjoy **books.** | Gerunds have the same form as present participles (simple form + *ing*), but they are used as nouns. |
| **Gerund Object of a Verb** | I enjoy **reading.** | |
| **Gerund Subject** | **Reading** is my favorite pastime. | |
| **Gerund Complement** | My favorite pastime is **reading.** | See Appendix 1 for spelling rules for the *-ing* ending. |
| **Gerund Object of a Preposition** | By **reading** a lot, I learn about the world. | |

| Active | Passive | Notes |
|---|---|---|
| **Governing** a country is difficult. | **Being governed** by a good leader is what most citizens want. | Passive gerunds are formed by using *being* + past participle. |
| **Not dedicating himself to peace** is unthinkable for a man like Jimmy Carter. | **Not being dedicated** to peace is unthinkable for a man like Jimmy Carter. | *Not* comes before the gerund. Possessive nouns or pronouns may also be used before gerunds. |
| Everyone was delighted by the **committee's inviting** Jimmy Carter. | Everyone was delighted by **Jimmy Carter's being invited** (by the committee). | As with most passive sentences, the *by* phrase is commonly omitted. |
| Everyone was moved by **Carter's committing himself** to the poor. | Everyone was moved by **his being committed** to the poor. | In formal English, a possessive is used before a gerund. In informal English, nouns or object pronouns are often used. See below. |

| **Use of Possessives and Pronouns with Gerunds** | | |
|---|---|---|
| | Active | Passive |
| **Formal** | Everyone was delighted by **the committee's inviting** Jimmy Carter.<br>Everyone was delighted by **its inviting** Jimmy Carter. | Everyone was delighted by **Jimmy Carter's being invited.**<br>Everyone was delighted by **his being invited.** |
| **Informal** | Everyone was delighted by **the committee inviting** Jimmy Carter.<br>Everyone was delighted by **it (them) inviting** Jimmy Carter.* | Everyone was delighted by **Jimmy Carter being invited.**<br>Everyone was delighted by **him being invited.** |

*See Chapter 6, Part 1, for information about collective nouns such as *committee*.

**1**   Make six sentences with active gerunds after the verb *like* or *enjoy*. Use these ideas and add some of your own.

     **Example:**    *I (don't) like reading about political leaders.*

> read books about politicians
> listen to speeches
> see films about political events
> learn about humanitarians* like Jimmy Carter
> hear about the accomplishments of leaders like Carter
> discuss the lives of remarkable people
> argue about who was a great leader
> sightsee at the home of a famous person
> find out about the lives of great leaders

**2**   Make complete sentences from the following. Begin your sentences with *We appreciate* . . . Use the example as a model.

     **Example:**    Carter / think about the need for world peace

> *We appreciate Carter's thinking about the need for world peace.*

---

*A *humanitarian* is someone who works for the good of all humankind.

1. you / interpret Ghandi's ideas for us
2. he / discuss the accomplishments of Jimmy Carter
3. Bob / record his conversation with Jimmy Carter
4. Grace / invite Thich Nhat Hanh* to speak at our peace conference
5. they / analysis of Mikhail Gorbachev's contribution to world peace
6. Phil and Maria / volunteer to take our guest speaker, former President Jimmy Carter, to his hotel

**3** Complete the second sentence in each pair with a passive gerund. Use the example as a model.

**Example:** We like reading to our children. Our children like _being read_ to.

1. We like inviting friends to our house. Our friends like _____

2. We enjoy teaching children about peace. Children enjoy _____

3. We enjoy including our friends. Our friends enjoy _____

4. We like reading to each other. Each of us likes _____

5. We like sending our friends newspaper articles. Our friends like _____

6. We enjoy applauding a good speaker. A good speaker enjoys _____

**4** Complete the following sentences with active or passive gerunds formed from the verbs in parentheses. Include negatives when indicated.

**Culture Note**

*Mother Teresa was an Albanian Catholic nun born in the city of Skopje in what was then the Turkish Empire. She spent her life working with the poor of Calcutta, India. She won the Nobel Prize for Peace in 1979.*

Mother Teresa inspired many people with her dedication.

**Example:** _Reading about_ (read about) Mother Teresa is _inspiring_ (inspire).

1. _____ (read about) Mother Teresa has inspired many people to help others.

2. Mother Teresa's message was that _____ (help) the poor was important work for humankind.

*Thich Nhat Hanh (pronounced *Tick Naught Han*) is a Vietnamese Buddhist monk famous for his efforts to create a peaceful world.

3. By _____ (not give up) and by _____ (continue) to fight against poverty and disease, she gave hope to millions.

4. People everywhere appreciate _____ (hear about) Mother Teresa's story.

5. _____ (serve) others was a full-time job for this humble woman.

6. _____ (go without) her own basic needs and even _____ (sacrifice) her health were part of her daily life.

7. Anyone who visited Mother Teresa could not help _____ (inspire) by her dedication.

8. _____ (award) the Nobel Peace Prize was a fitting tribute to her work.

## B. Gerunds Following Prepositions

|  | **Examples** | **Notes** |
|---|---|---|
| **Noun Object of a Preposition** | Thanks **for the invitation.**<br>Thanks **for the performance.** | Only the gerund form of verbs may be used to replace nouns as the objects of prepositions. Infinitives may *not* be used. |
| **Gerund Object of a Preposition** | Thanks **for inviting us.**<br>Thanks **for performing for us.** | |

| **Common Expressions with Prepositions That Are Often Followed by Gerunds** | | |
|---|---|---|
| be accused of | be sick of | plan on |
| be afraid of | be tired of | put off |
| be famous for | approve of (disapprove of) | talk about (talk over) |
| be fed up with | blame (praise) someone for | think about |
| be good at | complain about | worry about |
| be interested in | excuse someone for | How about . . . ? |
| be satisfied with (dissatisfied with) | | get through |

| **Expressions with *To* That Are Often Followed by Gerunds** |
|---|
| In the following idiomatic expressions, *to* is a preposition, and the gerund form follows it if a verb form is used. Do not confuse the preposition *to* with the *to* used in infinitives (*to* + verb). |

|  | **Examples** | **Expressions** |
|---|---|---|
| **Noun Object of *to*** | I am looking forward **to the party.** | be accustomed to<br>be opposed to |
| **Gerund Object of *to*** | I am looking forward **to seeing you.** (*Not* I am looking forward to see you.) | be subjected to<br>be used to<br>look forward to<br>object to<br>plead guilty (innocent) to |

 **5** Henry Ford of the United States and Akio Morita of Japan were two remarkable inventors and businessmen of the 20th century. In this activity, let's imagine that Ford and Morita were friends and often talked to each other. (In reality they did not live at the same period of time.) Complete the following three conversations by adding prepositions and forming gerunds from the verbs that follow. You must use every verb and preposition at least once. The first two are done for you.

**Culture Note**

*Henry Ford lived and worked in the first part of the 20th century. He invented the assembly line system of assembling automobiles. He founded the Ford Motor Company in the United States.*

*Akio Morita founded SONY Corporation in Japan. His creativity and leadership in producing electronic products such as radios, stereos, portable CD players, and hand-held television has made him and his company famous.*

*Both Ford and Morita are on* Time Magazine's *list of the "100 Most Remarkable People of the Twentieth Century." See them all on this Website:* http://www.time.com

| choose | market | about | on | ✓of |
| ✓discuss | ✓see | at | to | ✓complain |
| go | sell | ✓in | with | |
| look at | test-market | | | |

1.  *Akio:* I'm tired <u>*of discussing*</u> business. Let's find something else to do.

    *Henry:* Well, there's an auto show downtown. Are you interested <u>*in seeing*</u> it?

    *Akio:* No, I'm not. I'm fed up _____ machines, too.

    *Henry:* If you want a change, how _____ to a baseball game?

2.  *Akio:* You look upset. What's the matter?

    *Henry:* I'm dissatisfied _____ only a few automobile models each year. I'm sick _____ the same car year after year.

    *Akio:* You probably need to relax and think it over. There's no use _____ it when you're not good _____ straight.

3.  *Henry:* Aren't you looking forward _____ your new mini CD burner?

    *Akio:* I like the product in general, but the colors we're planning _____ just don't inspire me.

*Henry:* Well, would you object _____ those colors to Ford customers? If my customers don't like them, then you can complain _____ the wrong colors.

**6**   Morita's company, SONY, is famous for its high-quality stereos, TVs, and CD players. Do you have a certain way of choosing a new stereo or CD player? Use this activity to tell your classmates about it.

Complete the following sentences by using gerunds after the prepositions and by adding any other necessary information. You may want to use the verbs *do, watch, listen (to), try, study,* and *buy.*

**Example:**   Some people choose a product . . . by . . .
*Some people choose a product by listening to their friend's advice.*

1. Some people choose best by . . .
2. Other people learn from . . .
3. Here are my recommendations for . . .
4. You should start by . . .
5. Before . . . , you should . . .
6. While . . . , you should . . .
7. Instead of . . . , you should . . .
8. After . . . , you . . .

## C. Forms and Functions of Infinitives

| | **Examples** | **Notes** |
|---|---|---|
| **Noun Phrase Object of a Verb** | I would like **a new CD player.** | The infinitive is *to* + simple form. Like the gerund, it is a verb form that can replace a noun. It can also be used with or without *in order* to show purpose. It may *not* be the object of a preposition. |
| **Infinitive Object of a Verb** | I would like **to buy a new radio.** | |
| **Infinitive Subject** | **To choose** the right one takes a little time. | |
| **Infinitive Complement** | It is fun **to try out** all the models at a stereo store. | |
| **Infinitive of Purpose** | **To buy** a really good CD player costs a lot of money. He'll save for a year **(in order) to buy** that stereo. | |

| **Active** | **Passive** | **Notes** |
|---|---|---|
| We wanted **to tell** John about the stereo sale. | John has **to be told** about the stereo sale. | Passive infinitives are formed by using *to be* + the past participle. |
| Mary said **not to tell** him. | There is a reason for him **not to be told.** | *Not* comes before the infinitive. |
| It's important **for John to know** about this. | It's important **for John to be told.** | *For* + a noun or pronoun may also be used as the subject of an infinitive. |
| It's important **for him to know** about this. | It's important **for him to be told.** | |

*Note:* When two or more infinitives appear in a series, it is not necessary to repeat *to.* Compare these: *He loves to eat, to drink, and to be merry.* Or *He loves to eat, drink, and be merry.* In any series, it is important to use parallel structure. Do *not* mix infinitives and gerunds, if possible. INCORRECT: *He loves to eat, drinking, and to be merry.*

**7**  Let's suppose that Akio Morita, the founder of SONY Corporation, was asking you about your purchasing habits. Make six statements with active infinitives after the verb *like*. Use these ideas and add some of your own.

> **Example:**  *I (don't) like to shop for new CD players.*

| | |
|---|---|
| buy things over the Internet | purchase speakers on a friend's advice |
| buy products that have bright colors | choose name brands all the time |
| listen to a salesperson talk | discuss how much I paid for something |
| wander around a stereo store | have to read directions to use a CD player |
| compare prices by going to lots of stores | |

**8**  Here is some advice about international business that Akio Morita has given in the past. Pretend you are Morita advising the CEO* of a new company. Make complete sentences from the following. Begin your sentences with *It's important*. Use the example as a model.

> **Example:**  companies / find a competitive advantage
>
> *It's important for companies to find a competitive advantage.*

1. a company / include its workers in decision making
2. a CEO / know her product well
3. managers / include workers in product design
4. companies / to encourage creativity in their workers
5. managers / manage their work teams fairly
6. a new company / come up with new ideas

**9**  Gerunds are used more often than infinitives as subjects of sentences. However, infinitives are frequently used with anticipatory *it* as a subject. Change the following sentences to begin with *it*.

> **Example:**  Competing in the world market is difficult for a new company.
>
> *It's difficult for a new company to compete in the world market.*

1. For many companies, selling in the global marketplace is hard.
2. For name brand companies, selling their products abroad is easy.
3. Succeeding in the global economy is not simple.
4. Learning to compete for a share of the market takes a long time.
5. Educating consumers about your product is necessary.
6. For new companies, gaining a competitive advantage is essential.

---

*\*CEO* stands for chief executive officer. This is the person who is ultimately responsible for a company's performance.

**10**  Imagine that you are a music reporter who is interviewing the Beatles during the 1960s. Complete the second sentence in each pair with a passive infinitive.

**Example:**   **You the reporter say:** Do you like singing to children?

   **The Beatles answer:** We like to sing songs to children. Children like _to be sung_ to.

**Culture Note**

*The Beatles, an English pop music group, became world famous in the 1960s. They transformed U.S. rock 'n' roll in innovative and appealing ways. Their sense of style and their creativity began a musical and cultural revolution during the 1960s. Can you name the four Beatles?*

1.  *Reporter:* And do you entertain your friends too?

    *Beatles:* We like to entertain our friends. Our friends like _____

2.  *Reporter:* I see. How about large audiences?

    *Beatles:* We love to entertain large audiences. Large audiences _____

3.  *Reporter:* Do you ever include your friends?

    *Beatles:* Yes, we like to include our friends. Our friends like _____

4.  *Reporter:* This might seem like an odd question, but do you like to sing to each other?

    *Beatles:* Sure, we like to sing to each other. Each of us likes _____

5.  *Reporter:* And your girlfriends?

    *Beatles:* We like to send them presents. Our girlfriends like _____

*(John Lennon, Paul McCartney, George Harrison, and Ringo Starr)*

6.  *Reporter:* One last question. Would you like to send your fans a message?

    *Beatles:* Yes, we'd love to send our fans a message. Our fans _____

**11**  Test your knowledge of the Beatles by matching the following sentences. Make sentences with infinitives of purpose by combining the sentences. Match the items or events on the left with the purposes for them on the right in order to create new sentences.

**Example:**   **(1) He liked to wear a lot of rings. (h) He wanted to impress his fans.**
*He liked to wear a lot of rings to impress his fans. (Ringo)*

1.  He liked to wear a lot of rings.✓
2.  This Beatle traveled to India.
3.  He wrote a song, "Julia," about his mother.
4.  This Beatle was the last to join the group.
5.  He moved to a farm in Scotland.
6.  This Beatle formed a band named Wings.
7.  He went to the United States in the 1990s.
8.  This Beatle wrote the song "Imagine."

a.  He wanted to raise his family in the country.
b.  He replaced their drummer.
c.  He formed a group with Bob Dylan and Tom Petty.
d.  He wanted to keep playing music.
e.  He learned the sitar.
f.  He wanted to show the world his vision of peace.
g.  He wanted to remember her musically.
h.  He wanted to impress his fans.✓

## D. Infinitives Following Adjectives, Adverbs, and Nouns

| Adjectives + Infinitives | |
| --- | --- |
| **Examples** | **Notes** |
| I am **pleased to see** the new book about the Beatles. | Many adjective/infinitive combinations follow this pattern: *it* + *be* + adjective + infinitive. |
| It is **great to hear** one of them sing live. | |
| It was **nice of Paul to give** money for breast cancer research. | *Of* + an object often follows adjectives such as *nice, good,* and *polite.* |
| John was **the first Beatle to star** in a movie. | Infinitives often follow ordinals (*the first, the second,* and so on) or adjectives such as *the last* and *the only.* |

| Adverbs + Infinitives | |
|---|---|
| **Examples** | **Notes** |
| John Lennon's tragic story is **too** sad for me to **think about.** | *Too* often implies a negative result: *John Lennon's story is too sad; I can't think about it.* |
| Most Beatles' fans aren't old **enough to remember** the Beatles' first record. | *Not enough* also implies a negative result: *Most Beatles' fans aren't old enough; they can't remember the Beatles' first record.* |
| The Beatles' music is old **enough to make** it seem very familiar, yet fresh **enough to seem** like it is new. | *Enough* implies a positive result: *the Beatles' music is old enough to seem familiar, but it is fresh enough to seem like it is new.* |
| I would like to learn **how to play** some Beatles' songs. | Phrases with *what, when, where,* and *how* are reduced forms of noun clauses: *I would like to learn how I can play some Beatles' music.* |
| I would like to know **where to buy** a book of their music. | *I would like to know where I can buy a book of their music.* |

Let's suppose that it is 1968, and we are backstage at a Beatles' concert.

| Nouns + Infinitives | |
|---|---|
| **Examples** | **Notes** |
| Is this a good time **to go** backstage? | Infinitives are often used in the following |
| That would be a great thing **to do.** | combination: *this/that/it + be* + adjective + |
| **In order to go** backstage, we have to have a pass. | noun + infinitive. |
| (**To go** backstage, we have to have a pass.) | Infinitives are also used to express purpose or goals. |
| There are free passes **to be had.** | *In order* is not necessary for this meaning; |
| I have a pass **to use.** | it may be omitted. |
| She needs a pass **to get in.** | Similarly, infinitives can be used after nouns to show what should or can be done with |
| Do you have an extra pass **to give me?** | the nouns. |
|  | *There + be* + noun + infinitive is a common combination. |

**12**   Imagine the Beatles backstage at a concert in the late 1960s. Might they have a conversation like the following one? Complete the following by using either active or passive infinitive forms of the verbs in parentheses. Be sure to include negatives or subjects (phrases with *for*) when indicated. The first two are done as examples.

**At the Concert**

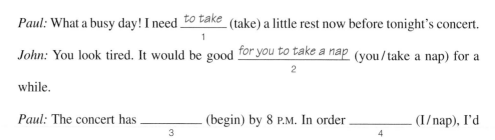

*Paul:* What a busy day! I need <u>*to take*</u> (take) a little rest now before tonight's concert.
                                      1

*John:* You look tired. It would be good <u>*for you to take a nap*</u> (you/take a nap) for a
                                                      2
while.

*Paul:* The concert has _____ (begin) by 8 P.M. In order _____ (I/nap), I'd
                            3                                          4

have _____ (rush) back to the hotel. You know it'd be terrific _____
       5                                                   6

(have / not) _____ (perform) tonight.
              7

*John:* Wouldn't it be great _____ (take) a month off from this concert schedule?
                                8

It would be nice _____ (do) nothing but relax.
                9

*Paul:* It would be even nicer _____ (the manager / give) us a year off. Then I
                                10

wouldn't need _____ (feel) so tired all the time. Well, it's easy _____
              11                                          12

(dream), isn't it?

**13**    You attended the Beatles' concert, and now you want to play guitar. Add infinitive phrases to complete the following.

    **Example:**  I'm interested in learning how *to play guitar.*

     1.  I'm looking for a good cheap guitar. Can you tell me where . . . ?
     2.  Have you considered lessons? It would be a good idea . . .
     3.  Many beginners have a hard time because playing the guitar is a difficult skill . . .
     4.  It usually takes several years . . .
     5.  Where can I get a guitar? Do you know of a good place . . . ?
     6.  I don't want to look for a guitar by myself. Do you have time . . . ?
     7.  I don't know anything about the guitar. Can you tell me what . . . ?
     8.  You can always rent a guitar if you don't have enough money . . .
     9.  Can you tell me where I can rent a guitar? I don't know where . . .
   10.  Thanks for your time. It was really nice of you . . .

**14**    Complete the following passages by filling in the gerund or the infinitive forms (active or passive) of the verbs in parentheses. Be sure to include negatives or subjects (*for* + noun / pronoun) when indicated.

### 1. Learning to Appreciate the Beatles' Music

    *Appreciating* (appreciate) the Beatles' music should be easy, but many people are so
        1

used to _____ (think about) its message that it is difficult _____
            2                                                   3

(they / enjoy) the music.

    Instead of _____ (take it easy) and _____ (enjoy) the music, they
                      4                               5

immediately get caught up in _____ (analyze) it. It is hard _____
                                   6                                    7

(they / not be) analytical. The best way to appreciate the music of the Beatles is just by

_____ (listen) to it.
  8

### 2. Watching *A Hard Day's Night*

_____ (watch) *A Hard Day's Night,* the Beatles' first movie, is a good way
   9

_____ (you/get to know) the Beatles if you don't know them. Each Beatle has a
   10

way _____ (make) laugh. You will forget about _____ (worry). Even if you
       11                                             12

don't know how _____ (sing), you can enjoy yourself by _____ (hum
                 13                                              14

along) to the music in the film. _____ (not know) the words well shouldn't bother
                                  15

you. It's more important _____ (you/enjoy) the music and _____ (see)
                          16                                     17

the joy and humor the Beatles found in life.


### 3. Playing Guitar Like the Beatles

Interest in _____ (play) guitar has always been high, and with good reason.
              18

Many people know the joy of _____ (have) music in their lives because the
                              19

Beatles inspired them _____ (learn) guitar. Playing guitar teaches you how
                       20

_____ (discipline) yourself because you can't learn an instrument without
   21

_____ (practice). Beatles George, Paul, and John all played guitar well.
   22

However, they learned _____ (play) well by _____ (perform) night after
                        23                          24

night during the early part of their career in Germany. _____ (entertain) night
                                                          25

after night in clubs enabled _____ (they/perfect) their skills on the guitar.
                              26


## Using What You've Learned

**15**   What do you feel like doing this afternoon? Tonight? Take turns making suggestions
with *how about* + gerund. Make a chain around the class. One student can begin:
turn to your neighbor and make a suggestion. Your neighbor will respond and then
turn to his or her neighbor with a suggestion. Continue until the whole class has had
a turn.

**Example:**   A.   **How about going to a movie tonight?**
                 B.   **Sorry, but I have a lot of homework.**
                 B.   **How about ordering a pizza for dinner?**
                 C.   **That sounds great!**

**16** In pairs or small groups, use the following phrases in a discussion about a remarkable person, someone you admire. After you have finished, choose one member of your group to give a brief summary of your discussion for the entire class.

I'm interested in . . .          It's fun . . .
I'm excited about . . .          It's enjoyable . . .
I'm turned off by . . .          It's boring . . .
I'm good at . . .                It's great . . .

**Example:   I'm interested in the life of Mother Teresa. She was like Ghandi.**

**Example:   I'm good at thinking up new ideas. I'd like to start a company like Akio Morita.**

**Example:   It's fun to sing and play. I'd like to start a group like the Beatles.**

---

**PART 2**

# Verbs Followed by Gerunds or Infinitives

---

## Setting the Context

**Prereading Questions**   Have you ever heard of Jerry Garcia? What do you know about San Francisco in the 1960s and the Hippie movement?

### Jerry Garcia—An American Original

Jerry Garcia was an American original. He lived life according to his artistic and personal values. He was the leader of the Grateful Dead, a rock band known for involving its audiences in its performance. The Grateful Dead believed  **5**
that each member of the band was an equally important member of their musical group. The band was famous for creating a business structure that respected the values of equality and collaboration.  **10**

Garcia was a virtuoso performer on his instrument, the guitar. But he was not only a musician, he was also an artist. His paintings and clothing designs show his unique artistic vision. He exhibited his paintings in art  **15** galleries and he marketed his ties in clothing stores. His influence extended beyond popular music. An ice cream company even named one of its flavors after him, Cherry Garcia.

**Discussing Ideas.**   Can you think of a musician like Jerry Garcia, one whose influence extended beyond the world of music to society as a whole? How has that person affected the society in which he or she lives?

## Verbs Followed by Gerunds or Infinitives

Some verbs may be followed by gerunds, some by infinitives, and some by either. Here are two lists. More verbs are covered later in the chapter. See Appendix 6 for a complete list of verbs followed by gerunds or infinitives with examples.

| Verbs Followed by Gerunds | | |
|---|---|---|
| | | **Examples** |
| anticipate | imagine | **Can** you **imagine being** a great performer? |
| be worth | involve | I **can't help wondering** what Jerry would |
| can (not) help | mind | be doing now if he were alive. |
| consider | recommend | |
| enjoy | suggest | |

| Verbs Followed by Infinitives | | | |
|---|---|---|---|
| | | | **Examples** |
| appear | have | seem | Would you **dare to live** an unconventional life? |
| be | hope | want* | I **would like to learn how** to play the banjo. |
| be able | know (how) | would like* | I**'ve decided to take** art lessons. |
| be supposed | learn (how) | would love* | I **need to register** for my art class today. |
| dare* | need* | | |
| decide | plan | | |

*More information about these verbs is in Part 3.

**1**   Think about a musician or music student (or student of anything!) that you know. Form complete sentences about this person from the following cues. Use the pattern of verb + gerund or verb + infinitive.

**Example:**   want / study

   *José wanted to study musical composition.*

1.  appear / be
2.  decide / stay
3.  enjoy / listen
4.  hope / return
5.  not mind / help
6.  plan / study
7.  be worth / learn
8.  would like / visit
9.  recommend / practice
10. need / know
11. anticipate / work
12. consider / go

**2**    Jerry Garcia designed neck ties, but he wasn't trained as a designer. Most people who work as clothing designers are trained. Imagine that you want to be a clothing designer. Rephrase each sentence using the cues that follow. Pay attention to the use of infinitives and gerunds.

> **Example:**    Would you enjoy learning to design clothing?
>
> *Would you like to design clothing?*
> *Can you imagine designing clothing?*

1.  Do you want to learn how to design clothing?
    Would you like  . . .
2.  You need to find a good instructor.
    I recommend  . . .
3.  I hope to begin design classes soon.
    I anticipate  . . .
4.  Becoming a designer involves spending years as an apprentice.
    Someone who is becoming a designer has  . . .
5.  Some student designers decide to start their own labels.
    Some student designers are able  . . .
6.  My instructor wants to rent a shop.
    My instructor suggests  . . .
7.  He mentioned designing it with me.
    He suggested  . . .
8.  I intend to start on it this week.
    I'm preparing  . . .

**3**    Complete the following, using gerund or infinitive forms of the verbs in parentheses. Be sure to include subjects when indicated.

### Watching a Great Musician Improvise

There are some things that are special treats in life—like watching a great jazz musi-

cian improvise. Jazz  *improvising*  is an art that few musicians master completely. It's
                       1 (improvise)

really thrilling _____ a great improviser at work. To _____ a great jazz
                 2 (see)                                     3 (observe)

musician _____ is rewarding for anyone who enjoys _____ present at the
          4 (improvise)                                  5 (be)

creation of art. Before _____ a performance by a great jazz musician, I recom-
                         6 (attend)

mend _____ familiar with the music that he or she plays, and even buy one or
      7 (you / become)

two essential CDs for close _____
                            8 (listen)

I suggest _____ your local jazz club regularly and perhaps _____
                    9 (visit)                                                                                   10 (get)

involved in the local jazz society. Then you will be able _____ jazz improvisation.
                                                                    11 (appreciate)

**4**   Complete the following passage by adding the gerund or infinitive form of the verbs in parentheses.

## Dancing the Night Away

Can you imagine _standing_ on a dance floor and _____ around in time to the
                  1 (stand)                              2 (move)

music? Some people never dare _____ _____ because they believe they
                                  3 (try)      4 (dance)

have no rhythm. But they're wrong. Instead of _____ about not _____
                                                5 (worry)              6 (be)

good dancers, they should dream of _____ in time to the rhythm of the music.
                                        7 (sway)

_____ can fulfill all your romantic fantasies. On the dance floor, you'll be able
8 (dance)

_____, _____, and _____ the music. Perhaps you won't be
9 (see)       10 (hear)          11 (feel)

able _____ _____ a little nervous, but you can anticipate
       12 (help)      13 (feel)

_____ your self-consciousness after a few dances. There's nothing
14 (lose)

_____, so why not dance?
15 (lose)

**5**   Complete the following passage by adding the gerund or infinitive form of the verbs in parentheses.

### Jerry Garcia and the Grateful Dead

Imagine ___*growing up*___ at a time when society was changing? Jerome John Garcia,
      1 (grow up)

Jerry to his friends, got used to _____ many changes in his life. As a child of
                                    2 (experience)

five, he saw his father drown. He was unable _____ him.  Then Jerry lost a fin-
                                              3 (save)

ger, yet he decided _____ the guitar. He disliked _____ to school so much
                    4 (play)                           5 (go)

that he dropped out of high school.

      Jerry began _____ folk music in Palo Alto, California, with a friend named
                  6 (play)

Ron McKernan. At that time, university scientists had started _____ with the
                                                              7 (experiment)

hallucinogenic drug LSD. Many famous individuals such as the writer, Ken Kesey, and

the poet, Allen Ginsberg, volunteered _____ part of these experiments. The
                                      8 (be)

1950s "Beat" culture, the new psychedelic drugs, the artistic community, and rock

music combined _____ a new culture. This new culture eventually became the
               9 (create)

"Hippie" Movement. The Civil Rights Movement and the Anti-Vietnam War Movement

also contributed _____ the anti-establishment feeling of the Hippies. Timothy
                 10 (provide)

Leary, who had been a Harvard psychologist, gave the Hippies their motto of "Tune In,

Turn On, and Drop Out." _____ , _____ , and _____ of society is pre-
                        11 (tune-in)   12 (turn on)     13 (drop out)

cisely what Jerry Garcia did. He became more and more interested in _____ a
                                                                    14 (create)

life for himself as a musician. He switched from folk music to rock. Then he formed the

rock band that became the Grateful Dead.

      The Grateful Dead moved into a house in the Haight-Ashbury district of San

Francisco. Their concerts soon became the center of Hippie social life, their fans

_____ themselves to the rhythm of the Dead's music, which often continued for
15 (give)

hours at a time. The band became well known for its ability _____ and its desire
                                                            16 (improvise)

_____ the audience _____ in their concerts. _____ all of this was
17 (see)                 18 (participate)              19 (lead)

Jerry Garcia. He was able _____ a life for himself that was unique because it
                              20 (imagine)

blended artistic devotion, anti-establishment feeling, and social consciousness. For

many people, Garcia's dream of _____ a better world through a common musi-
                                    21 (build)

cal experience was also their dream. For 30 years, until his death in 1995, Jerry Gar-

cia believed that music was capable of _____ human consciousness.
                                            22 (transform)

## Using What You've Learned

**6**  Have you ever purchased a musical instrument? Most people at one time or another
have had an instrument in their hands. Today use your grammar book to help this customer who has come into your music store. Work in pairs or in small groups and role-
play a visit to a music store. One partner is a customer who is looking for an instrument
that he or she can learn to play. The other partner works in the store. Use the following gerunds or infinitives in your role plays.

**Example:**   Do you really want . . . ?
> *Do you really want to learn a brass instrument?*

1.  It will involve . . .
2.  You seem . . .
3.  Your interest appears . . .
4.  I can't help . . .
5.  You can anticipate . . .
6.  You had better (not) . . .
7.  Have you considered . . . ?
8.  You must learn . . .
9.  You need . . .
10. I suggest . . .

**7**  Think about something you know how to do: dancing, singing, playing an instrument,
designing clothing, and so on. Write a brief paragraph about the subject, using at least
five of the verbs + gerunds and verbs + infinitives that appear in the charts on
page 216.

---

**PART 3**

# More Verbs Followed by Gerunds or Infinitives

## Setting the Context

**Prereading Questions**   Imagine living in the harshest climate on earth. What qualities would a person need not only to survive but also to be well-adjusted in a very
difficult setting?

**Culture Note**

*Antarctica belongs to no country. It is patrimony of the world. The 1959 Antarctica Treaty established a legal framework for managing Antarctica. Above all, the continent may be used only for peaceful purposes and all military activity is prohibited. Today, almost twenty countries maintain research stations on Antarctica year-round.*

### Living in Antarctica

Antarctica is a frozen continent where the temperature seldom manages to reach 25°F (−4°C). It tends to hover around −20°F (−30°C), and it can plunge to −100°F (−80°C) or less. The winds can reach 200 miles per hour (320 km). The sun shines most of the day during the very short summer, but the winter is month after month of dusk and darkness. 5

You might like to pay a short visit to Antarctica to see its frozen beauty from the warmth of your cruise ship, but would you like to live there? Approximately 1000 people live in Antarctica year-round, and two of those remarkable people are Adriana Romero and Victor Figueroa, from Argentina.

Victor Figueroa has spent almost five years in Antarctica, and the last full year 10 he spent there, he was joined by his wife Adriana. Victor was commander of the scientific station at Esperanza (Hope), named because of a shipwrecked group from Sweden that managed to survive an Antarctic winter there in 1903. Adriana was hired to help run the Antarctica radio station, and she also volunteered to teach in the Esperanza school, to help with the *Adelie* penguin counts, and to 15 translate for foreign visitors.

For them, living in Antarctica was exciting, but both also admit being bored and even being frightened at times. Through all, they persisted with high spirits and courage, both making major contributions to our knowledge of this forbidding continent. 20

**Discussing Ideas.** Have you (or someone close to you) ever had any experiences similar to those of Adriana Romero and Victor Figueroa—living for an extended time in a very difficult environment? Can you describe the experience?

## A. More Verbs Followed by Gerunds

| | | | Examples |
|---|---|---|---|
| admit | finish | regret | **I appreciated** your **explaining** the rules. |
| appreciate | forgive | risk | You should **spend** some **time reading** about Antarctica. |
| avoid | keep (on) | spend (time) | |
| delay | miss | tolerate | We can't **tolerate having** problems. |
| dislike | postpone | understand | |
| escape | practice | | |

## B. More Verbs Followed by Infinitives

| | | | Examples |
|---|---|---|---|
| afford | hesitate | refuse | Can you **afford to buy** that? |
| agree | intend | tend | I would **hesitate to spend** so much money. |
| care | manage | threaten | We **meant to tell** you about the cost. |
| deserve | mean | volunteer | I'll **wait to make** my decision. |
| fail | offer | wait | |
| forget | prepare | wish | |
| happen | pretend | | |

**1** Complete the following, using gerund or infinitive forms of the verbs in parentheses. Be sure to include negatives and make other changes when indicated.

**Example:**   We can't afford  . . . (take that trip)

*We can't afford to take that trip.*

1.  They agreed  . . . (not tell anyone)
2.  We appreciated  . . . (he / tell us that)
3.  He had avoided  . . . (tell us)
4.  She deserved  . . . (tell) (*passive*)
5.  I can't forgive  . . . (they / not tell us)
6.  He happened  . . . (mention / the subject)
7.  We regretted  . . . (not tell) (*passive*)
8.  He waited  . . . (tell / officially) (*passive*)

Adriana Romero, radio broadcaster and teacher, bicycling near Argentina's Esperanza Station in Antarctica.

**2** Going to Antarctica was a major move for Adriana Romero, and living there was seldom easy. Following is information about her experiences and daily life. Rephrase each sentence using the cues below. Pay attention to the use of infinitives and gerunds.

**Example:**   Adriana was able to spend an entire year in Antarctica.

Adriana managed *to spend an entire year in Antarctica.*

1.  Adriana decided to move with her husband to Antarctica.
    Adriana agreed  . . .
2.  She was interested in living in Antarctica for a year.
    She wished  . . .
3.  When Adriana was in Antarctica, she managed to do some exercise almost every day.
    When Adriana was in Antarctica, she spent time  . . .
4.  At first, she didn't want to exercise outside.
    At first, she hesitated  . . .
5.  Later, she really enjoyed getting on her bicycle and riding on the ice.
    Later, she really appreciated  . . .

6.   Adriana missed not being able to swim.

She regretted not  . . .

7.   She offered to teach at Argentina's School No. 38 on the base.

She volunteered  . . .

8.   While there, Adriana was able to speak English and French through her radio broadcasts at Station LRA 36.

While there, Adriana practiced  . . .

9.   She was also always ready to speak with visiting scientists and tourists.

She was always prepared  . . .

10.   Adriana disliked not having a lot of fresh fruit to eat.

Adriana missed  . . .

11.   She couldn't help feeling afraid sometimes.

She admitted  . . .

12.   Adriana hopes to return to Antarctica someday.

Adriana intends  . . .

## C. Verbs That May Be Followed by a (Pro)Noun Object Before an Infinitive

Infinitives may follow these verbs directly, or a noun or pronoun object may come between the verb and the infinitive. The meaning of the sentence changes with the use of a (pro)noun. Note that *for* is not used before the (pro)noun.

| Verb [+ (Pro)Noun] + Infinitive | | |
|---|---|---|
| | | **Examples** |
| ask | promise | She **asked to play** soccer with us. |
| beg | want | She **asked her friend to play** soccer with us. |
| dare | would (may, might) like | She **wanted to play.** |
| expect | use | She **wanted her friend to play.** |
| need | | |

## D. Verbs That Must Be Followed by a (Pro)Noun Object Before an Infinitive

A noun or pronoun object *must* follow these verbs if an infinitive is used. The object comes between the verb and the infinitive. Note that *for* is not used before the (pro)noun.

| Verb + (Pro)Noun + Infinitive | | | |
|---|---|---|---|
| | | | **Examples** |
| advise* | get | remind | The doctor **encouraged him to get** more exercise. |
| allow* | hire | require | |
| cause* | invite | teach* | She **persuaded him to start** a regular exercise program. |
| convince | order | tell | |
| encourage* | permit* | urge | She **told him to begin** today. |
| force | persuade | warn | |

*These verbs are followed by gerunds if no (pro)noun object is used after the main verb.

**3**  Complete the following sentences by using *for* or *X* (to indicate that nothing is needed).

**Example:**   We asked ___*X*___ Victor to go camping with us.

It was difficult ___*for*___ him to decide.

1.  We had expected _____ him to say yes immediately.

2.  He promised _____ us to ask for vacation time.

3.  It wasn't easy _____ him to get time off from work.

4.  We told _____ him to keep trying.

5.  We finally convinced _____ Victor to come.

6.  Then, he invited _____ his friends to come.

7.  In order _____ all of them to come, we had to find more tents.

8.  Our neighbor wanted _____ us to use his tent.

**4**  Complete the following, using gerund or infinitive forms of the verbs in parentheses. Be sure to include subjects when indicated.

### Watching Birds and Counting Penguins

Some pastimes can be done almost anywhere—observing birds, for example. Bird ___*watching*___ (watch) is a pastime, even a competitive sport, for millions of people around the world. And for Adriana Romero and many scientists in Antarctica, it is an important job. The work of many of the scientists there is _____ (keep) track of the penguins. They spend a lot of time _____ (observe) and _____ (count) penguins, especially the *Adelie* penguins. Observing and counting penguins is a way for _____ (scientists/notice) possible changes in the environment. It allows _____ (scientists/detect) changes in the ecosystem of Antarctica and even warns _____ (they/expect) weather disturbances. Over the long term, penguin births and migration seem _____ (be) important indicators of global weather changes. Warmer temperatures cause penguins _____ (stay) longer in Antarctica and _____ (have) more babies. Colder temperatures bring shorter stays and earlier migrations. Because polar weather changes indicate changes

worldwide, scientists from many countries are urging _____ (governments/fund)
                                                         11
more programs like the penguin observation programs in Antarctica.

**5**   Adriana's husband, Victor Figueroa, was commander of Esperanza Station and later
was the leader of Argentina's 1999–2000 expedition to the South Pole. Learn about his
trek by completing the following passage with appropriate gerund or infinitive or
forms of the verbs in parentheses.

**Trekking to the Pole**

1.   All of us were used to _____ (spend) long hours outdoors in the frigid
     weather.

2.   All of us were accustomed _____ (hike) long distances with heavy loads.

3.   Because of our _____ (train), each one of us knew how _____ (survive)
     under terrible conditions.

4.   All of us looked forward to _____ (trek) to the Pole. Of course, we all felt
     nervous, too.

5.   It was thrilling for _____ (me / lead) the 1999–2000 expedition.

6.   Of course, I was worried about _____ (have) accidents or injuries.

7.   I anticipated _____ (encounter) some very bad weather.

8.   In fact, we delayed _____ (start) our expedition because of an accident and
     some bad weather.

9.   And, we weren't able _____ (arrive) at the Pole for 1/1/2000 because of bad
     snow storms.

10.  All of us risked _____ (lose) our lives on this trek, but none of us regret
     _____ (make) the trip.

11.  Amazing sights such as the *aurora* or the beautiful star-filled nights never failed
     _____ (boost) our courage.

12.  And, none of us will ever forget _____ (stand) at the bottom of the world, the
     South Pole!

**6**   Complete the following, using gerund or infinitive forms (active or passive) of the verbs
in parentheses. Be sure to include negatives, possessives, or subjects when indicated.

**Amateur Astronomy**

Would you like _to know_ (know) more about the stars but don't know where _____
                   1                                                              2
(begin)? Well, even though there appear _____ (be) millions of stars, only about six
                                             3

thousand are visible. The visible stars are the brightest but not necessarily the closest.

Many of these seem _____ (group) together. These groupings are called constella-
                            4

tions, and many have unusual names, such as Taurus the Bull and Orion the Hunter.

You can learn _____ (recognize) many of them by _____ (remember) what they
                    5                                              6

represent.

The best time for _____ (you/study) the stars is during cold, clear nights. It is
                        7

easier _____ (see) many of the fainter stars then because the atmosphere lets more
            8

light reach the earth. Don't be discouraged by _____ (not/have) a telescope. You
                                                      9

can always see important stars—like Polaris, the North Star, or the Southern Cross.

Early navigators knew how _____ (tell) direction by _____ (find) Polaris because
                                10                              11

it is almost directly over the North Pole. In order _____ (keep) a steady direction
                                                          12

east or west, you have _____ (make) sure Polaris is in the same position each night.
                            13

Explorers have used this method of _____ (navigate) for over three thousand years.
                                          14

If you are interested in _____ (learn) more, consider _____ (enroll) in a
                              15                                    16

course or _____ (join) a local group of astronomers. And, of course, before
                17

_____ (invest) in a telescope or any expensive equipment, ask your local science
    18

museum or school department for advice.

**7**    Imagine that your class will live on a base in Antarctica for one year. You are the commander. Life will be very difficult, so you will need to have clear rules. Make a list of
rules for your subordinates (your classmates). Complete the following sentences. Then
share your lists of commands.

**Example:**   I advise *you to take this mission seriously.*

1.  I encourage . . .
2.  I expect . . .
3.  You must (not) finish . . .
4.  It's (not) important . . .
5.  It's (not) necessary . . .
6.  I promise . . .
7.  I will require . . .
8.  I will (not) allow . . .

9.  I will (not) force . . .
10. I will (not) forgive . . .
11. I will (not) permit . . .
12. I will (not) tolerate . . .
13. You will risk . . . if you . . .
14. I urge . . .
15. I would like . . .

## Using What You've Learned

**8**  Think about a special trip that you've taken or a special thing that you've observed. It doesn't have to be as exotic as an *Adelie* penguin or the southern *aurora,* much less a trek to the South Pole. It only needs to be special to you. Take fifteen minutes and write about this place or thing. Then go back and try to rephrase some of your sentences to use gerunds or infinitives.

**9**  Living in Antarctica is not easy, and sometimes for Adriana Romero it was lonely and frightening. She found ways to keep herself encouraged and optimistic. One source of inspiration for her was a giant petrel, a sea bird that flew near Esperanza Station often.

Read her description of this petrel and its impact on her. Then, think of something from nature that has had an impact on you—that has inspired you or has helped give you courage or peace or persistence. It could be a place, a bird or animal, or a thing: a beautiful meadow, a mountain peak, a special bird or animal, for example. Finally, spend 15–20 minutes writing about it and its inspirational impact on you. Try to use infinitives and gerunds in your writing. If you wish, share your piece with the class.

### My Magnificent Bird

Driven by gusts of freezing wind of the Antarctic Peninsula, the Giant Petrel kept soaring higher and higher. This magnificent bird coasted across Hope Bay from one extreme to the other in just a few minutes. Then it disappeared behind the huge glacier in front of me.

I could follow his flight from my house at Esperanza Station. I saw him gliding    5
effortlessly and I heard him cawing his message to me often during the year I lived and worked in the "uttermost confines of the world," as people who'd been in Antarctica for a while used to say. The Giant Petrel was a winged presence that constantly reminded me "to reach for the skies." He invited me to dream and to imagine great adventures. His presence encouraged me to explore the frigid    10
spaces around me. As he gave me hope and courage, he persuaded me to become completely wrapped up in my fascination with the cruel, glacial beauty of this frozen continent.

Adriana Romero, Esperanza Station, Antarctica

| PART 4 |
|---|

# Verbs Followed by Either Gerunds or Infinitives

## Setting the Context

**Prereading Questions**   Are you a fan of bicycle racing?  What do you know about the Tour de France or the Tour de Espana?  What do you know about the American cyclist Lance Armstrong?

### Lance Armstrong: An Inspiration to All

Some people love to compete on the tennis court or the track field. Others like to compete on the golf course or on the soccer field. Lance Armstrong prefers to compete on the roadway—or rather "the bike" path. The multiple winner of the Tour de France is an outstanding bicycle racer, but more so, he is an outstanding human being and a cancer survivor.                                                                  5

Lance Armstrong has always tried hard to do everything well—whether that has meant training long hours every day of the week in order to be fit enough to win "the big race" or whether that has meant fighting the cancer that had spread to his lungs and his brain.

It was in 1996 that Armstrong was named the top cyclist in the world. It was   10 also in 1996, just four months before his 25th birthday, that Armstrong was diagnosed with advanced stages of cancer. Chances for his recovery were fifty-fifty.

Very soon thereafter, Armstrong started taking chemotherapy treatments— the most aggressive form available. This therapy was so potent that it completely weakened Armstrong—a young athlete in peak physical form. Miraculously, the   15 chemotherapy began to work, and Armstrong allowed himself to think about racing once again. In May of 1998, Lance Armstrong celebrated his return to cycling, and in 1999, 2000 and 2001 he won the prestigious Tour de France.

Armstrong has won an even greater race, the race against cancer. And he has survived with a remarkable spirit. He says, "It's ironic, I used to ride my bike   20 to make a living. Now I just want to live so that I can ride."

**Discussing Ideas.**   Lance Armstrong is considered truly remarkable, in sports and in the medical world. What characteristics do you think he has—characteristics that helped him in bicycling and in facing cancer?

## A. Verbs Followed by Either Gerunds or Infinitives

These verbs may be followed by either gerunds or infinitives without affecting the basic meaning of the sentence.

| | Examples | | |
|---|---|---|---|
| **Verb + Gerund** | It **began raining.** | begin | like* |
| **Verb + Infinitive** | It **began to rain.** | can't bear | love* |
| | | can't stand | neglect |
| | | continue | prefer |
| | | hate | start |

*Remember that *would like* and *would love* are followed by infinitives.

## B. Verbs Followed by Gerunds or Infinitives, Depending on the Use of a Noun or Pronoun Object

These verbs are followed by gerunds if no noun or pronoun object is used. If a noun or pronoun object is used, it must be followed by an infinitive.

| | Examples | | |
|---|---|---|---|
| **Verb + Gerund** | We **don't permit smoking** here. | advise | encourage |
| **Verb + Noun or Pronoun + Infinitive** | They **permitted him to smoke** in the other room. | allow | permit |
| | | be worth | teach |
| | | cause | |

**1**   What sports or other activities do you enjoy?  Which do you dislike?  Complete the following sentences in your own words. Use at least one infinitive or gerund in each.

**Example:**   I like *to bicycle a lot*.

Or:   I like bicycling *a lot*.

1.   I like ⎯⎯⎯⎯⎯⎯⎯⎯.

2.   I love ⎯⎯⎯⎯⎯⎯⎯⎯.

3.   I would like ⎯⎯⎯⎯⎯⎯⎯⎯.

4.   I don't like ⎯⎯⎯⎯⎯⎯⎯⎯.

5.   I can't stand ⎯⎯⎯⎯⎯⎯⎯⎯.

6.   I prefer ⎯⎯⎯⎯⎯⎯⎯⎯.

7.   Last year (month, summer, and so on), I began ⎯⎯⎯⎯⎯⎯⎯⎯.

8.   I still haven't started ⎯⎯⎯⎯⎯⎯⎯⎯.

9. My teachers always encourage me _____.

10. My parents usually allowed me _____.

11. My parents never permitted _____.

12. I'd advise _____.

**2** Complete the following passage by using active or passive infinitive or gerund forms of the verbs in parentheses. Be sure to include negatives or noun objects when indicated.

**Bicycling**

Bicycles were invented in the early nineteenth century as "toys" for the rich, the only

people who could afford _to buy_ (buy) the early models. Later, bikes became more
                              1

affordable, but few people would dare _____ (risk) _____ (fall) in order
                                              2                    3

_____ (try) _____ (ride) one.
       4                   5

   By 1899, however, one out of every six Americans had bought a bike and started

_____ (ride). The bicycle boom was on! People everywhere began _____
       6                                                                              7

(ride) for pleasure, and many began _____ (race). Even the *New York Times*
                                            8

hired _____ (reporters/cover) races and encouraged _____ (local
           9                                                          10

groups / sponsor) bicycle events. But then the automobile was invented, and its popularity threatened _____ (eliminate) the bicycle entirely.
<br>11

Of course, the bicycle was not eliminated by the car. People everywhere have continued _____ (ride) their bicycles for pleasure. Likewise, many people bicy-
<br>12

cle _____ (stay fit)—especially as doctors have been advising _____
<br>13                                                       14

(people / reconsider) their lifestyles and encouraging _____ (they / get) more ex-
<br>15

ercise. At the same time, various energy crises have caused _____ (many
<br>16

people / leave) their cars at home and _____ (use) their bicycles for commuting
<br>17

too. During one energy crisis alone, bicycle sales skyrocketed—from fewer than 7 million in 1970 to over 15 million in 1973. This trend has continued, and today in Washington, D.C. alone, for example, over seventy thousand bicyclists commute to their jobs daily.

So bicycles don't seem _____ (be) disappearing. In fact, the popularity of
<br>18

_____ (cycle) is expected _____ (increase) as millions of people world-
<br>19                                                    20

wide rely on bikes for transportation and recreation.

**3**   Two great female athletes of the 20th century are Olga Korbut, from Russia, and Nadia Comaneci, from Romania. Learn more about them by completing this passage, using gerund or infinitive forms of the verb in parentheses. Note any instance where either an infinitive or a gerund is possible.

### Gymnastic Superstars

Olga Korbut and Nadia Comaneci are two remarkable athletes who changed the world of gymnastics forever. Both began _practicing/to practice_ (practice) and
<br>                                                          1

_____ (compete) in the sport at a very early age, and both continued
<br>2

_____ (develop) excellent athletic and artistic skills.
<br>3

Olga Korbut was born in 1956 in what is now Belarus. At age 11, she started

_____ (study) gymnastics at a government school and within a few years
<br>4

became one of the best Soviet gymnasts. Her persistence paid off, but it wasn't easy.

She tells many stories of her early years of _____ (train). For example, the first
                                               5

time she stood on the high beam, she fell off and was close to tears. She wanted

_____ (quit) then and there.
       6

    Her coach told _____ (she/get up) and start over. He encouraged
                            7

_____ (she/be) more relaxed. He asked _____ (she/imagine)
       8                                                    9

_____ (walk) in a beautiful meadow, not on a thin beam. Olga hated
      10

_____ (hear) these things, and she almost refused _____ (continue).
      11                                                              12

She was frightened, and as she said, "I was too young _____ (know) that this
                                                             13

was the greatest wisdom that a coach can have. After a fall, a tiny molecule of fear is

born, somewhere deep in the soul. If time is lost—even an hour or two—that molecule

will grow into an enormous beast. This beast will push you off the apparatus every time

you climb on to it, and one day, you will simply be too scared _____ (ap-
                                                                       14

proach) it at all." Olga learned _____ (overcome) her fears, kept on
                                        15

_____ (practice), and soon became a star.
      16

    Nadia Comaneci was born in Romania in 1961 and began _____ (do)
                                                                    17

serious gymnastics after she'd been "discovered" at age 6 by the national coach. The

coach taught _____ (she/do) many amazing exercises, and she herself cre-
                   18

ated others. Even as a very young athlete, Nadia was rarely afraid of anything—of

_____ (try) difficult or dangerous moves or of _____ (perform) in
      19                                                        20

front of millions of people. Perhaps the truly difficult thing for her was press confer-

ences. Journalists seemed _____ (forget) her age, and they would ask
                                21

_____ (she/respond) to every kind of question imaginable! Once a journalist
      22

asked her about her greatest wish, and she answered, "I want _____ (go)
                                                                     23

home." Another journalist questioned her about her plans for _____ (retire),
                                                                     24

and she responded, "I'm only 14."

Both Olga Korbut and Nadia Comaneci achieved greatness in gymnastics. They

created new and beautiful moves, they received incredibly high scores from judges,

and they won numerous medals—Olympic and others. Their infectious smiles and

great performances captured the hearts of people around the world and caused

_____ (millions of young girl / take up) gymnastics. Above all,
        25

perhaps, the talent and persistence of these two athletes encouraged people every-

where _____ (work) hard, _____ (be) persistent, and _____
        26                              27                                   28

(follow) their dreams.

**4**   A great American female athlete is the tennis player Billie Jean King. Learn more
about her by completing this passage. Use gerund or infinitive forms of the verbs in
parentheses. Note any instance where either an infinitive or a gerund is possible.

**Example:**   Billie Jean King always liked _to do / doing_ (do) sports.

1.   From a very early age, Billie Jean King loved _____ (play) tennis.

2.   She continued _____ (practice) and _____ (play) as an amateur even

though she was seldom invited _____ (participate) in important tennis com-

petitions because she didn't have "the right connections."

3.   People often neglected _____ (inform) her about key amateur competitions.

4.   Billie Jean King also began _____ (notice) how little female tennis stars

were paid and how much male stars could earn.

5.   She couldn't stand _____ (see) good female athletes treated poorly, so she

decided _____ (do) something about the problem.

6.   She started _____ (discuss) the issue with other female tennis players and

asked if they would like _____ (to join) together in contract negotiations.

7.   Billie Jean King's breakthroughs into the "male" world of sports encouraged

_____ (many young females / get) involved.

8.   Her efforts allowed _____ (young women everywhere / dream) of

_____ (be) successful in professional sports.

## C. Verbs That Change Meaning Depending on the Use of Infinitives or Gerunds

These verbs may be followed by either infinitives or gerunds, but the choice between
infinitives and gerunds affects the meaning of the sentence. In general, the infinitive

refers to the future and often involves a purpose, whereas a gerund refers to the past. The clearest example of this is with the verb *remember*.

| | **Examples** | **Meanings** |
|---|---|---|
| **mean + Infinitive**<br><br>**mean + Gerund** | I **meant to visit** Brazil.<br><br>A trip to Brazil **meant spending** much more money. | I planned to visit Brazil, but I couldn't.<br><br>A trip to Brazil involved spending much more money. |
| **remember + Infinitive**<br><br>**remember + Gerund** | I always **remember to buy** the paper.<br>I **remember buying** the paper. | I never forget to buy the paper.<br>I remember that I bought the paper. |
| **stop, quit + Infinitive**<br><br>**stop, quit + Gerund** | He **stopped (quit) to smoke.**<br><br>He **stopped (quit) smoking.** | He stopped his work in order to smoke a cigarette.<br>He does not smoke any more. |
| **try + Infinitive**<br><br>**try + Gerund** | The room was hot, so we **tried to open** the window.<br>The room was hot, so we tried the fan, but it didn't work. Then we **tried opening** the window. | We were not able to open the window.<br>Opening the window was another possibility. |

**5**   Complete the following by using the infinitive or the gerund forms of the verbs in parentheses.

1.  After the volleyball game, we all stopped ___*to have*___ (have) a cup of coffee, but Joanie didn't join us. She said that she'd stopped _____ (drink) coffee because the caffeine bothered her.

2.  Everyone at work was surprised when John quit _____ (work) _____ (take) a long vacation in South America. He said that we should quit _____ (work) so hard and take off for faraway places too!

3.  "I tried _____ (open) the front door, but it seems _____ (be) stuck."
    "Have you tried _____ (use) the key? It's locked, you know."

4.  "Did you remember _____ (buy) some golf balls?"
    "Of course, I didn't remember _____ (buy) any. I didn't know that you needed some."
    "You knew, but you forgot _____ (get) some. I distinctly remember _____ (tell) you _____ (buy) some this morning.
    "Oh no . . . you meant _____ (tell) me, but *you* forgot. I didn't forget!"

**6** Complete the following by using the infinitive or the gerund forms of the verbs in parentheses.

**A Golf Phenomenon:  Tiger Woods**

1.  Tiger Woods has used his fame and fortune from golf ___*to help*___ (help) _____ (foster) self-esteem in young children.

2.  The Tiger Woods Foundation "encourages _____ (youth/dream) big dreams."

3.  It tries "_____ (engage) communities in _____ (help) youngsters pursue their goals."

4.  The Foundation looks for ways _____ (teach) children "_____ (care) about and _____ (share) with others."

5.  His work involves _____ (team) up with other organizations interested in _____ (help) kids.

6.  Tiger Woods tries hard _____ (foster) in young children the same qualities he himself values the most.

7.  That means _____ (help) "_____ (foster) tenacity, integrity, courage, self-esteem and drive for excellence".

8.  He wants _____ (kids/keep on) _____ (improve) themselves. He says, "Never quit _____ (try) hard!  Never stop _____ (work) toward your dream."

9.  Tiger Woods speaks from experience because he remembers _____ (do) all those long hours of practice and exercise.

10. He always kept on and on even though many times he wanted _____ (quit) _____ (work) so hard.

11. He urges _____ (kids/do) the same—keep on _____ (strive) forward.

12. Above all, Tiger hopes _____ (show) young children everywhere "the power they possess to improve their own circumstances."

**7** **Review.** Complete the following sentences by using either the infinitive or gerund form (active or passive) of the verbs in parentheses. Include negatives and subjects where indicated.

**Mastering Golf**

**Example:** <u>_Mastering_</u> (master) golf may be frustrating, but it can also be rewarding.

1. It will take time and patience for _____ (you/learn) the game of golf well.

2. _____ (learn) the uses of each club is the first step.

3. In order _____ (learn) faster, it is best for _____ (you/watch) other players.

4. It is also helpful _____ (teach) by a good player.

5. Good players will advise _____ (you/spend time) _____ (walk) around the golf course in order _____ (get) _____ (know) its contours.

6. _____ (plan) a sequence of moves, rather than just one at a time, is one secret to good strategy.

7. _____ (not pay) attention to your opponent's moves can be disastrous.

8. _____ (watch) by spectators distracts some golfers.

9. Some spectators need _____ (tell) _____ (be) quiet.

10. _____ (win) the game is important, but _____ (play) well, _____ (develop) strategies and _____ (not get) nervous are just as important.

## Using What You've Learned

**8** In pairs or in small groups, use as many of the following verbs as possible to talk about and explain your favorite outdoor activity or game. It may be an organized sport, or it may be an activity such as camping or hiking. As you talk, be sure to explain any rules involved.

| allow | hate | remember |
|-------|------|----------|
| begin | like | start |
| can't stand | love | stop |
| continue | permit | try |
| dislike | prefer | |

**Example:** *In golf, you begin by looking over the course, by choosing your first club (usually a driver), and by teeing up. Then . . .*

**9** Are you frustrated about something? How about getting it out of your system? In groups or as a class, vent your frustrations by making complaints with *can't bear, can't stand,* and *hate* + gerund or infinitive or with *be fed up with, be sick of, be tired of,* and *be sick and tired of* + gerund. Make sure that everyone has the chance to make at least one complaint. Some of you may have more!

**Example:** *I can't stand to do any more homework!*

**10** In small groups, make up a story together. One member of your group will begin, and the rest will add to it to create an entire story. Each student must talk continuously for at least thirty seconds. Use as many verbs as possible. (To make this activity more difficult, you may use the rule that no verb can be repeated!) Try to use an infinitive or gerund with each. You may use your own opening to begin the story, or you may use one of the following lines:

1. "It was a dark and stormy night." (from *Paul Clifford*)
2. "Romeo, Romeo, wherefore art thou Romeo?" (from *Romeo and Juliet*)
3. "As Gregor Samsa awoke one morning from uneasy dreams, he found himself transformed in his bed into a gigantic insect." (from *The Metamorphosis*)
4. "Once upon a time there lived . . ."
5. "This is the tale of a meeting of two lonesome, skinny, fairly old men on a planet which was dying fast. . . ." (from *Breakfast of Champions*)

<table><tr><td>**PART 5**</td></tr></table> # Special Uses of Other Verb Forms

## Setting the Context

**Prereading Questions** Barbara McClintock was a very successful American scientist who did research in the field of genetics beginning in the 1920s. What characteristics do you think a woman of that time needed to have in order to succeed in such a field?

**Culture Note**

*Maize (corn) is a gigantic domesticated grass that originated in tropical Mexico and has been cultivated by humans for over 8000 years. Many crops from the "New World" were brought back to Europe by the Spaniards, but corn quickly became one of the most popular. A taste for corn spread through Africa, India, and China during the 1500s; in fact, a Chinese drawing of an ear of corn has been dated to 1597. Today, the United States, Peoples Republic of China, and Brazil together produce almost 75 percent of annual global production. Mexico, the world's fourth largest producer, currently produces almost 15 million tons yearly.*

### Barbara McClintock: A Pioneer in Genetic Research

As a young child, Barbara McClintock was always interested in science and the natural world around her. She would look carefully at the plants growing in the yard and could notice even small variations among the same types of plants.

By the time she entered Cornell University just after World War I, she was fully committed to botany. Plants of all kinds were interesting to her, vegetables were  5
definitely inspiring to her, but she was absolutely fascinated by corn (maize). Needless to say, Barbara McClintock was unusual.

Her incredible interest in plants was not the only unusual thing about her. Being a woman in science was also unusual, though in her day, botany was somewhat "acceptable" for women to study. However, being a woman made it very dif-  10
ficult for her to become a researcher. Many universities "let" women study or teach but did not "let" them do research. So despite her tremendous talents and ground-breaking* work, Barbara McClintock never obtained a permanent position as a researcher at any university.

Barbara McClintock's long and productive career greatly helped expand our  15
knowledge of plant genetics. And her work most certainly helped open the path for other women to work in the field of genetics.

**Discussing Ideas.**   Since Barbara McClintock began her career in the 1920s, the world of scientific work has changed a great deal for women. Can you give examples of other areas of science where women are very active in research or development today?

## A. Causative Verbs and Related Structures

*help, let,* and *make*

These verbs are followed by the simple form of a second verb. They are not generally followed by passive constructions. Note that the use of *to* after *help* is optional.

*ground-breaking* innovative, first-of-its-kind

| | Examples | Notes |
|---|---|---|
| *help* | I **helped** (him) **carry** the packages. <br> I **helped** (him) **to carry** the packages. | *Help* may take the simple form or the infinitive of another verb as an object. |
| *let* | I **let** him **borrow** my car. <br> I **let** them **help** me. | *Let* is followed by a noun or a pronoun and the simple form of another verb. It *does not* take an infinitive. |
| *make* | I **made** him **wash** my car. <br> I **made** them **help** me. <br> The news **made** me **unhappy.** <br> The bad weather **made** us **late.** | *Make* is followed by a noun or pronoun and the simple form of another verb. *Make* + noun or pronoun + adjective is also frequently used. |

*have, get,* and *need*

These verbs are often followed by the active or passive form of a second verb.

| | Examples | Notes |
|---|---|---|
| **have** <br> **Active** <br><br> **Passive** | I **had** him **wash** my car. <br> I **had** the barber **cut** my hair. <br> I **had** my car **washed** (by him). <br> I **had** my hair **cut** (by the barber). | With *have*, the active form is *have* + noun or object pronoun + simple form. The passive form is *have* + noun or object pronoun + past participle. These constructions are often used when you pay for a service. You *have* someone *do* something, or you *have* something *done* by someone. |
| ***get* and *need*** <br> **Active** <br><br> **Passive** | I **got** him **to wash** my car. <br> I **needed** him **to wash** my car. <br> I **got** my car **washed** (by him). <br> I **needed** my car **washed** (by him). | With *get* and *need*, the active form is *get / need* + noun or object pronoun + infinitive. The passive form is *get / need* + noun or object pronoun + past participle. The passive form of *get* is similar in meaning to the passive form of *have*. *Get* is frequently used in conversational English. |

**1**  Barbara McClintock succeeded despite many obstacles in her path. Use the following cues to form complete sentences with *make*. The sentences will tell about her struggle to succeed.

**Example:**  being a female researcher / try twice as hard

> *Being a female researcher made her try twice as hard.*

1.  being a woman / others suspicious of her work
2.  one colleague's support / her feel confident
3.  her research / think differently about genetic transfer
4.  what she found out about jumping genes in corn / believe that genes could move
5.  the first reaction of the scientific community / feel rejected

6. eventually her careful and innovative research / earn the respect of the world
7. her discovery of transposable elements in genetic structure / win the Nobel Prize
8. this final recognition / her friends happy for her

**2**   Answer the following questions. Use *let* in your answer.

1. Do you let other people tell you how to think?
2. In general, do you let others decide things for you?
3. Do you sometimes let yourself do less than your best?
4. Do you ever let yourself daydream about doing one great thing?
5. Did your parents let you follow your dreams?
6. What situations let you do your best?
7. Do you know anyone who doesn't let society tell him / her how to lead his / her life?
8. Have you ever let someone know he / she has done something great for you?

**3**   You are a scientific researcher. Imagine you are beginning a great project, something that you have really been wanting to do. Imagine what preparations you would need before getting into your work. Complete each sentence with appropriate past participles.

**Example:**   I'll have my daily schedule _____*cancelled*_____ by my secretary.

1. I'll have a team of co-workers _____ to help me on the project.
2. I'll have important meetings _____ until we are done with the work.
3. I'll get my ideas _____ down on paper before we begin.
4. I'll have my assistant _____ a quiet place for us to work.
5. I'll get my friends to _____ me relax after working sessions.
6. I'll have all our lunches _____ so we can work through lunch.
7. I'll get all my colleagues to _____ me their wildest dreams for the project.
8. I'll have a big party _____ when we finish the work.

**4**   You have lots of responsibilities at home and at work. Sometimes we need to get things done, to take care of these responsibilities, before we can do our best work. Follow the cues to form complete sentences with *have, need,* or *get.*

**Example:**   children / pick up from school
*I'll need the children picked up from school.*

1. shopping / do
2. dinner / prepare for tonight
3. my appointments / cancel
4. someone / walk the dog

5. someone / clean up the house
6. my assistant / screen my calls
7. someone / bring my car in for servicing
8. my neighbor / pick up my mail

**5** The following passage is an imaginary conversation that Barbara McClintock might have had with her personal assistant Judy before taking a trip away from her laboratory. Complete the passage with appropriate forms of the verbs in parentheses.

*Barbara:* Judy, I'm scheduled to present at the genetics conference in Berlin. Have the travel agent _book_ (book) me a round-trip ticket to Berlin, please. Oh, and get her
1

_____ (reserve) an aisle seat for me.
2

*Judy:* Anything else you want?

*Barbara:* Yes, if it wouldn't be too much trouble, get my red suit _____ (press)
3

and my black coat _____ (clean). Have my bags _____ (pack) ready to go
4           5

by morning. Oh, I also need _____ (cancel) classes for the next week. Have the
6

work-study student _____ (put) a note on my office door. I'll let you _____
7                                 8

(take care of) the rest of the details.

*Judy:* All right. Have a nice time in Berlin. When are you returning?

*Barbara:* Next Tuesday. Have someone _____ (meet) me at the airport. And
9

thanks.

## B. Verbs of Perception

The verbs *see, look (at), watch, observe, listen (to), hear, smell, taste, perceive* and *feel* can be followed by a second verb. The second verb can be in the simple or the present participle form. Often, there is little difference in meaning between the two forms but the *-ing* form usually stresses an action in progress.

| | Examples | Notes |
|---|---|---|
| **Present Participle** | We **heard** the bell **ringing.** | action in progress |
| **Simple Form** | We **heard** the bell **ring.** | action completed |
| **Present Participle** | We **saw** the building **burning** down. | action in progress |
| **Simple Form** | We **saw** the building **burn** down. | action completed |

**6**  Imagine that you have just had a tour of a botanist's laboratory. Use the information in parentheses to complete the following sentences describing what you saw, felt, and so forth.

**Example:**   While we were in the lab, we saw (a lab assistant / examine plant cells under a microscope.)

*While we were in the lab, we saw a lab assistant examining plant cells under a microscope.*

Or:   *. . . we saw a lab assistant examine plant cells under a microscope.*

1. We watched (a scientist / perform an experiment).
2. We heard (a parrot / speak). It was Polly, the lab mascot.
3. We felt (the humid air / wet our faces).
4. We looked at (the many species of corn / grow in the greenhouse).
5. We observed (the scientists / concentrate on their work).
6. We felt (the air temperature / grow warmer as we entered the greenhouse).
7. We smelled (roses / give off their fragrance).
8. We listened to (Polly / say hello and goodbye a thousand times).

## C. Present and Past Participles Used as Adjectives

The participle forms of many verbs may also be used as adjectives after linking verbs such as *be, become, feel,* and *get.* In particular, verbs that express emotions are often used in this way.

|  | **Examples** | **Notes** |
|---|---|---|
| **Verb** | The ideas in that botany book **interested** me. The descriptions of plants **fascinated** me. | Verbs that are often used this way include *amaze, annoy, astonish, bore, confuse, disappoint, excite, fascinate, frighten, inspire, interest, please, relax, satisfy, surprise, thrill, tire,* and *worry.* |
| **Present Participle** | The ideas in that botany book were very **interesting** to me. | The present participle expresses the effect of the subject on someone or something. |
| **Past Participle** | I was very **interested** in the ideas in that botany book. I am getting more **excited about** botany every day. I never feel **bored with** that botany book. | The past participle expresses the reaction of the subject to someone or something. Note the variety of prepositions used with the past participle. |

**7**  Think about a plant, a tree, or a flower that you've learned about recently or seen recently in nature. Describe how you felt at that time by answering the following questions.

1. How did you become interested in learning about it?
2. Is its appearance interesting?

3.   Were you surprised by anything you found out about it?
4.   Was there anything confusing about it?
5.   Was it satisfying to learn about it?
6.   Were you excited about it?

**8**   Complete the following by using either the present or the past participle of the verbs in parentheses.

**Example:**   Walking alone in the forest is _frightening_ (frighten) to many people.

1.   Some people get _____ (worry) about eating wild mushrooms.

2.   Yet people everywhere are _____ (interest) in trying new foods.

3.   Looking for new varieties of mushrooms is _____ (excite) to many people.

4.   They are _____ (thrill) at the thought of finding food in the wild.

5.   It is _____ (amaze) to think that we could survive on wild plants and other foods if we had to.

6.   City folk are _____ (surprise / often) by what country people eat from nature.

**9**   **Review.**   Complete the following passage with gerund or infinitive forms of the verbs in parentheses. Include negatives and objects where indicated.

**How Corn Can Change Lives**

Life in rural China can be very, very hard. An example is the province of Guizhou. There, typical farms are less than one hectare (two acres) and are often perched on almost inaccessible mountainsides. Until recently, annual incomes were less than $50 per person. For up to three months a year, families had almost no food because of weather conditions and crop cycles.

**Culture Note**

*"Corn Flakes," perhaps the world's most popular breakfast cereal, had an accidental beginning. In 1894, Dr. John Kellogg and his brother W. K. Kellogg were trying to create a new breakfast idea for patients at a health resort in Michigan. First they created a new, more digestible form of wheat bread, but due to an unrelated problem, they had to let the thin bread sit in the oven overnight. The next day, they discovered "wheat flakes," which they liked, so they then tried the process with corn. The results were "Kellogg's Corn Flakes." W. K. Kellogg had his name and signature printed on each box. To distinguish his flakes from the competition, Kellogg could say, "The original has this signature." According to Kellogg's, today they remain the original and the best!*

In 1994, life began *to change/changing* (change) for many farmers in Guizhou,
                        1
and today it promises _____ (get) even better. In 1994, technicians from the
                              2
Guizhou Academy of Agricultural Sciences offered _____ (help) farmers in
                                                         3
the area and encouraged _____ (they/plant) "quality protein maize." They
                                4
recommended _____ (plant) this high-quality corn because it is a hybrid that
                      5
grows well in difficult areas. In fact, its yields are about 10 percent higher than normal

yields, and it has a high content of certain amino acids that are vital for children's

growth.

The corn is also used _____ (feed) animals, especially pigs. By _____
                               6                                            7
(raise) larger, healthier pigs, farmers have been able _____ (make) major
                                                              8
changes in their lives. By _____ (sell) thirty pigs during three years' time, one
                                  9
farmer was able _____ (build) a new house, _____ (educate) his children,
                        10                              11
and _____ (get) new equipment for _____ (irrigate) and _____
            12                                     13                          14
(compost).

The Guizhou Academy of Agricultural Sciences has been responsible for

_____ (educate) and _____ (work) with the farmers on _____ (intro-
    15                          16                                      17
duce) this hybrid corn. _____ (Develop) the corn itself involved _____
                                18                                          19
(cross) traditional Chinese corn with international varieties. First, the technicians had

_____ (several farmers/try) the new seeds, and after others saw this spe-
    20
cial corn _____ (grow) and _____ (produce) well, many wanted
                  21                      22
_____ (join) in the project. The university technicians didn't even need
    23
_____ (persuade) _____ (other farmers/try) it because the good results
    24                      25
were obvious.

The university technicians themselves were very _____ (excite) about the
                                                          26
project and willing to work in difficult conditions. They were _____ (thrill)
                                                                        27

_____ (see) the tremendous results, and many became more deeply involved in
28

_____ (help) _____ (educate) and _____ (introduce) other farming
29                 30                              31

innovations.

Today, it is in rural corners like these in China that you can see agricultural re-

search _____ (have) a major impact on people's lives. You can look at corn
32

stalks _____ (burst) with ears of corn, and you can watch healthy children
33

_____ (play) and _____ (work).
34                 35

Above all, you can hear these subsistence* farmers _____ (tell) their stories.
36

As a 78 year-old woman who had obviously gone through many, many hard times said,

"We have always worked hard, but this barely kept us alive until [the researchers and

the high protein corn] arrived. Thank you for helping us. Now my family is happy, I

have a good house, good clothes, and I can travel to the local town."

**10** Reread the passage "Barbara McClintock" on page 238. Look at the variety of verb
forms used in the passage. Try to find examples for each of the categories shown in the
following chart.

| Expressions with Causative Verbs | Expressions with Verbs of Perception | Participles Used as Adjectives |
|---|---|---|
|  |  |  |

---

*subsistence farmer* a farmer able to produce only the minimum necessary for survival

## Using What You've Learned

**11**   What is on your *To Do* list? What are some repairs or services that you need to take care of? What are some that you have had done lately? Go around the room in a chain, giving statements with *get, have,* or *need.*

**Examples:**   | **To Do** | **Done** |

I have to get my          I had my teeth checked
glasses repaired.         last week.

**12**   When your life is busy, it's hard to find time to get everything done that you need to do. It can also be very pleasant to have things done for you. First, make a list of things you enjoy having done for you. Try to give at least five. Then, make a list of things you don't like having done for you. After you have made your lists, work in pairs or small groups. Compare your lists, explaining why you do or do not enjoy each.

**Examples:**        **Like**                        **Don't Like**

I like getting my laundry done.    I don't like having my teeth cleaned.

**13**   Think of a place with lots of unusual sights and sounds. It may be a place that you've visited recently, or it may be a place that you remember from the past. In small groups, take turns telling about the place. Use verbs of perception to describe things that you saw, smelled, heard, and so forth. As an alternative, write a short composition about your place and then share it with your classmates.

**Examples:**   *There's a beautiful place in the mountains where we used to camp. From the camp, we could see the mountains rising sharply above us. We would sit and watch deer and moose eating in the meadow below us.*

*Last week I went to Disneyland, and it was incredibly crowded. In every direction, I saw thousands of people walking, standing, eating, laughing, arguing, getting sunburned and tired. I heard hundreds of people screaming as they rode on the different rides.*

**14**   Think about a trip you've taken; a sport you've played; or a restaurant, store, or museum you've visited during the past few weeks. Give several original sentences using either present or past participles. Choose from the following verbs or add your own.

| **Positive Feelings** | | **Negative Feelings** | |
|---|---|---|---|
| amaze | interest | annoy | disappoint |
| amuse | intrigue | bewilder | shock |
| excite | relax | bore | tire |
| fascinate | surprise | confuse | worry |

**15**  Traveling to faraway places is one of the most fascinating ways to spend your leisure time. Imagine yourself in the Middle East, in the Amazon, or in Paris. Imagine where you have been and how you arrived at this destination. Imagine what you will do next. As you imagine, describe everything that you see, hear, smell, feel, perceive. Are you excited? Are you nervous? What are the most interesting things around you?

# Video Activities: Overcoming Serious Illness

**Before You Watch.**   Discuss these questions in small groups.

1.  When you are paralyzed, _____.
    a.  you cannot move some muscles          c.  your bones are broken
    b.  you are in a lot of pain

2.  A stroke affects your _____.

    a.  heart                 b.  brain                 c.  lungs

**Watch.**   Circle the correct answers.

1.  Brian Davis became paralyzed when he had _____.

    a.  an accident           b.  a stroke              c.  a heart attack

2.  What part of Brian Davis's body was paralyzed?

    a.  his arms              b.  his left leg          c.  his right side

3.  What did Brian Davis have to relearn?

    a.  walking          b.  thinking          c.  talking          d.  swallowing

4.  What part of Brian Davis's body is still paralyzed?

    a.  one arm               b.  one leg              c.  one hand

5.  Who promised to ride with Brian?

    a.  his brother           b.  his friend           c. his doctor

6.  Circle the adjectives that describe Brian.

    determined     depressed     courageous     weak     hardworking     content

**Watch Again.**   Compare answers in small groups.

1.  How long ago was Brian's accident?

    a.  1 year                b.  6 months             c.  6 years

2.  What is Brian's advice to people in his situation?

3.  What is Brian's next challenge?

    a.  to climb a mountain             c.  to ride without training wheels
    b.  to become a doctor

**After You Watch.**   Complete the following sentences with a word or phrase beginning with a gerund or an infinitive.

1.  Before his stroke, Brian enjoyed _____.

2.  Now that he has started _____, Brian hopes _____.

3.  For along time after his stroke, Brian was unable _____.

4.  Brian doesn't want to delay _____.

5.  Brian was always an active person so he hated _____.

## Focus on Testing

### Use of Verb Forms

Gerunds, infinitives, and other verb forms are frequently tested on standardized English proficiency exams. Review these commonly tested structures and check your understanding by completing the sample items below.

**Remember that . . .**

■ Different verbs are followed by different forms. Make sure the appropriate form is used.

■ Gerunds, not infinitives, are used after prepositions.

■ In lists containing verb forms, make sure that the same form is used whenever possible. Don't mix forms (for example, gerunds and infinitives) unless it is unavoidable. Try to use parallel structures.

**Part 1:** Circle the correct completion for the following.

**Example:** John appears _____ happy with his work.
    a. to be
    b. be
    c. been
    d. being

1. The pitching of the waves on the open sea caused the small vessel

    _____.

    a. capsize
    b. capsizing
    c. to capsize
    d. have capsized

2. It will always be helpful _____ a map while hiking in wilderness areas.
    a. to carry
    b. to carrying
    c. carrying
    d. carry

3. Of the various activities she does, Mary likes swimming and _____ the best.
    a. to ride a horse
    b. to horseback ride
    c. horses
    d. horseback riding

4. _____ a mistake is not to bring on the end of the world.
    a. To made
    b. Making
    c. To make
    d. Having made

**Part 2:**   Circle the letter below the underlined word(s) containing an error.

**Example:**   An individual <u>may</u> feel frustrated and <u>confusing</u> if <u>she</u> doesn't know
                                        A                                    Ⓑ              C
the language of the country <u>where she is living</u>.
                                                    D

1.   The Park Service always advises visitors <u>using</u> extra caution when <u>hiking</u> or
                                                                        A                                      B

camping in areas <u>where</u> bears <u>have been sighted</u>.
                                    C                          D

2.   The <u>popularity</u> of bicycles increased <u>greatly</u> during the 1970s, as more
                    A                                              B

people began to ride them for pleasure and <u>using</u> them <u>to commute</u> to work.
                                                                    C                    D

3.   Polaris, <u>the North Star</u>, has helped <u>guiding</u> seafarers <u>ever since</u> ancient times
                            A                                  B                        C

when <u>sophisticated</u> navigational tools did not exist.
                D

4.   Do <u>you</u> really <u>want</u> <u>learn</u> <u>to play</u> a musical instrument?
            A                  B            C          D

# Chapter 8

## Creativity

# Introduction

In this chapter, you will review the variety of sentence types in English, and you will study both compound and complex sentences. This chapter focuses on complex sentences with adverb clauses of time and condition. Later chapters cover other types of complex sentences. As you study this chapter, pay close attention to the time frames expressed by the different constructions.

The following passage introduces the chapter theme, "Creativity," and raises some of the topics and issues you will cover in the chapter.

---

### The Creative Urge

If an inventor builds an astounding machine or an artist produces a stunningly original work, we call this creative genius. Yet, creativity is not only in the realm of artists and scientists: it is an attribute we all have within us. The creative urge is the most profoundly human—and mysterious—of all our attributes. Without fully understanding how or why, each of us is creative.                                                    5

Since earliest times, humans have produced marvelous creations. Learning to use fire and to make tools were incredibly creative achievements. Above all, early humans produced our most extraordinary creation: language.

After our ancestors had learned to communicate with each other, a long series of amazing developments began. Creativity flourished among such peo-    10
ples as the ancient Egyptians, Minoans, Greeks, Mayans, and the Benin of Africa. Long before the modern age of machines, our ancestors had already developed sophisticated techniques and systems in mathematics, astronomy, engineering, art, architecture, and literature.

Of course, not every society has made tremendous achievements by today's    15
standards. While the Egyptians were developing mathematics and building libraries, other societies were still learning to use fire. By the time Europeans began to use money, the Chinese had already been trading with paper currency for hundreds of years. Nevertheless, every new achievement represents human creativity. If one attribute characterizes humans, it is our creative urge to improve,    20
to find new ways of doing things.

---

**Discussing Ideas.**   Who are some creative people you know about? They may be living now or they may be from another time. Take a few minutes to think and make some notes. Then share your thoughts with the class.

PART 1 # Compound Sentences

## Setting the Context

**Prereading Questions**   Creativity is a difficult concept to define because it means different things to different people. What is your definition of creativity?

---

### What Is Creativity?

To *create* means "to bring into being, to cause to exist." According to this dictionary definition, ordinary people are creative every day. We are creative whenever we look at or think about something in a new way.

---

 **Discussing Ideas.** Can you identify the activities in these drawings? Can you add three or four more examples of creative activities? With a partner, make a list of at least ten activities and then share your ideas with the class.

## A. Review of Sentence Types

Sentences may be simple, compound, complex, or a combination of compound and complex.

|  | **Examples** | **Notes** |
|---|---|---|
| **Simple** | Creativity is part of everyday life. | Simple sentences have one subject/verb combination. |
| **Compound** | Many artists are highly creative, **but** ordinary people can be just as creative. Some people are creative from childhood; **however,** others show their genius later in life. | Compound sentences are two simple sentences connected by *and, but, for, nor, or, so,* or *yet.* A compound sentence may also be formed by joining two sentences with a semicolon. Transition words or phrases are often used with compound sentences. |
| **Complex** | **Although** some people are creative from childhood, others show their genius later in life. | Complex sentences consist of two or more clauses: a main clause that is complete by itself and one or more dependent clauses introduced by a connecting word such as *although, because, if, that, when,* or *who.* |
| **Compound/ Complex** | Some people are creative from childhood, **but** others show their genius **when** they are much older. | Sentences can have several clauses. There is always one main clause, but other clauses can be joining a variety of connecting words. |

## Punctuation Guidelines

### Coordinate Clauses

A comma is normally used before conjunctions that join two independent clauses.

*Note:* The comma is optional in short sentences.

_____, and

_____.

### Transitions

Most transitions are used at the beginning of a sentence or after a semicolon. They are normally followed by a comma. In some cases, transitions may be used in the middle or at the end of a sentence.

In addition, _____.

_____; in addition,

_____.

### Subordinate Phrases and Clauses

Most adverb phrases and clauses may begin or end sentences. A comma is normally used after introductory phrases and clauses.

_____ while

_____

While _____,

_____.

**1** **Review.** Label subject(s) and verb(s) in the following sentences. Then indicate what type of sentence each is (simple, compound, or complex). If the sentence is compound or complex, circle the connecting word. Underline the *dependent* clauses in complex sentences.

**Example:** We are creative (whenever) we look at or think about something in a new way. *complex sentence*

1. First of all, creativity involves an awareness of our surroundings.
2. It is the ability to notice things that others might miss.
3. A second part of creativity is an ability to see relationships among things.
4. Creativity is involved when we remake or reorganize the old in new ways.
5. We might find a more efficient way to study, or we could rearrange our furniture in a better way.
6. Third, creativity means having the courage and drive to make use of our new ideas.
7. To think up a new concept is one thing; to put the idea to work is another.
8. These three aspects of creativity are involved in all the great works of genius; however, they are also involved in many of our day-to-day activities.

**2** **Review.** Label subject(s) and verb(s) in the following quotations. Then indicate what type of sentence each is (simple, compound, or complex). If the sentence is compound or complex, circle the connecting word. Underline the *dependent* clauses in the complex sentences.

**Examples:** In order to create, there must be a dynamic force. *simple sentence*

What force is more potent (than) love is? —*Igor Stravinsky* *complex sentence*

1. The creative person is both more primitive and more cultivated, more destructive, a lot madder, and a lot saner than the average person is. —*Frank Barron*
2. Creative minds always have been known to survive any kind of bad training. —*Anna Freud*
3. All men are creative, but few are artists. —*Paul Goodman*
4. Human salvation lies in the hands of the creatively maladjusted. —*Martin Luther King, Jr.*
5. In creating, the only hard thing's to begin; a grass blade's no easier to make than an oak. —*James Russell Lowell*
6. One must still have chaos in oneself to be able to give birth to a dancing star. —*Friedrich Nietzche*
7. He who does not know how to create should not know. —*Antonio Porchia*
8. A creative artist works on his next composition because he was not satisfied with his previous one. —*Dmitri Shostakovich*
9. The urge for destruction is also a creative urge. —*Michael Bakunin*
10. Two roads diverged in a wood, and I—
    I took the one less traveled by,
    And that has made all the difference. —*Robert Frost*

## B. Coordinating Conjunctions

*And, but, for, or, so, yet,* and *nor* are used to join two independent clauses into one compound sentence. A comma is normally used between the two clauses. In short sentences, however, the comma can be omitted. Note that *and, but, or,* and *yet* are often used to join words or phrases also.

| And, But, For, Or, So, Yet | | |
|---|---|---|
| **Examples** | | **Notes** |
| Martin is easy-going, | **and** he is quite funny. | *and* = addition |
| | **but** he sometimes loses his temper. | *but* = contrast |
| | **for** he enjoys just about everything. | *for* = reason |
| | **or** at least he seems that way. | *or* = choice |
| | **so** many people like him. | *so* = result |
| | **yet** he gets nervous about tests. | *yet* = contrast |

| Nor | | |
|---|---|---|
| **Simple Sentences** | **Compound Sentences** | **Notes** |
| The box is not very big. It is not very heavy. | The box is not very big, **nor** is it very heavy. | *Nor* is used to join two negative clauses. When *nor* begins the second clause, the auxiliary or the verb *be* is placed before the subject. A negative is not used in the second clause. |
| Ann doesn't like cold weather. She doesn't enjoy snow. | Ann doesn't like cold weather, **nor** does she enjoy snow. | |
| Ben hasn't done his homework. He hasn't cleaned the house. | Ben hasn't done his homework, **nor** has he cleaned the house. | |

**3**  Form compound sentences using the coordinating conjunctions indicated for each set. Change word or sentence order when necessary. Also change nouns to pronouns and add commas. For sentences with more than one possibility, form two sentences and try to explain any difference in meaning or emphasis.

**Example:**    (nor) Some people do not use all their senses very often. They do not have a very great awareness of their surroundings.

*Some people do not use all their senses very often, nor do they have a very great awareness of their surroundings.*

1. (but / yet) Some people use all five senses often. Most of us rely heavily on our sight.
2. (nor) Many people do not pay attention to sounds. Many people do not take time to listen.
3. (for / so) Musicians pay attention to all types of sounds. Musicians want to find interesting new combinations.
4. (and / yet) A musician can find music in exotic sounds. A musician may also hear music in ordinary noises.
5. (or / and) A car horn may produce a new rhythm. A bird may sing a new sequence of notes.

6.  (but / yet) Another person may not hear these combinations. A music lover will find these combinations.
7.  (but) Smell is important in chocolate tasting. Taste is perhaps more important.
8.  (or) A chocolate taster must have a good sense of taste. A chocolate taster won't last long on the job.
9.  (and) A chocolate taster must be able to recognize the smell of a high-quality chocolate. A chocolate taster must be able to recognize the flavor of a high-quality chocolate.
10. (but) Chocolate tasters and musicians may use their sight while working. Sounds and tastes are very important in their work.

## C. Transitions

Transitions are words or phrases that link two related ideas. The accompanying list contains some of the most frequently used. In the following chapters, you will study these and other transitions in more detail.

| | Examples | Notes |
|---|---|---|
| **Provide Examples** | Anyone can be creative. **For example,** a cook who tries a new recipe is creative. | *For instance* is also used to give examples. Like *for example*, it is common in conversational English. |
| **Express Emphasis** | Each of us is creative and, **in fact,** we are creative more often than we realize. | *In fact* emphasizes important or little-known information. |
| **Give Additional Information** | Creativity involves looking at things in a new way; **in addition,** it means trying new things. | *In addition* has the same meaning as "also." |
| **Show Contrast** | Everyone can be creative; **however,** many people are afraid to try.<br>Some people never try new ideas; **on the other hand,** there are many people who constantly try new things. | *However* has the same meaning as "but."<br>*On the other hand* refers to the opposite side of an issue. *In contrast* is also common. |
| **Provide a Reason or Result** | Creativity is a mysterious process; **therefore,** it is difficult to define. | *Therefore* means "as a result" or "so." |
| **Show Sequence (by Time or Order)** | Creativity involves several steps. **First,** it is being aware of something. **Next,** it involves seeing a relationship with something else. **Then,** it means using the new ideas. | Some of the most common sequence transitions are *first, second, now, then, next, earlier, later, after that, finally.* Sequence transitions are not normally used with a semicolon. Commas are sometimes used after these transitions. |

**4** Describe the process of taking a photo by putting the following steps in order. Use sequence transitions (*first, second,* and so on) as you reorder the sentences. More than one sequence is possible.

**Example:**   First, buy a roll of film.

1. Focus the lens on your subject.
2. Shut off the camera.
3. Open the back cover in order to load your film.
4. Turn on the "flash," if necessary.
✓5. Buy a roll of film.
6. Take the photo.
7. Close the back cover.
8. Hold the camera steady.
9. Look through the view finder and compose your photo.
10. Remove the lens cap.
11. Load the film.
12. Turn on the camera.

**5**   Two of the 20th century's most creative musicians have been the jazz greats Louis Armstrong and Miles Davis. Both played the trumpet, but in other aspects, they were two very different individuals. Read the following information about them. Then write sentences with *in contrast* and *on the other hand*.

**Example:**   Louis Armstrong always tried     Miles Davis did not seem to
to please his audiences and his fans.    care about popularity.

*Louis Armstrong always tried to please his audiences and his fans; in contrast, Miles Davis did not seem to care about popularity.*

**Culture Note**

*Jazz began in the late 1800s in the U.S. South. Jazz started as a mix of African rhythms and European styles of music, such as minuets, polkas, and marches. Scott Joplin, and his "Maple Leaf Rag," published in 1899, made jazz instantly popular across the United States.*

Louis Armstrong

Miles Davis

1. Louis Armstrong came from a relatively poor family in New Orleans.

Miles Davis was born into a prosperous middle-class family in East St. Louis.

2.  Louis Armstrong was friendly and fun-loving.

Miles Davis was often called mysterious, rebellious, and even shy.

3.  Armstrong was a film star and comedian as well as a musician.

Davis concentrated only on jazz.

4.  Armstrong maintained a consistent style throughout his career.

Miles Davis changed his musical style numerous times.

5.  There is a simplicity and clarity to most of Louis Armstrong's music.

The music of Miles Davis is often abstract and complex.

6.  Louis Armstrong was noted for his singing style as well as his playing style.

Miles Davis did not sing at all.

7.  Armstrong's speaking voice was warm and sunny with a pleasant New Orleans twang.

Davis's voice was thin and raspy,* almost as if it hurt him to speak.

8.  Louis Armstrong generally wore suits on stage.

Miles Davis was well-known for his unusual and trendy clothes.

9.  Armstrong's sound was bold and brassy.**

Davis's sound was mellow† and moody.

10.  Louis Armstrong was part of the "mainstream" of American music.

Miles Davis was always on the "cutting edge" of music.

**6**  This passage is about the artist Georgia O'Keeffe and her husband, Alfred Stieglitz. First, read the passage to understand the ideas. Then, complete it by adding transitions: *however, in addition, in fact, therefore.* Use each at least once. You will also need to add punctuation.

*Note:* In general, a writer would not use this many transitions in one short passage. Other connecting words such as *although, because, but,* and so on would also be used to give more variety.

### Georgia O'Keeffe and Alfred Stieglitz

Georgia O'Keeffe was perhaps the most famous female artist of the 20th century. She

was born and raised on a large farm in Wisconsin; <u>*therefore*</u>, she felt more at home in
                                                            1

wide open spaces than she did in cities. _____ O'Keeffe moved to New York City in
                                              2

the 1920s because of the large artist community there.

It was difficult for a woman to be an artist at that time _____ she had to work
                                                              3

very hard to support herself. She sold paintings _____ she worked as a teacher in
                                                      4

order to make a living. In her early years, O'Keeffe received little recognition for her

---

*raspy*   harsh sounding, irritating
**brassy*   noisy and metallic sounding
†*mellow*   soft and rich sounding

work, and her life in New York was difficult. _____ after her marriage to the famous
                                                        5
photographer Alfred Stieglitz, she became very well known.

Stieglitz and O'Keeffe were a brilliantly creative couple. _____ together, they
                                                                      6
produced more creative works than perhaps any other 20th-century couple.

Alfred Stieglitz and Georgia O'Keeffe

*Jack-in-the-Pulpit #2* by Georgia O'Keeffe

**7**  Combine the following sentences, using *for example, however, in addition, in fact, on the
other hand,* or *therefore.* Use each transition once. Add appropriate punctuation and make
other necessary changes. For example, change nouns to pronouns when appropriate.

**Example:**    Being creative involves making the best use of your senses.
                Being creative means looking at the same object from many different
                perspectives.

*Being creative involves making the best use of your senses; for example, it
means looking at the same object from many different perspectives.*

1.  A good photographer looks at the object itself. A good photographer considers the
    distance, angle, texture, and light.
2.  Light is one of the most important aspects of a good photo. The same scene can be
    either unusual or boring, depending on the light.
3.  Creative photographers experiment with light. They may take the same photo at
    many different times of day.
4.  Mornings and evenings give warm light, rich colors, and long shadows. Noon
    gives harsh, bright light to a photo.
5.  Morning and evening light is richer. Most outdoor photographers work between
    sunrise and 10:00 A.M. and between 4:00 P.M. and sunset.
6.  Bright sunlight makes colors seem pale. Good photos can be produced even on
    very sunny days by using a "sunlight" filter.

7. Today, most people take color snapshots. Art photographs are still mostly done in black and white.

8. Good photographers share a bond with their subjects. Good photographers know how to "bring out the best" in their photos.

## Using What You've Learned

**8** In pairs or in small groups, discuss the quotations from Activity 2, page 255. After your discussion, choose one quotation that particularly interests you. Express your own thoughts about it in a paragraph or brief composition. You might explain the quotation, or you might describe a person or activity that illustrates the idea of the quotation.

**9** Do you have a pastime or hobby that you enjoy? It might be taking photos, drawing, playing an instrument, or making crafts. Think about how you do this activity. Then, work in pairs or small groups, and take turns describing some of the steps involved in the activity. Try to include sequence transitions in your description.

**10** Reread your comparisons of Louis Armstrong and Miles Davis in Activity 5, page 258. Then think of two other individuals who do the same activity but who have very different styles or personalities. The two may be musicians, artists, sports figures, actors or actresses, or politicians, for example. Write a brief composition comparing the two individuals, using transitions when possible. Then work in pairs or small groups and tell each other about these people.

**PART 2**

# Adverb Clauses of Time and Condition: Unspecified or Present Time

## Setting the Context

**Prereading Questions** In the following quotation, Theodore Levitt talks about thinking versus doing. As you read, try to decide if you agree with his thoughts on creative ideas and innovation.

### Creativity and Innovation

If creativity is thinking up new things, innovation is doing them. Ideas are useless unless they are used, and the proof of their value is in their implementation.*

There is no shortage of creativity or creative people. . . . If there is a shortage, it is a shortage of innovators.

Theodore Levitt, Harvard University

---

*implementation* being put into action

**Discussing Ideas.**   Do you agree with Levitt? Is there a shortage of innovators in our world?

## A. Clauses of Time: Unspecified or Present Time

Time clauses can relate ideas or actions that occur at the same time or in a sequence. These may be habitual, repeated activities, or they may be occurring in the present. Note that these clauses may begin or end sentences.

| Habitual Activities | | |
|---|---|---|
| | **Examples** | **Notes** |
| **when** <br><br> **whenever** | **When** Tim Astor gets a new idea for a novel, he writes it down immediately. <br> He begins a new book **whenever** he gets an inspiration. | *When* joins two actions that happen at the same time or in sequence. In many cases, *when* means "at any time" and is the equivalent of *whenever*. The simple present is generally used in both clauses. |
| **after** <br><br> **before** <br><br> **until** | He edits his material **after** he finishes the entire first draft. <br> He never starts a new project **before** he has completed the current one. <br> He works on a project **until** he is fully satisfied with it. | *After, before,* and *until* join actions that occur in sequence. Either the simple present or the present perfect may be used in the dependent clause. The present perfect emphasizes the completion of the action. |
| **as** <br><br> **while** | **As** he is writing, he often listens to classical music. <br> He often listens to music **while** he is writing. | *As* and *while* may join two actions that happen at about the same time. The present continuous can be used in the dependent clause to emphasize continuity. The verb in the main clause shows whether the action is habitual or happening at the moment of speaking. |

| Present Activities | | |
|---|---|---|
| | **Examples** | **Notes** |
| **as** <br><br> **while** | Tonight he is listening to Beethoven's Fifth Symphony **as** he is writing. <br> He is humming **while** he is writing. | *As* and *while* can join two actions that are happening at the present. In this case, both clauses are in the present continuous. |

| Past and Present Activities | | |
|---|---|---|
| | **Example** | **Notes** |
| **since** | He has been writing **since** he woke up at six this morning. | *Since* joins a previous action or situation to an action or situation in progress. The main clause is in the present perfect (continuous). |

**1** Complete the following with present forms of the verbs in parentheses. The first one is done as an example.

### A Method to Our Madness

For most of us, when we ___think___ of the work of creative artists and scientists, we
1 (think)

_____ a mysterious world of geniuses. When an inventor _____ an
2 (imagine)                                                                                 3 (develop)

amazing new machine, when a musician _____ a beautiful piece of music, or
4 (create)

when a scientist _____ a major discovery, we _____ in awe. We
5 (make)                                                  6 (feel)

_____ that these geniuses _____ very different from us. Yet, geniuses
7 (assume)                              8 (be)

or not, we all _____ a similar creative process whenever we_____ at
9 (use)                                                              10 (look)

something in a new way or _____ new solutions to a problem. It _____
11 (try)                                                      12 (be)

a process of first looking at a situation carefully and then making and following a plan

of action.

**2** Think about the process of writing a composition or essay. Make a step-by-step plan of action for writing by forming complete sentences from the following clauses. Try to give at least two completions for each step. You may want to add more steps.

**Example:** Whenever you write something, . . .

*you have to concentrate on your ideas.*

Or: *you should find a quiet place without distractions.*

1. Before you begin to write a composition, . . .
2. While you are thinking about the topic, . . .
3. After you have gathered your ideas, . . .
4. When you need more information on a topic, . . .
5. . . . as you are writing.
6. After you have finished writing, . . .
7. . . . until you are satisfied with your composition.
8. . . . before you hand in your composition.

**3** Describe the following processes by making statements with time clauses.
Explain (a) what you should do before you begin . . . , (b) what you should do while you are . . . , and (c) what you should do after you have finished. Add modal auxiliaries such as *can* or *should* and combine steps when necessary.

**Example:** *Before you begin painting, you should choose a good piece of watercolor paper. After you have sketched your drawing lightly, wet the paper with water . . .*

1. Painting a watercolor
   - ■ Choose a good piece of watercolor paper.
   - ■ Sketch your drawing lightly.
   - ■ Wet the paper with water.
   - ■ Use watery paint for large areas.
   - ■ Catch any drips.
   - ■ Use a drier brush for details.
   - ■ Let your painting dry completely.
   - ■ Mount your picture.

2. Sculpting clay
   - ■ Put a mat down to protect the table.
   - ■ Work the clay with your hands.
   - ■ Add water to soften the clay.
   - ■ Shape individual parts of the sculpture.
   - ■ Attach each part by pinching it on.
   - ■ Smooth the sculpture with water.
   - ■ Use tools to draw any details.
   - ■ Carefully put the sculpture on a piece of paper.
   - ■ Let the sculpture dry at least twenty-four hours.

3. Designing a Webpage
   - ■ Spend some time looking at other Webpages.
   - ■ Think of a URL that is not already taken.
   - ■ Make some sketches of how you want the Webpage to look.
   - ■ Choose a background pattern and color for the first page.
   - ■ Decide on the font styles and sizes that you wish to use.
   - ■ Create a logo for your Webpage.
   - ■ Enter your information.
   - ■ Add hypertext to link parts of your document and to link to other Websites.

## B. Clauses of Condition: Unspecified or Present Time

|  | Examples | Notes |
|---|---|---|
| **if** | **If** Tim writes a lot during the week, he usually has time to relax on the weekend.<br><br>Tim usually has time to relax on the weekend **if** he writes a lot during the week. | The main clause is the effect or result of the dependent clause. These sentences refer to habitual activities or activities that are true in general. |
| **unless** | Tim rarely writes on the weekend **unless** he has a deadline.<br><br>**Unless** he has a deadline, Tim doesn't work on the weekend. | *Unless* is used similarly to *if . . . not* in many sentences. However, *unless* is more emphatic. |

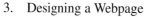

**4**  According to Paul Heist in *The Creative College Student,* the following are some of the chief characteristics of creative students and creative people in general. *Creative people are flexible, independent, innovative, spontaneous, and open to a wide range of experiences. They develop their own styles and their own sense of beauty.*

The following deals with some of these characteristics. Form complete sentences from each pair by matching a main clause with a dependent clause. Be sure to pay attention to the difference in meaning of *if* and *unless.*

**Example:**  If you develop your own style, . . .  _b_

Unless you develop your own style, . . .  _a_

    a.  you end up imitating other people.

    b.  you don't have to imitate other people.

1.  If a person is independent, . . .  _____

Unless a person is independent, . . .  _____

    a.  he or she usually relies on others for support or encouragement.

    b.  he or she doesn't have to depend on others for support or encouragement.

2.  If you are flexible, . . .  _____

Unless you are flexible, . . .  _____

    a.  you can adapt more easily to new situations.

    b.  it may be difficult for you to adapt to new situations.

3.  If people are open to new ideas, . . .  _____

Unless people are open to new ideas, . . .  _____

    a.  they can take better advantage of unusual opportunities.

    b.  they may miss many unusual opportunities.

4.  If you are innovative, . . .  _____

Unless you are innovative, . . .  _____

    a.  it may be difficult for you to find solutions for many problems.

    b.  you can usually find solutions for most problems.

5.  If you have your own sense of style, . . .  _____

Unless you have your own sense of style, . . .  _____

    a.  you will merely copy what is in fashion.

    b.  you will create a unique image for yourself.

6.  If you have your own sense of beauty, . . .  _____

Unless you have your own sense of beauty, . . .  _____

    a.  you can find beauty in your work and in your life.

    b.  you won't really know how to judge a work of art.

**5**   Complete the following sentences in your own words.

**Example:**   I feel most creative when . . .
*I am relaxed (I am a little tired, I listen to music).*

1.   It is easiest for me to write (sing, draw, and so on) if . . .
2.   Most of my best ideas come after . . .
3.   It is hard for me to concentrate unless . . .
4.   I have done my best work since . . .
5.   I really enjoy listening to music while . . .
6.   I am fascinated whenever . . .
7.   It is not easy for me to start a project before . . .
8.   I am often afraid to . . . until . . .

**6**   What type of student are you? What type of person are you? Answer the following questions in complete sentences.

1.   When do you do two things at once?
2.   Do you watch TV while you are doing your homework?
3.   What else do you do while you are doing your homework?
4.   Can you concentrate if people around you are talking or doing other things?
5.   Are you nervous before you take a test?
6.   Do you celebrate after you have turned in a big assignment?
7.   Do you always take notes (listen carefully) when you are in class?
8.   Do you get depressed if you get less than an A?

## Using What You've Learned

**7**   Who do you consider to be creative? Do you have a friend or relative who is good at making or fixing things, at painting, at cooking or baking, at playing or writing music? Give a brief presentation on a creative person you know. Use the following questions to help you prepare.

1.   How is this person creative?
2.   When is he or she the most creative? What seems to inspire him or her?
3.   Has this person always been creative?
4.   What interesting things has he or she done or produced?
5.   What is this person doing now? Is he or she still involved in creative activities?

**8**   What do you consider to be a very creative work? Have you seen a piece of original art, a photograph, a play, a musical performance that you really liked? Give a brief presentation on this work. Use the following questions to help you prepare.

1. In what medium is this work? (plastic arts, performing arts, other?)
2. What makes this work creative?
3. How does it make you feel?
4. What do other people think of this work? Do they agree with you?
5. Do you know who created this work? Has this person or have these people created something else as good?

*Whistler in the Dark* (self-portrait)

---

**PART 3**

# Adverb Clauses of Time and Condition: Past Time with the Simple Past and Past Perfect Tenses

## Setting the Context

**Prereading Questions**    A Renaissance person is someone who is knowledgeable and accomplished in a wide variety of fields. The following passage is about such a person, Leonardo da Vinci (1452–1519). What do you know about his accomplishments?

The *Mona Lisa*

### Leonardo da Vinci

Most people recognize Leonardo da Vinci as the painter of the *Mona Lisa* and the *Last Supper*. Yet Leonardo was a master of design, engineering, science, and invention, as well as a master of art.

After Leonardo had painted his most famous works, he   5
began to spend more time on his other dreams. As a military engineer, Leonardo had drawn plans for primitive tanks and airplanes long before they were ever dreamed possible. He is also credited with having designed the first parachute and having constructed the first elevator.   10

In the sciences, Leonardo was equally amazing. He had discovered complex principles of physics nearly a century before Galileo did his own work. In anatomy, Leonardo studied muscle and bone structure to improve his painting, and even after he had tired of painting, he continued to study the workings of the heart.   15
He had even speculated on the circulation of blood a century before William Harvey proved it. Leonardo da Vinci was so far ahead of his time that not until this century did his genius become truly evident.

**Discussing Ideas.**    This passage tells about only some of da Vinci's works. Can you tell about any other of da Vinci's projects? Can you name other individuals who have been *ahead of their time?* For example, in the 1700s, Benjamin Franklin worked with electricity and created lending libraries, but it wasn't until much later that these were commonly used.

## A. Clauses of Time: Past Time with the Simple Past and Past Perfect Tenses

|  | **Examples** | **Notes** |
|---|---|---|
| **before** <br> **by the time (that)** <br> **until** <br> **when** | Leonardo da Vinci **had painted** the *Mona Lisa* **before he worked** on many of his ideas for inventions. | The past perfect is used to refer to an event or situation that came before another event or time in the past. With *before, by the time that, until,* and *when,* the past perfect is used in the main clause. |
| **after** <br> **as soon as** <br> **once** | **After** Leonardo da Vinci **had painted** his major artworks, he **spent** more time on his inventions. | In complex sentences with *after, as soon as,* and *once,* the past perfect (continuous) is used in the dependent (not the main) clause. |

## B. Adverbs of Frequency with Time Clauses

| **Examples** | **Notes** |
|---|---|
| Leonardo da Vinci **had already worked** as a civil engineer, military engineer, and architect **by the time** he **began** his major paintings. | Adverbs such as *already, hardly, just, scarcely,* and *not . . . yet* are often used with the past perfect. They generally come between *had* and the past participle. |

## C. After, Before, By, *and* Until *as Prepositions*

*After, before, by,* and *until* can also be used as prepositions in phrases of time. Sentences with *before, by,* and *until* may use the past perfect tense, whereas sentences with *after* would generally use the simple past tense. Compare these:

|  | **Examples** |
|---|---|
| **Subordinating Conjunction** | **Before** he began his major paintings, da Vinci had already worked as an engineer and architect. <br> **After** da Vinci had painted many of his major artworks, he spent more time on his inventions. |
| **Preposition** | **Before** 1495, da Vinci had already worked as an engineer and architect. <br> **After** 1500, da Vinci spent more time on his inventions. |

**1**   Reread "Leonardo da Vinci" on page 267. How many sentences can you find with adverb clauses of time? For each such sentence, find the connecting word. Then, explain which action came earlier and which action came later.

**2**   Everyone develops special talents during his or her lifetime, but few are able to equal the extraordinary feats of the following individuals. Complete the following passages by using simple past or past perfect forms (active or passive) of the verbs in parentheses. Note any case where you feel both tenses are appropriate. The first two are done as examples.

1. **Ibn Sina**

Ibn Sina ____*was*____ a Persian who ____*wrote*____ *The Canon of Medicine.* This
          1 (be)              2 (write)

medical encyclopedia _____ very advanced; as a result, scholars _____
                3 (be)                        4 (use)

it for five centuries. Before his death in 1037, Ibn Sina _____ an additional
                                                5 (complete)

150 books on such varied subjects as philosophy, mathematics, theology, and

astronomy. Like many learned* men, he _____ early. By the age of ten, he
                                  6 (begin)

_____ the Koran. By the age of eighteen, he _____ as a physician for a
7 (memorize)                                      8 (work)

sultan.

2. **King Sejong**

King Sejong _____ Korea from 1418 to 1450. He _____ a scholar as
                1 (rule)                           2 (be)

well as one of the greatest and most virtuous of Korean kings. Peace for Korea

_____ one of his finest accomplishments. Once he _____ the barbarians
        3 (be)                                  4 (defeat)

on Korea's northern border, Korea _____ a long period of peace. Within his
                                    5 (enjoy)

government, Sejong _____ men of talent, no matter what their social status.
                       6 (promote)

He _____, "The prosperity of the state depends upon the character of the
     7 (say)

government." He also _____ *hang'ul,* the Korean alphabet, which
                    8 (invent)

_____ literacy to the common people. By the time Sejong _____, he
9 (bring)                                            10 (die)

_____ culture blossom and _____ learning truly flourish in his
11 (see)                      12 (watch)

beloved** Korea.

---

*learned*   pronunciation: *lear' ned* (two syllables)
**beloved*   pronunciation: *be la' ved* (three syllables)

3.   **Sor Juana Inés De La Cruz**

Sor Juana, the great Mexican poet, was born in Mexico City around 1651. She

_____ to read before she _____ three years old. By her seventh birthday,
  1 (start/already)                        2 (be)

she _____ to enter the university. Because girls _____ in the university,
       3 (try)                                          4 (not allow)

Sor Juana eventually _____ the convent. During her life, she _____
                        5 (join)                                    6 (write)

extraordinary prose and poetry. Before she _____ in 1695, she _____ a
                                               7 (die)                8 (collect)

library of over 4000 books.

4.   **Johann Wolfgang Von Goethe**

Goethe _____ from 1749 to 1832. He _____ a scientist as well as the
          1 (live)                        2 (be)

greatest of German poets. By age 16, he _____ religious poems, a novel,
                                            3 (write/already)

and a prose epic. While continuing to write, he _____ both law and medicine.
                                                    4 (study)

After he _____ to live in Weimar, Goethe _____ minister of
            5 (invite)                              6 (become)

state. Because of his position, he _____ himself in agriculture, horticulture,
                                      7 (educate)

and  mining.  He  then  _____  to  master  anatomy,  biology,  optics,  and
                           8 (proceed)

mineralogy.

5.   **John Stuart Mill**

Perhaps John Stuart Mill _____ more at age thirteen than most people
                            1 (master/already)

learn in their entire lives. He _____ reading Greek at age three and Latin at
                                   2 (begin)

seven. By age 12, he _____ all the masterpieces in both languages. He then
                        3 (read)

_____ to logic and political economy; by age 18, he _____ articles on
   4 (turn)                                                     5 (write)

these topics for the *Westminister Review.*

6.   **Margaret Mead**

By the time Margaret Mead _____ twenty-six, she _____ curator of
                             1 (be)                    2 (name/already)

the American Museum of Natural History. Before she _____ age 30, she
                                                       3 (reach)

_____ two major books on people of Oceania. Before her death in 1978,
   4 (publish)

she _____ hundreds of articles and books on topics ranging from anthropol-
<br>5 (write)

ogy to nuclear warfare and disarmament.

**3**   The following sentences give you information about Michelangelo Buonarroti (1475–1564) and some of his accomplishments. The sentences are listed in chronological order. Use the cues in parentheses to combine each pair. Change nouns and verb tenses, omit words, and add punctuation when necessary.

**Example:**   Artists used methods of fresco* painting for many centuries. The Italians perfected the technique. (before)

*Artists had used methods of fresco painting for many centuries before the Italians perfected the technique.*

1.   Both Michelangelo and Leonardo da Vinci worked with fresco. Michelangelo and Leonardo were commissioned for a painting in Florence. (before)
2.   Michelangelo began his work on the Council Room in Florence. Michelangelo was called to Rome by Pope Julius II. (soon after)
3.   Michelangelo left for Rome. The two artists never worked together again. (once)
4.   Michelangelo arrived in Rome. The pope commanded Michelangelo to fresco the Sistine Chapel. (as soon as)
5.   Michelangelo didn't finish the ceiling. The pope impatiently opened the Sistine Chapel in 1509. (when / yet)
6.   Michelangelo, without help, covered 5800 square feet with fresco painting. Michelangelo finished the Sistine Chapel ceiling. (by the time that)

A detail from the Sistine Chapel ceiling painted by Michelangelo Buonarroti.

---

*fresco*   the art of painting on a moist plaster surface

**4**   First read the following passage for meaning. Then complete it by using appropriate connecting words. Choose from *after, but, by, by the time that, for example, in fact, once, whenever.* Use each at least one time.

### The Italian Renaissance

Many cultures have produced great thinkers and great artists, __*but*__ the collection
                                                            1
of brilliant minds that lived in Italy in the 1400s and 1500s may never be repeated. It

was a very special time for the world. _____ the end of the 13th century, Florence
                                          2
and other Italian cities had reached very high standards of living. The aristocracy used

its wealth to promote the arts and the sciences. _____ Leonardo da Vinci was born
                                                   3
in 1452, even the growing middle class of craftspeople and merchants had begun to

participate in and benefit from the "explosion of learning and creativity" evident in

Florence, Lucca, and other Italian cities. Knowledge was highly valued, _____
                                                                          4
learning was important even for the common people.

The creative and reflective atmosphere of that time led to great achievements

across many fields. New ideas about mathematical and geometric proportions led to

changes in music, architecture, and of course, art. _____ other thinkers had worked
                                                      5
out ideas about depth and perspective, masters such as Botticelli, da Vinci, and

Michelangelo began applying these theories in their paintings and sculptures.

_____, architecture changed dramatically. _____ various mathematical and
   6                                             7
structural theories had been developed, taller and wider buildings became possible.

_____, great new domed cathedrals like *Santa Maria del Fiore* in Florence were
   8
built, _____ old gothic styles were abandoned.
         9
The sciences also blossomed. Geniuses like Leonardo da Vinci and Galileo

Galilei worked across many disciplines. _____, Galileo worked with mechanics,
                                          10
astronomy, temperature, and magnetism. He invented the microscope, _____ he
                                                                       11

also built a telescope powerful enough to make the discovery of the satellites of the planet Jupiter. _____, he experimented with ideas of motion such as the pendulum
12
and gravitation. _____, it is said that he used the tilt of the Tower of Pisa to do his
13
experiments on the acceleration of falling bodies.

Renaissance Italy produced tremendous achievements that still impact us today.

_____ we admire great works of art, listen to lyrical music, appreciate beautiful
14
buildings, or look through a lens at the starry night sky, we must thank Italians of the Renaissance for their many creative contributions to our world.

Santa Maria del Fiore in Florence, Italy          The Campanile (Leaning Tower) in Pisa, Italy

## Using What You've Learned

5   Leonardo da Vinci was "far ahead of his time." He had drawn plans for a number of inventions that were not developed until centuries later. Some of these plans included an airplane, an elevator, a helicopter, lock gates for canals, a submarine, a tank.

In small groups, discuss one or more of these inventions. Try to imagine what da Vinci had been thinking, doing, or feeling before he created his plans and how he arrived at them. You might want to use the following questions to help you. After you have finished, choose one member to give a brief summary for the class.

1.   What do you think led da Vinci to these ideas? What problems had he been trying to solve?

2. Can you think of any reasons why he didn't develop the actual invention? (He *did* design and build a type of gate for canal locks.) Were all the necessary materials available at that time?

3. When were these inventions actually developed?

4. How have they changed since then?

5. How have they affected our lives?

Tank

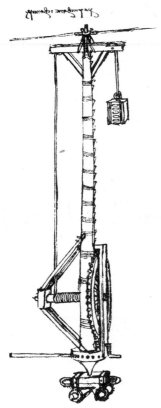

Movable derrick

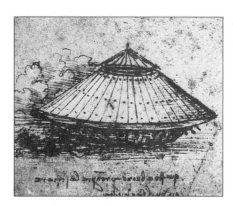

Submarine

**6** Is there someone whom you particularly admire for his or her knowledge or accomplishments? He or she may be a musician, a scholar, a sports figure, a politician, a friend, or a family member. What did this person do? How did he or she accomplish this?

Write a brief composition describing this person's accomplishments. Organize your composition in chronological order, and be sure to pay close attention to your use of verb tenses. Later, work in small groups and share your descriptions with your classmates.

<table>
<tr><td>**PART 4**</td></tr>
</table>

# Adverb Clauses of Time and Condition: Past Time with the Simple Past and Past Continuous Tenses

## Setting the Context

Albert Einstein in Princeton, New Jersey

**Prereading Questions**    Who was Albert Einstein? What do you know about his work?

### Creativity and Genius in Science

One of history's greatest revolutionary thinkers has been Albert Einstein, yet virtually no one foresaw his creativity. When he was a child, his parents actually suspected that he was mentally handicapped. For example, while he was learning to talk, he had great difficulties. When he entered school, he was considered "average" at best. Later, after he had finally graduated from a technical school, he was not able to find a job teaching science. Yet Einstein went on to become one of the world's greatest scientists, and today his name is synonymous with genius.

5

**Discussing Ideas.**    In many ways, Einstein was what we call a *late bloomer,* someone who develops his or her potential later than other people do. Do you know of other people who began great accomplishments later in life? What about the opposite? Do you know of people who were *precocious,* who produced a great deal early in life and then stopped?

## Clauses of Time and Condition: Past Time with the Simple Past and Past Continuous Tenses

|  | Examples | Notes |
|---|---|---|
| **when** | **When** Einstein **had** extra time during the day, he **wrote** down his ideas. | The simple past tense is used with *when* to show a direct connection in the time of occurrence of two events. |
| **if**<br><br>**unless** | **If** he **had** enough time, he **wrote** out long mathematical equations.<br>**Unless** he **had** no time, he **would** usually **write** down notes each day. | *If* and *unless* express a cause/effect relationship between two events. The main clause is the effect or result of the dependent clause. |
| **as**<br><br>**while** | **As** Einstein **was doing** his work, he **was** also **thinking.**<br>**While** Einstein **was working** in the patent office, he **had** plenty of time to think. | The past continuous is used to express past actions in progress at a particular time. Both clauses may use the past continuous to emphasize that both activities were in progress at the same time. |

**1**   Complete the following passage by using simple past or past continuous forms of the verbs in parentheses. Include adverbs where indicated. The first one is done as an example.

### Albert Einstein

When Einstein ___was___ a child, he _____ no early evidence of genius. While
       1 (be)             2 (show)

he _____ to talk, he _____ tremendous difficulties, and his
    3 (learn)          4 (have)

parents _____ him of being mentally handicapped. In high school, he
    5 (suspect/even)

_____ an average student. When he _____ from a technical
  6 (be)           7 (graduate/finally)

institute in Zurich, Switzerland, he _____ able to find a teaching ap-
          8 (not be)

pointment in science. He _____ up working in a patent office in Bern,
       9 (end)

Switzerland.

    Einstein _____ that type of job, but as he _____ in the office,
       10 (not want)          11 (work)

he _____ able to spend time thinking. Several years later he _____
  12 (be)                13 (publish)

five papers in one year, 1905. These papers _____ an explanation of his
14 (include)

special theory of relativity, which _____ a worldwide scientific revolution.
15 (begin)

**2** Many of science's greatest findings or events have come as a result of good luck as
well as hard work. Complete these passages by using simple past or past continuous
forms of the verbs in parentheses. The first verb is done as an example.

1. During the late 1800s, Louis Pasteur __*was experimenting*__ with bacteria. When
1 (experiment)

   Pasteur _____ chickens old bacteria by accident, they _____
   2 (give)                                                                3 (become)

   sick but they _____. When he _____ the injections several
   4 (not die)                        5 (repeat)

   times, the chickens _____ a resistance to infection. This discovery
   6 (develop)

   _____ his work on immunization.
   7 (begin)

2. While von Mering and Minkowski _____ the pancreas (which helps to
   1 (study)

   metabolize sugar), they _____ the organ from several dogs. Later, a
   2 (remove)

   laboratory assistant _____ something unusual. Flies _____
   3 (notice)                                                      4 (swarm)

   around the cages of these dogs, but they _____ near the cages of other
   5 (not go)

   dogs. When the two researchers _____ the dogs without pancreases,
   6 (test)

   they _____ that the dogs _____ the symptoms of diabetes.
   7 (discover)                      8 (have)

   This incident _____ medical science the first information connecting
   9 (give)

   the pancreas to the cause of diabetes.

3. In 1929, the English bacteriologist Alexander Fleming _____ with a
   1 (experiment)

   bacteria culture when it _____ contaminated by a mold. When the
   2 (become)

   mold _____ the bacteria, the bacteria _____. Fleming
   3 (touch)                                      4 (die)

   _____ this mold and _____ it grow in a liquid. While this
   5 (save)                       6 (let)

   mold _____, it _____ a substance that _____
   7 (grow)          8 (produce)                          9 (be)

   able to kill a number of bacteria. Moreover, the substance _____ ani-
   10 (harm / not)

   mals. This substance later _____ known as penicillin.
   11 (become)

**3**   Complete the following sentences about Marie Curie by using simple past, past continuous, or past perfect forms (active or passive) of the verbs in parentheses.

Marie Curie

1.  Born in Poland in 1867, Marie Sklodowska __was not allowed__ to attend
    (not allow)

    school there beyond the high school level.

2.  After an older brother and sister _____ for university education in Paris,
    (leave)

    Marie _____ to send them money and to save for her own education.
    (work)

3.  While she _____, Marie _____ herself from family books.
    (work)  (teach)

4.  As soon as she _____ enough money, she _____ to Paris.
    (save)  (go/also)

5.  While Marie _____ at the Sorbonne, she _____ as
    (study)  (live)

    economically as possible and _____ all her time studying.
    (spend)

6.  When she _____, Marie Sklodowska _____ at the top of her class.
    (graduate)  (be)

7.  In 1894, she _____ to Pierre Curie, who _____ somewhat
    (introduce)  (become/already)

    famous for his work in physics.

8.  After Marie _____ Pierre Curie, she _____ to apply his
    (marry)  (begin)

    earlier discoveries to the measurement of radioactivity.

9.  Scarcely six years after Marie _____ in Paris, she _____
    (arrive)  (make)

    major discoveries about radioactivity; Pierre _____ the potential and
    (see)

    _____ his own research to join her.
    (drop)

10. In December 1898, the Curies _____ other experiments with uranium
    (conduct)

    ore when they _____ a new radioactive substance: radium.
    (detect)

11. In 1903, Marie Curie _____ her dissertation on radioactivity, and for
    (write)

    it, she and Pierre _____ that year's Nobel Prize with Antoine Becquerel.
    (give)

12. After Pierre Curie's death in 1906, Marie _____ her study of radioac-
    (continue)

    tive elements, and in 1911 she _____ the Nobel Prize in chemistry.
    (award)

**Culture Note**

*As of 2000, 29 women have been awarded Nobel Prizes. Marie Curie is the only woman to receive two awards, both in sciences: 1903 for physics and 1911 for chemistry. Her daughter, Irene, also won a Nobel Prize in chemistry in 1935.*

**4**   The following sentences tell about the life of Albert Einstein. Combine each group of sentences by using coordinating or subordinating conjunctions or transitions. You can choose from the following connecting words or you can use others: *after, and, as soon* *as, as a result, before, for example, in addition, when, while, until.* Change words, phrases, verb tenses, and punctuation when necessary.

**Example:** In 1900, Albert Einstein graduated from the Polytechnic Academy in Zurich. Later that year, Albert Einstein became a Swiss citizen. Later that year, Albert Einstein took a job in a Swiss patent office.

*In 1900, after Albert Einstein had graduated from the Polytechnic Academy in Zurich, he became a Swiss citizen and took a job in a Swiss patent office.*

1. Albert Einstein worked in the patent office for three years. Then, Albert Einstein married Mileva Marié.

2. Albert Einstein worked in the patent office for several years. During that time, he developed many of his theories.

3. Albert Einstein worked at the patent office. He financed some of his research by writing patents for better refrigerators.

4. Einstein did not produce any notable scientific work. Then he published five papers in 1905.

5. These papers were published. Einstein immediately became famous in the scientific community. These papers contained many revolutionary ideas. They outlined the "special theory of relativity," the "equivalence of mass and energy ($E = mc^2$)," and the "photon theory of light."

6. Einstein published his papers in 1905. Before then, he had been completely unknown in the scientific community.

7. During the next six years, Einstein continued to develop his theory of relativity. During that time, Einstein continued to study the relationship between mass and energy. During that time, Einstein tried to incorporate gravity into his theory.

8. Einstein taught in Prague for a brief time. Then the Einstein family returned to Switzerland. Einstein was offered a position at the Polytechnic Academy in Zurich.

**5** The following is a continuation of the chronology of Albert Einstein's life. Use the information to write a short paragraph about him. Combine ideas by using coordinating conjunctions, subordinating conjunctions, and transitions. Change words, phrases, verb tenses, and punctuation when necessary.

**1914** Einstein accepted a position at the Prussian Academy of Sciences.

The Einstein family moved to Berlin.

Einstein's wife and sons vacationed in Switzerland.

World War I began.

His family was unable to return to Germany.

This forced separation eventually led to divorce.

**1916** Einstein published his paper on the general theory of relativity.

This theory was revolutionary.

It contradicted Newton's ideas on gravity.

It predicted irregularities in the motion and light from Mercury.

During this time, Einstein devoted much of his time to pacifism.

Einstein began to write and distribute antiwar literature.

**1919** The Royal Society of London verified Einstein's predictions about Mercury.

Einstein quickly became famous.

Einstein married Elsa, the daughter of a cousin of his father.

Einstein stayed in Berlin.

Einstein continued to work for pacifism.

**1921**    Einstein was awarded the Nobel Prize in physics.

## Using What You've Learned

**6**    On the Internet or at the library, research the later part of Albert Einstein's life. Use this information along with information from this section to write a short biography of Einstein. Pay close attention to use of verb tenses and connecting words when you edit your composition.

**7**    Use information from this section, along with other information you can gather from the Internet or the library, to write a short composition about one of the following:

Marie Curie and the discovery of radium

Alexander Fleming and the discovery of penicillin

Louis Pasteur and immunization, pasteurization, or other processes

**8**    M. C. Escher was a Dutch artist who lived from 1902 to 1972. He created some of the most unusual and stimulating drawings in history. The drawing here is his interpretation of *Relativity*. In pairs or in small groups, discuss the following questions about this work. Be sure to include your own questions too.

1.  How do you react when you see a drawing like this?
2.  Try to imagine what Escher was thinking about while he was planning this.
3.  Why do you think he called it *Relativity?*
4.  How do you think he drew the picture? For example, do you think he drew several separate pictures and later put them together?

*Relativity* by M. C. Escher, National Gallery of Art, Washington, D.C. Gift of Mrs. C. V. S. Roosevelt

## PART 5   Adverb Clauses of Time and Condition: Future Time

### Setting the Context

**Prereading Questions**   How do you go about making decisions? Do you simply "decide"? Or do you look carefully at alternatives? Have you ever seen or used a "decision tree" like the following one?

---

#### Decision Making

Making a good decision is one of the most creative things we do. In many ways, creativity is the ability to see all the alternatives. It can be an analytical process. Using a decision tree can be a great help, especially if the decision is a complicated one.

*Supplier A:*   higher grade silk, cost is $0.50 more per meter, delivery is cheaper than supplier B, supplier A wants to dye silk, won't ship otherwise

*Supplier B:*   slightly lower grade silk, cost is cheaper than supplier A, delivery costs about $0.25 more per meter of silk fabric, supplier B will ship raw fabric, not dyed

I am in charge of identifying a supplier of silk fabric for our company.

If our company buys from supplier A, we will have to spend more for the fabric. → If we spend more, we'll have to charge more.

If our company buys from supplier A, we will have to take what colors they give us. → If the colors aren't good, they won't sell.

If our company buys from supplier A, delivery will be cheaper. → If we can save here, we can cut down on cost.

If our company buys from supplier B, the fabric will be cheaper, but not as good. → If the fabric is poor, it won't sell.

If our company buys from supplier B, we can choose our own colors. → If we can choose our own colors, we might sell more.

If our company buys from supplier B, our delivery costs will be higher. → If the fabric cost is cheap enough, we can handle the extra cost of delivery.

---

**Discussing Ideas.**   Think this process through some more. What other repercussions does this decision have on the company and on the individual who makes the decision?

## A. Clauses of Time: Future Time

| | **Examples** | **Notes** |
|---|---|---|
| **after** | **After I finish,** I will take a long vacation! | The verb in the dependent clause is in the simple present or the present perfect tense. The present perfect emphasizes the completion of the action. |
| **as soon as** | I'm going to call you **as soon as I finish.** | |
| **before** | I won't call you **before I have finished.** | |
| **once** | **Once I've finished,** I'll call you. | The verb in the main clause is in a future tense. Modal auxiliaries such as *can* and *should* are often used in either clause. |
| **until** | I should work **until I have finished.** | |
| **when** | **When I finish,** I'll give you a call. | |
| **as** | I'll have to concentrate a lot **as I'm working.** | The present continuous is often used in dependent clauses with *while* or *as* to emphasize an action in progress. |
| **while** | **While I'm working,** I won't think about my vacation. | |

**1**  Imagine that you have a business that offers a service such as insurance, travel, or computer consulting. In your own words, complete the following about "your business."

1. After the sales meeting is over, . . . *we'll make some decisions.*
2. When we have finished our business plan, . . .
3. Tonight, I'm going to finish my work before . . .
4. While I'm reviewing our balance sheet tonight, . . .
5. As soon as I get to the office, . . .
6. I'll call them once . . .
7. As we're redoing our office, . . .
8. I will keep on trying to contact the buyer until . . .

**2**  Imagine that you're going to start your own online business. What are you going to do before you start the business? While you are thinking about the product you will sell? After you have decided on a product? Form complete sentences from the cues. Add specific information about your own "business."

**Example:**  Think of a product to sell online.

*Before I start this business online, I am going to think about what my product will be. While I am thinking about the product, I'll do market research on . . .*

1. research the competition
2. decide what advantage selling online can give
3. find a supplier
4. set up a distribution system
5. design a Website

6.   create packaging
7.   market my product on the Internet
8.   hire an accountant to handle my record keeping


**3**   Complete these sentences, giving more ideas about your "company."

**Example:**   If the product sells, _we'll expand our company._

1.   If we make a profit, . . .
2.   If the product is successful, . . .
3.   If we add a new product, . . .
4.   If we don't sell a lot of the product, . . .
5.   If my friends want to invest in my company, . . .
6.   If my financial backers are willing to lend me more money, . . .
7.   If we sell a lot of products online, . . .
8.   If we get more orders than we planned in the first year, . . .


## B. Clauses of Condition: Future Time

Factual conditional sentences that refer to the future generally express predictions or intentions. The main clause shows the effect or result of the *if* clause.

|  | **Examples** | **Notes** |
|---|---|---|
| **if** | **If I finish** my work, **I will** (may, might, and so on) go to the party. <br> **I am not going** to go (can't go, shouldn't go, and so on) **if I haven't finished** my work. | The verb in the dependent clause is in a present tense. The verb in the main clause is *be going to* or a modal auxiliary: *will, may, might, should,* and so on. |
| **unless** | **Unless I finish** my work, **I am not going** to go (can't go, shouldn't go, and so on) to the party. | *Unless* is similar in meaning to *if . . . not* in many sentences, but *unless* is more emphatic. |


**4**   Complete the following in your own words.

**Example:**   If the weather is nice this weekend, _we'll take a trip._

1.   If I have enough money, . . .
2.   If it rains tomorrow, . . .
3.   If I finish my homework early, . . .
4.   If I don't finish my homework, . . .
5.   If my friends invite me to visit, . . .
6.   If my parents don't call soon, . . .
7.   If I win a scholarship, . . .
8.   If I get 600 on the TOEFL test, . . .

**5**   Imagine that you are trying to decide about a place to live. Use the following decision tree, similar to the one on page 281, to help you decide what to do. Use the correct forms of the verbs in parentheses and add more information. Then make your decision and explain why you made that decision.

I can spend up to $500 a month for my expenses (housing, meals, transportation).

*Apartment A:*   with Americans; $280 a month; near school
*Apartment B:*   with people from my own country; $200 a month; far from school

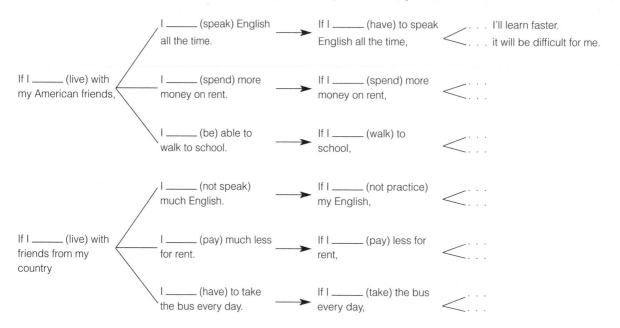

**6**   Combine the following pairs to form new sentences with *unless*.

**Example:**   I should speak English more often. If I don't, I'll never become fluent.
*Unless I speak English more often, I'll never become fluent.*

1.   I should find a cheaper place to live. If I don't, I'll run out of money soon.
2.   We should save more money. If we don't, we'll never be able to take a long vacation.
3.   You should send your application for school soon. If you don't, you may not be accepted this year.
4.   I should write my parents soon. If I don't, they'll start to get worried about me.
5.   You should start your research project soon. If you don't, you may not be able to finish in time.
6.   They should prepare more for the test. If they don't, they may not pass.
7.   Deb should see the doctor soon. If she doesn't, her condition may get worse.
8.   Jack should take a long vacation. If he doesn't, he might have a nervous breakdown.

**7**   The following guidelines for excellence in business are from *In Search of Excellence* by Thomas J. Peters and Robert H. Waterman. According to Peters and Waterman, these are the eight attributes of "excellent, innovative companies." After reading the list, think about the causes and effects of these attributes. Then think about the consequences for a company that does not have them. Form sentences using *if, unless, before, after,* and *when* to express your ideas. You may have several opinions for each.

**Excellent, Innovative Companies**

1. take action

   They make theories and analyses, but most important, they try new ideas.

   *If a company is innovative, it will try new ideas.*

   *When a company takes action, it will be able to see results, rather than guess the results.*

   *If a company doesn't try something new, another company will probably try it first.*

   *Unless a company tries new ideas, it won't make any progress.*

2. are close to the customer

   They get their ideas from the people they serve; they listen carefully to their customers.

3. encourage independence and ingenuity

   They don't hold people back. They encourage employees to be creative and to take risks. They support experimentation.

4. work for productivity through people

   They treat everyone in the company as an important source of ideas. They never encourage a "we / they" management / worker situation.

5. keep "quality" as the basic philosophy of the organization

   Quality is the most important thing, not status, organization, resources, or technology.

6. stick to their own business

   They don't get involved in things that are outside of their area of expertise. They don't acquire jobs or businesses they don't know how to run.

7. keep their organization simple and their staff to a minimum

   Their structures and systems are simple; they avoid having too many managers.

8. are both centralized and decentralized

   Control is loose because workers at all levels have authority and responsibility; on the other hand, control is tight because top management decides the basic direction of the company.

## C. Sentence Problems: Fragments, Comma Splices, and Run-ons

Fragments, comma splices, and run-on sentences are some of the most common errors in writing. These errors involve incomplete ideas or incorrect punctuation.

|  | **Examples** | **Notes** |
|---|---|---|
| **Fragment** | Thinking up new ideas. | Fragments are incomplete sentences. |
| **Comma Splice** | Thinking up new ideas can be difficult, it is important. | A comma splice is two sentences combined with a comma but without a connecting word. |
| **Run-On Sentence** | Thinking up new ideas can be difficult it is important. | A run-on sentence is two sentences combined without proper punctuation. |

**8**   **Error Analysis.**   Some of the following sentences are well written. Others are incomplete or are punctuated incorrectly. For each sentence, indicate complete (C), incomplete (I), or punctuation error (PE). Then, rewrite the incorrect sentences correctly.

**Example:**   ___I___ If a scientist makes an outstanding discovery.

*A scientist may make an outstanding discovery.*

Or:   *If a scientist makes an outstanding discovery, we call this creativity or genius.*

1.   _____ When an artist produces a masterpiece.

   _____

2.   _____ People are creative not only in art or science, they are also creative in their daily lives.

   _____

3.   _____ Ordinary people are creative every day.

   _____

4.   _____ Creativity involves awareness it means noticing the world around us.

   _____

5.   _____ To think up a new concept.

   _____

6.   _____ It is the courage and drive to make use of new ideas.

   _____

7.   _____ Creativity combining old ideas in new ways.

   _____

8.   _____ According to an old saying, there is nothing new under the sun.

   _____

9.   _____ Is not always easy to look at the same ideas in a different way.

   _____

10.   _____ Being open to new ideas is sometimes difficult, however, every one of us has the ability to do it.

   _____

**9**   **Error Analysis.**   The following passage contains errors in punctuation: sentence fragments, comma splices, and run-on sentences. First, read the passage once to understand the ideas. Then, correct the passage by changing or adding punctuation when necessary.

## Creativity

One form of creativity is the sudden flash of insight. When an idea pops into your head. This is what Arthur Koestler called the Eureka process. *Eureka* comes from the story of the ancient Greek scientist Archimedes. Archimedes supposedly leapt naked from his tub. Shouting "Eureka!" *Eureka* mean "I have found it." He had suddenly figured out why some things float.                                    5

Not all creative discoveries come like a flash of light, however. In fact, Thomas Edison, the inventor of the light bulb, tried hundreds of metal combinations in his laboratory. Before he found the right one to conduct electricity. Edison was able to create something new and valuable because of his energy and tenacity. He gave his own definition of genius it is 1 percent inspiration and      10
99 percent perspiration.

Despite their differences, Edison and Archimedes had much in common, they followed the same process. First, both recognized a problem. And were aware of previous steps to solve it. Both consciously or unconsciously worked toward a solution. Finally, both arrived at a solution, this was the creative idea.      15

## Using What You've Learned

**10**  Consider the world of business. In small groups, share some of your ideas about business in your culture. Look at the following questions. Discuss them, and add your own ideas. After you talk in the small group, share your ideas with the whole class.

What happens in your culture . . .
- if someone opens a new business?
- if you need start up money?
- if your children don't want to work in the business?
- if you sell an imported product?

**11**  Rube Goldberg was a creative American cartoonist. He "created" some of the world's most amazing "inventions." The invention in the accompanying cartoon is designed to attract a waiter's attention. Read the text and then follow the drawing to give the step-by-step process involved. Use *if, when, before,* and *after* to join the steps.

**Example:**  *If you light the skyrocket, the string will open the jack-in-the-box. When the skyrocket goes off, . . .*

**12** Consider the world of myths and superstitions. In small groups, share some traditional beliefs and/or superstitions. Use these ideas and add some of your own. Then, share your information with the whole class.

What will happen . . . {
if you break a mirror?
if you step on a crack in the sidewalk?
if you walk under a ladder?
if a black cat crosses your path?
}

**13** Think about the various descriptions of creativity, innovation, and excellence in this chapter. Try to put these ideas to use as you consider the problems of teaching and learning a language. Imagine that you and your classmates are educational consultants. You have been asked to design a program for a language school.

Work in small groups. Discuss your ideas on the best ways to learn languages. Then make a list of recommendations for planning a language program. Consider the following questions, and add ideas of your own.

1. How many students should there be per class? How many different teachers should students have?
2. How many hours a day should students have classes? When should the classes be offered?
3. What kinds of classes should be offered?
4. Should there be a language lab? Should use of the lab be optional or mandatory?

Remember that both money and time may be problems for the students. Some may be working. Some may have families. Many will not be able to afford expensive classes. How should you plan if you want to offer economical and effective classes?

**14** Short essay tests are frequently used in both the sciences and the humanities. Your scores are usually determined by the content, not correct grammar usage. However, an answer with few grammatical errors will most likely receive a better score than one with many answers. Practice your skills at writing short answers to these questions regarding content in this chapter. Try to spend no more than ten minutes per answer.

**Hint:** You can often begin your answer by making the question into a statement.

1. Who is the only woman to have been awarded two Nobel Prizes? Give a brief history of her life. Be sure to include information on the Nobel Prizes she received.
2. Create a decision tree for one of these situations. Make your decision regarding the situation. Use your decision tree to justify your choice.

   ■ Toshio has been awarded two scholarships: one full scholarship to a smaller state university and one a partial scholarship to a well-known and expensive East Coast college. His parents cannot afford to pay for his tuition.

■ Anna has two job offers: one at a small firm in her hometown and the other in a large firm in a large city about five hours from her home. The job offers are similar in terms of money and benefits. In her hometown, she can live with her parents and use public transportation. In the city, she will need to have a car and an apartment.

3. Briefly describe the steps involved in taking a good photograph.

## Video Activities: A Life of Painting

**Before You Watch.**   Discuss these questions in small groups.

1. At what age do people usually retire?
2. Do you know any elderly people who are still working? If so, how do they feel about their work?

**Watch.**   Answer the following questions.

1. What was Harry Sternberg's occupation? _____

2. What is his occupation now? _____

3. Why did he move from New York City to Escondido, California?

   a. for health reasons            c. to be near his children
   b. for financial reasons         d. to be near his wife's family

4. The narrator uses a nickname for New York City. What is it? _____

5. How did Harry feel when he first moved to Escondido?

   "It was a _____!"

6. What did Harry discover when he drew pictures of people on the New York

   City subway? Most people hated _____.

7. How do we know that Harry loves his work?

   a. He sleeps in his studio.
   b. He sometimes forgets to eat.
   c. When he goes away, he can't wait to get back.
   d. He paints every day.
   e. He gets excited before he starts every new painting.

**Watch Again.**   Compare answers in small groups.

1. What are the names of the first two paintings? _____ and _____
2. Complete the name of the exhibition in the beginning of the video.

   "No _____ Without _____"

3. Listen for the numbers.

    1. the number of years Harry Sternberg has been painting _____

    2. the number of years he lived in New York City      _____

    3. the year he moved to Escondido      _____

    4. the number of self-portraits he has painted      _____

    5. his age      _____

4. Complete the quotation.

    "I'm as _____ now when I _____ as I was _____."

**After You Watch.**   Combine each group of sentences using coordinating or subordinating conjunctions or transitions. You can choose from the following connecting words or you can experiment with others: *after, although, and, as soon as, as a result, before, for example, in addition, when, while, until.* Change words, phrases, verb tenses, and punctuation when necessary.

1. Harry Sternberg was born in 1904. He became a professional painter at the age of 26.

2. Harry Sternberg lived in New York City for 60 years. In 1966, he moved to Escondido, California for health reasons.

3. He realized that Escondido was very different from New York. He fell in love with the desert.

4. Harry Sternberg loves his work. He never gets bored.

5. In the 1960's Harry drew pictures of people on the New York subway. He realized that many people hated their work.

## Focus on Testing

*Objective Tests: Use of Connecting Words*

Connecting words are frequently tested on standardized English proficiency exams. Review these commonly tested structures and check your understanding by completing the sample items that follow.

**Remember that . . .**

■ Subordinating conjunctions must be followed by a subject/verb combination.

■ Prepositions are followed by nouns or noun forms.

■ Transitions use semicolons when joining two sentences.

**Part 1:**   Circle the correct completion for the following.

**Example:**   _____ John is satisfied with his work, he will submit the project.

    (a.)  When

    b.  Therefore

    c.  During

    d.  In fact

1. _____ Georgia O'Keeffe was living in New York, she worked as a teacher to support herself.
   a. If
   b. Unless
   c. While
   d. After

2. _____ you have problems with motion sickness, you can take over-the-counter antihistamines before traveling.
   a. If
   b. On the other hand
   c. Unless
   d. After

3. In Europe, most Internet users pay per message; _____, Internet users in the United States usually pay flat rates.
   a. in contrast
   b. while
   c. therefore
   d. once

4. _____ the age of ten, the Persian scholar Ibn Sina had memorized the Koran.
   a. During
   b. By the time that
   c. When
   d. By

**Part 2:**   Circle the letter below the underlined word(s) containing an error.

**Example:**   An individual often <u>feels frustrated</u> <u>unless</u> she has difficulties
                                        A              (B)
             in <u>speaking</u> the language of the country <u>where she is living</u>.
                   C                                            D

1. Louis Armstrong was one of <u>the</u> twentieth <u>century's</u> greatest jazz musicians;
                                  A                  B
   <u>in contrast</u>, he starred in movies and <u>did</u> comedy shows.
       C                                         D

2. <u>While</u> April <u>of</u> 1999, Europeans sent <u>more than</u> a billion messages on their
       A          B                              C
   <u>mobile phones</u>.
       D

3. <u>During</u> Pope Julius II opened <u>the</u> Sistine Chapel in 1509, Michelangelo
       A                               B
   Buonarroti had <u>not yet</u> finished his <u>fresco painting</u> of the ceiling.
                     C                          D

4. <u>Before</u> her death in 1978, Margaret Mead <u>was written</u> hundreds of articles
       A                                          B
   and books on numerous subjects <u>including</u> anthropology, museum <u>curating</u>,
                                      C                                    D
   and nuclear disarmament.

| PART 6 | # Review: Chapters 5 to 8 |

**1**  **Review.**   First read this passage for meaning. Then complete it by choosing the appropriate word(s) from each set in parentheses. If nothing is needed, choose *X*. The first two are done as examples.

## Inventions and the Patent System

In 1790, only a few years after the Revolutionary War (ended / (had ended)) in the
1

United States, a new revolution (((began)/had begun). This revolution (was/is) fairly
2                                               3

peaceful, but it involved large amounts of (the / X) money, creativity, and emotion. It in-
4

volved patents. According to the dictionary, (a / an) patent is a government grant to
5

(a / an) inventor for a specific period of time to make, use, and (sell / to sell) an inven-
6                                                                           7

tion. Every part of this definition (changes / has changed) since the beginning of the
8

patent system in (the / X) 1790. In the beginning, an invention (can be / could be) al-
9                                              10

most anything. The invention simply had (to be / be) unusual. Later it (became / was be-
11                                          12

coming) something "new and useful." By 1880, it had to be (the / X) result of a "flash of
13

genius." In (the / X) 1950s, a patented invention (defined / was defined) as something
14                                                   15

that (might not have occurred / should not have occurred) to the ordinary person.
16

Patents gave inventors rights to the invention for a period of years, usually seven-

teen. Inventors had to explain their inventions publicly, however. (Until / After) the
17

patent had expired, anyone (can / could) make the invention.
18

Since it (begins / began), the patent system has encouraged (many / much) in-
19                                                        20

ventors (developing / to develop) their ideas, but it has made (few / little) inventors
21                                                        22

(become / to become) rich. Many inventors have had serious financial problems, and
23

(other / others) people—not the inventors—have often made fortunes from their ideas.
24

During (the / X) 19th century, a tremendous number of patents (was given / were
25                                                                    26

given). For example, Cyrus McCormick (gave / was given) the patent for the
27

McCormick reaper and Charles Goodyear (awarded/was awarded) the patent for
28
(vulcanizing/to vulcanize) rubber. But the giant of all inventors was Thomas Alva
29
Edison. Edison (holds still/still holds) the record for the number of patents given to a
30
single inventor. He (has/is having) a total of 1093. Edwin Land, who (invented/was
31                                                                                              32
invented) the Land camera and (founded/was founded) Polaroid, is second
33
with 533.

Today, the patent system is incredibly complex, (but/however) the 21st century
34
may bring radical changes. The United Nations is stepping in and promoting a simple,
global system for patent filing. (In fact/On the other hand), more than 40 countries
35
have already signed a new world patent law treaty, and over 60 other countries should
sign soon.

**2**  **Review.**  Following is information about Thomas Edison and some of his accomplishments. The pairs of sentences are listed in chronological order. Use the cues in parentheses to combine each pair. Use a past perfect verb in each new sentence. Change nouns, and adverbs, omit words, and add punctuation when necessary.

**Example:**  Thomas Edison ended his formal education.
           Thomas Edison became a teenager. (long before)
           *Thomas Edison had ended his formal education long before he became a
           teenager.*

1. Thomas Edison invented dozens of practical tools and machines.
   Thomas Edison reached his early twenties. (before/already)
2. Edison made some money from an invention for the stock market.
   Edison set up a factory in Newark, New Jersey. (soon after)
3. Edison ran the factory for just two years.
   Edison decided to organize the first U.S. industrial research park in Menlo Park, New Jersey. (when)
4. In his attempts to create a light bulb, Edison tried hundreds of metal combinations.
   Edison finally found the right one to conduct electricity. (before)
5. Edison developed the first commercial light bulb.
   Edison created the mimeograph, dictating machines, early motion picture cameras and projectors, and an iron-alkaline battery, among other inventions. (after)
6. Edison received over 1000 patents for practical applications of scientific principles.
   Edison died. (by the time that)

**3**   **Review.**   Work in pairs. One partner should use charts 1 and 2 and the other should use charts 3 and 4. Take turns asking and answering questions in order to complete the following charts. Do not look at each other's charts. Here are some sample questions. Try to add your own questions too.

Who invented _____?

Who was _____ invented by?

By whom was _____ invented?

What did _____ invent?

When was _____ invented?

What could _____ do?

What impact has _____ had on our lives?

What are some of the effects of _____?

| Inventions: Chart 1 | | | | | |
|---|---|---|---|---|---|
| **Inventor with patent** | | | Joseph Glidden | Alexander Graham Bell | |
| **Invention** | cotton gin | sewing machine | | telephone | |
| **Year of patent** | | | 1874 | | 1880 |
| **Function** | took seeds out of the cotton | | provided cheap, practical fencing material | | provided economical and safe lighting |
| **Impact on the world** | | built the garment industry; created the first millionaire inventor | | began a communications revolution; produced the world's largest company—ATT— until it was broken up in 1984 | |

| Inventions: Chart 2 | | | | | |
|---|---|---|---|---|---|
| **Inventor with patent** | Eli Whitney | Elias Howe | | | Thomas Edison |
| **Invention** | | | barbed wire | | light bulb |
| **Year of patent** | 1794 | 1846 | | 1876 | |
| **Function** | | mechanized sewing | | allowed long-distance communication | |
| **Impact on the world** | made cotton the world's most important crop; made slavery profitable in the United States; helped start the Civil War | | allowed ranchers to close the plains of the American west | | gave a new dimension to life around the world; began the electronic age |

**Inventions: Chart 3**

| | | George Selden | | Chester Carlson | |
|---|---|---|---|---|---|
| **Inventor with patent** | | George Selden | | Chester Carlson | |
| **Invention** | machine gun | | airplane | | transistor |
| **Year of patent** | 1890 | 1895 | | | |
| **Function** | allowed bullets to be fired rapidly | | allowed humans to fly | created a "dry" process for copying paper documents | could change weak electrical signals into strong ones |
| **Impact on the world** | | did not invent the automobile, but got the patent and delayed the development of cars in the United States until 1911, when Henry Ford won in court | | | became the basis for all solid state technology; formed the basic device in miniature electronic systems like radios; led to development of the silicon chip for computers |

**Inventions: Chart 4**

| | | | | | |
|---|---|---|---|---|---|
| **Inventor with patent** | Hiram Maxim | | Orville and Wilbur Wright | | John Bardeen, Walter Brattain, William Shockley (ATT) |
| **Invention** | | automobile | | xerography | |
| **Year of patent** | | | 1906 | 1942 | 1950 |
| **Function** | | provided a motorized vehicle for rapid transportation | | | |
| **Impact on the world** | completely changed wars and ways of fighting | | changed trans-portation forever; was the begin-ning of hundreds of industries connected with flight | allowed documents to be copied easily using electricity; began a multibillion dollar company named Xerox | |

## Focus on Testing

*Review of Problem Areas: Chapters 5 to 8*

A variety of problem areas are included in this test. Check your understanding by completing the sample items that follow.

**Part 1:**   Circle the correct completion for the following.

**Example:**   When John _____ satisfied with his work, he will submit the project.

a.   is being
b.   is
c.   will be
d.   is been

1.   By 1911, Marie Curie _____ two Nobel Prizes in science.
a.   had been awarded
b.   had being awarded
c.   awarded
d.   was being awarding

2.   Professional musicians often rehearse their music mentally in order

_____ better.
a.   performing
b.   being performed
c.   to perform
d.   to be performed

3.   Until barbed wire was invented, _____ land in the Great Plains had been fenced.
a.   few of
b.   few of the
c.   little of
d.   little

4.   Most minerals near the earth's surface are located in _____ amounts.
a.   a small
b.   small
c.   the small
d.   the very small

5.   The light bulb, along with over 1000 other useful items, _____ by Edison.
a.   were patented
b.   patented
c.   patenting
d.   was patented

6.   Einstein had some of his most brilliant ideas _____ he was working in a Swiss patent office.
a.   by the time that
b.   unless
c.   in addition
d.   while

7.   The child appears healthy; _____, it's a good idea for her to have a check up soon.
a.   otherwise
b.   therefore
c.   nevertheless
d.   moreover

8.   _____ I agree with you, you're happy.
a.   Whenever
b.   While
c.   How
d.   Everywhere

**Part 2:** Circle the letter below the underlined word(s) containing an error.

**Example:** An instructor may <u>feel frustrated</u> <u>if</u> the students
                                       A         B

            <u>come prepared</u> with the assignment <u>that had been given</u>.
               Ⓒ                                        D

1. Physically fit people <u>should be able</u> <u>to stay</u> the same weight over a period of
    A                     B         C

   several years <u>unless</u> they maintain good health habits.
                D

2. Keynesian economics <u>has influenced</u> a number of <u>key governmental</u> policies
                     A                          B

   and policy makers involved with <u>monetary decision making</u> during the last
                                  C

   five <u>decade</u>.
        D

3. The <u>physiological and psychological</u> benefits of exercise <u>has been shown</u>
                  A                            B

   through numerous studies <u>done</u> on <u>stress reduction</u>.
                      C       D

4. When Einstein's five papers, <u>including</u> his special theory of relativity,
         A               B

   <u>were published</u> in 1905, a scientific revolution began <u>to unfolding</u>.
      C                                     D

5. After Leonardo da Vinci <u>had painted</u> the *Mona Lisa,* he <u>had gone</u> on to pursue
                            A                     B

   research in <u>such</u> varied fields as physics, anatomy, and <u>military science</u>.
            C                                      D

6. <u>Unless</u> you want to explore <u>much of</u> Lanai, the most secluded of <u>the</u>
   A                         B           C              D

   Hawaiian Islands, you will need a four-wheel drive vehicle.

7. <u>If</u> he decides <u>to tell</u> the truth, we <u>will</u> know who <u>kills</u> the old woman.
   A          B                   C         D

8. <u>Do you</u> like your coffee <u>with</u> <u>nor</u> without <u>cream</u>?
   A                      B  C        D

# Chapter

# 9

# Human Behavior

# Introduction

In this chapter, you will review basic word order of modifiers, and you will study adjective clauses. As you study the chapter, pay close attention to the role of punctuation with these clauses.

The following passage introduces the chapter theme, "Human Behavior," and raises some of the topics and issues you will cover in the chapter.

---

### Religion and Human Behavior

Does life have meaning? What gives it meaning? Why do we act the way we do? What is the best way to live? How can we be happy? How can we find peace? How can we find fulfillment in our lives?

These are questions that people have struggled with throughout human history. Philosophers, psychologists, sociologists, and physicists all have tried to give us answers. We also look for answers within ourselves. We try to cultivate the spiritual side of our lives. For many people in the world, spiritual questions are answered by organized religion.                                                    5

Hundreds of spiritual traditions exist in the world, yet they all try to answer the same questions. They teach basic ideas that help humans understand their nature and their behavior. They describe oppositions between the spirit and the body, good and evil, earthly and divine. Often these opposites cause conflict in people. Each spiritual tradition gives people a method that they can follow to walk the path of goodness. Each spiritual tradition moves toward a goal. Often that goal involves moving from earth to the divine and from the body to the spirit. This goal has names like heaven, nirvana, and salvation.                                          10

                                                                                                            15

All cultures in the world have spiritual traditions and usually some form of organized religion. The spiritual side of existence, whether organized into a religion or not, has a strong effect on the daily lives of people around the world.

---

**Discussing Ideas.**     Think about religion in your culture. Is there one major religion? Or are there several? Is religion an important influence in your culture? To what extent does it affect or control the way people think and behave?

Islamic mosque

Christian church

Jewish synagogue

Hindu temple

| PART 1 |

# Review of Modifiers and Introduction to Adjective Clauses

## Setting the Context

**Prereading Questions**    This chapter talks about five of the major world religions. It begins with Hinduism, the oldest of the five. What do you know about Hinduism? Is it practiced in your area or country?

### Hinduism

The religious tradition that we call *Hinduism* is the product of 5000 years of development. The name, however, dates only from about C.E. 1200, the time when the invading Muslims wished to distinguish the faith of the people of India from their own.

    *Hindu* is the Persian word for *Indian*. Hindus themselves, however, call their    **5** religious tradition the eternal teaching or law *(sanatana dharma)*.

    Hinduism has no founder and no prophet.* It has no specific church structure, nor does it have a set system of beliefs defined by one authority. The emphasis is on a way of living rather than on a way of thought. Radhakrishnan, a former president of India, once remarked: "Hinduism is more culture than a creed."    **10**

**Discussing Ideas.**    Where did the name *Hindu* come from? Who founded Hinduism? Does Hinduism have a strictly organized system of beliefs? Do you think Hinduism is somewhat different from other religions in these regards? Do you know of any Hindu customs or Hindu beliefs?

## A. Review of Modifiers

Remember that English has fairly strict rules for the word order of modifiers in a sentence. To review the order of modifiers, see Chapter 1, pages 9–15.

**1**    Look at the italicized modifiers in the following sentences and indicate which word(s) each modifies. Try to identify the modifiers (adjective, adverb, article, and so on).

        *article    preposition        preposition*
                    *noun*               *noun*

**Example:**    *The* majority *of Hindus* believe *in karma.*

1.    *An important* concept *of Hinduism* is karma, *which means "action" or "work."*
2.    Because *most* Hindus believe *in reincarnation,* karma *also* means the consequences *of actions from one life to the next.*
3.    To *some* social scientists, karma is *heredity,* or genetic inheritance, and dharma is *free will,* the ability to make choices.
4.    Reincarnation means *an* individual has lived *many* lives and will live many more until the *final* liberation.

*prophet    a person who claims to speak for God

5.  Because of karma and reincarnation, respect *for life, customs, and laws* is very important to Hindus.

6.  *Some* Hindus believe that being a vegetarian is *the best way* to show respect *for life.*

The Ganges River

**2**  Quickly reread the passage "Hinduism" on page 302. Then do the following:

1.  Read the first sentence of the passage. Name the subject, verb, and complement in the main clause. Name the subject, verb, and connecting word in the dependent clause.

2.  In the same sentence, name the parts of speech of the following:
    a.  *religious*       d.  *of*
    b.  *Hinduism*       e.  *development*
    c.  *the*

## B. Introduction to Adjective Clauses

An adjective clause is a dependent (relative) clause that modifies a noun or pronoun. An adjective clause usually comes immediately after the word(s) it modifies. In some cases, a pronoun or prepositional phrase may come between the (pro)noun and the clause. English has several different types of adjective clause constructions. You will study each one in detail in later sections.

|  | **Examples** |
|---|---|
| **Subject Clauses: *that*, *which*, and *who*** | Hinduism is a religion **that** did not have one founder. |
| **Object Clauses: *that*, *which*, and *who(m)*** | The man **whom** I met yesterday is a Hindu. <br> The man **to whom** I was introduced is a Hindu. |
| **Possessive Clauses: *whose*** | Hinduism is a religion **whose** beliefs form a major part of Hindu culture. |
| **Time and Place Clauses: *when* and *where*** | India is a country in Asia **where** a majority of the population is Hindu. |

**3**    Each of the following sentences has an adjective clause. Underline the dependent clauses and circle the word(s) they modify.

**Example:**    The Ganges is a (river) that flows through northern India.

1.    It is a river whose water is sacred to Hindus.
2.    Hindus from all over the world travel to the Ganges, which is the symbol of life without end.
3.    Every day, the Ganges is filled with hundreds of thousands of people who come to drink or bathe in the sacred water.
4.    Millions of people come for the great Kumbh Mela Festival, which is held once every twelve years.
5.    This festival takes place at Allahbad, where the Ganges and the Jumna rivers join.
6.    The Kumbh Mela Festival is a special time when all Hindus hope to bathe in the sacred waters of the Ganges.
7.    A very important festival is the Kumbh Mela Festival, during which millions of people drink or bathe in the sacred river.
8.    Varanasi, which is another city on the Ganges, is the most sacred for Hindus.
9.    Varanasi is the city that Hindus believe to be the most sacred.
10.    All Hindus hope to die at Varanasi, where the sacred water gives eternal life.
11.    A hope that all Hindus have is to die at Varanasi.
12.    The sacred ashes of those who have died at Varanasi are thrown on the river, and their lives will continue forever.

**4**    Work with a partner. Reread the sentences in Activity 3. Decide whether the noun or pronoun is modified by an adjective clause that is a subject clause, an object clause, a possessive clause, or a time and place clause. Use the chart on page 303 as a guide.

**Example:**    The Ganges is a river <u>that flows through northern India</u>. *subject clause*

**5**    Reread the sentences in Activity 3 one more time. On a separate piece of paper, try to rewrite each sentence as a simple sentence, but try to include all the important information, information which might be expressed in the adjective clause.

**Example:**    It is a river whose water is sacred to Hindus.

> *The water of the Ganges River is sacred to Hindus.*

## Using What You've Learned

**6**    The word *holiday* originally was "holy day," and it had a strictly religious meaning. Today, we use *holiday* to mean any vacation day. Just as religions celebrate special holidays, so do cities, states, countries, and cultures.

Get into four groups. Each group will take a season (spring, summer, winter, or fall). In your group, make a list of holidays you know that are celebrated during that season. Include a brief description of how and where they are celebrated. After you have finished, share your information with the rest of the class. Later, you will be asked to give a brief presentation about one holiday.

<table>
</table>

| **PART 2** |
|---|

# Clauses with *That, When,* and *Where:* Replacement of Subjects, Objects, and Adverbials of Time or Place

## Setting the Context

**Prereading Questions**   Hinduism and Buddhism are closely related in many ways. Siddhārtha Gautama was a Hindu who sought knowledge throughout his life, and his teachings developed into Buddhism. Why do you think Buddhism became a separate religion? Has this happened in other religions?

The Great Buddha of Kamakura, Japan

### Buddhism

Buddhism developed from the teachings of Siddhārtha Gautama (the Buddha or "enlightened one"). However, it is not a religion that honors one person, human or divine. Buddha is neither a god nor a god-sent mediator. He is   **5** not a "redeemer" who can save others.

In Buddhism, teaching *(dharma)* and knowledge are more important than the person, Buddha. This knowledge is a special religious knowledge that people attain through   **10** transcending human limitations. It is knowledge that goes far beyond the limits of thought. It leads to the ultimate goal, where the personality is transformed. The path to this transformation is a method of forming "right"   **15** habits.

Today, Buddhists refer to Buddha as the great example, but every person has to seek his or her own enlightenment. Selflessness and the seeking of peace on earth are the   **20** ways to enlightenment.

**Discussing Ideas.**   According to the passage, every person has to seek his or her own enlightenment. What does *enlightenment* mean to you?

## A. Clauses with That: *Replacement of Subjects*

When two sentences share an identical noun or noun phrase, you can use *that* to replace the noun or noun phrase in the second sentence. *That* is used for ideas and things. In informal spoken English, *that* is sometimes used to refer to people; *who* is generally preferred, however. Commas are *not* used with adjective clauses beginning with *that*.

|  | **Examples** |
|---|---|
| **Simple Sentences** | Buddhism is a **religion. This religion** teaches a way of life. |
| **Complex Sentence** | Buddhism is a religion **that** teaches a way of life. |
| **Simple Sentences** | Siddhārtha was a **person. This person** tried to overcome suffering. |
| **Complex Sentence** | Siddhārtha was a person **that (who)** tried to overcome suffering. |

**1** Combine the following sentences to form adjective clauses with *that*. Make any necessary changes in the sentences.

**Example:**   We visited a Buddhist temple. The temple was in Tokyo.

*We visited a Buddhist temple that was in Tokyo.*

1.   I bought a book. The book was about Buddhism.
2.   Buddhism is a religion. It has over 300 million followers.
3.   Buddhism has many beliefs. These beliefs help people to deal with their problems.
4.   I have a problem. It has been bothering me for a while.
5.   I talked about it with a friend. The friend had a similar problem.
6.   My friend had some ideas for me. These ideas were very helpful.
7.   I visited a Buddhist temple. The temple was made of wood.
8.   Buddhists often sit in meditation. Meditation quiets the mind and body.

**2** Combine the following sentences to form adjective clauses with *that*. Make any necessary changes in the sentences.

**Example:**   Buddha is a word from Sanskrit. This word from Sanskrit means "the enlightened one."

*Buddha is a word from Sanskrit that means "the enlightened one."*

1.   Through meditation, Buddha learned laws of life. Laws of life include the "Four Noble Truths" of Buddhism.
2.   The first law is about suffering. The suffering comes from our past actions or "karma."
3.   The second law talks about desires. The desires are for the wrong things.
4.   The third law says changing our lives will solve the problems. The problems come from desires.
5.   The fourth law describes a way of living. The way of living is Buddha's path to inner peace.
6.   According to Buddha, these "Four Noble Truths" are the laws. These laws will lead us to enlightenment.
7.   Funerals in East Asia are often marked by Buddhist services. These services are a little different in each country of that region.
8.   Buddhists believe in the unity of all living things. Living things are part of this world.

**3** Summarize the information given in Activity 2 by completing the following in your own words:

Buddha taught a way of thinking and acting that . . .

## B. Clauses with That: *Replacement of Objects of Verbs*

To form an adjective clause, the relative pronoun *that* can replace the object of the verb in a simple sentence. *That* normally refers to things or ideas, and in informal English it may be used to refer to people. In addition, *that* is sometimes omitted in informal English; this is possible only when *that* replaces an object (not the subject).

| | Examples |
|---|---|
| **Simple Sentences** | The **ideas** helped relieve suffering. Siddhārtha taught **these ideas.** |
| **Complex Sentences** | The ideas **that** Siddhārtha taught helped relieve suffering. The ideas Siddhārtha taught helped relieve suffering. |

## C. Clauses with When *or* Where: *Replacement of Adverbials of Time or Place*

*When* and *where* can be used as relative pronouns that replace adverbials of time or place. Do not confuse adjective clauses with *when* or *where* (which follow the noun(s) they modify) with adverb clauses (which may begin or end sentences).

| | Examples |
|---|---|
| **Simple Sentences** | Siddhārtha lived at a **time.** People suffered tremendously **then.** |
| **Complex Sentence** | Siddhārtha lived at a time **when** people suffered tremendously. |
| **Simple Sentences** | Nepal is a **country.** Buddhism and Hinduism are practiced **there.** |
| **Complex Sentence** | Nepal is a country **where** Buddhism and Hinduism are practiced. |

**4** Combine the following sentences by using *that, when,* or *where.* Eliminate words whenever necessary.

**Example:** Nirvana is a state of being. People can reach nirvana through learning.

*Nirvana is a state of being that people can reach through learning.*

1. The word is *nirvana.* Buddhists use this word to describe inner peace.
2. Nirvana is the goal. Every Buddhist hopes to achieve this goal.
3. It is a feeling. People describe the feeling as inner peace.
4. According to an early Buddhist scripture, nirvana is a place. There is no earth, water, fire, and air there.
5. It is a time. An individual achieves the end of suffering then.

6. The way is through meditation. People can reach nirvana this way.
7. Some people know the way. The way follows the practice of Siddhārtha.
8. The stillness of the very early morning is a time. Many people feel meditation is best then.

Buddhist monk meditating

**5** Whenever you study a new subject, you need to define and understand key words. Definitions often use adjective clauses. In order to understand Activity 6, which follows, you will need to know the meanings of the following words. Complete their definitions by choosing the appropriate adjective clause.

1. Our lifestyle is the way . . .           a.  that we gain through study and experience

2. Our livelihood is the way . . .          b.  that we choose to live, act, and think

3. Discipline is the effort . . .            c.  that we plan to do

4. Wisdom is knowledge and understanding . . .    d.  that we earn money

5. Our intentions are actions . . .         e.  that we use to determine right from wrong

6. Our morals are the guidelines . . .      f.  that we use to control our thoughts and actions

7. Suffering is the sad part of life . . .    g.  that a Buddhist believer must work in the world

8. Right livelihood is the way . . .        h.  that we cannot avoid

**6** **Error Analysis.**   Many of the following sentences have errors in the formation of adjective clauses. Find the errors and correct them. Indicate sentences that have no errors.

**Examples:**    The way to nirvana is a method that Buddhists call the "Eightfold Path."  *correct*                                                                      *where*
People who follow the Eightfold Path reach a point ~~that~~ extremes and impulses are avoided ~~there~~.

1. The Eightfold Path gives a moral way of living that it includes "right speech, action, and livelihood."
2. It has instructions on discipline that they involve "right effort, mindfulness, and concentration."
3. The Eightfold Path also discusses the wisdom that we develop this wisdom through "right views and intentions."
4. It is not a set of teachings that emphasizes strictness or severity.
5. It teaches a moderate lifestyle where avoids strong feelings.
6. The Eightfold Path leads to Nirvana, a feeling of peace when a person no longer has inner conflicts or suffering.
7. Vegetarianism is a diet choice means you don't eat meat.
8. Vegetarians honor the right that all things have to live.

**7**   Summarize the information given in Activity 6 by completing the following in your own words:

The lifestyle that Buddha . . .

**8**   Have you felt moments of real inner peace? Describe one by completing the following sentences. Add other information if you wish.

1. I've felt the kind of peace that . . .
2. It was at a time (in my life) when . . .
3. I had reached a point (in my life) where . . .
4. It gave me the sensation that . . .
5. For me, inner peace comes at the times when . . .
6. Peace is a feeling that . . .
7. There is a place where . . .
8. To achieve inner peace, you need a personal space where . . .

**9**   Quickly reread the passage "Buddhism" on page 205. Then answer the following:

1. What is the function of *that honors one person* in line 2?
2. What is the function of *that people attain through transcending human limitations* in lines 6 to 7?

## Using What You've Learned

**10**   After you have completed this section, there still may be words that confuse you. Make a short list of new vocabulary that you don't completely understand. Then, in small groups, write your own definitions for them.

After you have written your own definitions, check with other groups, with your teacher, or with your dictionary to see if the definitions are correct. You may also want to define some of the following words:

| | | |
|---|---|---|
| atheism | festival | ritual |
| belief | prayer | sin |
| doctrine | prophet | tradition |
| faith | religion | worship |

## PART 3

# Restrictive and Nonrestrictive Clauses; Clauses with *Who, Which,* and *Whose:* Replacement of Subjects and Possessives

## Setting the Context

**Prereading Questions**   The following passage tells about the third major world religion, Judaism. What do you know about Judaism? Are you familiar with any of its customs, traditions, or teachings?

### Judaism

Judaism, which is the parent of both Christianity and Islam, is the oldest of the world's three great monotheistic* religions. The core of Judaism is the belief in only one God who is the creator and ruler of the whole world. He is transcendent† and eternal.‡

We can trace the origin of Judaism to the time of Abraham. According to Jew-    **5**
ish tradition, Abraham made an agreement with God that he and his family would teach the doctrine of only one God. In return, God promised Abraham the land of Canaan for his descendants.

Judaism is based on two fundamental texts: the Old Testament of the Bible (the Torah) and the Talmud, which is a collection of poetry, anecdotes, laws,    **10**
traditions, biographies, and prophecies of the ancient Jews. All of Judaism's teachings, laws, and customs are also called the *Torah,* which means "to teach."

---

*monotheistic*   believing in one God
†*transcendent*   going beyond the limits of time and space
‡*eternal*   forever

**Discussing Ideas.** About one-half of the world's religions are monotheistic (believing in one God), while the others are polytheistic. In your opinion, is this a major difference in beliefs? Is this more important than any similarities among religions?

## A. Restrictive and Nonrestrictive Clauses

Restrictive clauses identify the nouns they describe. Restrictive clauses give *essential* information about these nouns. *No* commas are used with restrictive clauses.

   Nonrestrictive clauses do *not* define or identify the nouns they describe. Nonrestrictive clauses give *extra* information: the identity of the noun is already known. A comma is used at the beginning and at the end of a nonrestrictive clause. *That* may not be used with nonrestrictive clauses (with commas).

|  | **Examples** | **Notes** |
|---|---|---|
| **Restrictive** | I met a professor **who teaches a religious studies course at the college.** | Restrictive clauses explain *which* people, places, things, or ideas are being described in the sentence. |
| **Nonrestrictive** | I met Dr. Chang, **who teaches a religious studies course at the college.** | Nonrestrictive clauses add information. They do *not* explain *which* people (places, and so on). Clauses that modify proper names, entire groups, or nouns that are unique (the sun, and so on) are normally nonrestrictive. |

In some cases, the same clause may either identify or give extra information, depending on the situation. Compare the following examples.

|  | **Examples** | **Notes** |
|---|---|---|
| **Restrictive** | My brother **who lives in Iowa** is a teacher. (I have several brothers; the brother in Iowa is a teacher.) | This clause tells *which* brother. No commas are used. |
| **Nonrestrictive** | My brother, **who lives in Iowa,** is a teacher. (I have only one brother, or I'm talking about one brother now. By the way, he lives in Iowa.) | This clause gives extra information. Commas are used. |

*Note:* In spoken English, speakers often pause before and after a nonrestrictive clause. This tells you that the information is *extra*. Thus, pauses are likely in the second sentence but not in the first.

**1**   As your teacher reads the following sentences aloud, underline the adjective clause in each. Then decide whether the information is *essential* (telling *which* person, thing, and so on) or *extra*. Add commas if the information is extra.

**Example:**   People who believe in Judaism are called Jews.

*essential information; no commas*

1. Steve Wise who comes from Maryland is Jewish.
2. Steve's brother who lives in Chicago is a rabbi. (Steve has only one brother.)
3. Joan's brother who lives in Chicago is a rabbi. (Joan has several brothers.)
4. Judaism is based on the Talmud and the Old Testament which is also part of the Christian Bible.
5. The Bible which has two parts is the basis for both Judaism and Christianity.
6. A synagogue is a place where Jews worship and study.
7. The Touro Synagogue which is in Rhode Island is the oldest in the United States.
8. The synagogue which is in Rhode Island is the oldest in the United States.
9. The Talmud which is part of Judaism's holy texts is not part of Christianity's holy texts.
10. The Sabbath which is the weekly holy day for Jews falls on Saturday.

## B. Clauses with Who or Which: *Replacement of Subjects*

To form an adjective clause, the relative pronoun *who* or *which* can replace the subject of a simple sentence. *Who* refers to people only. It may be used in both restrictive and nonrestrictive clauses. *Which* refers to things or ideas. In nonrestrictive clauses (with commas), *which* (not *that*) must be used. In restrictive clauses (without commas), either *which* or *that* may be used, but *that* is preferred.

| | **Examples** |
|---|---|
| **Simple Sentences** | We spoke with **Dr. Chang. Dr. Chang** is an exchange scholar. |
| **Complex Sentence** | We spoke with Dr. Chang, **who** is an exchange scholar. |
| **Simple Sentences** | Dr. Chang will lecture on **Judaism. Judaism** is his specialty. |
| **Complex Sentence** | Dr. Chang will lecture on Judaism, **which** is his specialty. |
| **Simple Sentences** | Dr. Chang will lecture on a **topic. This topic** is very interesting. |
| **Complex Sentence** | Dr. Chang will lecture on a topic **that (which)** is very interesting. |

**2**   Use *who* or *which* to form an adjective clause from the second sentence in each pair. Combine the sentences, omitting words and adding commas when necessary.

**Example:**   Yesterday I met Mr. Preston. Mr. Preston is a world-famous scholar.

*Yesterday I met Mr. Preston, who is a world-famous scholar.*

Archeological dig in Israel.

1. Mr. Preston will give a talk about archeology. Archeology is the study of past human life and activities.
2. Mr. Preston will speak about various ruins in the Middle East. Mr. Preston has spent many years doing archeology.
3. The Middle East includes countries in Southwest Asia and North Africa. The Middle East is also called the Mideast.
4. The Middle Eastern countries are Egypt, Israel, Jordan, Saudi Arabia, and Yemen. These Middle Eastern countries are on the Red Sea.
5. The Red Sea borders the Sinai. The Sinai is a vast desert of plains, mountains, and white sandy beaches.
6. Mr. Preston used to live in Jerusalem. Jerusalem is a very important center for Judaism, Christianity, and Islam.
7. Mr. Preston told me about several archeologists. These archeologists are doing interesting work in Jerusalem.
8. Mr. Preston conducts archaeological digs. Archaeological digs uncover artifacts from past civilizations.
9. Jerusalem has many important archaeological sites. Jerusalem is an ancient city.
10. The City of David is visited by thousands of tourists each year. The City of David is a very large and ancient ruin in Jerusalem.

**3**   Use *who* or *which* to form an adjective clause from the second sentence in each pair. Combine the sentences, omitting words and adding commas when necessary.

**Example:**   Many religions have spring festivals like Passover.
Passover marks the end of winter.

*Many religions have spring festivals like Passover, which marks the end of winter.*

1. Passover commemorates the Jews.
   These Jews made the Exodus from Egypt.
2. Rosh Hashanah celebrates the "birthday of the world."
   Rosh Hashanah is the Jewish New Year's festival in the fall.
3. The Shofar is a trumpet.
   This trumpet is blown at Rosh Hashanah.
4. The ten days are a time for confessing sins and asking forgiveness.
   These ten days follow Rosh Hashanah.
5. This period ends with Yom Kippur.
   Yom Kippur is the "Day of Atonement."
6. On Yom Kippur, the synagogues are filled with people.
   These people are praying and asking forgiveness for their sins.
7. At Passover Jews prepare a special meal.
   This meal is called a seder.
8. Jews follow ancient traditions.
   These ancient traditions have their roots in the Bible and the Talmud.

**4**    Summarize the information given in the preceding exercise by completing this sentence in your own words: *Three important Jewish holidays are Passover, which . . . ; Rosh Hashanah, which . . . ; and Yom Kippur, which . . .*

**5**    In the following sentences, decide whether you may change *who* or *which* to *that*. If you cannot, explain why not.

**Examples:**    A rabbi is a person who teaches and leads worship.

*A rabbi is a person that teaches and leads worship.*

*You can change who to that because the clause is restrictive (no commas are necessary).*

1.  *Rabbi* is a Hebrew word which means "teacher" or "my master."
2.  Only a person who has learned the Torah may be called a rabbi.
3.  A rabbi has many duties, which include interpreting Jewish law and giving spiritual guidance.
4.  Originally, rabbis were scholars who lived and studied at the synagogues.
5.  Rabbis were the people who taught young children the Jewish faith.
6.  Rabbi Gordon, who is a friend of ours, teaches several classes each week.
7.  Rabbi Gordon's oldest brother, who teaches at a university, is a world-famous scholar.
8.  Rabbis often counsel people who find themselves in a spiritual or emotional crisis.

## C. Clauses with Whose: *Replacement of Possessives*

The relative pronoun *whose* can be used to form an adjective clause. It replaces a possessive. *Whose* normally refers to people, but it may also refer to places, ideas, or things.

|  |  | **Examples** |
|---|---|---|
| **Simple Sentences** | | I never miss a class with **Dr. Chang. Dr. Chang's (his)** lectures are always fascinating. |
| **Complex Sentence** | | I never miss a class with Dr. Chang, **whose** lectures are always fascinating. |
| **Simple Sentences** | | I particularly enjoyed **the last lecture. Its** topic was "Judaism and the Legal System." |
| **Complex Sentence** | | I particularly enjoyed the last lecture, **whose** topic was "Judaism and the Legal System." |

**6**    The following sentences include adjective clauses with *whose*. Rephrase these sentences to form two complete sentences by eliminating *whose* and adding a possessive (or a prepositional phrase).

**Example:**    The Jewish tradition of learning comes from the Bible, whose chapters stress the importance of education.

*The Jewish tradition of learning comes from the Bible.*

*The Bible's chapters (the chapters of the Bible) stress the importance of education.*

1. The tradition of learning centers around children, whose education begins at an early age.
2. Education begins with the parents, whose duty is to teach the commandments.
3. The education of the child continues with the rabbi, whose teaching includes both religious and social ideas.
4. Traditionally, all rabbis were scholars whose studies and teachings have shaped modern Judaism.
5. Religious education follows a strict progression whose order and methods have changed little over centuries.
6. Countries everywhere have been influenced by Judaism, whose teachings form the basis of many legal systems.
7. Judaism offers an ancient spiritual message to modern people, whose lives are often filled with doubt.
8. Judaism is a religion whose tenets* have remained the same over thousands of years.

**7**  Complete the following ten sentences with *who, which, that, whose,* or *X* to indicate no relative pronoun is needed. In some cases, more than one relative pronoun may be used. In other cases, the relative pronoun may be omitted. In these cases, give all possibilities, but indicate the preferred form.

**Examples:**   The Talmud, __*which*__ is a sacred Jewish text, gives detailed rules about daily life. *only one possibility*

The Talmud was developed by ancient rabbis _*who (that)*_ wrote stories and parables about daily life. *who is preferred*

1. The Talmud explains rituals _____ many Jews perform every day.
2. Children learn Jewish rituals from their parents and from the rabbi, _____ work includes teaching as well as leading worship.
3. The first rituals _____ Jews perform in the morning are to thank God and to wash their hands.
4. Washing the hands is a ritual _____ symbolizes purity.
5. Cleanliness, _____ is very important in Judaism, is the basis for many Jewish customs.
6. The Talmud gives many rules _____ cover food preparation.
7. Food _____ has been prepared in special ways is called "kosher."
8. Foods like pork, _____ spoils easily, have traditionally been forbidden.

---

*tenets*   basic beliefs

9.   This is an example of a religious custom _____ basis was practical. It protected against food poisoning.

10.  Jews _____ follow these rules strictly are called "orthodox."

**8**   **Error Analysis.**   Many of the following sentences have errors in their use of adjective clauses. Correct the errors. Then look for the sentences in the passages "Hinduism" on page 302, "Buddhism" on page 305, and "Judaism" on page 310 to see if your answers are correct.

**Example:**   Judaism which is the parent of both Christianity and Islam is the oldest of the world's three great monotheistic religions.

*The clause is nonrestrictive and needs commas.*

*Correction: Judaism, which is the parent of both Christianity and Islam, is the oldest of the world's three great monotheistic religions.*

**Culture Note**

*In the past in the United States, many schools had Christmas and Easter holidays and stores were closed on Sunday for the Christian sabbath. Nowadays, most schools schedule winter and spring holidays and many stores are open for business on Sundays in recognition of other religions.*

1.   The religious tradition that we call *Hinduism* is the product of 5000 years of development.

2.   Buddhism is not a religion that it honors one person.

3.   Knowledge in Buddhism is a special kind of religious knowledge people attain through transcending human limitations.

4.   It is knowledge goes far beyond the limits of thought.

5.   In Buddhism, knowledge leads to the ultimate goal where the personality is transformed there.

6.   The core of Judaism is the belief in only one God who is the creator and ruler of the world.

7.   Judaism is based on the Old Testament and the Talmud, which it is a collection of poetry, anecdotes, and so on.

8.   All of Judaism's teachings are also called the *Torah* which means "to teach."

## Using What You've Learned

**9**   What is your favorite holiday? Is it a religious, cultural, or national holiday? How is it celebrated? Is there special food, clothing, dancing, or music? Prepare a brief (three- to five-minute) presentation on the holiday of your choice. If possible, bring any special clothing, music, or pictures to show the class as you are describing the holiday.

**Example:**   This is a picture of the Passover celebration at my parents' home. My father is the man who. . . . He is wearing a yarmulke, which symbolizes . . .

**10**   Write definitions for the following words and expressions from American popular culture. You may need to ask people outside your class for help. When you prepare your definitions, use adjective clauses whenever possible. Then try to add one or two other expressions you are familiar with. Finally, work in small groups and share your definitions.

**Example:**   What is a yuppy?

A yuppy is a "young urban professional." It is someone who might be single or married, but who probably doesn't have children. It's a person who has a good job and a fair amount of money. . . .

| | |
|---|---|
| What is a potluck? | What is a skateboard? |
| What is a fender bender? | What is the tooth fairy? |
| What is a nerd? | What are "jammies"? |
| What are jelly beans? | What is leap year? |
| Who is Pokemon? | What was the Twist? |
| What is an all-nighter? | |

**11** Write at least three sentences describing one of your classmates. Use adjective clauses in your descriptions. Then, read your descriptions to the class, but don't say the person's name. Can the other students guess who you are describing? (Don't make your description too easy!)

**Example:** *I'm thinking of someone who is in this class. She's a woman who has been in this city only a few months. She's someone who wants to study business. I think she will succeed because she's responsible and hardworking.*

---

**PART 4**

# Clauses with *Whom* and *Which:* Replacement of Objects

## Setting the Context

**Prereading Questions**   The teachings of Jesus have had a tremendous impact on our world. What do you know about his teachings?

---

### Christianity

Christianity is based on the teachings of Jesus Christ, whom Christians call the "Son of God." At the same time, Christians commemorate Jesus as an actual historical figure. He was a man of lowly social standing who was unknown outside of the small part of the Roman Empire where he lived and died.

Jesus was born in Bethlehem, in Judea, in about 4 B.C.E.* and was raised in    5
Galilee, where he spent most of his short life. Little is known about Jesus' early years. Our knowledge of Jesus comes from the last three years of his life, which he spent preaching a doctrine of brotherly love and repentance. During these three years of teaching, he and his closest followers traveled throughout Palestine. Wherever Jesus went, he drew large crowds. Before long, he was known as    10
a healer, and people came from far and wide to ask his help.

As Jesus grew popular with the common people, who saw him as their long-awaited savior, he became a political threat. Within a short time, Jesus was arrested as a political rebel and was crucified.

---

**Discussing Ideas.**   Christianity has many different sects (or divisions). Are you familiar with any of them? Which?

---

*B.C.E.   before the common era

## A. Clauses with Whom and Which: *Replacement of Objects of Verbs*

The relative pronouns *who(m)* and *which* can replace the object of a verb in a simple sentence. *Whom* is used to refer to people only. Note that *whom* is used in formal speaking and writing; *who* is often substituted in informal English. *Which* is used to refer to things or ideas. *Which* must be used in nonrestrictive clauses (with commas). *That* is preferred in restrictive clauses (without commas) that describe things or ideas.

|  | **Examples** |
|---|---|
| **Simple Sentences** | **Dr. Gill** will teach a class on the early Christians. I met **Dr. Gill** last week. |
| **Complex Sentences** | Dr. Gill, **whom** I met last week, will teach a course on the early Christians. (formal) |
|  | Dr. Gill, **who** I met last week, will teach a course on the early Christians. (informal) |
| **Simple Sentences** | **History 410** covers early Roman history. Dr. Gill teaches **History 410.** |
| **Complex Sentence** | History 410, **which** Dr. Gill teaches, covers early Roman history. |

**1**   Underline the adjective clauses in the following sentences. Then decide whether the clauses are restrictive or nonrestrictive. Add commas if the clauses are nonrestrictive.

**Example:**   After Christ's death, the followers <u>whom Jesus had chosen</u> met privately.
*no commas needed*

1. Peter was a fisherman whom Jesus had selected to lead his new religion.
2. Peter whom Jesus had chosen as leader kept the followers together.
3. The followers of Jesus were Jews, and they believed in Judaism which they continued to practice.
4. Christianity as a separate religion actually began with Saint Paul whom many scholars consider to have been the main organizer of the new movement.
5. Both Peter and Paul were probably executed around 60 A.D. in Rome which Christians had made the center of the new religion.
6. At that time, only a small sect of "fanatics" believed in Christianity which most people ignored.
7. By 400 C.E., however, Christianity was the official religion of the Roman Empire which the Emperor Trajan had extended throughout the Mediterranean.
8. Today over 1 billion people believe in the group of religions which we call Christianity.
9. The largest denomination of Christianity is Roman Catholicism which has several hundred million followers.
10. In the latter part of the 20th century, many Christians returned to a literal interpretation of the Bible which is the basis of Christian belief.

**Culture Note**

*The United States began as a Christian country but now respects the variety of religions of its citizens. Most schools began the day with a Christian prayer until 1962, when the Supreme Court ruled against it. School prayer remains a controversial issue in the United States.*

**2**   Combine the following sentences by using *whom* or *which*. Form an adjective clause from the second sentence in each pair. Change words and add punctuation when necessary.

**Example:**   The word *holiday* actually came from the words *holy* (religious) and *day.* We use the word *holiday* to mean a vacation day.

*The word holiday, which we use to mean a vacation day, actually came from the words holy and day.*

Decorating a Christmas tree

1. Holidays such as Christmas have become more like social occasions than religious events. Christianity instituted Christmas.

2. Christmas originally honored only the birth of Jesus Christ. People of many religions now celebrate Christmas.

3. Perhaps the best-known character in the Christmas celebration today is Santa Claus. We see Santa Claus in every store window.

4. The symbol of Santa Claus came into being in 1822 in the poem *The Night Before Christmas.* Clement Clark Moore wrote this poem.

5. The Christmas tree is a popular tradition. German farmers began this tradition many, many years ago.

6. The custom of decorating the tree began in the 1800s. Bohemians started this custom.

7. The manger or nativity scene is one of the oldest Christmas symbols. St. Francis of Assisi first created a manger in 1223.

8. The birth of Jesus Christ marks the beginning of the Roman calendar. Much of the world uses the Roman calendar.

9. A Roman abbot and astronomer set Christ's birth as the beginning of the calendar. The Catholic Church commissioned this person.

10. Other calendars include the Islamic, the Chinese, and the Jewish calendars. Many groups or countries follow these calendars.

## B. Clauses with Whom *and* Which: *Replacement of Objects of Prepositions*

Relative pronouns may replace the object of a preposition. Several constructions are possible, depending on how formal or informal the statement should be. In formal English, the preposition begins the adjective clause. In informal English, the preposition usually follows the verb in the adjective clause. If the preposition begins the clause, *whom, which,* or *whose* must be used. In restrictive clauses with the preposition at the end, the relative pronoun may be dropped.

|  | **Examples** |
|---|---|
| **Simple Sentences** | **Dr. Church** teaches a course in Roman history. |
|  | I was introduced to **Dr. Church** yesterday. |
| **Complex Sentences** | Dr. Church, **to whom** I was introduced yesterday, teaches a course in Roman history. (*formal*) |
|  | Dr. Church, **who(m)** I was introduced **to** yesterday, teaches a course in Roman history. (*informal*) |
| **Simple Sentences** | **Bascom Hall** is the building. |
|  | The course is taught in **Bascom Hall.** |
| **Complex Sentences** | Bascom Hall is the building **in which** the course is taught. (*formal*) |
|  | Bascom Hall is the building **which** the course is taught **in.** (*informal*) |
|  | Bascom Hall is the building **that** the course is taught **in** (*or* **where** the course is taught). (*informal*) |
|  | Bascom Hall is the building **the course is taught in.** (*Note:* This construction is possible only with restrictive clauses with the preposition at the end.) |

**3**  Combine the following sentences by using *whom* or *which* with prepositions. Form adjective clauses from the second sentence in each pair. Use the adjective clause to modify the italicized word(s). Change words and add commas when necessary.

**Example:**  The Greek word *biblia* simply means "the books." The word *Bible* is derived from *biblia.*

*The Greek word biblia, from which the word Bible is derived, simply means "the books."*

1. The Bible is a collection of *books.* Both Christians and Jews take their doctrines from these books.
2. These books were written over a period of more than one thousand *years.* During that time, numerous authors contributed their own styles and perspectives.
3. The *Old Testament* is the longer of the Bible's two sections. Judaism is based on the Old Testament.
4. The Old Testament has given us many rules of behavior such as *the Ten Commandments.* Most Western legal codes are founded on the Ten Commandments.
5. The *New Testament* consists of 27 writings completed during the first century C.E. Christianity derives its teachings from the New Testament.
6. Its gospels, revelations, and letters were written by *many authors.* We get a variety of perspectives on the life and teachings of Jesus from these authors.
7. *The message of the gospels* is the central teaching of Christianity. Christians lead their lives according to this teaching.
8. Many politically active Christians base their work on *the New Testament.* The New Testament provides a justification for their actions.

**4**   **Review.**   Complete the following sentences by adding *which, whose, that,* or *X* to indicate that no relative pronoun is needed. Give all possibilities, but indicate the preferred form. Add commas when necessary.

1. The name *Christianity* _____ includes all Christian sects was not used during the lifetime of Jesus.

2. *Jesus* is the Greek name for Joshua _____ means "Jehovah is salvation" in Hebrew.

3. *Christ* comes from a Greek word _____ means "messiah" or "anointed one."

4. *Christ* was a name _____ the people of Antioch, Syria, gave to Jesus.

5. The ending *-ian* _____ comes from Latin was added to Christ.

6. The name *Christian* _____ was soon adopted by the followers of Jesus appeared in later portions of the New Testament.

7. Many words in Christianity come from Greek _____ the Romans used as the common language of their empire.

8. Greek was the language of the great missionary Saint Paul _____ thirteen letters (or *epistles*) are an important part of the New Testament.

**5**   **Review.**   Combine the following sentences by using *who, which, whose, that,* or *when.* Form adjective clauses from the second sentence in each pair. Omit or change words when necessary and pay close attention to punctuation.

1. Christianity consists of three major branches: Roman Catholic, Eastern Orthodox, and Protestant. Christianity has over 1 billion followers.

2. The largest branch is the Roman Catholic church. The Roman Catholic church is headed by the Pope, the bishop of Rome.

3. The origins of Christianity's major branches were two historic movements. The attempts of these movements to make reforms divided the Roman Catholic Church.

4. The second branch, Eastern Orthodox, dates from 1054. The "great schism" occurred between East and West (Greek and Latin Christianity) in 1054.

5. Actually, differences had begun centuries before 1054. These differences centered around authority and control.

6. The third branch developed from a sixteenth-century movement. The movement is called the Reformation.

7. The Protestant Reformation began as a protest against some practices. German Catholics opposed these practices.

8. Protestants had hoped to reform the Catholic Church. Protestants saw abuse of faith, power, and money in the Catholic Church.

9. The Protestant Reformation was led by Martin Luther. The Catholic Church excommunicated Martin Luther.

10. Martin Luther then founded his own religion. This religion became known as Lutheranism.

11. Eventually, other divisions led to the formation of over 250 Protestant sects. The divisions concerned specific beliefs and practices.

12. Lutheranism is the largest branch of Protestantism. The various churches of Protestantism are now loosely united by the World Council of Churches.

**6** Summarize the information given in the preceding activity by completing this sentence in your own words: *Christianity has three major branches: Roman Catholic, which . . . , . . .*

## Using What You've Learned

**7** Most religions and cultures have special ceremonies to mark important stages in life. Birth, adolescence, and death are commemorated in special ways around the world. In pairs or in small groups, discuss one or more of these ceremonies and prepare a brief presentation for the entire class. Make sure to include descriptions of actions, food, special clothing or music, and so forth.

**Example:**   *Baptism, or christening, is the ceremony that Christians use to welcome a child into the world and into the faith. The ceremony often uses a baptismal font, which is a large basin filled with holy water.*

**8** Think about the high points and low points of your life. Think about the best and worst, the most interesting, and the most frightening. Tell or write several brief stories about them. Following is some vocabulary to give you ideas. Begin your story with *The* (adjective + noun) *that (whom) I have ever . . .*

**Examples:**   The strangest dream that I have ever *had was when I was about seventeen . . .*

Or:   The most embarrassing situation that I have ever *been in was during eighth grade . . .*

Or:   The most interesting teacher whom I have ever *known was . . .*

| **Adjectives** | | **Nouns** | |
|---|---|---|---|
| best | funny | dream | person |
| bizarre | interesting | experience | situation |
| embarrassing | strange | friend | teacher |
| exciting | worst | meal | trip |
| frightening | | nightmare | |

| **PART 5** | # Clause to Phrase Reduction; Agreement with Adjective Phrases and Clauses |
|---|---|

## Setting the Context

**Prereading Questions**   Islam is the "youngest" of the five major world religions. What do you know about Islam? Who founded it? When?

---

### Islam

Beginning in Mecca about 610 C.E., Islam is the youngest of the great religions. It was founded by Muhammad, a respected and influential citizen of Mecca. Not feeling satisfied with success and security, Muhammad continued to search for answers to the many questions that bothered him. Finally, leaving friends and family, Muhammad sought the desert and its solitude. In the desert, an event   5 occurred which changed his life and affected the history of the world. According to Islamic tradition, on a lonely night, the angel Gabriel appeared to Muhammad. Muhammad returned from the desert to proclaim the words of Allah, revealed to him by the angel. This event began the religion we now call Islam.

---

Millions of pilgrims at midday prayer at the mosque in Mecca, Saudi Arabia.

A page from a 13th century Koran.

**Discussing Ideas.**   Most religions have some form of meditation. Many great thinkers have gone to the desert or the mountains in order to be alone, to think, and to search for answers. What is the role of solitude in this search?

## A. Appositives

Appositives are nouns or noun phrases that describe nouns. Nonrestrictive adjective clauses (clauses that use commas) can be shortened to appositives by eliminating the relative pronoun and the verb *be*. The order of the noun and the appositive can usually be reversed without affecting the meaning of the sentence. Appositives, like nonrestrictive clauses, are normally preceded—and may be followed—by commas.

|  | **Examples** |
|---|---|
| **Clause** | We recently met Dr. Carlson, **who is a professor of Islamic studies.** |
| **Appositive Phrases** | We recently met Dr. Carlson, **a professor of Islamic studies.** |
|  | We recently met a professor of Islamic studies, **Dr. Carlson.** |

**1**   In the following sentences, change the adjective clauses to appositive phrases.

**Example:**   The Koran, which is the sacred book of the Muslims, takes its name from the Arabic word meaning "recite."

*The Koran, the sacred book of the Muslims, takes its name from the Arabic word meaning "recite."*

1. The Koran is based on revelations to Muhammad, who was the founder of Islam.
2. The whole book, which is the length of the Christian New Testament, is memorized by many Muslims.
3. Those who memorize the Koran earn a special title, which is "Hafiz."
4. The first chapter, which is *Sura 1,* is the most common prayer among Muslims.
5. The followers of Islam, who are perhaps 600 million worldwide, say prayers from the Koran five times each day.

**2**   Summarize the information given in the preceding exercise by completing this sentence in your own words: *The Koran, . . .*

## B. Past Participial Phrases

Adjective clauses with verbs in the passive voice may be shortened to phrases that use the past participle. To form a phrase with a past participle, eliminate the relative pronoun and the verb *be* from an adjective clause.

|  | **Examples** |
|---|---|
| **Clause** | Dr. Carlson recently taught a course **that was called Islam and the Arts.** |
| **Phrase** | Dr. Carlson recently taught a course **called Islam and the Arts.** |

**3**   In the following sentences, change adjective clauses to phrases with past participles.

**Example:**   Muslims follow a set of rules and traditions that is called the "Five Pillars of Islam."

*Muslims follow a set of rules and traditions called the "Five Pillars of Islam."*

1. The *shahada,* which is repeated each day, is the Muslim's statement of faith.
2. The second pillar consists of prayers that are said five times a day while facing toward Mecca.
3. The third pillar is a donation of money that is determined by a Muslim's income.

4. The fourth pillar is to fast during the ninth month of the Muslim calendar, which is known as Ramadan.

5. The last pillar of Islam is a pilgrimage to Mecca, which is made at least one time in a person's life if health and finances permit.

## C. Present Participial Phrases

Some adjective clauses with verbs in the active voice may be shortened to phrases using present participles. The adjective clause must have *who, which,* or *that* in the subject position. To form a phrase, omit *who, which,* or *that* and use the present participle of the verb. The order of the noun and the phrase can often be reversed.

|  | **Examples** |
|---|---|
| **Clause** | Over 600 million people, **who represent** every race and continent, believe in Islam. |
| **Phrase** | Over 600 million people, **representing** every race and continent, believe in Islam. |
| **Clause** | Islam, **which began** in Arabia, spread quickly throughout the world. |
| **Phrases** | Islam, **beginning** in Arabia, spread quickly throughout the world. |
|  | **Beginning** in Arabia, Islam spread quickly throughout the world. |

**4** In the following sentences, change the adjective clauses to phrases with present participles.

**Example:** Islam, which spread from Spain to Indonesia, brought new art forms to many parts of the world.

*Islam, spreading from Spain to Indonesia, brought new art forms to many parts of the world.*

Or: *Spreading from Spain to Indonesia, Islam brought new art forms to many parts of the world.*

1. Islam contributed to numerous art forms, which included weaving, painting, metalwork, literature, and architecture.

2. Islamic architects, who followed the plan of Muhammad's seventh-century house in Medina, designed magnificent mosques such as the Great Mosque in Córdoba, Spain, and the Royal Mosque in Isfahan, Iran.

3. A Muslim who travels in a foreign country will find the same design in all mosques.

4. Mosques may be large or small, but they have the same design, which consists of an open courtyard and enclosed prayer halls.

5. Artisans who work with ceramic, wood, and metal have created magnificent decorations, such as at the mosque in Medina.

Interior of mosque dome, Córdoba, Spain

**5**   **Review.**   First, underline the appositive or participial phrase in each of the following sentences. Then expand the sentences by changing the phrases to adjective clauses.

**Example:**   Modern science owes a tremendous debt to the Islamic Empire, <u>the center of Western learning from the ninth to the fourteenth centuries.</u>

*Modern science owes a tremendous debt to the Islamic Empire, which was the center of Western learning from the ninth to the fourteenth centuries.*

1. Islam has given us the knowledge of Greek science, preserved and developed by the Muslims.
2. Much of Islam's scientific development was done at Baghdad, the capital of the Islamic Empire.
3. Caliph Ma'mum, ruler from 813 to 833, created the "House of Wisdom."
4. The House of Wisdom, containing a library, a translation bureau, and a school, was a sophisticated center of learning.
5. At the House of Wisdom, scholars studied Greek, Persian, and Indian scientific works translated into Arabic.
6. Scientists studying ancient Greek manuscripts developed the foundations for modern medicine.
7. Muslim scientists experimenting with a variety of laboratory techniques developed the foundation for modern chemistry.
8. In mathematics, Muslims gave us three extremely important ideas—the use of numerals, the decimal system, and the concept of zero.

## D. Agreement with Adjective Phrases and Clauses

The subject of a sentence determines if the verb should be singular or plural. Adjective phrases and clauses that come between the subject and verb do not affect the agreement. Adjective clauses are singular or plural, depending on the noun(s) they modify. In adjective clauses with their own subjects (object clauses), however, the subject and verb of the clause should agree.

|  | **Singular verb** | **Plural verb** |
|---|---|---|
| **With Adjective Phrases** | The **Koran,** the sacred book of the Muslims, **comes** from the Arabic word "recite." | **Muslims,** followers of Muhammad, **recite** from the Koran each day. |
| **With Adjective Clauses** | The **Koran,** which **is** the sacred book of the Muslims, **comes** from the Arabic word "recite."<br><br>*Sura I,* which **a believer** in Islam **recites** daily, comes from the Koran. | **Muslims,** who **are** followers of Muhammad, **recite** from the Koran each day.<br><br>*Sura I,* which **Muslims recite** daily, comes from the Koran. |

**6**   Choose the correct form of the verbs in parentheses to complete the following sentences.

1. The Koran, the sacred book of the Muslims, (take /(takes)) its name from the Arabic word meaning "recite."
2. Many scholars who study Christianity (consider / considers) St. Paul to have been the main organizer of Christianity as a separate religion.

**Culture Note**

*There are many Muslims in the United States. In addition, there are Black Muslims, who were originally members of the African American nationalist movement started in 1930, called the Nation of Islam. Malcom X, about whom a motion picture was made, was a significant political/religious figure in the 1960s in this movement.*

3. Peter, who was one of the fishermen, (was / were) chosen by Jesus to be a leader.

4. Traditionally, all rabbis were scholars whose knowledge (has / have) shaped modern Judaism.

5. Rituals that are explained in the Talmud (is / are) performed by many Jews every day.

6. Judaism, which is the parent of both Christianity and Islam, (is / are) the oldest of the world's three great monotheistic religions.

7. Muslims follow a set of rules and traditions that (is / are) called the "Five Pillars of Islam."

8. Mosques may be large or small, but they have the same design, which (consist / consists) of an open courtyard and enclosed prayer halls.

9. The House of Wisdom, containing a library, a translation bureau, and a school, (was / were) a sophisticated center of learning.

10. Santa Claus, whom we see in store windows and television commercials, (is / are) one of the most popular Christmas symbols.

## Using What You've Learned

**7** George Bernard Shaw said, "There is only one religion, though there are a hundred versions of it." After studying this chapter, do you agree with Shaw's thoughts? If this is true, why have the religions of the world created so many divisions among people? How would the world be different if everyone believed in only one religion? Use information from this chapter and your own ideas and opinions to write a short essay agreeing or disagreeing with Shaw's thoughts.

**8** How many adjective clauses can you put in one sentence? While this may be very poor writing style, it certainly is a test of your knowledge of adjective clauses!

First read the following attempt by one student. How many clauses do you find? (The answer is on page 330.) Then try an original one. *But remember that this is only for practice.* We do not recommend using dozens of adjective clauses in your sentences!

---

There was an old man who lived in Mexico City, which is the capital of Mexico, which is situated between North and South America, who had a big house that was surrounded by a large garden in which a lot of old trees grew and where sat the old Rolls-Royce, in which the old man had driven through the city until he had an accident in which he hurt his legs and arms, which were then put 5
in casts by a doctor who came from the hospital that had been built by the father of the old man who had the accident, and it is now the best hospital in Mexico, the one in which all the most talented surgeons work, most of whom come from the University of Mexico City, which has a large painting on its front wall that was done by Salvador Dali, who is a Spanish surrealistic painter and who is, unbelievably, 10
related to our old man who had the accident in Mexico City, which is, as mentioned above, the capital city of Mexico.

---

—Hans Jurgen

# Video Activities: People Skills

**Before You Watch.**   Discuss these questions in small groups.

1.   How do people greet each other in different cultures?

2.   Which of these do you think are "people skills"?

a. being a good listener        c. being a good actor
b. being athletic               d. being smart

**Watch.**   Answer the following questions.

1.   The reporter says that this is National _____ Month

a. People to People        b. Friendly People        c. People Skills

2.   Match the types of handshakes with the descriptions.

a. wimpy              1. too strong
b. bonecrusher        2. correct strength
c. perfect            3. too weak

3.   The telephone game shows that most people _____.

a. don't have good memories        c. aren't good listeners
b. don't speak clearly             d. aren't competitive

4.   Here is the message used in the telephone game. How did it change?

The Jenkins project will be put on hold for three weeks until Connie's digital
pager returns from the shop in Ohio.

_____

_____


**Watch Again.**   Compare answers in small groups.

1.   The man in the video thinks that his handshake is _____.

a. wimpy                b. perfect                c. a bonecrusher

2.   The man he shakes hands with thinks that it is _____.

a. wimpy                b. perfect                c. a bonecrusher

3.   What are the names of the people the woman has to remember?

_____    _____    _____

4.   The woman says, ". . . you put me on the spot!" She means that the reporter

_____.

a. tricked her
b. made her stand in the wrong place
c. asked her a difficult question

**After You Watch.**   Combine these sentences using *who* or *that*.

1.   People have "people skills." People have a lot of friends.
2.   This is the month. This month people should think about their listening skills.
3.   Telephone is a game. Telephone tests your listening skills.
4.   People can't remember names. People are at a disadvantage.
5.   The man is in the video. The man thinks he has a perfect handshake.

## Focus on Testing

### *Use of Adjective Clauses and Phrases*

Modifiers such as adjective phrases and clauses are frequently tested on standardized English proficiency exams. Review these commonly tested structures and check your understanding by completing the sample items that follow.

**Remember that . . .**

- *That* may not be used in nonrestrictive clauses (with commas).
- In formal English, *who* (not *that*) is preferred when describing people.
- In formal English, *whom* (not *who*) must be used with object clauses.
- When adjective clauses are reduced, the appropriate participle form must be used.
- Subjects and verbs must agree in number.

**Part 1:**   Circle the correct completion for the following.

**Example:**   John appears happy with his new boss, _____ is from Spain.

     a.   that           c.   whose
     b.   whom         (d.)  who

1.   *Hindu* is a word _____ Persians gave to the people of India.

     a.   that           c.   who
     b.   that was      d.   whose

2.   The Old Testament, _____ Judaism is based, is the longer of the Bible's two sections.

     a.   which        c.   on whom
     b.   on which     d.   what

3.   The gentleman _____ we were introduced is an archaeologist.

     a.   to whom      c.   who
     b.   whom        d.   to who

4.   The desert is the place _____ Mohammed meditated to find answers to his question.

     a.   which        c.   where
     b.   that which    d.   when

**Part 2:**   Circle the letter below the underlined word(s) containing an error.

**Example:**   <u>Overseas</u> travelers <u>often</u> experience culture shock, <u>which are a</u>
                      A                        B                                              Ⓒ
combination of <u>confusion</u>, frustration, and depression.
                          D

1.   *Nirvana* is the word <u>that</u> Hindus <u>use it</u> to <u>describe</u> <u>a</u> sense of inner peace.
                                    A                B            C          D

2.   Sociologists are researchers <u>who</u> <u>studies</u> the science of society, <u>along with</u>
                                               A        B                                           C
<u>its</u> social institutions and social relationships.
  D

3.   Mosques <u>may be</u> large or small, but <u>they</u> have the same design <u>consist of an</u>
                     A                                 B                                      C
open courtyard and <u>enclosed</u> prayer halls.
                                 D

4.   Christ, <u>born</u> a Jew, preached a message of brotherly love <u>that</u> <u>it</u> <u>is</u> now part
                    A                                                                   B     C   D
of Christianity.

# Chapter 10

# Crime and Punishment

# Introduction

In this chapter, you will look at the difference in expressing hopes, wishes, and dreams, in contrast to describing reality. To do so, you will review the modal auxiliaries, and you will study the verbs *hope* and *wish* and various conditional sentences.

The following passage introduces the chapter theme, "Crime and Punishment," and raises some of the topics and issues you will cover in the chapter. Note that many of the selections in this chapter come from people who have spent time in prisons for a variety of crimes—both violent and nonviolent.

### Crime in Our Society

Imagine what you would do if you were in the following situations. If you didn't have enough money to pay your income taxes, would you cheat on them? If you were drunk, would you drive your car? If you were the president of a corporation, would you allow your employees to dump waste into the ocean? Would you ever take something from a store without paying if you didn't have the money for it?  **5** Would you become violent if you were angry with your friends or family? These are just some examples of the types of situations in which people may make a decision that can lead to criminal behavior.

Why do people do things that are illegal and can hurt others? Criminologists suggest that the reason we have so much crime is that it is a symptom of other  **10** social problems, such as a poor educational system, lack of family values, unemployment, and drug use.

Everybody hopes that crime will decrease, but what can we do to prevent it? Some people wish that we had tougher judges and mandatory sentences for those people who break the law. Others wish that more tax money were spent to  **15** fight crime; they wish we had more police on the streets. Still others believe we need to work on changing society. These people hope that social change will lead to a reduction in crime. No matter how we choose to fight crime, everyone wishes we could feel safer in our homes and on the street.

**Discussing Ideas.**   In your opinion, what causes crime? If you were working on a crime prevention committee, what would you suggest we do to prevent crime?

## PART 1    *Hope* **and** *Wish*

## Setting the Context

**Prereading Question**   What does *doing time* mean?

### Doing Time

When I was a child, my ma* always talked about taking responsibility for your own actions. Sometimes I don't care anything about what she said, but many days I wish I'd listened to her and I'd thought about what she was trying to teach me.

---

*\*ma*   Mother, Mama

Here I am—doin' time in the joint.* I'm caged like an animal because I did some horrible things to some people who were probably nice. Sure, I wish I weren't here. Sure, I wish they'd never caught me.    5

But that ain't† all. I wish this life I've got now had never happened. I wish I'd done it differently. I wish I'd believed that someday I'd be responsible for what I'd done. I hope somebody will look at my life and will learn from it. I hope somebody will pay attention to the words of people like my ma.    10

I wish I'd known . . . I wish I'd listened. And I wish I were out on the street.

Phillip Moton, A Quad, California Men's Colony

**Discussing Ideas.**   Do you think that most prisoners have feelings such as Phillip Moton's? Why or why not?

## A. Hope *Versus* Wish

The verb *hope* is generally used to express optimism; the speaker feels that something is possible. The verb *wish* is often used to express impossibility or improbability; the speaker wants reality to be different than it is. To show the contrast to reality, *would, could,* or a special verb form—the subjunctive mood—is used after *wish*. The subjunctive mood shows that the ideas are imaginary, improbable, or contrary to fact.

|  | **Examples** | **Implied meaning** |
|---|---|---|
| **hope** | I **hope** (that) he **will visit** us. | It is quite possible that he'll visit us. |
| **wish** | I **wish** (that) he **would visit** us. | It is doubtful that he'll visit. |
| **hope** | I **hope** (that) they **are going.** | I think that they are going to go. |
| **wish** | I **wish** (that) they **were going.** | I don't think they're going to go. |

---

*\*the joint*   slang for *jail, the prison*
†*ain't*   slang for *am not, isn't,* or *aren't*

## B. The Subjunctive with Wish

Wishes are expressed by using *would, could,* or a subjunctive verb form in the dependent clause. For present and future wishes, in most cases the subjunctive is the same as the simple past tense. However, in formal English, *were* is used for all forms of the verb *be.* In informal English, *was* is often used with *I, he, she,* and *it,* although this is considered incorrect.

Past wishes are also expressed by using a subjunctive verb form in the dependent clause. In all cases, this form is the same as the past perfect tense (*had* + past participle).

| | **Examples** | **Implied Meaning** |
|---|---|---|
| **Wishes About the Future** | I **wish** (that) I **could go** home soon. | I can't go home soon. |
| | I **wish** (that) things **would change.** | Things probably won't change. |
| **Wishes About the Present** | I **wish** (that) I **weren't** here. | I am here, but I'm not happy about it. |
| | I **wish** (that) I **weren't living** here. | I am living here, but I don't like it. |
| | I **wish** (that) I **didn't have** to be here. | I have to be here, but I don't like it. |
| **Wishes About the Past** | I **wish** (that) my life **had gone** differently. | I don't like the way my life has gone. |
| | I **wish** (that) I **had been** good. | I wasn't good then, and I regret it. |

**1**    Underline the verbs in the dependent clauses, and indicate the time frame of each. Then rephrase each sentence to show its meaning.

**Examples:**    I wish I <u>were going</u> to see my family soon. *present-to-future*
            *(I'm not going to see my family soon, but I would like to.)*
            I wish that you <u>were</u> here. *present (You're not here, and I miss you.)*
            I wish that I <u>hadn't done</u> it. *past (I did it, but I regret it now.)*

1. I wish that I'd done a lot of things differently.
2. I wish I'd worked harder at my old job.
3. I wish I'd finished school.
4. I wish that my husband (wife) could find a better job.
5. I wish that I had more free time.
6. I wish that I were sleeping.
7. I wish I were living on a Caribbean island.
8. I wish that my friends lived closer to me.
9. I wish that I hadn't stolen the money.
10. I wish I had a better place to live.
11. I wish that my landlord would lower the rent.
12. I wish I could understand myself better.

**2**   Quickly reread the passage "Doing Time" on page 332. Underline the dependent clauses that follow the verbs *hope* and *wish*. Identify the verb(s) in these clauses and tell the time frame (past, present, or future) for each.

**3**   Anyone who is spending time in prison would most likely rather be somewhere else and be doing something else. Rephrase the following sentences to use *wish*.

**Example:**   I'd rather be with my friends.

*I wish I were with my friends.*

1. I'd rather be outside in the fresh air.
2. We'd rather be jogging.
3. I'd rather be home.
4. I'd rather be at the beach.
5. I'd rather be driving.
6. We'd rather be playing soccer.
7. I'd rather be with my children.
8. I'd rather be free.

**4**   In pairs, take turns making statements and responses.

**Example:**   My cousin graduated last year.
   A:   **My cousin graduated last year.**
   B:   **Don't you wish that you had graduated last year too?**
   A:   **Of course. (or: Not really.)**

1. My friend traveled around the world last year.
2. My sister will get married next year.
3. My brother got a scholarship at the university.
4. My father learned to speak German.
5. My mother is a computer whiz.
6. My brother-in-law is trilingual.
7. My nephew is a professional football player.
8. My cousin won the lottery!

**5**   The following are quotes from people who have been convicted of crimes and who have spent time in prison. Complete them by adding appropriate forms of the verbs in parentheses. Add modal auxiliaries when necessary.

1. You don't want to know about what I've done. I wish I __*had never done*__ it, that's
      _____(do/never)_____

   for sure. Look at me. Do I look like a criminal? No, but I am. I wish I

   _____ in prison, but that's only part of it. I wish I _____.
      (not/be)                                          (be born/never)

                                                        —Jack B., bank robber

2. I did something I believed was right. I still don't know if it was the right thing to

   do. I wish that I _____. I kidnapped someone. I kidnapped someone
                      (know)

important. I wanted to create a revolution because I wanted social justice. Here I am behind bars, and the revolution never came. I hope someday we _____
(have)
justice in our society. I wish I _____ the answers because what I did
(know)
hasn't seemed to help.

—Bill H., kidnapper

3.  I carried drugs across the border. For that, I got five years to life here in the U.S. I wish I _____ what was going to happen. I thought I was going to
    (know)
    make some money. Now here I am and my wife's alone with my kids and they don't even remember their father. I hope that someday they _____ me
    (love)
    again. I wish I _____ them. I am so sad and lonely.
    (see)

    —Ramón G., drug smuggler

4.  I killed some people, famous people. The family—we killed some people. I don't think about it much now. I have asked forgiveness from my God, and I hope he _____ me. Many people in the joint, we find religion. I found it here.
    (forgive)
    Today, I can hope that tomorrow I _____, tomorrow I _____.
    (sleep)                          (rest)
    I wish I _____ to be here, but it has led me to some hope.
    (not have)

    —Tex W., murderer

## Using What You've Learned

**6**   Each one of us has choices to make, and sometimes we make the wrong ones. Think of three bad choices you have made: in your studies, your career, or your personal life, for example. Looking back, what do you wish that you had done? Write a short paragraph telling what you wish had happened. Later, in a small group discussion, share your composition with your classmates.

**7**   Aladdin found his Genie of the Lamp. Imagine that you've found yours! What three wishes would you wish for? Orally or in writing, tell what you desire and why you'd like to make those particular wishes.

 **8**   North Americans love to put bumper stickers on their cars. One popular type of bumper sticker begins, "I'd rather be . . . ," meaning "I wish I were . . ." Such bumper stickers usually tell about our hobbies and interests. In pairs or small groups, create your own bumper stickers with *wish*. Try to create at least five slogans beginning with *I wish I were* or *I wish we were*.

**Examples:**   *We wish we were sailing.*
                  *We wish we could be studying more grammar.*

 **9**   The verbs *hope* and *wish* often represent the attitudes of the optimist and the pessimist. The optimist hopes that everything will work out, while the pessimist *wishes* it would. In small groups, write short dialogues that include people who are optimistic and people who are pessimistic. The dialogue may be serious or it may be comical. Here are some suggestions for topics:

1.   The menu at the dormitory tonight: Imagine that you all live in a dormitory. The food is almost always bad! Some of you would like to send the cook to the moon or at least to a cooking school. Yet a few of you try to be kind in your attitude toward the cook. You optimistically hope for a miracle.

2.   The first date with a new boyfriend / girlfriend: Imagine that you are going out with a new person tonight. You will have to meet his or her family, and you hope to make a good impression on everyone. You are worried about not saying and doing the right things. The people in the family are nervous too. You imagine that your evening could be a complete disaster, or perhaps it could be the beginning of a wonderful relationship.

Be sure to include a role for everyone in your group. After you have finished, role-play your dialogues for the class.

## PART 2

# Conditional Sentences: Present or Unspecified Time

## Setting the Context

**Prereading Questions**   Do you feel safe? What can you do to lower your risk of becoming a victim of crime?

### The Risk of Being a Victim

In a recent survey, 17 percent of the people interviewed said that at least one member of their household had been either a victim or a witness to a crime in the past year. However, if you had been a victim of a crime, it most likely wouldn't have been a violent one. Even though a violent crime is three times more likely to occur now than it was 30 years ago, today 94 percent of all crimes don't involve any   5
threat of violence. Most crimes are not the sensational type that become headlines or top stories on the evening news.

So what are your chances of being involved in a crime? If it were 1960 and you were living in the United States, the chances of your experiencing a crime would be low. Today, the odds of experiencing a crime vary. For example, if you   10
lived in an impoverished household, you would be at a greater risk than if you lived in a well-to-do household. If you were an adult, you would be less likely to be victimized than if you were a youth. If you used drugs and committed crimes yourself, you would raise your chances. Interestingly, the odds of being a victim are highest for criminals themselves.   15

**Discussing Ideas.**   Why do you think youths, criminals, and people living in poverty have the greatest chances of being victims of crimes? What does this tell us about how we can prevent crime?

## A. Otherwise

*Otherwise* is a transition that contrasts reality with wishes and dreams. It means "if the situation were different" or "under other circumstances." The auxiliaries *could, might,* and *would* are often used after *otherwise.* As with other transitions, a semicolon is used when two sentences are joined into one.

| Examples | Implied Meaning |
|---|---|
| I'm scared to walk alone at night; **otherwise,** I would go to the party. | I am scared to walk home alone at night, so I won't go to the party. |
| I don't have any money. **Otherwise,** I might buy a new car. | I don't have any money, so I can't buy a new car. |
| No one knows where the criminal is hiding. We could arrest him, **otherwise.*** | We don't know where the criminal is hiding. As a result, we cannot arrest him. |

*This placement of *otherwise* is informal. It is used in conversation only.

**1**   Complete the following sentences in your own words.

**Example:**   I don't have a car; otherwise, I could *take a trip to the mountains.*

1. I don't have much money this month. Otherwise, I might . . .
2. I have a lot of homework tonight; otherwise, we could . . .
3. The reviews of that movie weren't very good; otherwise, . . .
4. I have to work during vacation. Otherwise, . . .
5. I'm out of shape. Otherwise, I . . .
6. I'm afraid of the ocean; otherwise, . . .
7. My roommate is taking a test on Saturday. Otherwise, . . .
8. I don't know how to . . . ; otherwise, . . .

## B. Imaginary Conditionals: Present or Unspecified Time

Imaginary conditions express ideas that the speaker or writer thinks are unlikely, untrue, or contrary to fact. They may be wishes or dreams, or they may express advice to others. To show this, *could, might,* or *would* is used in the main clause, and a sub-junctive form is used in the *if* clause. In most cases, the subjunctive form is the same as the simple past tense, but with the verb *be, were* is used for all persons in formal English.

| Examples | Implied Meaning |
|---|---|
| If I **had** more money, I **could take** some trips. | I don't have much money, so I am not able to take many trips. |
| If I **were** rich, I **would** never **worry.** | I'm not rich, so I worry sometimes. |
| If I **were** you, I **would save** money. | My advice to you is that you should save money. |
| If I **was** you, I **would save** money.* | My advice to you is that you should save money. |

*This form is incorrect but is frequently used in conversation.

**2**   Combine the ideas in the following sentences by forming sentences with *if.* Use the example as a model.

**Example:**   I wish this town were stricter about drinking and driving. Then I wouldn't worry so much about driving at night.

*If this town were stricter about drinking and driving, I wouldn't worry so much about driving at night.*

1. I wish that there weren't so much crime in this neighborhood. Then I wouldn't feel so nervous about living here.
2. I wish the streets were safer here. Then I could walk home at night.
3. I wish that there weren't so many robberies. Then I wouldn't need five locks on my door.
4. I wish there were more police walking through this neighborhood. Then I would feel safer.
5. I wish that this town were stricter about drinking and driving. Then I wouldn't worry when I drive at night.

6.   I wish there weren't so many bike thefts. Then I could park my bike outside.

7.   I wish apartments weren't so expensive here. Then I could get a bigger place.

8.   I wish that I had a car. Then it would be much easier to get around.

**3**   Crime isn't the only way to get money or things without working long and hard. Imagine that the following situations happened to you through good luck. How would you feel? What would you do? What wouldn't you do? Make at least three statements for each, using *if* clauses.

**Example:**   Imagine that you were awarded a one-year scholarship at your school—all expenses paid.

*If I were awarded a scholarship, I would feel very proud.*

*If I had a full scholarship, my parents wouldn't have to send me more money.*

*If I didn't have to pay tuition, I could concentrate more on my work because I wouldn't be worried about money all the time.*

1.   Imagine that you were offered a special promotion by the phone company for one month's long distance calls—*free.*

2.   Imagine that you were the winner of a sweepstakes at your grocery store—for $500 worth of purchases.

3.   Imagine that you won a shopping spree at the mall—for everything you could purchase in three hours.

4.   Imagine that you had a winning ticket in the local lottery—for $10,000.

5.   Imagine that you won an unlimited mileage air pass from an international airline—for one month of travel to anywhere.

6.   Imagine that you hit the jackpot in Las Vegas—for $1 million.

**4**   We often use *If I were you* . . . instead of *you should* . . . or *you'd better* as a way of giving advice. In pairs, take turns giving advice for the following. If possible, give two pieces of advice for each.

**Example:**   A:   I often leave my room unlocked.

B:   **If I were you, I wouldn't do that. I would lock the door whenever I left.**

1.   I don't feel very safe in my apartment. The windows are very low, and the locks are not very good.

2.   I worry about parking my car on the street.

3.   I usually leave my backpack (briefcase, purse, and so on) in my office near my desk, but I often forget to lock the door when I go out.

4.   I often stay late at the lab. Sometimes I work until 12:30 or 1:00 A.M. and then I walk home by myself.

5.   All my important documents, such as my passport, are in a box in my closet, I think. I'm not really sure where I put them.

6.   I don't believe in banks, so I keep all my cash in my home.

## Using What You've Learned

**5**  Both crimes and punishments vary from culture to culture. Consider the following crimes:

| | | | |
|---|---|---|---|
| arson | drug possession | speeding | theft |
| assault | kidnapping | tax evasion | vandalism |
| burglary | littering | | |

Do you know how these crimes would be punished in your country? In small groups or as a class, share any information you have on your country's justice system.

**6**  Is crime a serious problem in your hometown or in the town where you live now? If you had the chance, how would you deal with the problem? In a short composition, explain how you would handle it. Begin with *If I were the chief of police in (your city)* . . . . Then, in pairs, small groups, or as a class, share your ideas.

**7**  Check your local newspaper, watch the television news, or listen to the radio. Make notes about any recent crimes. Come to class prepared to discuss crime in your town or in the nation.

**8**  Are you talkative, shy, impatient, calm? Are you a good listener? Do you have a good memory? Reflect for a moment on your personality. Is there anything about yourself that you'd like to change? What are some characteristics or traits that you wish you had? Are there any you wish you didn't have? Give several original sentences using *If I were* . . . or *If I weren't* . . . .

**Example:**   *If I weren't so careless, I would do better on tests.*

*If I were more patient, I'd have less stress.*

**9**  In a speech at Harvard University in 1953, future president of the United States John F. Kennedy said, "If more politicians knew poetry, and more poets knew politics, I am convinced the world would be a better place in which to live."

In your opinion, how might the world be a better place? Share your ideas in a discussion with your classmates or in a brief composition.

<hr>

**PART 3**   # Perfect Modal Auxiliaries

### Setting the Context

**Prereading Questions**   Crimes do not always involve hurting someone or damaging property. What other types of crime are there?

### Crimes Without Violence

*Wife:* I can't believe this!

*Husband:* What happened? What's wrong?

*Wife:* Someone must have gotten my credit card number and used it. I've got charges here that I never made!

*Husband:* But how could it have happened?                                                    5

*Wife:* Well, lately, I haven't asked for the carbon paper when I've made charges. Someone may have gotten my number out of a wastebasket in some store. Or maybe it happened because I gave my credit card information for an Internet auction. Do you remember those "Beanie Babies" I bought online? Somebody might have gotten access to my        10 account there. Oh, I should have been more careful. . . .

*Husband:* No matter what, these things shouldn't happen. It's wrong. Well, let's call the credit card company and put a stop on the card. . . .

Unfortunately, this scenario is not unusual. Worldwide, nonviolent but equally reproachable criminal acts take place all too frequently. These nonviolent crimes are often called white collar crimes. They do not hurt us physically, but they can have other terrible effects.

**Discussing Ideas.**   Have you ever been a victim of a nonviolent crime, such as the one described in the reading? What happened? What did you do about it?

## A. Perfect Modal Auxiliaries

Perfect modal auxiliaries express past activities or situations that were not real or that did not occur. Often, they express our wishes in hindsight.

| | Examples | Notes |
|---|---|---|
| **Unfulfilled Intentions and Preferences** | | |
| **would** | I **would have gone,** but it was impossible. | *Would have* refers to past intentions that were not fulfilled. |
| **would rather** | I **would rather have gone** with you than stay here. | *Would rather have* refers to past preferences that were not fulfilled. |
| **Unfulfilled Advice** | | |
| **should** | You **should have gone** too. | *Should have* and *ought to have* refer to actions that were advisable but did not take place. |
| **ought to** | He **ought to have stayed** longer. | *Ought to have* is less common than *should have*. |

**Culture Note**

*With the increasing use of telemarketing and the Internet for sales, consumer fraud is becoming more and more common. In 1997, the United States and Canada signed an agreement to work together on combating telemarketing fraud. In 1999, the U.S. Department of Justice also began its "Internet Fraud Initiative." Today, the most common types of fraud involve auctions or sales, business opportunities, work at home schemes, and identity issues (using someone else's identification, credit card number, and so on). You can get more information about these crimes and what to do if you are a victim at www.usdoj.gov/criminal/ fraud.*

| Past Possibilities | | |
|---|---|---|
| *could*<br>*might*<br>*may* | I **could have gone** later.<br>He **might have called.**<br>He **may have left** already. | *Could have, may have,* and *might have* refer to past possibilities. In many cases, the speaker or writer is uncertain whether the action took place. In some contexts, *could have* also refers to past abilities. |
| Past Probabilities | | |
| *must* | He **must have left.** | *Must have* refers to past probabilities. The speaker or writer is fairly certain that the action took place. |

*Note:* See Chart B on page 344 for more examples of unfulfilled advice (advice not taken).

**1** Quickly reread "Crimes Without Violence" on page 342. Underline all the modal auxiliaries in the passage and give the function and time frame of each.

**2** Change the modals to perfect forms in the following sentences. Then listen carefully as your teacher reads both the present and past forms rapidly. Try to distinguish between the two. What clues can you find to help you distinguish the two forms in rapid speech?

**Example:**   He may go to jail.
*He may have gone to jail.*

1. She may get fired.
2. Someone might steal your bike.
3. It must be dangerous to walk on that path.
4. He might cheat on his taxes.
5. John must be worried.
6. John should be more careful.
7. We could have a serious problem.
8. They may use someone else's credit card.
9. Sandy could have an accident.
10. Jim should think more about that.
11. They might rob a bank.
12. Debbie could do very well on the test.

**3** We often use responses with modal auxiliaries as a way of empathizing, saying that we understand how someone else feels. In pairs, take turns making statements and responses based on the model. Use *would (not) have* and *too* or *either* in your responses.

**Example:**   Someone found out my credit card number and used it. I was really shocked.
   A:   **Someone got my credit card number and used it. I was really shocked.**
   B:   **I would have been shocked too!**

1. Someone stole my bicycle. I felt just awful.
2. Someone broke into our apartment, and it scared me to death. I wasn't able to sleep for a week.

3. Another student took my ideas for a project. I was infuriated!

4. Someone sent me some threatening e-mails. I was scared and nervous.

5. Someone stole my purse with my address book in it. I felt terrible.

6. Someone got access to my computer and erased several files. I was furious.

7. Someone picked my pocket on the bus. I got so angry!

8. My landlord wouldn't fix the plumbing, so I had to pay the plumber. I was not very happy about that.

9. I had to go to the police station to file a complaint. I felt really nervous.

10. Someone on the Internet tried to get personal information about my son. I was so upset and worried.

**4**  In each of the following statements, a person had a problem but did something wrong to solve it. What could, should, or might the person have done instead? Give at least two alternative actions for each. Use *could have, should have,* or *might have* in your suggestions.

**Culture Note**

*With the spread of Internet use, online harassment and threats are, unfortunately, increasingly common. What can people do? Especially, what can parents do to protect their children? Contact www.fbi.org for more information and a copy of "Parents Guide to Internet Safety."*

**Example:**  Pedro didn't study for his math exam, so during the exam he cheated and copied down the answers from the test of the woman sitting next to him.

*He should have studied for his exam.*

*He could have tried his best on the exam.*

1. Jack was failing his history course and needed a high score on his final exam. The class was very large, and the final exam was given in a large hall. He paid someone to take his test for him.

2. Mary had a term paper due for a history class. She would fail the course if she didn't complete it. She did not finish her work, so instead, she bought a term paper from another student.

3. Taka did not want to pay for a book for his class, so he photocopied it chapter by chapter, even though the photocopies cost almost as much as the book.

4. Ravi didn't want to buy lots of CDs, so he downloaded hundreds of songs from the Internet. This was still technically legal, but then Ravi began to sell "pirate" CDs to his friends.

## B. Perfect Modal Auxiliaries and Past Advice

In the present, English has words to express advice, such as *ought to* and *should.* When you want to show that the advice was not taken in the past, use *ought (not) to have* + past participle or *should (not) have* + past participle.

| Present-to-Future Advice | Past Advice Not Taken |
|---|---|
| He **ought to go.** | He **ought to have gone.** |
| He **ought not to say** that. | He **ought not to have said** that. |
| He **should go.** | He **should have gone.** |
| He **should not say** that. | He **should not have said** that. |

*Note:* See Chart A on page 342 for more examples of unfulfilled advice (advice not taken).

**5**   In pairs, take turns making the following statements and responding to them. Use *should (not) have* or *ought (not) to have* in your responses. Then add a few original statements and your partner will respond to them.

**Example:**   A:   Eun didn't want to wrinkle her blouse, so she didn't wear her seatbelt.

B:   **She really should have worn her seatbelt.**

A:   **Yes, if she had worn her seatbelt, she might not have been injured in the accident.**

B:   **Right, maybe she would be home and not in the hospital right now.**

1.   Miki was in a hurry, so she parked her car in a "handicapped" zone.
2.   Bill wasn't paying attention and ran a red light. He almost hit another car.
3.   Dorothy didn't have any change, so she didn't put any money in the parking meter.
4.   Abdul didn't pay any of his parking tickets, and one day his car was impounded.
5.   While David was driving, he didn't notice his children were throwing candy wrappers out of the car window.
6.   Maria was late for an appointment, so she drove 50 miles per hour through a residential area in order to get to a highway.

**6**   Rephrase the following sentences to use *otherwise*. Use *may have, might have, could have,* or *would have* in your new sentences.

**Example:**   He was a dangerous criminal, so I was nervous to be near him.

*He was a dangerous criminal; otherwise, I wouldn't have been nervous to be near him.*

1.   There was a lot of crime in that part of town, so I didn't go there very often.
2.   The man knew she was a thief, so he didn't hire her.
3.   Her boyfriend never paid his parking tickets, so the police towed his car.
4.   I worry about Internet fraud; that's why I don't use my credit card to buy things online.
5.   There are so many social problems; that's why we have so much crime.
6.   The prisons are overcrowded, so we need to build more jails.

## Using What You've Learned

**7**   We often use *otherwise* to make excuses when we haven't done something. What haven't you done recently that you should have done? Think of at least six original sentences that use *otherwise* and perfect modals. Some ideas for topics are assignments, trips or vacations, calls or letters home, problems with a roommate or friend, cleaning, and fixing things.

**Example:**   *I didn't have much free time last weekend; otherwise, I would have written my family.*

**8** The American poet Robert Frost wrote about choices in his poem *The Road Not Taken.*

### The Road Not Taken
Two roads diverged in a yellow wood,
And sorry I could not travel both
And be one traveler, long as I stood
And looked down one as far as I could
To where it bent in the undergrowth;
Then took the other, as just as fair,
And having perhaps the better claim,
Because it was grassy and wanted wear;
Though as for that the passing there
Had worn them really about the same,
And both that morning equally lay
In leaves no step had trodden black.
Oh, I kept the first for another day!
Yet knowing how way leads on to way,
I doubted if I should ever come back.
I shall be telling this with a sigh
Somewhere ages and ages hence:
Two roads diverged in a wood, and I—
I took the one less traveled by,
And that has made all the difference.

What do you think Frost is telling us about choices in this poem? What does this poem tell us about his life?

Whenever we make a choice, it gives us new possibilities, but at the same time, it usually eliminates others. Think about the "crossroads" in life, when several "roads" are possible. In small groups, discuss some of these. You may want to use your ideas for the basis of a composition too.

---

**PART 4**

# Conditional Sentences:
# Past and Past-to-Present Time

---

## Setting the Context

**Prereading Questions**   Do you believe that abuse of the environment is a criminal act? Can you give any specific examples?

---

### Crimes Against Our Environment
Ok, it's true. We humans have made a mess of our world. We've committed many criminal acts against our environment. If we'd been a little smarter, if we had done more planning, if we hadn't been so greedy, our world would be a much better place. We wouldn't have created giant cities without efficient transportation systems. We wouldn't have polluted our air, land, and water. We wouldn't have let     **5**
people become so desperate that drugs and crime were their only escape. We

would have created healthy, *livable* cities that showed respect for humanity and for the environment.

Is it too late? Absolutely not! We got ourselves into this mess; we can certainly get ourselves out.

10

Jack Powers, age fortyish

**Discussing Ideas.** Can you give any examples of cases where individuals or companies have been found guilty of environmental crimes?

## A. Imaginary Conditionals: Past Time

Conditional sentences with *if* can be used to describe past situations or events that did *not* take place. A subjunctive form, which is the same as the past perfect tense, is used in the *if* clause, and perfect modal auxiliaries are used in the main clause.

| Examples | Implied Meaning |
|---|---|
| If I **hadn't needed** the money, I **wouldn't have done** that. | I did something because I needed the money. |
| We **would have taken** better care of our environment if we **had been** wiser. | We didn't take good care of our environment because we were not wise. |

**1**  Complete the following sentences with the appropriate form of the verbs in parentheses.

**Examples:**  If I have time, I <u>will go</u> (go) to the party.

If I had time, I <u>would go</u> (go) to the party.

If I had had time, I <u>would have gone</u> (go) to the party.

**Culture Note**

*In 1998, over seven billion pounds of hazardous waste was released by U.S. companies into the air, land, water, or underground. The primary releasers of toxins were metal mining and electrical utility companies. For its "Toxic Release Inventory" and information about your specific geographical area, contact the U.S. Environmental Protection Agency at www.epa.gov/enviro.*

1.  If she _____ (be) here, I'm sure she will help us.

    If she were here, I'm sure she _____ (help) us.

    If she _____ (be) here, I'm sure she would have helped us.

2.  If he _____ (want) a raise, he would have worked hard.

    If he wants a raise, he _____ (work) hard.

    If he wanted a raise, he _____ (work) hard.

3.  We _____ (visit) him in prison, if you tell us the address.

    We _____ (visit) him in prison, if you had told us the address.

    We _____ (visit) him in prison, if you told us the address.

4.  If they _____ (need) money, they will rob a bank.

    If they needed money, they _____ (rob) a bank.

    If they _____ (need) money, they would have robbed a bank.

5.  If I _____ (study) harder, I'd get better grades.

    If I _____ (study) harder, I'd have gotten better grades.

    If I _____ (study) harder, I'll get better grades.

## B. Imaginary Conditionals: Past-to-Present Time

Conditional sentences with *if* can be used to describe past actions or situations that have affected the present. A subjunctive form (*had* + past participle) is used in the *if* clause, and a simple modal auxiliary is used in the main clause.

| Examples | Implied Meaning |
|---|---|
| If we **hadn't bought** the house, we **might** still **be** in an apartment. | We bought a house, so we don't live in an apartment now. |
| If we **hadn't bought** the house, we **would** still **have** to pay rent. | We bought a house, so we don't have to pay rent. |
| We **would have** much less space if we **hadn't bought** the house. | We have much more space now because we bought a house. |

**2**  Imagine the following possible situations and how they might have affected your life. Complete the following sentences in your own words. Give at least two sentences for each item.

**Example:**   If I had been born a millionaire, . . .

> *If I had been born a millionaire, my money problems today would be completely different! I would have trouble spending it, not making it.*

1.   If I had never studied English, . . .
2.   If I had not come to this school, . . .
3.   If I had been born the opposite sex, . . .
4.   If I had been born thirty years ago, . . .
5.   If I had been elected president of my country ten years ago, . . .
6.   If I had gotten married at age 15, . . .

**3**   Imagine how our lives might be different today if these events had not occurred. Make notes in the following chart. Try to give at least one negative and one positive effect or result for each event. Then write complete sentences with *if*.

| | Negative | Positive |
|---|---|---|
| *example:* If internal combustion engines hadn't been developed, . . . | If internal combustion engines hadn't been developed, we wouldn't have cars, buses, and taxis. Transportation and travel would be much more difficult. | If they hadn't been developed, however, we also wouldn't have so much air pollution. |
| 1.   If petroleum hadn't been discovered, . . . | | |
| 2.   If cars hadn't been invented, . . . | | |
| 3.   If no one had invented paper clips, . . . | | |
| 4.   If zippers hadn't been created, . . . | | |
| 5.   If computers hadn't been invented, . . . | | |

**4**   Boston is a very "liveable" city. In recent years, many major improvements have been made. The following sentences tell about some of the changes that have made Boston more pleasant. Rewrite them to show what *might, could* or *would (not)* have occurred if things had been the opposite. Use clauses with *if* and appropriate modal auxiliaries.

**Example:**   Bostonians valued their past; as a result, they restored their historic buildings.

*If Bostonians had not valued their past, they would not have restored their historic buildings.*

1.   Bostonians were concerned about historic parts of the city; as a result, they fought very hard to preserve them.
2.   Bostonians cared about the beauty of the city; as a result, they preserved many historic areas.
3.   The city made major improvements in the old waterfront area; as a result, it is a great attraction today.
4.   The old waterfront warehouses in Boston were renovated; as a result, a wide variety of shops and restaurants opened there.
5.   The city developed parks and gardens along the harbor; as a result, the waterfront area is very attractive.
6.   The city needed new income to pay for some of the improvements; as a result, it tried to attract more tourists.
7.   Boston wanted to attract more visitors; as a result, it promoted the development of hotels and tourist facilities.
8.   The Boston community was very proud of its history and beauty; as a result, citizens invested in its preservation.

Faneuil Hall, a preserved historic
site in Boston

**5**   **Review.**   Complete the following passage with the appropriate forms of the verbs in parentheses. Be sure to add modal auxiliaries when necessary. The first one is done as an example.

## City Living

My name's Mario. I live in a big city. It's a beautiful city in a lot of ways, but our neigh-

borhood is pretty tough. I wish things _____*were*_____ a lot different. For example, I
                                              1 (be)

live a long way from school. I wish that I _____ to get up at 6:00 A.M. to take
                                              2 (not have)

a bus to school. I wish my school _____ right next door. And I wish the
                                        3 (be)

whole neighborhood _____ nicer and cleaner. I wish people _____
                          4 (be)                                              5 (clean)

up around here—and not just the garbage! I wish there _____ any drugs
                                                            6 (not be)

on the streets. I wish I _____ out alone at night. Sometimes I wish that my
                            7 (go)

parents _____ here. I hope things _____. I hope I _____
          8 (never move)                        9 (change)              10 (go)

to college and help my family.

**6**   **Review.**   First read the following passage for meaning. Then choose the appropriate form from the words in parentheses to complete the passage.

## Los Angeles

At the beginning of this century, Los Angeles ((was)/were) a sleepy little town, and
                                              1

even as recently as the 1950s and early 1960s, there (was/(were)) farms and
                                                          2

orchards close to our house. Gardens (thrived/had thrived) here, and you
                                          3

(could find/could have found) an incredible variety of exotic plants and shrubs. Of
  4

course, there (wasn't/weren't) any freeways, and there (used to be/used to being) a
                    5                                      6

good transportation system of electric trains. The air (was usually/usually was) very
                                                            7

clear, and as a young child, I (could see/could have seen) the mountains to the north
                                    8

and east almost every day.

     Now, we (get/have got) freeways, traffic, and pollution. What a shame! If you
                  9

(had seen/would have seen) Los Angeles forty years ago, you (had been/would
    10                                                            11

have been) amazed.

     If the city (knew/had known) what (was/was going to) happen. . . . If Los
                      12                      13

Angeles (kept/had kept) its train system, we (might/should) have avoided some of
            14                                      15

the traffic problems. If city planners (had only thought/had thought only) more about
                                            16

the future, they could (have put/had put) more money into public transportation. If
                                      17

fewer people (have/had) moved to southern California, the population wouldn't have
                  18

(grew/grown) so fast. If L.A. (didn't grow/hadn't grown) so fast, we (might not have/
  19                                    20                                          21

might not have had) so many problems today. No one (anticipates/anticipated) all
                                                                    22

these things; otherwise, we (had been/might have been) a lot more careful. I certainly
                                          23

(hope/wish) that we (had/had had) better foresight and planning. I (hope/wish) that
  24                    25                                                    26

things (will improve/would improve) in the future. Otherwise, we (might have/might
                      27                                                            28

have had) even worse problems in the upcoming years.

—Debra Love, 49, second-generation native of Los Angeles

## Using What You've Learned

**7**  Think about your hometown or the town where you are living now. Have changes
taken place in recent years? Have these been good or bad? What if these changes
hadn't taken place? What would your area be like? Make at least four statements using
conditional sentences with both past and present time.

**8**  "What if" you had been born at a different time? How would your life be different?
"What if" you had been born in a different place? How would your life be different
today? Test your knowledge in a game like Trivial Pursuit. Separate into four different
groups. In your groups, make up questions about history, geography, languages, social
customs, and so on. (Be sure that you know the answers!) The questions should use
clauses with *if.*

**Example:**    *If you had lived in London in 1900, who would have been the ruler of your
country? (Queen Victoria)*

*If you had been in Buenos Aires in 1930, what kind of music might you have
listened to? (tangos)*

When you have prepared eight to ten questions, get together with another group.
Take turns asking the other group members your questions and answering theirs. Keep
a count of correct answers, and the group with the highest score wins.

**9**  As a class or individually, see the video "Life on Death Row," *Amazing Stories,* by
Steven Spielberg. Discuss the video and then write a brief summary of it or your reactions to it.

**10**  Read the following passage, and think about *second chances,* the opportunities to try
again.

### If I Had My Life to Do Over

I'd make a few more mistakes next time. I'd relax. I would limber up. I would be sillier than I had been this trip. I would take fewer things seriously. I would climb more mountains and swim more rivers. I would eat more ice cream and fewer beans. I would perhaps have more actual troubles, but I'd have fewer imaginary ones. **5**

You see, I'm one of those people who live sensibly and sanely hour after hour, day after day. Oh, I've had my moments, and if I had it to do over again, I'd **10** have more of them. In fact, I'd try to have nothing else. Just moments, one after another, instead of living so many years ahead of each day. I've been one of those persons who never goes anywhere without a hot water bottle and a parachute. If I had it to do again, I would travel lighter.

If I had my life to do over again, I would start barefoot earlier in the spring and **15** stay that way later in the fall. I would go to more dances. I would ride more merry-go-rounds. I would pick more daisies.

Nadine Stair, 85, Louisville, Kentucky

Is this passage about reality or dreams? How do you know? Look at the title of this passage. What verb is used? Does it refer to the past or the present? Most of the passage is written in the conditional with *would*. What is the meaning of *would* in these sentences?

Are there things you would do differently if you had the chance? Tell or write about your ideas.

## Video Activities: Victim Support Groups

**Before You Watch.**   Discuss these questions in small groups.

1. What do you think a support group is? Who is in it? What is the purpose of the group?
2. What murder cases have you heard about? What was the punishment? Do you think it was fair?
3. In most countries, convicted criminals have the right to appeal their conviction. What do you think *appeal* means?

**Watch.**   Answer the following questions.

1. The video is about a support group for _____.
   a. families of murderers        c. families of murder victims
   b. murder victims               d. murderers
2. Who are the "monsters" referred to in the video? _____
3. According to Susan Field, how is murder different from a natural death for the victim's family?

a. The grief period is longer.
b. They feel angrier.
c. There is a lot of publicity.
d. They have had no time to prepare for it.
e. They have to deal with the judicial system.

4. According to Jim Roche, what should the United States Supreme Court do to help the families of murder victims?
   a. Put more murderers in prison.
   b. Change the appeal process.
   c. Stop all appeals.
   d. Get rid of the death penalty.

5. According to Kate Elke, execution is state law and it should be _____.
   a. changed                b. abolished                c. enforced

**Watch Again.**   Compare answers in small groups.

1. Write these names in the correct row.

| Ron Russe | Susan Fisher | Linda Ricio | Virgina Allen |
| Pamela Allen | Sammy Smith | Kate Elke | Jim Roche |

**Murder Victims**               _____   _____
**Murderer**                     _____
**Relatives of Murder Victims**  _____   _____   _____
**Government Officials**         _____   _____

**After You Watch.**   Match the two columns to make sentences.

1. If John hadn't been murdered,
2. If you commit murder,
3. If a murderer isn't punished,
4. If your family member is killed,
5. If the Supreme Court shortens the appeals process,

a. the family often feels angry.
b. you should join a support group.
c. today would have been his 40th birthday.
d. murderers will die sooner.
e. you might receive a death sentence.

## Focus on Testing

### Use of Conditional and Subjunctive Forms

Conditional and subjunctive forms of verbs are frequently tested on standardized English proficiency exams. Review these commonly tested structures and check your understanding by completing the sample items that follow.

**Remember that . . .**

■ *Hope* is followed by an indicative verb form but *wish* is generally followed by a subjunctive form.

■ In formal English, *were* (not *was*) is used with *I, he, she,* and *it* in present *if* clauses.

■ In formal English, modal auxiliaries are used in *if* clauses only in specific cases.

**Part 1:**   Circle the correct completion for the following.

**Example:**   John wishes that his boss _____ him a long vacation.

    a.   gave                          c.   will give
    (b.)  would give                  d.   was giving

1.   If she _____ chosen to study in San Francisco, she would have had to find a new house.

    a.   has                          c.   will have
    b.   would have               d.   had

2.   If Los Angeles had not dismantled its system of electric trains, mass transportation there _____ better today.

    a.   might be                  c.   might have been
    b.   might                    d.   might had been

3.   John's roommate wishes that John _____ a set of drums.

    a.   would never have bought     c.   had never bought
    b.   would have never bought     d.   never bought

4.   Al has used up all of his vacation time _____ to Mexico with us.

    a.   ; otherwise, he would go     c.   ; otherwise, he will go
    b.   , otherwise, he would go     d.   . Otherwise, he will go

**Part 2:**   Circle the letter below the underlined word(s) containing an error.

**Example:**   It's a good idea <u>for overseas</u> travelers <u>to know</u> something of the
                      A                 B

language of the new country; <u>otherwise</u>, they <u>might have had</u> many
                           C             (D)

difficulties in adapting.

1.   If Einstein, <u>perhaps</u> the greatest scientist of the twentieth century,
              A

<u>did not propose</u> his theories of <u>atomic</u> structure, production of the atomic
    B                 C

bomb <u>might have been delayed</u> another ten or fifteen years.
        D

2.   Companies <u>may have</u> <u>respond</u> more quickly if the United States
            A     B

<u>had imposed</u> stricter penalties for pollution much <u>earlier on</u>.
    C                                D

3.   One of <u>the greatest</u> wishes of <u>humans</u> today is that we
          A             B

<u>could have discovered</u> a cure for cancer in <u>the next few</u> years.
    C                          D

4.   <u>It is hoped</u> <u>that</u> computerized health care <u>would help</u> to reduce the mistakes
    A    B                       C

that are currently <u>being made</u>—causing injuries to about 20 percent of U.S.
              D

patients.

# Chapter 11

# The Physical World

# Introduction

In this chapter, you will study compound and complex sentences that show cause, comparison, contrast, effect or result, and purpose. As you study the chapter, note the relationships between ideas and the variety of ways these relationships can be expressed. Also pay attention to the ways these sentences are punctuated and how the sentence focus can change, depending on the choice of connecting word. The following passage introduces the chapter theme, "The Physical World," and raises some of the topics and issues you will cover in the chapter.

### The Hydrologic Cycle

Every day, approximately 4 trillion gallons of fresh rainwater or snow falls on the United States. Americans use only one-tenth of this fresh water, and most of the water returns to the system, to be recycled and used again. The renewal process is called the *hydrologic cycle*. Each day the sun evaporates* 1 trillion tons of water from the oceans and land and lifts it as vapor into the atmosphere. This is the greatest physical force at work on earth.  **5**

Nevertheless, the United States, as well as most of the world, faces serious water problems, of both quality and quantity. Because rain and snow do not fall evenly across the land, the western United States, with 60 percent of the land, receives only 25 percent of its moisture. Although the East receives a tremendous  **10** amount of moisture, it faces problems of quality. Because of large population centers, old sewage systems,† and pollution, most of the East—from New England to Florida—faces a lack of *clean* water.

As the U.S. population grows, demands for clean water will be greater than ever before. Even if an increased population uses the same amount of water as we do  **15** now, the United States will face severe shortages. Because water—clean water—is essential to all life, we must begin now to care for this resource adequately.

**Discussing Ideas.**   In the area where you live, what are the primary sources of water for human use? Is the water supply adequate for the population?

## PART 1

# Clauses and Related Structures of Cause, Purpose, and Effect or Result

## Setting the Context

**Prereading Questions**   What is the climate of the area where you live now? What is the climate of your hometown or region?

---

*\*evaporates*   changes from liquid to gas
*†sewage systems*   water purification systems

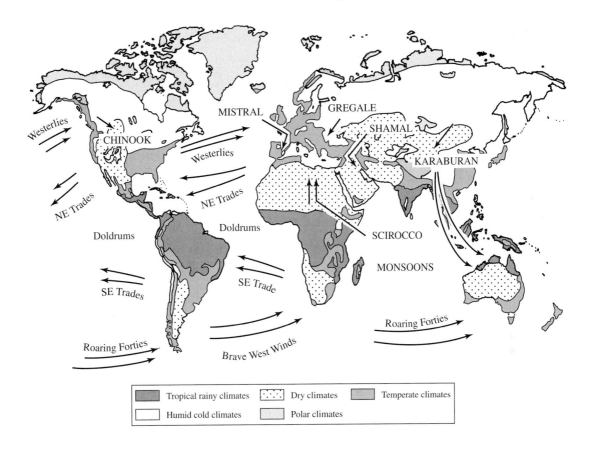

| | | | | | |
|---|---|---|---|---|---|
| ■ | Tropical rainy climates | ⋯ | Dry climates | ■ | Temperate climates |
| □ | Humid cold climates | ■ | Polar climates | | |

## World Weather Patterns

Because all weather is interconnected, a change in one area affects other areas. Today, scientists collect information worldwide so that they can understand and predict changes in the weather more accurately. Due to technological advances in the last several decades, meteorologists can now gather detailed information on cloud cover, precipitation, temperature changes, wind speed and direction,    **5** and energy from both the sun and earth.

This collection of data reveals some interesting facts. For example, winds in one region are accompanied by opposite winds in another; therefore, if north winds are extremely cold in one part of the world, south winds are abnormally warm in another part. Since winds affect precipitation, changes in wind patterns    **10** alter the amount of rainfall.

**Discussing Ideas.**   What kinds of data do scientists collect to study the weather? Why is it important to have information about weather from other parts of the world?

## A. Clauses and Phrases of Cause

|  | Examples | Notes |
|---|---|---|
| **With Clauses**<br>**because**<br><br>**since** | **Because** there was a drought, Californians had many problems with water.<br>California had many problems with water **since** there was a drought. | Most adverb clauses may begin or end sentences. Introductory clauses are generally followed by a comma. A comma is not usually used when the main clause begins the sentence. |
| **With Phrases**<br>**because of**<br><br>**due to** | **Because of** the drought, California had many water shortages.<br>California had many water shortages **due to** the drought. | Prepositions are followed by phrases, *not* clauses. A comma is generally used after an introductory phrase. |

**1**  Complete the following in your own words.

**Example:**   Because the weather was terrible, *I decided to stay home and study.*

1. Because of the high winds . . .
2. Due to the dry climate . . .
3. Because the weather was great . . .
4. The highway was closed because . . .
5. Classes were cancelled due to . . .
6. . . . since the rains flooded the streets.
7. . . . due to the freezing temperatures.
8. . . . because of the danger of tornadoes.
9. . . . because the hurricane destroyed the bridge.
10. Because of the drought . . .

**2**  Complete the following passage by adding *because, because of, due to,* and *since*. Use each word once.

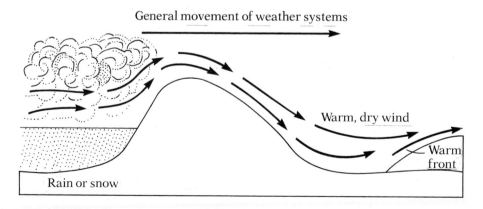

General movement of weather systems

Warm, dry wind

Warm front

Rain or snow

### Mountains and Weather

_____ their height, mountains are important in the making of weather. When
1

moisture-filled air encounters mountains, it is forced upward. _____ the air cools
2

at higher altitudes, water vapor in the air turns to rain or snow. By the time the air

passes over the mountaintops it has lost its moisture.

_____ the air is much cooler and thinner then, it sinks. _____ the
3                                                              4

dryness of these downward winds, Native Americans in the western United States call

them "snow eaters." They can evaporate snow at the rate of two feet a day.

## B. Clauses and Phrases of Purpose

|  | Examples | Notes |
|---|---|---|
| **With Clauses**<br>**so that** | During droughts, governments often set monthly limits **so that** they can control water use.<br>Los Angeles set limits **so that** it could control water use. | *So that* is used only between clauses. Clauses with *so that* use modal auxiliaries *(can, could, may, might, will, would)*. Commas are not used with *so that*. |
| **With Phrases**<br>**in order to** | The city has begun rationing **in order to** conserve more water.<br>The city has begun rationing **to** conserve more water. | In written English, *in order to* is used more frequently than *so that*. *In order* can usually be omitted; using *in order* emphasizes the idea of purpose. |

*Note: That* is sometimes omitted and *so* is used alone in conversational English. Do not confuse *so (that)*, meaning purpose, with the conjunction *so*, meaning result. Compare: *I went to the store so (that) I could buy bread.* (purpose) *I needed bread, so I went to the store.* (result)

**3**   Complete the following passage by adding *so that* or *in order to.*

### El Niño and La Niña

In recent years, the public has been made aware of the effects that El Niño and La Niña

have on the world's weather. El Niño is the warming of water in the Pacific Ocean. A

change in water temperature disrupts the food chain of fish, birds, and sea mam-

mals. During the years of El Niño, these creatures have to struggle greatly for food

_____ they can survive. It changes weather inland, too. For example, meteorolo-
1

gists in the Southern United States have needed to be more alert _____ predict
2

the more frequently occurring thunderstorms and tornadoes that El Niño brings.

La Niña is the cooling of water in the Pacific Ocean. In the Atlantic Ocean, La

Niña is associated with an increase in the number of hurricanes. Therefore, ships have

to schedule trans-Atlantic crossings carefully _____ keep away from these awful
3

storms. Farmers in the southwest of the United States have had to plan irrigation better

_____ the droughts that La Niña brings will not ruin their crops. Researchers are
4

studying underwater volcanoes _____ to learn the role that they play in creating
5

El Niño and La Niña. Perhaps one day these powerful negative influences on the

world's weather can be controlled _____ lives and crops can be saved from
6

harm.

**Culture Note**

*The United States has the most tornadoes of any country. Most occur in an area called "Tornado Alley" in the Midwest. Tornadoes are classified on the "F" scale. An F5 tornado, the strongest, has wind gusts clocked at between 260 and 300 miles per hour. In the United States, 75 percent of hurricanes are F0 or F1 and only one percent are F5.*

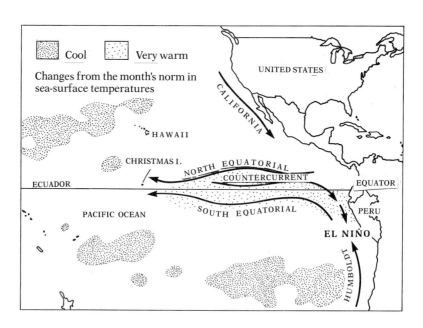

**4**  In the following sentences, change *so that* to *in order to* or *in order to* to *so that*. Make all other necessary changes.

**Example:**  Meteorologists collect data in order to find patterns in the weather.

*Meteorologists collect data so that they can find patterns in the weather.*

1. Meteorologists study mountainous regions so that they can learn how mountains affect weather.
2. Meteorologists take smog samples in order to study the effects of air pollution on weather.
3. Meteorologists work with oceanographers and geologists so that they can understand the roles of oceans and land formations in weather.
4. Scientists fly into the eye of a hurricane in order to make observations and take measurements.
5. Geologists gather rock samples in order to analyze the earth's crust.
6. Astronomers use high-powered telescopes in order to view distant stars.
7. Oceanographers analyze ocean currents and temperatures so that they can understand changes in fish population.
8. Volcanologists study volcanoes so that they can predict dangerous eruptions.

**5** Complete the following eight items in your own words.

**Example:** Astronomers use telescopes so that _they can see farther into the sky_.

1. Doctors use stethoscopes so that . . .
2. Doctors take X rays in order to . . .
3. Dentists use drills in order to . . .
4. Plumbers use wrenches so that . . .
5. People use computers in order to . . .
6. People use telescopes so that . . .
7. People use calculators in order to . . .
8. I bought a computer so that . . .
9. People use dictionaries in order to . . .
10. I bought a good dictionary so that . . .

## C. Transitions of Effect or Result

|  | **Examples** | **Notes** |
| --- | --- | --- |
| consequently<br>therefore<br>thus<br>as a result<br>for this reason<br>for that reason | During the drought, rainfall was far below normal; **therefore,** farm production fell dramatically.<br>Rainfall was far below normal. **Consequently,** farmers lost many crops.<br>Everyone used less water. **As a result,** we were able to survive the drought. | Transitions may be used to relate the ideas in two different sentences, or they may be used with a semicolon (;) in a compound sentence. *Consequently, thus,* and *therefore* are more common in formal English. The other transitions are used in both formal and informal English. |

**6**   Change the following sentences from complex to compound. Rewrite them to use *consequently, therefore, thus, as a result,* and *for this reason.* Use each transition once.

**Example:**   Because the equator is closest to the sun, the atmosphere there absorbs the most solar energy.

*The equator is closest to the sun; consequently, the atmosphere there absorbs the most solar energy.*

1.   Because the air at the equator absorbs the most solar energy, it is much hotter than the air near the poles.
2.   Since hot air rises, low-pressure areas develop at the equator.
3.   Because low-pressure areas are like holes in the atmosphere, cold air moves in from the poles to fill them.
4.   Because this pattern is a cycle, air almost always moves toward the equator on the surface and away from it at high altitudes.
5.   Since hot and cold air flow in this cycle, our atmosphere is continually in motion.
6.   Because our atmosphere is always in motion, our weather changes frequently.
7.   Since this cycle is important yet easy to understand, it is often taught in schools.
8.   Because of computer technology, students can view simulations that more clearly illustrate the cycle.

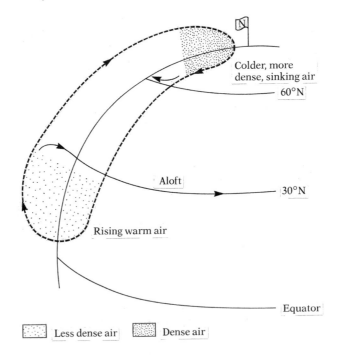

## D. Sentence Focus in Compound and Complex Sentences

In complex sentences, the main clause usually carries the idea that the speaker or writer wants to emphasize. The main clause is, therefore, the focus of most complex sentences. It gives the topic or main idea, while the subordinating clause gives additional information. In contrast, in compound sentences, both clauses generally have equal importance. Compare the following:

| Examples | Focus |
|---|---|
| **Complex Sentences** | |
| Because there was a drought, California had serious water shortages. | serious water shortages in California |
| Because California was experiencing water shortages, the state imposed limits on daily consumption. | limits imposed by the state on daily consumption |
| **Compound Sentence** | |
| California suffered from a long drought; therefore, the state had serious water shortages. | the long drought in California **and** the serious water shortages. |

**7**   Read the following sets of sentences and underline the main clause in each. With a partner, discuss the differences in focus in each set. In some cases, there may be only main clauses.

**Example:**   The equator is closest to the sun; therefore, the atmosphere around it absorbs the most solar energy.

*Focus: both the equator and the atmosphere around it*

Since the equator is closest to the sun, the atmosphere around it absorbs the most solar energy.

*Focus: the atmosphere around the equator and the energy it absorbs*

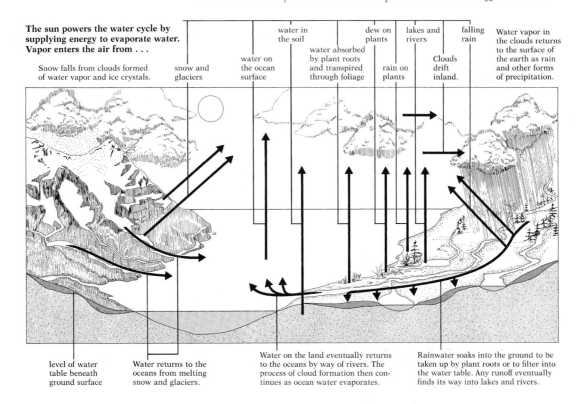

**The sun powers the water cycle by supplying energy to evaporate water. Vapor enters the air from . . .**

Snow falls from clouds formed of water vapor and ice crystals.

snow and glaciers

water in the soil

water on the ocean surface

water absorbed by plant roots and transpired through foliage

dew on plants

rain on plants

lakes and rivers

Clouds drift inland.

falling rain

Water vapor in the clouds returns to the surface of the earth as rain and other forms of precipitation.

level of water table beneath ground surface

Water returns to the oceans from melting snow and glaciers.

Water on the land eventually returns to the oceans by way of rivers. The process of cloud formation then continues as ocean water evaporates.

Rainwater soaks into the ground to be taken up by plant roots or to filter into the water table. Any runoff eventually finds its way into lakes and rivers.

1.  Since hot and cold air flow in a cycle, our atmosphere is continually in motion.
    Hot and cold air flow in a cycle; as a result, our atmosphere is continually in motion.
2.  Because air cools at higher altitudes, water vapor in the air turns into rain or snow.
    Air cools at higher altitudes; therefore, water vapor in the air turns into rain or snow.
3.  Meteorologists study mountainous regions to learn their effect on weather.
    Meteorologists study mountainous regions so that they can learn the effect of mountains on weather.
4.  The mountains in California absorb much of the moisture coming from the Pacific Ocean; as a result, the states to the east—Utah, Nevada, and Arizona—are extremely dry.
    Because the California mountains absorb much of the moisture from the Pacific Ocean, the states to the east—Utah, Nevada, and Arizona—are extremely dry.
5.  Due to its scarcity in many populated areas, control of water is becoming a major political and economic issue worldwide.
    Fresh water is scarce in many populated areas; consequently, control of this valuable resource is becoming a major political and economical issue worldwide.

**8**  Complete the following sentences in your own words.

**Example:**   We had to cancel the soccer games due to *the terrible weather.*

1.  In extremely cold weather, you shouldn't stay outside for very long because . . .
2.  During electrical storms, it is not recommended to be in open areas due to . . .
3.  When a tornado has been spotted, people are told to take cover in their basements so that . . .
4.  I wouldn't like to live near a volcano because . . .
5.  That region is suffering from a serious drought. Therefore, . . .
6.  She studied meteorology because of . . .
7.  During a flood, people often use sand bags in order to . . .
8.  Air pollution can strongly affect the elderly and the very young. For this reason, . . .

**9**  Combine the following sentences, using *because, since, therefore, thus, as a result, consequently,* and *for this reason.* Use each at least once. Change words and add punctuation when necessary.

**Example:**   The rotation of the earth and its atmosphere affects air patterns. Air does not move directly north and south.

*The rotation of the earth and its atmosphere affects air patterns; as a result, air does not move directly north and south.*

1.  Outer space is frictionless. The earth's atmosphere moves at the same speed as the earth.
2.  The earth's circumference at the equator is almost 25,000 miles. The air at the equator travels 25,000 miles each day.

**Culture Note**

*The strongest hurricane in the Western Hemisphere was Hurricane Gilbert, which devastated Jamaica and parts of Mexico in 1988. In 1992 in the United States, Hurricane Andrew caused 15.5 billion dollars in damage and left 50 people dead and thousands homeless.*

3.   There is little surface wind at the equator. The earth and the air move at the same speed.

4.   Away from the equator, the surface speed of the earth decreases. The earth's circumference grows smaller toward the two poles.

5.   Away from the equator, the air and the earth do not move at the same speed. The mid latitude winds are born.

6.   The earth's surface often affects wind patterns. Wind patterns become extremely complicated.

7.   The oceans and mountains break wind patterns. High-altitude winds going to the poles can lose their heat.

8.   These high-altitude winds lose their heat. These high-altitude winds sink and mix with the surface winds below.

## Using What You've Learned

**10**   Every culture has topics for conversation that are *taboo* (considered inappropriate) and others that are *safe*. Generally speaking, the weather is one of the safest topics for conversation worldwide. In pairs, practice the skill of *small talk*—conversation on a safe topic with strangers or people you don't know well—by talking about the weather. Be creative and see just how long you can keep the conversation going. Your teacher will time you, and the pair who can talk the longest may win a prize—a weather map!

**11**   Doctors take X rays in order to look for broken bones. A businesswoman buys a computer program so that she can manage her personal finances. Scientists worldwide use e-mail so that they collaborate on research. What equipment or processes are used in your career or hobby? Choose an area of interest to you—your work or your pastimes—and write a short paragraph about it. Tell some of the tools or processes you use and explain the purpose of each. Then work in small groups and take turns telling (not reading) your information. Use structures covered in this section whenever possible.

**12**   Choose one of the following questions to answer in a brief composition. Use information from this section to help you, but try to use your own words.

■   Why is our atmosphere continually in motion?

■   Why do winds develop away from the equator?

■   Why is there normally little wind at the equator?

■   How do mountains and other geographical features affect the weather?

■   What types of weather data do meteorologists study? Why?

**13**   Choose a city in the world. For one week check the weather every day and record it on a chart. You can use the Internet, newspapers or television. At the end of a week, pretend that you are a meterologist and present a weather report for a small group.

| PART 2 | # Clauses and Related Structures of Contrast: Concession and Opposition |

## Setting the Context

Most freshwater is frozen in glaciers and polar ice caps.

**Prereading Questions**   How much water is there on earth? Where is it located?

---

### Consumable Water

Of the total surface of the earth, 75 percent is covered by water. Nevertheless, only a small portion can be used for human needs. Only about three percent of the water on earth is fresh water, whereas 97 percent is saltwater. And, although three percent is fresh, three-quarters of that is ice, primarily in the polar ice caps. Thus, just less than one percent of the earth's water is available for human use.     **5**

Despite its lack of taste, color, odor, and calories, water is a powerful beverage. It is the only substance necessary to all life. Many organisms can live without oxygen; however, none can survive without water. The human body itself is 78 percent water.

Even though water is critical to all life, it is often taken for granted until a disaster occurs. Some may be natural disasters, such as droughts or floods; on the other hand, many are human caused, such as pollution of surface water or groundwater.     **10**

---

**Discussing Ideas.**   Either too much or too little water can be a disaster. Has drought or flooding been a serious problem in your area or country? Is water pollution a serious problem? Is clean drinking water available for most people?

## A. Clauses, Phrases, and Transitions of Concession

The following clauses, phrases, and transitions are used to express ideas or information that is different from our expectations.

|  | **Examples** | **Notes** |
|---|---|---|
| **With Clauses**<br>**although**<br>**even though**<br>**though** | **Although** water covers much of the earth, very little is usable. | These conjunctions are commonly used in speaking and writing, but *although* is preferred in formal English. |
| **With Phrases**<br>**despite**<br>**in spite of** | **Despite** technological advances, removing salt from ocean water is still very expensive. | *Despite* and *in spite of* are followed by phrases, not clauses. The phrases may contain nouns, pronouns, or gerunds. |
| **With Transitions**<br>**however**<br>**nevertheless** | Several countries have large desalinization projects; **however,** no country gets the majority of its water through this process. | *Nevertheless* is used in formal English. *However* is frequently used in both speaking and writing. *However* may appear at the beginning or end or in the middle of a sentence. |

**1**   Complete the following in your own words.

**Example:**   I like winter despite *the cold and snow.*

1. Although snow can be beautiful, . . .
2. The weather was perfect that day; nevertheless, . . .
3. Even though it was raining, . . .
4. I enjoy hot weather though . . .
5. Many people dislike humid weather. However, . . .
6. We decided to go camping in spite of . . .
7. Some people choose to live in desert areas even though . . .
8. Water can wear away a mountain; however, . . .
9. Fishermen sometimes go out to sea in storms in spite of . . .
10. Many people enjoy living on tropical islands; nevertheless, . . .

**2**   Combine each of the following pairs of sentences in two ways. First, combine them with *although* or *even though*. Then combine them with *however* or *nevertheless*. Be sure to change or omit words and to add punctuation when necessary. Finally, tell the primary focus of each of your new sentences.

**Example:**   We usually think of water as a liquid. Water exits in three forms: gas, liquid, and solid.

*Although we usually think of water as a liquid, it exists in three forms: gas, liquid, and solid.*

*Focus: the three forms of water*

*We usually think of water as a liquid; however, it exists in three forms: gas, liquid, and solid.*

*Focus: water as a liquid and the three forms of water*

1. All precipitation begins with the cooling and condensing of water vapor. Precipitation may reach earth as rain, sleet, snow, or hail.

2. The actual locations of rainfall depend on geography and winds. The total annual rainfall in the world is enough to provide every human with about 22,000 gallons of fresh water every day.

3. Meteorologists do not know all the effects of air pollution. Many fear that pollution is changing rainfall worldwide.

4. Some countries are finally beginning to react to the problem. Acid rain has already damaged buildings, forests, lakes, and streams around the world.

5. El Niño warms the water of the Pacific Ocean. This warming is not beneficial to sea creatures.

6. La Niña sometimes occurs for four-year periods. It sometimes occurs only for two-year periods.

## B. Clauses, Phrases, and Transitions of Opposition

The following clauses, phrases, and transitions are used to express an opposite view of the same idea or information.

|  | **Examples** | **Notes** |
|---|---|---|
| **With Clauses**<br>**Whereas**<br>**Where**<br>**While** | **While** some countries rely on water conservation, others find ways to increase the water supply.<br><br>Some countries rely on water conservation, **whereas** others find ways to increase their water supply. | *While, where,* and *whereas* are usually used to contrast direct opposites. *Whereas* is used in formal English.<br><br>Note that in many cases the connecting word may begin either clause. The focus of the sentence changes, but not the general meaning. |
| **With Phrases**<br>**Instead of** | **Instead of** importing water, some Middle Eastern countries are importing icebergs from the Arctic. | *Instead of* is followed by a noun phrase or a gerund, not a clause. |
| **With Transitions**<br>**In contrast**<br>**On the other hand**<br><br>**On the contrary** | This is not the most practical way to get more water; **on the other hand,** it is creative.<br>This is not an economical way to get more water; **on the contrary,** it is very expensive. | *In contrast* and *on the other hand* relate different points that are not necessarily direct opposites.<br><br>*On the contrary* is used differently than other transitions of contrast. It often reinforces a negative idea in the preceding sentence. In many cases, it means the opposite of *in fact*. |

**3**   Complete the following in your own words.

**Example:**   Despite the rain, *we decided to take a long walk.*

1.   Although summer weather can be great, . . .
2.   Despite the bad weather, . . .
3.   While some people enjoy the snow, . . .
4.   Even though we are learning more and more about the weather, . . .
5.   In the middle latitudes of the earth, four distinct seasons exist. In contrast, . . .
6.   I don't like hot weather. On the other hand, . . .
7.   I don't enjoy hot weather. On the contrary, . . .
8.   Instead of drinking water from the tap, my family . . .
9.   Even though much of the earth is covered with water, . . .
10.   Meteorologists don't know all the effects of air pollution. On the contrary, . . .

**4**   Combine each of the following pairs of sentences in three ways. First, combine them in two different ways with *while* or *whereas*. Then, combine them with *in contrast* or *on the other hand*. Change or omit words and add punctuation where necessary. Finally, tell the primary focus of each of your new sentences.

**Example:**   Each year, 80,000 cubic miles of water evaporates from the oceans. Only 15,000 cubic miles of water evaporates from the land.

*Each year, while 80,000 cubic miles of water evaporates from the oceans, only 15,000 cubic miles of water evaporates from the land.*

*Focus: water evaporation from the land*

*Each year, 80,000 cubic miles of water evaporates from the oceans, while only 15,000 cubic miles of water evaporates from the land.*

*Focus: water evaporation from the oceans*

*Each year, 80,000 cubic miles of water evaporates from the oceans; in contrast, only 15,000 cubic miles of water evaporates from the land.*

*Focus: water evaporation from both the oceans and the land*

1.   The oceans cover 71 percent of the earth's surface. Land covers only about 25 percent of the earth's surface.
2.   Less than 15 percent of the water vapor in the air evaporates from the land. Over one-quarter of the world's annual rainfall (approximately 24,000 cubic miles) falls on the land.
3.   Mt. Waialeale in Hawaii receives 470 inches of rain annually. Desert regions in Africa receive less than 1 inch of rain each year.
4.   Only 1.7 inches of rain fall annually in California's Death Valley. A few hundred miles north along the coast of the Pacific Ocean, 140 to 150 inches of rain fall.

**5**   Complete the following with *instead of, despite, although,* and *while.* Use each one time.

**Example:**   In clear air, only temperature and humidity determine when vapor condenses* into water, *while* in polluted air, chemicals and dust affect this process.

---

*condense   change from gas to liquid or liquid to solid

1. _____ research on pollution is incomplete, scientists now know that it affects weather.

2. In clear air, condensation happens slowly, _____ in particle-filled air it occurs much more rapidly.

3. _____ serious problems with pollution worldwide, many countries have not yet begun to look for solutions.

4. _____ investing money in mass transportation systems, many countries continue to promote the use of automobiles, a major source of pollution.

**6** Each of the following selections uses both conjunctions and transitions of contrast. Rewrite the sentences shown in bold type, changing transitions to subordinating conjunctions and subordinating conjunctions to transitions. Be sure to make all necessary changes.

**Example:    CIRRUS CLOUDS**

Pulled apart by winds, the wispy cirrus often look like spider webs. **Cirrus clouds often mean warm weather is on the way;** *however,* **they are actually the coldest clouds of all.** Cirrus can rise to over 40,000 feet, and the moisture in them is frozen into ice crystals.

*Even though cirrus clouds often mean warm weather is on the way, they are actually the coldest clouds of all.*

1. **FOG**

When the earth cools at night, water vapor condenses in damp areas, such as river valleys, producing fog. **We call it by a different name;** *nevertheless,* **fog is simply a cloud that forms near the ground. Clouds are formed when warm air rises and is cooled,** *whereas* **fog is formed when air cools near the ground or ocean.**

2. **CLOUDS AND OCEANS**

Because the land and the sea affect clouds differently, sailors often use clouds to help navigate. **Clouds will often form over land; the skies out at sea,** *in contrast,* **will remain cloudless.** *Although* **early Polynesian navigators did not have compasses, they could sail from island to island by reading the clouds.**

3. **LIGHTNING**

**Lightning is not entirely understood;** *however,* **we do know that powerful electrical charges build up inside a thundercloud.** *While* **a positive electrical charge builds up near the top of the cloud, a negative charge builds up near the bottom.** The negative charge is attracted to the ground below. When enough voltage builds up, a powerful electric current travels between the earth and sky. This current is lightning.

4. **DOES LIGHTNING STRIKE TWICE?**

Many myths exist about lightning. **For example, an old saying tells us that "lightning never strikes twice."** *On the contrary,* **almost every bolt of lightning strikes the same place several times. Each bolt is actually a series of "strokes" traveling to and from the earth,** *even though* **we perceive only a single flash of light.**

5. **SNOWFLAKES**

*Although* all snowflakes are six-sided, they have an infinite variety of forms. The most beautiful are delicate starlike flakes. *In contrast,* others may look like flat plates, needles, cups, or spools.

**7**   **Error Analysis.**   Many of the following ten sentences contain errors in the use of connecting words or phrases or in punctuation. Find and correct all errors.

**Examples:**   *Although*
~~Despite~~ water exists in three forms—gas, liquid, and solid—the most common fresh water form on earth is ice.

Around three-quarters of the earth's surface is water; however, we cannot use most of it easily. *correct*

1. Although we call the earth "the water planet," most of its water is not easily used.

2. Even though the amount of water on earth, most of it would be very difficult to recover for human use.

3. Seventy-one percent of the earth's surface is covered by oceans however humans cannot drink untreated saltwater.

4. Saltwater cannot be used easily; on the contrary, consuming saltwater can be very harmful to humans.

5. However in theory fresh water is plentiful 75 percent of it is frozen in glacial ice.

6. The Arctic is a frozen ocean, covered by sea ice and surrounded by land, on the other hand, the Antarctic is a frozen continent, covered by glacier ice and completely surrounded by sea.

7. Water normally freezes at 32°F (0°C) the presence of snow and ice depends on other facts that influence temperature, such as altitude.

8. Although snow and ice cover the peaks of many mountains the regional "snow line" varies greatly according to latitude.

9. Near the poles, the snow line is at sea level. While in the tropics, the snow line is above 20,000 ft (6,000 m).

10. Glaciers can exist on moderately high mountains in the middle latitudes. In contrast, near the equator they exist on only the highest peaks, such as Chimborazo, Kilimanjaro, and Mount Kenya.

**8**  Complete the passage with appropriate connecting words. Then look back at the passage "Consumable Water" on page 368 to check your answers. Of course, in some cases, more than one possibility exists.

### Consumable Water

Of the total surface of the earth, 75 percent is covered by water. _____ ,
<br>1

only a small portion can be used. Only about three percent of the water on earth is

fresh water, _____ 97 percent is saltwater. And, _____ 3 percent
<br>2                          3

is fresh, three-quarters of that is ice, primarily in the polar ice caps. _____ ,
<br>4

just less than 1 percent of the earth's water is available for human use.

_____ its lack of taste, color, odor, and calories, water is a powerful
<br>5

beverage. It is the only substance necessary to all life. Many organisms can live with-

out oxygen; _____ , none can survive without water. The human body itself
<br>6

is 78 percent water. _____ water is critical to all life, it is often taken for
<br>7

granted until a disaster occurs. Some may be natural disasters, such as droughts or

floods; _____ , many are human caused, such as pollution of surface water
<br>8

or groundwater.

## Using What You've Learned

**9**  In pairs or small groups, use the following map for a weather report. First, make notes. Choose a day, month, or season, and add high and low temperatures in Fahrenheit for each city and area of the U.S.—for example, *June 10, early summer, Houston 96/70.* Then use the symbols on the map to understand current weather conditions and to predict the future. Create a brief weather report for your class. Tell what you are basing your predictions on, using as many connecting words of cause, contrast, purpose, or result as you can.

**Example:**    *It's June 10th, early summer in Houston. The weather is hot and dry. Therefore, we can expect drought conditions to continue.*

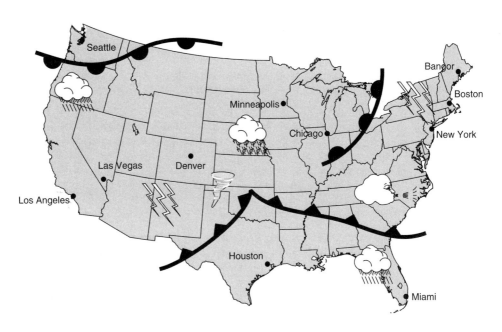

 **10** Let's forget the weather and talk about English! First, complete the following by writing your own ideas. Then, get together with a partner and share how you feel about English and your experiences learning it. Try to express your feelings without looking at the sentences you wrote, though.

- ■ I'm studying English because . . .
- ■ Although my English isn't perfect, . . .
- ■ Instead of studying English, . . .
- ■ In spite of all the hours I've been studying English, . . .
- ■ Because I want to improve my English, . . .
- ■ I've got to work hard so that . . .
- ■ I need English in order to . . .

**PART 3** # Comparative and Superlative Adjectives and Adverbs

## Setting the Context

**Prereading Questions**   What are the major bodies of water in the world? What are the major bodies of water in or surrounding your region or country?

### The World's Oceans

Geographers and mapmakers recognize four major oceans: the Pacific, the Atlantic, the Indian, and the Arctic. The Pacific is the largest of the four oceans.

At 64,186,300 square miles,* it is almost twice as large as the Atlantic Ocean (33 million square miles) and more than twice as large as the Indian Ocean (28 million square miles). The Arctic Ocean is much smaller than the other three major **5** bodies of water. At five million square miles, the Arctic Ocean is only one-twelfth the size of the Pacific. It is much shallower than the Pacific too. The average depth of the Pacific is 13,739 feet, whereas the average depth of the Arctic Ocean is 4362 feet. In averages, the Atlantic and Indian Oceans are almost as deep as the Pacific. Although the Indian Ocean is smaller than the Atlantic, its average depth **10** is greater than that of the Atlantic.

Other major bodies of water include the South China Sea, the Caribbean Sea, the Mediterranean Sea, and the Bering Sea. In total, 75 percent of the world's surface is covered by water.

**Discussing Ideas.** Of the oceans and other bodies of water mentioned in the passage, which have you seen? Have you lived near one? If so, describe it for your classmates.

## Comparisons with Adjectives and Adverbs

The positive forms of adjectives and adverbs are used in expressions with *(not) as . . . as (as slow as, not as slowly as)*. Comparative forms are used to compare two things. Superlative forms are used to discuss three or more things. *The* is normally used with superlative forms. Note that spelling rules for adding *-er* and *-est* are the same as for adding *-ed* (see Appendix 1).

| | **Positive** | **Comparative** | **Superlative** |
|---|---|---|---|
| <u>**Add *-er* and *-est* to:**</u> | | | |
| **One-Syllable Adjectives** | nice | nicer | the nicest |
| | young | younger | the youngest |
| **Adjectives and Adverbs that Have the Same Form** | early | earlier | the earliest |
| | fast | faster | the fastest |
| | hard | harder | the hardest |
| | late | later | the latest |
| <u>**Add *-er* and *-est* or use *more, less, the most, the least* With:**</u> | | | |
| **Most Two-Syllable Adjectives** | clever | cleverer | the cleverest |
| | | more clever | the most clever |
| | funny | funnier | the funniest |
| | | more funny | the most funny |
| | shallow | shallower | the shallowest |
| | | more shallow | the most shallow |
| | simple | simpler | the simplest |
| | | more simple | the most simple |

*Note:* With words ending in *-y* and *-le,* the *-er* and *-est* forms are more common than forms with *more, less,* and so on.

---

**square mile*    a square area measuring one mile on each side

| | Positive | Comparative | Superlative |
|---|---|---|---|
| **Use *more, less, the most, the least* With:** | | | |
| **Two-Syllable Adjectives That End in *-ed, -ful, -ing, -ish, -ous, -st,* and *-x*** | worried | more worried | the most worried |
| | harmful | more harmful | the most harmful |
| | caring | more caring | the most caring |
| | selfish | more selfish | the most selfish |
| | joyous | more joyous | the most joyous |
| | robust | more robust | the most robust |
| | complex | more complex | the most complex |
| **Longer Adjectives and Most *-ly* Adverbs** | difficult | more difficult | the most difficult |
| | quickly | more quickly | the most quickly |
| | slowly | more slowly | the most slowly |

| Irregular Adjectives and Adverbs | | | |
|---|---|---|---|
| **Adjective** | **Adverb** | **Comparative** | **Superlative** |
| bad | badly | worse | (the) worst |
| good | — | better | (the) best |
| well | well | better | (the) best |
| far | far | farther | (the) farthest (*distance*) |
| | | further | (the) furthest |
| little | little | less | (the) least |
| many | — | more | (the) most |
| much | much | more | (the) most |

**1**  For each word that follows, give the two forms that are missing.

**Example:** _____*far*_____ farther \_\_\_*the farthest*\_\_\_

| Positive | Comparative | Superlative |
|---|---|---|
| 1.  good | _____ | _____ |
| 2.  simple | _____ | _____ |
| 3.  _____ | _____ | the worst |
| 4.  _____ | younger | _____ |
| 5.  handsome | _____ | _____ |
| 6.  _____ | later | _____ |
| 7.  _____ | _____ | the least |
| 8.  carefully | _____ | _____ |
| 9.  _____ | further | _____ |
| 10.  early | _____ | _____ |
| 11.  _____ | _____ | the nicest |

12.   much          _____        _____

13.   quickly       _____        _____

14.   _____     _____        the fewest

15.   worried       _____        _____

16.   _____     harder          _____

**2**   Reread the passage "The World's Oceans" on pages 375–376. Then do the following:

1.   Underline all the comparatives (*more . . . than, less . . . than, -er than,* and so on) and superlatives (*the . . . -est*) in the passage.

2.   How many bodies of water are being compared in sentence 2? Which form of the adjective is used? (*The Pacific is . . .*)

3.   How many bodies of water are being compared in the sentence in line 7? Which form of the adjective is used? (*It is . . .*)

4.   Can you explain the comparison in the sentence in lines 9 to 10? Which form of the adjective is used? (*In averages, . . .*)

**3**   Complete the following superlative forms of the words in parentheses.

**Example:**   _The greatest_ tides in the world occur in the Bay of Fundy.

1.   _____ waterfall in the world is Salto Angel (Angel Falls) in Venezuela.
     (high)

2.   _____ active geyser in the world is Steamboat Geyser in Yellowstone
     (tall)
     National Park.

3.   _____ fjord (inlet) in the world is in eastern Greenland, extending inland 195
     (long)
     miles from the sea.

4.   _____ water currents in the world are the Nakwakto Rapids in British
     (strong)
     Columbia, Canada, which may reach 18.4 mph.

5.   _____ waterfall in the world is Khone Falls in Laos.
     (wide)

6.   _____ place in the world is the Atacama Desert in Chile, which had no
     (dry)
     measurable rainfall for 400 years.

7.   _____ port in the United States is the Port of South Louisiana.
     (busy)

8.   _____ inland waterway in North America is the St. Lawrence and Great
     (large)
     Lakes waterway.

**4** Complete the following with comparative (+) or superlative (++) forms of the words in parentheses. Be sure to add *the* when necessary. The first one is done as an example.

Vernal Falls, Yosemite National Park

Lake Michigan and the Chicago skyline

### Waterfalls: Wonders of the World

In 1935, Jimmy Angel, an American looking for gold in Venezuela, discovered

*the highest* waterfall in the world, Salto Angel (Angel Falls). Angel Falls (3212 ft) is
1 (++ high)

only slightly _____ than its _____ rival, Tugela Falls (3110 ft) in South
                    2 (+ high)           3 (++ close)

Africa. At about 700 feet _____ than Tugela Falls is Yosemite Falls (2425 ft) in
                          4 (+ low)

California.

High waterfalls may be _____ than _____ falls, but _____ and
                       5 (+ spectacular)   6 (+ low)        7 (+ short)

_____ falls are in general _____. For example, Khone Falls in Laos drops
8 (+ wide)                      9 (+ powerful)

only 72 feet, yet it often discharges _____ than 400,000 cubic feet of water per
                                       10 (+ many)

second.

Perhaps _____ "falls producer" of all is the Rio Paraná in South America. It
         11 (++ great)

produces Iguassú Falls and Guaíra Falls. Many visitors say that Iguassú Falls is

_____ on earth. At _____ than two miles wide, it certainly is one of
12 (++ beautiful)        13 (+ many)

**Culture Note**

*In the mid-20th century, Niagara Falls, located between Canada and the United States, was a popular honeymoon spot. It has also been a sight where daredevils have attempted to go over the falls in barrels or boats, often with disastrous results.*

_____ in the world. And Guaíra Falls is definitely _____ worldwide,

14 (++ awe inspiring)                                                    15 (++ mighty)

with an average of 470,000 cubic feet of water per second thundering through a series of 18 cascades.

**5**   The Great Lakes of North America form the largest body of fresh water in the world and, with their connecting waterways, are the largest inland water transportation system. Use the information in the following chart to complete the sentences. Be sure to add *the* when necessary.

| The Great Lakes | | | | | |
|---|---|---|---|---|---|
| | Length (miles) | Width (miles) | Deepest Point (feet) | Volume (cubic miles) | United States and Canada total area (square miles) |
| Erie | 241 | 57 | 210 | 116 | 32,630 |
| Huron | 206 | 183 | 750 | 850 | 74,700 |
| Michigan | 307 | 118 | 923 | 1,180 | 67,900 |
| Ontario | 193 | 53 | 802 | 393 | 34,850 |
| Superior | 350 | 160 | 1,330 | 2,900 | 81,000 |

**Example:   LENGTH**

Lake Erie is _shorter_ than Lake Michigan, but it is _longer_ than Lake Huron or Lake Ontario.

1. **WIDTH**

   a.   Lake Superior is a little _____ than Lake Huron.

   b.   Lake Ontario is _____ of the five lakes.

   c.   Lake Huron is _____ of the five lakes.

2. **DEPTH**

   a.   Lake Superior is by far _____ of the five lakes.

   b.   Lake Erie is _____ of the five lakes.

   c.   Lake Ontario is _____ than Lake Huron, but it is _____ than Lake Michigan.

3. **VOLUME**

   a.   Lake Erie holds _____ water of the five lakes.

   b.   Lake Huron holds _____ water than Lake Michigan.

   c.   Lake Superior holds over twice as _____ water as Lake Michigan.

   d.   Lake Michigan holds _____ water than Lakes Erie and Huron combined.

4.  **TOTAL AREA**

a.  Lake Erie covers _____ area of the five lakes.

b.  Lake Superior covers _____ area of the five lakes.

**6**   Without looking back at the opening passage, try to complete the following, using the appropriate adjectives. Be sure to add *the* when necessary.

**Example:**   The Pacific is <u>*the largest*</u> of the four oceans.

1.  The Pacific is almost twice as _____ as the Atlantic.

2.  The Pacific is _____ than twice as _____ as the Indian Ocean.

3.  The Arctic Ocean is _____ than the other three oceans.

4.  At an average depth of 4362 feet, the Arctic is _____ than the Pacific.

5.  The Atlantic and Indian Oceans are almost as _____ as the Pacific Ocean.

6.  At an average depth of 13,739 feet, the Pacific is _____ of the four oceans.

7.  The Indian Ocean is _____ in size than the Atlantic.

8.  The average depth of the Indian Ocean is _____ than that of the Atlantic.

**7**   Complete the following with comparative or superlative forms of the words in parentheses. Be sure to use *the* when necessary.

**Lake Baikal**

Lake Baikal is a place of superlatives. It is <u>*the deepest*</u>, _____, and
1 (++ deep)   2 (++ old)

_____ lake in the world. It is also the home of _____ than a thousand
3 (++ voluminous)                                    4 (+ much)

species found nowhere else, including the world's only fresh water seal.

Lake Baikal

Baikal's volume of 5500 cubic miles is

_____ than the combined volume of the Great
5 (+ great)

Lakes. However, its surface area is _____ than
6 (− little)

half of Lake Superior's. All together, Lake Baikal and

the five Great Lakes hold _____ than 40 per-
7 (+ much)

cent of the world's fresh water.

Lake Baikal is _____ and _____ than
8 (+ clear)        9 (− polluted)

almost any other major lake in the world. Overall, its water is, perhaps, _____ of
10 (++ pure)

all major lakes and can be drunk without treatment. Some problems with pollution in

Lake Baikal do exist, however. _____ threat is from manufacturers on the
11 (++ immediate)

shores of the lake. However, Russians have responded very quickly to the concerns,

perhaps _____ than to any other issue. In fact, concerns about Lake Baikal have
12 (+ quickly)

drawn _____ reaction from citizens to almost any environmental concern in the
13 (++ strong)

last 30 years.

Of the world's natural resources, Lake Baikal is one of our _____
14 (++ important)

treasures. Its unique environment and its wealth of clean water should be protected. It

is one of the world's _____ sources of life-giving water.
15 (++ valuable)

Adapted from *Horizons,* Sigurd Olson Environmental Institute

| Comparison of Lake Baikal and Lake Superior | | |
|---|---|---|
|  | **Lake Baikal** | **Lake Superior** |
| Surface area *(square miles)* | 12,160 | 31,820 |
| Volume *(square miles)* | 5550 | 2900 |
| Average depth *(feet)* | 5313 | 1333 |
| Retention time *(years)* | 317 | 191 |

**8**   Use the preceding chart to write at least five sentences comparing Lake Superior and
Lake Baikal.

**Example:**   *Of the two lakes, the surface area of Lake Baikal is much smaller.*

## Using What You've Learned

**9** Look back at the world map on page 359. Can you label all the oceans? Do you know the most important rivers, lakes, and mountains on each continent? Work in small groups. Combine your knowledge of geography to make lists for each continent. Write as many "superlatives" as you can. Then compare your lists with those of other groups. As a class, are you fairly knowledgeable about geography?

**Example:**   Asia: the highest mountain   *Mt. Everest*

**10** Choose a topic that interests you and do some comparison research. Use your local library or the Internet to learn more about this topic. Gather data that you can later share with your classmates. Choose at least three items to study and prepare a comparison for your classmates in terms of distances, longevity, sizes, shapes, speed, and so on. Prepare a brief report to give in a small group or for the whole class. Here are some topics that may interest you:

- Architecture or engineering: bridges, buildings, dams, tunnels, and so on
- Biology: animals, birds, plants, trees, and so on
- Geography: lakes, mountains, rivers, and so on

**Example:**   *I like birds, so I researched the three that interest me most. The first is the hummingbird, which is the smallest bird in the world. The second is the ostrich, which is the largest bird in the world . . .*

**11** In pairs or in small groups, make up quizzes based on information given in this section. Try to write at least ten questions per quiz. In your quizzes, make statements that compare two or more items. Set a time limit for completing the quizzes, and then exchange them with a classmate or with another group. Return your quiz to the author(s) to be corrected.

**Example:**   T /(F)   *Yosemite Falls in California is higher than Tugela Falls in South Africa.*

**PART 4**   # Comparisons with *As* and *Than*

## Setting the Context

**Prereading Questions**   The world has a tremendous variety of climates. Which climate do you prefer?

---

### World Climates

Climates can change greatly. Even in a "steady" climate, an area can receive much more rain in some years than it does in others. Too, some areas may get less rain in an entire year than they normally get in one month. Temperature sometimes varies as much as rainfall does. An area with winters that are normally severe may have temperatures above freezing during an entire winter season.   **5**

---

**Discussing Ideas.** Do you think different climates produce differences in lifestyles, even differences in cultures?

## *Clauses and Phrases with* As *and* Than

Clauses of comparison can be formed with *as* or *than*. Positive adjectives and adverbs are used with *as*, whereas comparative forms are used with *than*. The clause may use an appropriate auxiliary verb, or it may repeat the first verb. In conversational English, these clauses are often shortened to phrases. In formal English, subject pronouns follow *than* or *as*. In informal English, object pronouns are often used, though this is considered incorrect.

| | With Clauses (more formal) | With Phrases (less formal) |
|---|---|---|
| **as . . . as** | Al likes winter **as much as he likes** summer.<br>Al likes winter **as much as he does** summer.<br>Al likes winter **as much as I do**. | Al likes winter **as much as** summer.<br><br>Al likes winter **as much as** me. |
| **not as . . . as** | I **don't like** the heat **as much as Al likes** the heat.<br>I **don't like** the heat **as much as Al does**.<br>Summer isn't **as pleasant as** fall or spring is. | I **don't** like heat **as much as** Al.<br><br>I **don't** like heat **as much as** him.<br><br>Summer isn't **as pleasant**. |
| **more . . . than**<br>**-er . . . than** | The weather here gets **more humid than it gets** in my hometown.<br>The weather here gets **hotter than it does** in my hometown. | The weather here gets **more humid than** in my hometown.<br><br>The weather here gets **hotter**. |
| **less . . . than**<br>**-er . . . than** | This year, we have gotten **much less rain than we got** last year.<br>This year, we have gotten **much less rain than we did** last year.<br>This year, we've had **many fewer storms than we did** last year. | This year, we've gotten **much less rain than** last year.<br><br><br>This year, we've had **many fewer storms than** last year. |

*Note: Many, much,* and *even* are often used to intensify *more* or *less: He has much more money. I've written many fewer checks. I wrote even fewer than last month. Not quite* is often used with *as* when the difference between the two items is not great: *It's not quite as hot today as it was yesterday.*

**1   Rapid Oral Practice.**   For each of the following, give a phrase using *as* or *than*. With positive adjectives and adverbs, use *as*. With comparative forms, use *than*.

**Examples:**   hot
*as hot as*
hotter
*hotter than*

1. quickly
2. easier
3. less difficult
4. friendly
5. more complex

6. harder
7. beautiful
8. angrily
9. brilliant
10. fewer

**2**  Complete the following passage by adding *than* or *as*. The first one is done as an example.

### The Sun and Weather

Four main factors determine weather: temperature, pressure, humidity, and wind. The

sun, more <u>*than*</u> our own earth, has the greatest effect on these factors. The earth re-
$\quad\quad\quad$ 1

ceives less _____ two-billionths of the sun's total energy, yet it receives more
$\quad\quad\quad\quad\quad$ 2

energy in one minute _____ we can produce in an entire year through power plants.
$\quad\quad\quad\quad\quad\quad\quad$ 3

$\quad\quad$ The earth loses _____ much energy _____ it absorbs because of reflection
$\quad\quad\quad\quad\quad\quad\quad$ 4 $\quad\quad\quad\quad\quad\quad\quad$ 5

from cloud tops, ice fields, and snow. In addition, water vapor in our atmosphere

shields the earth because it absorbs more energy _____ it allows to pass through.
$\quad\quad\quad\quad\quad\quad\quad\quad\quad\quad\quad\quad\quad$ 6

When the water vapor absorbs more energy _____ it can hold, it begins to con-
$\quad\quad\quad\quad\quad\quad\quad\quad\quad\quad$ 7

dense and form clouds. In this way, the cycle of rainfall begins again.

$\quad\quad$ The sun, then, ultimately causes all weather. The sun determines why parts of

Hawaii receive _____ much rain in one month _____ parts of Chile have gotten
$\quad\quad\quad\quad\quad\quad$ 8 $\quad\quad\quad\quad\quad\quad\quad\quad$ 9

in sixty years.

**3**  Many comparisons are "understood." Complete the shortened comparisons in the following sentences by adding *as* or *than* and the understood comparison. Then change each comparison to use *than* instead of *as* or *as* instead of *than*.

**Example:**    Southwestern Canada has pleasant weather. The weather in northern Canada is much colder (than the weather in southwestern Canada is).

*Southwestern Canada isn't as cold as northern Canada is.*

1.  British Columbia has a lot of mountains. Alberta is much flatter.
2.  Manitoba is filled with lakes. Alberta doesn't have as many.
3.  Edmonton has harsh winters. The winters in Vancouver aren't as severe.
4.  Last year, eastern Canada got a lot of snow. This year it didn't get as much.
5.  Toronto is usually quite windy in the winter. Last winter it wasn't as windy.
6.  Montreal is humid, but Quebec City is often much more humid.
7.  Storms in Florida are often violent. Storms in New York are usually not as violent.
8.  Los Angeles is quite smoggy. Houston is smoggier.

**4**   The following sentences compare nouns. Complete them by using *fewer* or *less.*

**Example:**   Small towns generally have _fewer_ cars than large cities do.

1.   Small towns normally have _____ pollution than large cities because they have _____ traffic.

2.   In general, towns with _____ factories have _____ problems with pollution.

3.   Despite pollution, people continue to move to areas like southern California, which has _____ bad weather than most parts of the country.

4.   Southern California gets _____ inches of rain in one year than Vancouver, British Columbia, gets in one month.

5.   Southern California has _____ windy days than British Columbia does.

6.   Southern California gets _____ snow than British Columbia does.

7.   Vermont has _____ snow storms than Alaska.

8.   New York has _____ lakes than Minnesota.

9.   Australia has _____ fertile land than the United States.

10.   The United States has _____ frozen territory than Canada.

**5**   Rephrase the following sentences, changing clauses of opposition to clauses of comparison. Give at least two new versions for each.

**Example:**   Al Aziziyah, Libya, has reached 136°F, while Death Valley, California has reached 134°F.

*Two of the hottest places in the world are Al Aziziyah, Libya, and Death Valley, California. Death Valley has not gotten quite as hot as Al Aziziyah has.*
*Al Aziziyah has reached even higher temperatures than Death Valley has.*

1.   While Oymyakon, in Russia, has reached −96°F, Vostok, Antarctica, has reached −128.6°.

2.   Tutunendo, Colombia, gets 463 inches of rain annually, while Mt. Waialeale, Hawaii, gets 450 inches per year.

3.   While Death Valley, California, gets around 1.7 inches of rain per year, parts of the Atacama Desert in Chile receive no measurable precipitation annually.

4.   While winds at Mt. Washington, New Hampshire, have reached 231 mph, winds during a tornado in Wichita Falls, Texas, reached 280 mph.

## Using What You've Learned

**6**   Imagine that you could "custom-design" the perfect place to live. For you, what would it be like? It doesn't have to be a place that already exists, but if you know of a perfect place, you can describe it. Write a short composition describing your perfect place. Be sure to describe the climate, the geography, and so on. Later, share your description with your classmates.

**7**  Play a game with comparisons. First, everyone should stand up. Then, go around the room in a chain, giving adjectives or adverbs and making sentences from them. Choose any adjective or adverb. Your teacher will judge if the sentence is correct. If it is not, you must sit down. The last person standing wins.

**Example:**   A:   exciting

B:   **New York is much more exciting than here.**

B:   beautiful

C:   **No one is as beautiful as you are!**

**8**  Work in pairs, and use the following chart to help you create sentences using comparatives. Create as many sentences as you can.

**Examples:**   *Of the first two bridges, the Golden Gate Bridge in San Francisco is shorter.*

*The Verrazano-Narrows Bridge in New York City is longer.*

*The Verrazano-Narrows Bridge in New York City is longer than the Golden Gate Bridge.*

*The Golden Gate Bridge is not quite as long as the Verrazano-Narrows Bridge.*

| **Bridges** | Verrazano-Narrows Bridge in New York City | 4260 feet long | Golden Gate Bridge in San Francisco | 4200 feet long |
|---|---|---|---|---|
| | Bendorf Bridge on the Rhine River | 3378 feet long | Bosphorus Bridge in Istanbul | 3524 feet long |
| **Buildings** | Sears Tower in Chicago | 1454 feet tall | World Trade Center in New York City | 1368 feet tall |
| | Bank of China in Hong Kong | 1001 feet tall | Eiffel Tower in Paris | 984 feet tall |
| **Deserts** | Gobi Desert in Mongolia and China | 500,000 square miles | Libyan Desert in North Africa | 450,000 square miles |
| **Lakes** | Lake Baikal in southern Siberia | 5315 feet deep | Lake Tanganyika in east central Africa | 4823 feet deep |
| **Mountains** | Mount McKinley in Alaska | 20,320 feet tall | Mount Kilimanjaro in Tanzania | 19,340 feet high |

**9**  Look at the chart from Activity 8 again. Do some research and find another item to add to each group. Then, working in pairs, use each other's research to create new sentences with comparatives and superlatives. Create as many correct sentences as you can. The pair with the most new sentences wins!

<table>
<tr><td>**PART 5**</td></tr>
</table>

# Clauses of Result

## Setting the Context

**Prereading Questions**   Can you think of examples of how human beings have controlled their supply and use of water? For example, the ancient Romans built aqueducts, which moved water from place to place.

---

### Is Drip Irrigation the Future of Water Technology?

In recent years, the world has experienced the effects of too little water. For example, the Eastern Seaboard of the United States has gone through such a dry period that many towns and cities have become worried about the future of their water supply. Drought in Africa continues to cause famine and death to thousands of people. At the same time, people continue to misuse water. Green lawns use so  **5** much water that authorities have had to ban lawn irrigation in certain places during summer months when it is dry. Most frequently, plants, trees, shrubs, and flowers get water through spraying. However, spraying is so inefficient that more than half of sprayed water either evaporates or gets blown away before it reaches plant life. The most efficient way to water is to use drip irrigation. Slow and steady  **10** dripping of water onto plant life is both efficient and effective. Many farmers in the southwestern and western United States use drip irrigation on their crops. Drip irrigation wastes so little water that it is 95 percent efficient as a technology. Drip irrigation systems are simple to set up and to use. In a world where water is becoming such a scarce and expensive resource that some political scientists  **15** predict future wars will be fought over water, drip irrigation could hold the key to water needs, and perhaps, by extension, the key to a peaceful world.

---

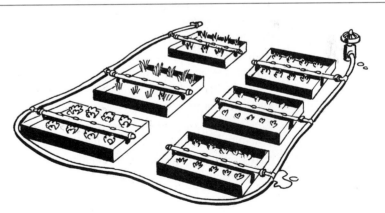

**Discussing Ideas.**   What irrigation systems are used by farmers in your region? Does your home have a lawn or garden? How is it watered?

## *Adverb Clauses and Related Structures Showing Result*

Clauses with *that* can be used to show the results or effect of a situation. See page 390 for transitions often used to show result.

|  | Examples | Notes |
|---|---|---|
| **so . . . (adjective/ adverb) . . . that** | Dams control the Tennessee River **so tightly that** it can be turned off like a faucet. | *So* may be followed by an adjective or an adverb. *So* often replaces *very* when two sentences are joined. |
| **so many** **so much . . . (noun)** **so few . . . that** **so little** | **So much water** has been pumped from beneath Houston **that** parts of the city are sinking. **So many wells** are dry now **that** the city is worried about its water supply. | *So much* or *so little* is used with a noncount noun. *So many* or *so few* is used with a count noun. |
| **such (a/an) . . . (noun) . . . that** | **Such great quantities** of water are used **that** the Colorado River dries up before it ever reaches the ocean. | *Such* is used with nouns. Remember to use *a* or *an* with a singular count noun. Plural and noncount nouns do not use an article. |

**1**  First, identify the noun, adjective, or adverb to be emphasized. Then combine each pair of sentences with *so  .  .  .  that.* Change or omit words when necessary.

**Example:**   In parts of the world, rainfall is sparse. People in those areas constantly conserve water.

*In parts of the world, rainfall is so sparse that people constantly conserve water.*

1.  The world is becoming forgetful. People don't realize water is our most precious resource.
2.  Water is now a scarce resource. People are beginning to fight over it.
3.  The world population is growing fast. Under current patterns of use, water resources cannot meet the needs of everyone on the planet.
4.  The world's fresh water remains at a constant level. We must find other ways to use our water resources.
5.  One out of three people in the world live with poor sanitation. They would benefit from a system equal to that of the ancient Romans.
6.  Nations without a good water supply often have a hard time feeding their people. Many go hungry.
7.  It takes a lot of water to make a little grain. The water scarcity might cause humanity to lose the capacity to feed itself.
8.  Lack of water creates many problems. It seems difficult to know where to start in solving them.

**2**  Before working with *such  .  .  .  that,* review the use of articles with count and noncount nouns by completing the following passage. Use *a, an,* or *X* to indicate that no article is needed.

**Culture Note**

*Desalination, or making fresh water out of seawater, is a solution to water shortages. In the United States, the first city to have a water desalination plant was Key West, Florida, in 1967. Now there are more than 500 such plants in the United States. This is a very expensive process and therefore limited in use.*

## Altering the Environment

_____ surface fresh water—_____ water in _____ lakes, _____ streams, and _____
   1                   2          3         4         5

rivers—is replenished about once _____ week. _____ groundwater—_____ water
                                 6          7                8

underground—is replenished much more slowly. Because _____ rainfall is not
                                                  9

dependable, _____ people dig wells to get _____ constant supply of _____ fresh water.
          10                      11              12

Because of _____ well digging, _____ parts of the United States are like _____
             13            14                     15

pincushion. Over 150,000 wells have been dug to tap the Ogallala aquifer, _____
                                                    16

underground reservoir beneath _____ eight states. It has taken nature at least
                                 17

25,000 years to fill this aquifer, and it is taking _____ humans only _____ few decades
                                         18                  19

to empty it.

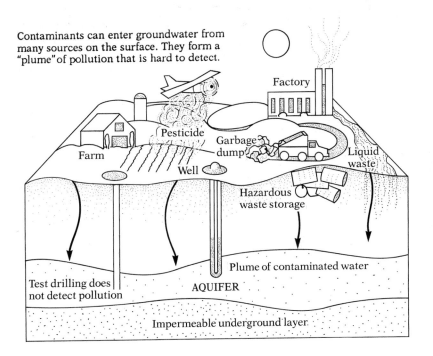

Contaminants can enter groundwater from many sources on the surface. They form a "plume" of pollution that is hard to detect.

Factory

Pesticide

Garbage dump

Farm

Liquid waste

Well

Hazardous waste storage

Test drilling does not detect pollution

Plume of contaminated water

AQUIFER

Impermeable underground layer

**3**  Rewrite the following sentences to use *such . . . that* instead of *because*. Use the example as a model.

**Example:**  Because there is a strong relationship among all living things, damage to one part of an ecosystem will hurt another part.

*There is such a strong relationship among all living things that damage to one part of an ecosystem will hurt another part.*

1. Because wetlands—marshes and swamps—were considered useless places, millions of acres world-wide have been filled.

2. Because large numbers of wetlands are being drained, the United States loses over 300,000 acres annually.

3. Because wetlands are a critical source of oxygen, we must protect them at all cost.

4. Because the plants in wetlands form strong filters, they are natural water purifiers.

5. Because wetlands capture large amounts of carbon in the form of peat, they protect the atmosphere.

6. Because wetlands are feeding and breeding grounds for fish, they provide the United States with over half its saltwater fish and shellfish each year.

**4**  **Review.**  Before working with *so . . . that*, review the use of *few, little, many,* and *much*. First identify the nouns as count or noncount. Then complete the sentences with *few, little, many,* or *much*.

1. The Los Angeles basin has so _____*little*_____ natural water that it can supply only about 200,000 people.

2. With so _____ people (around 8 million living in the basin alone), Los Angeles has to import large quantities of water.

3. Los Angeles gets as _____ as 80 percent of its total water supply through an aqueduct from the Owens Valley in east central California.

4. Most of this water is from surface streams, but at times as _____ as 30 percent comes from groundwater pumping.

5. _____ Owens Valley residents say that Los Angeles is turning their valley into a desert.

6. They claim that Los Angeles leaves them so _____ ground and surface water that it is destroying the environment of the valley.

7. For example, between 1900 and 1920, Los Angeles pumped so _____ gallons of water that it dried up 100-square mile Owens Lake.

8. _____ of the land is now covered with sagebrush, and _____ crops can grow.

**5**  Combine the following sentences with *so much . . . that* or *so many . . . that*.

**Examples:**  Government departments are involved in water management. Water use is almost impossible to control.

*So many government departments are involved in water management that water use is almost impossible to control.*

Groundwater has become polluted. It is becoming a severe national problem.

*So much groundwater has become polluted that it is becoming a national problem.*

1. Many urban water pipes are old and cracked. They leak millions of gallons of water.

2. Water is wasted on making lawns greener. Measures must be taken to limit the use of water on lawns in order to conserve it for more important purposes.

3. A thousand tons of water are needed to grow one ton of grain. Drought-stricken countries end up having to import food.

4. About one-fifth of the world's people do not have drinkable water. They become ill and die from easily preventable water-born diseases.

5. Underground water reserves are being used up rapidly. The cities and towns above them are sinking.

6. Farmers have lost land they once planted because of dams. Their situation has become a major problem all over the world.

**6**  **Review.**   Combine the following sentences, using a variety of connecting words and phrases. Change or omit words and add punctuation when necessary.

**Example:**   It doesn't rain frequently in the desert. Occasionally, rain comes down in torrents.

*Although it doesn't rain frequently in the desert, rain occasionally comes down in torrents.*

**Flash Floods**

1. Vegetation in the desert is very sparse. The desert ground is often very hard. The water from a heavy rain does not soak in.

2. Very little water is absorbed. Most of it runs off into dry riverbeds.

3. These riverbeds or gullies are very common in dry lands. Most languages have a name for them.

4. *Arroyo* and *wadi* are words from foreign languages. These names are also used in English to describe dry riverbeds or gullies.

5. The sandy bed of the arroyo may absorb some rainwater. Most of the rainwater begins to flow forward. The rainwater quickly picks up speed.

6. The arroyo acts as a funnel. The rainwater rushes faster and faster. The rainwater often builds a wall of water several feet high.

7. It is difficult to imagine the speed and force of a flash flood. Automobile-sized boulders in a dry arroyo demonstrate a flash flood's carrying power.

8. The carrying power of a stream increases dramatically with speed. Even a small flood can pull very heavy objects along with it.

9. Heavy rains fall quickly and unpredictably in the desert. Desert travelers should watch weather signs. They should move to high ground at any sign of rain.

10. Flash floods can be devastating. Damage seldom occurs on higher ground.

**7**   **Review.**   Combine the following sentences, using a variety of connecting words and phrases. Change or omit words and add punctuation when necessary.

**Tsunami**

*Tsunami* is a Japanese word that means "large waves in harbors." It is appropriate because only a major disturbance can produce large waves in sheltered bays.

1. In the United States, tsunami are often called "tidal waves." The name "tidal wave" is incorrect.

2. Tsunami have nothing to do with tides. The approach of tsunami on an open coast may look like a rapid rise of the tide.

3. Almost all tsunami have followed tremendous earthquakes. Some scientists believe a sudden lift or drop in the ocean floor produces these giant waves.

4. An alternative explanation is that huge submarine landslides produce them. There is no good proof of the idea of submarine landslides.

5. Tsunami move at enormous speeds in the open ocean. Tsunami can average 450 miles per hour.

6. Their height in the open ocean is small. They may have no effect on the deep sea floor. Along a coast, they become very destructive.

7. A major earthquake shook Alaska in 1946. A tremendous tsunami hit Hawaii several hours later.

8. The waves took only four hours to reach Hawaiian shores after the earthquake. Then the shallow waters off Hawaii slowed them down.

9. The waves slowed very much. The waves moved at a rate of only about 15 miles per hour near the coast.

10. Their depth was limited in the shallow water. They grew in height to the size of a three-story wall.

## Using What You've Learned

**8**   Think about yourself and your reactions to a disaster situation. You may have experienced a flood, an earthquake, a typhoon, or a blizzard. In small groups, describe the disaster and talk about how you felt and what you did. (If you have never experienced a disaster, you can make up a story.)

**Example:**   *When the earthquake hit Caracas, the buildings shook so much that I thought everything would fall. I was so frightened that I could hardly breathe.*

**9**   Individually or in pairs, use your sentences from Activities 6 and 7 to write short paragraphs. If you have other knowledge about these phenomena, add it to your composition.

**10**   Play a "chain" game with *so . . . that* and *such . . . that*. First, everyone should stand up. Then, go around the room in a chain. The first student should give an adjective, adjective + noun, or adverb. Then, the next student makes a sentence using the word(s). Choose any adjective, noun, or adverb. Your teacher will judge if the sentence is correct. If it is not, you must sit down. The last person standing wins.

**Example:**   A:  exciting class
             B:  **This is such an exciting class that I don't want to have a break!**
             B:  intelligent
             C:  **You are so intelligent that I'm sure you'll get 650 on the TOEFL.**

**11**   Test your knowledge of water trivia. How much water do you think it takes to do the following? Write your own answers. Outside of class, ask two people who are not classmates to give theirs. Afterward, analyze your data. Who guessed the most correct answers? The fewest? Then bring your data back to class and in groups of three, compare answers. Again, analyze the data. (The correct answers are at the bottom of page 398.)

| In the United States, How Many Gallons of Water Are Used . . . | Your Name | Name | Name |
|---|---|---|---|
| 1.  In an average household each year? | | | |
| 2.  By an average person daily? | | | |
| 3.  To flush a toilet? | | | |
| 4.  To take a shower? | | | |
| 5.  To brush your teeth (with the water running)? | | | |
| 6.  To shave (with the water running)? | | | |
| 7.  To wash dishes by hand? | | | |
| 8.  To run a dishwasher? | | | |
| 9.  To run a washing machine? | | | |
| 10. To produce a quart of milk? | | | |
| 11. To produce one tomato? | | | |
| 12. To produce the nation's newspapers for a day? | | | |
| **Extra Question**   What percentage of the world's population does not have clean water? | | | |

# Video Activities: Air Pollution

**Before You Watch.**   Answer the following questions in small groups.

1.  Smog is a kind of _____ pollution.
    a. air                          b. water                      c. noise

2.  What causes smog?
    a. cars and factories        b. bad weather              c. construction

3.  What problems does smog cause?

**Watch.**   Answer the following questions.

1.  The Environmental Protection Agency's new rules will _____ air pollution.
    a. decrease                  b. eliminate                 c. cause

2.  How does the oil industry feel about the new rules? Why?

3.  The new rules will make diesel fuel _____.
    a. cleaner and cheaper                c. safer but more expensive
    b. less expensive but more dangerous

**Watch Again.**

1.  The EPA's new rules will decrease sulphur emissions by _____.
    a. 90%                       b. 7%                        c. 97%

2.  The EPA is particularly worried about emissions from which two kinds of vehicles?
    a. cars      b. trucks      c. motorcycles      d. buses      e. motorhomes

3.  According to an official from the oil industry, the new rules will create new national standards that the industry cannot _____ for a _____ that fuel distributions systems cannot _____ at _____ American consumers cannot _____.

4.  What diseases does air pollution cause?
    a. cancer        b. tuberculosis        c. malaria        d. asthma

5.  When do the new rules start to go into effect?

6.  How long will old vehicles be on the roads?

**After You Watch.**   Complete these sentences logically and grammatically.

1.  The new EPA rules are very strict, as a result, _____.

2.  Air pollution is a big problem in some cities, consequently _____.

3.  Despite _____, car emissions continue to be a problem.

4.  Great strides have been made in reducing water pollution, in contrast _____.

5.  While _____, the oil industry continues to oppose them.

## Focus on Testing

### Use of Adverb Clauses and Phrases

Adverb clauses and phrases are frequently tested on standardized English proficiency exams. Review these commonly tested structures and check your understanding by completing the sample items that follow.

**Remember that . . .**

- Clauses follow subordinating conjunctions.
- Phrases follow prepositions.
- In formal English, *so that* (not *so*) must be used to express purpose.
- A modal auxiliary is generally used in clauses with *so that*.

**Part 1:**   Circle the correct completion for the following.

**Example:**   _____ he appears happy with his work, he often complains about the schedule.

    a.  In spite of            c.  Even
    b.  Despite               (d.)  Even though

1. The geologist was gathering rock samples _____ he could locate a site for drilling.
    a.  that                 c.  so
    b.  so that             d.  such that

2. It was _____ polluted well that we couldn't use water from it.
    a.  so                 c.  such a
    b.  such              d.  so many

3. Surface winds are rare at the equator _____ the earth and the atmosphere rotate at the same speed there.
    a.  because          c.  because of
    b.  so               d.  due to

4. _____ recent changes in weather patterns, scientists are predicting severe droughts and floods in many countries in the future.
    a.  Because          c.  Because of
    b.  So               d.  Due

**Part 2:**   Circle the letter below the underlined word(s) containing an error.

**Example:**   <u>Overseas</u> travelers frequently experience culture shock <u>even</u> they
          A                                          (B)
<u>may have spent</u> a <u>good deal of</u> time in foreign countries.
      C            D

1. The Great Lakes in <u>North America</u> form <u>the large</u> body of fresh water in <u>the</u>
    A                  B                 C                      D
    world.

2. In English, the expression *tidal wave* is often used despite these giant waves,
                                              A           B

   which are most likely caused by lifts or drops in the ocean floor,
    C

   have nothing to do with tides.
             D

3. Naturally occurring radon emits so large quantities of radiation that it poses
        A                    B                      C

   one of the most worrisome environmental problems in the United States
             D

   today.

4. Because many hurricanes are accompanied by a tornadoes in the
    A                           B         C

   surrounding areas, destruction often extends far beyond coastal areas.
                                  D

*Answers:*

**Extra** 30 percent

| | |
|---|---|
| 6. 10 to 15 gallons | 12. 300 million gallons |
| 5. 2 gallons | 11. 8 gallons |
| 4. 25 to 50 gallons | 10. 4 gallons |
| 3. 5 to 7 gallons | 9. 30 gallons |
| 2. 168 gallons | 8. 10 gallons |
| 1. 107,000 gallons | 7. 20 gallons |

# Chapter 12

# Together on a Small Planet

# Introduction

In this chapter, you will study some of the uses of noun clauses, including reported speech and embedded questions. You will also study how to reduce these clauses to phrases. Finally, you will review a variety of clauses and other structures covered in the text.

The following passage was written by the noted anthropologist Margaret Mead many years ago, yet its message holds true today. This passage introduces the chapter theme, "Together on a Small Planet," and raises some of the topics and issues you will cover in the chapter.

## Margaret Mead Speaking on the Future of Humanity

I am optimistic by nature. I am glad that I am alive. I am glad that I am living at this particular, very difficult, very dangerous, and very crucial period in human history. To this extent my viewpoint about the future reflects a personal temperamental bent—something that must always be taken into account. But, of course, unsupported optimism is not enough.      5

I support my optimism with my knowledge of how far mankind has come. Throughout the hundreds of thousands of years that human life has evolved, at first physically and later culturally, human beings have withstood tremendous changes and have adjusted to radically new demands. What we have to realize, I believe, is that human ingenuity, imagination, and faith in life itself have been      10 crucial both in initiating changes and in meeting new demands imposed by change.

As an anthropologist I also have seen how a living generation of men born into a Stone Age culture has moved into a modern world all at once, skipping the many small steps by which mankind as a whole moved from the distant past into      15 the present.

I find these things encouraging. An earlier generation invented the idea of invention. Now we have invented the industrialization of invention—a way of meeting a recognized problem by setting hundreds of trained persons together to work out solutions and, equally important, to work out the means of putting solutions      20 into practice.

This is what made it possible to send men to the moon and to begin the exploration of outer space. This should give us reason to believe also that we can meet the interlocking problems of runaway populations, war, and the pollution of the earth on which we depend for life. None of these problems is      25 insoluble.

What we need is the will to demand solutions and the patience to learn how to carry them out.

Margaret Mead

**Discussing Ideas.**   What do you believe about the future of our world? Are you optimistic, as Mead was? Or are you pessimistic? Why?

| PART 1 | # Clauses with *That* |
|---|---|

## Setting the Context

**Prereading Question**   What are the three most important things in your life? As you read the following passage, compare your own ideas to those of the author.

---

### On Friendship

If someone asked me to list the three most important things in my life, I'd have to tell the person my health, my family, and my friends. And I'd say that I worked very hard at all three of them. I know that you can't choose your family, and I realize sometimes you can't guarantee your health. But I believe that you are responsible for your friends. You make them and you keep them. Or, you lose them.  **5** Someone once said that a true friend was the best possession, and that's a proverb I believe in. I believe that you have to treat your friends accordingly. Treat them with care and affection just as you would your most valuable possession.

---

Edward Sonnenberg

**Discussing Ideas.**   Do you agree with Sonnenberg about his three choices? Would you add any others?

## A. Clauses with That

Noun clauses may replace nouns or pronouns as subjects, objects, or complements. These clauses often begin with the subordinating conjunction *that*. In conversational English, *that* is frequently omitted.

|  | **Examples** | **Notes** |
|---|---|---|
| **Noun or Pronoun Object** | I know **something.** | Noun clauses often follow such verbs as *agree, believe, feel, find, hope, know, mention, notice, realize, regret, remark, say, tell, think, understand,* and *wish.* |
| **Noun Clause Object** | I know **(that) friends are important.** |  |

**1** Answer the following questions. Use noun clauses after *learn, realize, know, regret,* and *believe.*

1. What have you learned about people in general during this class?
2. What are the three most important things about other cultures that you have learned during this class?
3. What have you realized about your own culture?
4. What are five new things that you now know about English?
5. Is there anything that you regret about your work in English?
6. What do you think is the most valuable thing about your experience here?
7. What do you suppose that you will do when you leave here?
8. Have you found that your English improved during this course?

**2** Work in groups of four to six students. Fill out the following chart by using your answers to Activity 1. Then use the chart to report to the rest of the class. Use "reporting clauses" such as *We (all) agree (believe, think) that . . . , several of us feel that . . . , some of us have found that . . . ,* and so on.

| |
|---|
| *We (all) . . .* |
| *Most of us . . .* |
| *Some of us . . .* |
| *A few of us . . .* |
| *None of us . . .* |

## B. Quotations and Reported Speech

Quotations are the exact words that someone says. They are used with quotation marks, and a comma often precedes or follows the quote. Reported speech gives the ideas, but *not necessarily* the exact words, of the original speaker or writer. Reported speech does not generally require commas or quotation marks.

| | Examples |
|---|---|
| **Quotation** | Ralph Waldo Emerson once said, "The only way to have a friend is to be one." |
| **Reported Speech** | Ralph Waldo Emerson once said that the only way to have a friend was (is) to be a friend to someone. |

## C. Sequence of Tenses in Reported Speech

Verbs and certain modal auxiliaries may shift to past forms in reported speech. These shifts most often occur when the report is being given at a different time or place from the action. If the information is still true at the moment of speaking, the shift from present to past may be optional. The changes must be consistent, however. *That* is also optional in most of these sentences.

| Changes in Verb Tense | | |
|---|---|---|
| **Quotations** | **Reported Speech** | **Notes** |
| "Max is at home."<br><br>"Max is studying."<br><br>"He is going to study all day."<br><br><br>"He has a lot of work."<br><br>"He hasn't finished yet." | Molly said Max was at home.<br><br>She mentioned that he was studying.<br><br>She remarked that he was going to study all day.<br><br>She said he had a lot of work.<br><br>She added he hadn't finished yet. | In reported speech, when the verb in the main clause (e.g., *Molly said, he mentioned*) is in the past, the verb in the noun clause is often in a past tense. The verb in the noun clause may shift from present to past or present perfect to past perfect. |
| "He started yesterday."<br><br><br>"He was working very hard." | She said he started (had started) yesterday.<br><br>She said he was working (had been working) very hard. | The shift of simple past and past continuous tenses in the noun clause to perfect forms is often optional. |

*Note:* In some cases, use of the past perfect or past perfect continuous changes the meaning. It can indicate that a situation is finished or is no longer true. Compare: *He said that he wanted to go.* (Perhaps he still wants to). *He said that he had wanted to go.* (He no longer wants to or he can't go.)

| Changes in Modal Auxiliaries | | |
|---|---|---|
| **Quotations** | **Reported Speech** | **Notes** |
| "Max can't go."<br><br>"Max may go later."<br><br>"He will tell us."<br><br>"He must finish his work." | She said that Max couldn't go.<br><br>She remarked that he might go later.<br><br>She added he would tell us.<br><br>She stressed that he had to finish his work. | *Can* often shifts to *could*.<br><br>*May* often shifts to *might*.<br><br>*Will* often shifts to *would*.<br><br>*Must* is sometimes changed to *had to* when need is expressed. |

*Note:* In reported speech, modals are changed less frequently than other verbs or auxiliaries because of the problems of differences in meaning.

| Changes in Commands | | |
|---|---|---|
| **Quotations** | **Reported Speech** | **Notes** |
| "Let's leave at 8:00."<br><br><br>"Be on time." | She said that we should leave at 8:00.<br><br>She told me very firmly that I must be on time. | In reported speech, an appropriate noun or pronoun is added to a command. *Should* or other modal auxiliaries are used, depending on the strength of the original command. |

**3**   Even good friends have problems, and one way to save friendships is by talking things over. In the following conversation, a group of roommates is trying to resolve a common problem, housework. Retell the conversation in reported speech by completing the sentences that follow. Be sure to use appropriate verb forms in your new sentences.

*Steve:* We're all good friends, but we've been having a lot of problems lately.

*Tom:* Well, in my opinion, the biggest problem is cleaning. The apartment is a mess. Nobody cleaned last week or the week before. We must find a way to keep things cleaner.

*John:* We can make a list of jobs to do, and each person can sign up for a job.

*Peter:* I'll be responsible for the kitchen area.

*Tom:* I'll do the living room, but we need a vacuum cleaner!

*Steve:* I'm going to check the newspaper. I may be able to find a good used one.

**Example:**   Steve said that they *had been having a lot of problems lately.*

1.   Steve remarked that they . . .

2.   However, he said . . .

3.   Tom felt the biggest problem . . .

4.   Moreover, he said . . .

5.   He added that nobody _____ and that they _____.

6.   John remarked that they _____ and that each person _____.

7.   Peter stated that he _____.

8.   Tom added that he _____ but that they _____.

9.   Steve mentioned that he _____.

10.   He added that he _____.

## D. Say *Versus* Tell

| Examples | Notes |
|---|---|
| Molly **said** that Max had to work. | In general, *say* is used when the listener is *not* mentioned. |
| Molly **told me** that Max had to work. | *Tell* is used when the listener *is* mentioned. (We say something, but we tell *someone* something.) |

**4**   Reread the conversation in Activity 3. Then complete the following with the past form of *say* or *tell*.

**Example:**   Steve _said_ that they'd been having a lot of problems lately.

1.   Steve _____ his roommates that they were all good friends.

2.   Tom _____ his roommates that cleaning was their biggest problem.

3.   Tom _____ that the house hadn't been cleaned in two weeks.

4.   John _____ that they could each choose a job to do.

5.   Peter _____ that he would clean the kitchen.

6.   Tom _____ everyone that he would take care of the living room.

7.   Finally, Steve _____ the others that he would try to find a vacuum cleaner.

## E. Pronoun and Adverb Changes in Reported Speech

In reported speech, pronouns are changed to show a change in speakers. Adjectives and adverbs are sometimes changed too. The use of *this, that, these, those, now, then, here,* and *there* depends on the time and place of the reported speech. *Today, tomorrow,* and *yesterday* may also change according to the time of the reported speech. Remember to be consistent. If you make the change in one place, you must make it in all cases.

|  | **Quotations** | **Reported Speech** |
|---|---|---|
| **Pronouns** | Mary said, "I need your help." <br> Mary said, "We must finish soon!" <br> Erik said, "You have to finish immediately." | Mary said that she needed my help. <br> Mary said they had to finish soon. <br> Erik said that we had to finish immediately. |
| **Demonstrative Pronouns and Adjectives** | Mary said, "This is important." <br> Mary said, "These papers are important." | Mary said that was important. <br> Mary said those papers were important. |
| **Adverbs** | Mary said, "I need them now." <br> Mary said, "T404he papers are here." | Mary said she needed them then. <br> Mary said that the papers were there. |

**5**   The following quotations are students' responses to various questions. Change each quotation to reported speech. Make all necessary changes in verb tenses, pronouns, and so on. Note that you do not need to use a "reporting clause" with every sentence; however, you do need to be consistent in all changes.

**Example:**   "I've really learned a lot here. I even learned how to surf!"
—Noriko, female, Japan

*Noriko said that she had really learned a lot there. She'd even learned how to surf.*

1.   What has been the best part of your stay in California?
  a.   "I've made wonderful new friends during my visit. I hope some of them will come to see me in Japan." —Masahiko, male, Japan
  b.   "I got married." —Walter, male, Poland

2. What do you like best about Boston?
   a. "I really enjoy the variety of people here."—Rita, female, Brazil
   b. "I can do almost anything here. This afternoon I may see a movie; there are at least ten good ones to pick from. Or I may go to a museum; there are several excellent ones."—Frank, male, Switzerland
3. How did you like the experience of spending a winter in Wisconsin?
   a. "We were extremely cold at first! We weren't used to cold weather at all. Little by little, my family is learning to adapt to it."—Lijia, female, Nicaragua
   b. "It was difficult at the beginning. Some days I almost froze while I was walking home. I'm finally getting used to it."—Bedi, male, Mauritania

## F. Verbs and Modal Auxiliaries That Do Not Change in Reported Speech

| | Quotations | Reported Speech | Notes |
|---|---|---|---|
| **No Tense Changes** | Molly says, "Max is at home." Molly adds, "He hasn't finished his work yet." | Molly says Max is at home. Molly adds that he hasn't finished his work yet. | In reported speech, no tense change occurs when the verb in the main clause is in the present tense. |
| **Optional Tense Changes** | Molly said, "Max is a hard worker." Molly said, "He works very hard." | Molly said Max was (is) a hard worker. Molly said he worked (works) very hard. | When the noun clause gives factual information that is true in general, either present or past forms may be used. |
| **No Change in Modal Auxiliaries** | Molly said, "Max should finish soon." | Molly said Max should finish soon. | *Could, might, ought to, should,* and *would* are not generally changed in reported speech. |
| | Molly added, "He must be tired." She remarked, "He ought to have started sooner." | Molly added that he must be tired. She remarked that he ought to have startedsooner. | *Must* does not change when it expresses probability. Perfect modals are not changed in reported speech. |

**6** **Error Analysis.** Many of the following statements have errors in their use of reported speech. Note that most of these statements can be true at any time, so certain changes will be optional. As you find the various errors, remember to be consistent in your corrections.

                                     *said*

**Example:**    Ralph Waldo Emerson (once said) that the only way to have a friend

         <u>was</u> to be one. *Either **was** or **is** is correct.*

1. Charles Colton once wrote that true friendship was like good health. The value of it is seldom known until it is lost.
2. Elbert Hubbard remarked that your friend is the person who knows all about me and still liked me.
3. In her book *Emma*, Jane Austen wrote that business might bring money, but friendship hardly ever did.

4. Ned Rorem once commented that sooner or later you've heard all my best friends have to say. Now came the tolerance of real love.

5. In his journals, Emerson remarked that one of the blessings of old friends was that you can afford to be stupid with them.

6. Kurt Vonnegut wrote that love was where you find it. It was foolish to go looking for it.

7. In the first century, a Roman author comments that the friendship that can come to an end had never really begun.

8. La Rochefoucauld wrote in his *Maxims* that however rare true love may be, it is less rare than true friendship.

**7** Ann Landers gave the following advice on love and friendship. Read her advice and make five statements using reported speech. Begin your sentences with a variety of openers: *She said, stated, mentioned, wrote,* and so forth. Use *should, ought to, have to, had better,* or *must* in the noun clause, depending on the strength of the advice.

**To Help You Improve the Quality of Life**
On this day—
Mend a quarrel,
Search out a forgotten friend,
Dismiss a suspicion and replace it with trust,
Write a letter to someone who misses you,
Encourage a youth who has lost faith,
Keep a promise,
Forget an old grudge,
Examine your demands on others and vow to reduce them,
Fight for a principle,
Express your gratitude,
Overcome an old fear,
Take two minutes to appreciate the beauty of nature,
Tell someone you love him.
Tell him again,
And again,
And again.

ANN LANDERS, *The Ann Landers Encyclopedia*

**Example:** *Ann Landers said that I (we, people) should mend a quarrel.*

**8** Answer the following questions, using reported speech where appropriate.

1. When did you last talk to your best friend or another friend whom you hadn't seen for a while? What did you talk about? What news did your friend tell you? What did you say about that? What news did you tell your friend?

2. Have you made a promise lately? To whom did you make the promise? What did you promise?

3. Have you had an argument lately? What was it about? Whom did you argue with? What did you say to each other? How did you settle the argument?

4. Have you had to make a decision or solve a problem lately? What was the situation? Did you discuss it with anyone? What did you talk about? What advice did the person give you?

5. When was the last time you were someplace you love with a friend? What did you say to each other then?

**9**   Look back at the opening passage by Margaret Mead on page 400. Then use the following cues to help you paraphrase her ideas. Use reporting clauses to begin at least some of your sentences. *Note:* Because Margaret Mead is now dead, any quotations about her *must* be changed to past forms. The changes are optional for more general quotations.

- ■ Margaret Mead said . . .
- ■ She told us . . .
- ■ She mentioned . . .
- ■ She believed . . .

**Example:**   optimistic by nature

   *Margaret Mead said that she was optimistic by nature.*

1. glad to be alive
2. glad / live
3. support / optimism
4. human beings / withstand tremendous changes
5. human ingenuity, imagination, and faith in life / crucial to change
6. see Stone Age cultures / move into the modern world in one generation
7. mankind as a whole / move by small steps into the present
8. be encouraged by these things
9. people / can solve the problems of population, war, and pollution
10. need the will and patience to find and carry out solutions

## Using What You've Learned

**10**   In pairs or small groups, take turns asking each other questions similar to those in Activity 5. Then briefly tell the whole group what your classmates said. Use reported speech when you talk to the whole group.

**11**   Reread the comments on friendship in Activity 6. Then, in small groups or as a class, share your own ideas. Do you agree with some or all of the statements? Do you disagree with any? Can you add any other sayings about love or friendship from your own culture?

**12**   Reread the advice from Ann Landers in Activity 7. Do you have any other suggestions to add? Share your ideas in a small group discussion or in a brief composition.

**13** In small groups, discuss the following quotations about friendship. After you have finished your discussion, choose a spokesperson to give a brief report to the class. Be sure to use reported speech in the summary of your discussion.

"No man is an island . . . ; every man is part of the main. . . . Any man's death diminishes me because I am involved in mankind, and therefore never send to know for whom the bell tolls; it tolls for thee."—John Donne

"He who has a thousand friends has not a friend to spare, And he who has one enemy will meet him everywhere."—Ali ibn-Abi-Talib, *A Hundred Sayings*

"I wish that people who are conventionally supposed to love each other would say to each other when they fight, 'Please—a little less love, and a little more common decency.'"—Kurt Vonnegut, *Slapstick*

---

**PART 2**

# Clauses with *If, Whether,* and Question Words

---

## Setting the Context

**Prereading Questions**  How do we learn? How can we use our knowledge? The following quotes look at learning and knowledge. As you read them, what are your reactions?

---

### Education, Learning, and Knowledge

"Education is an admirable thing, but it is well to remember from time to time that nothing that is worth knowing can be taught."—Oscar Wilde, *"The Critic as an Artist," Intentions,* 1891

"Experience is not what happens to you; it is what you do with what happens to you."—Aldous Huxley, *Reader's Digest,* March 1956                              5

"I learned to make my mind large, as the universe is large, so that there is room for paradoxes."—Maxine Hong Kingston

"I am convinced that it is of primordial* importance to learn more every year than the year before. After all, what is education but a process by which a person begins to learn how to learn?—Peter Ustinov, *Dear Me,* 1977                      10

---

"It is not a question of how much a man knows, but what use he makes of what he knows. Not a question of what he has acquired and how he has been trained, but of what he is and what he can do."—J. G. Holland

"Time will teach more than all our thoughts."—Benjamin Disraeli

"When hungry, eat your rice; when tired, close your eyes. Fools may laugh at me, but wise men know what I mean."—Lin-Chi

**Discussing Ideas.**   Which of these quotations do you find to be true? Discuss each one with a classmate. What do they tell you about education, learning, and knowledge?

## A. Clauses with If and Whether

| Yes/No Questions | Examples | Notes |
|---|---|---|
| Is he going? | I wonder **if** he is going. | Yes/no questions may be changed into noun clauses by using *if* and *whether.* The subject must come before the verb in the noun clause. Noun clauses with *if* and *whether* are often used in polite requests. |
| Has he left yet? | Do you know **whether** he has left yet? | |
| Can he go? | I wonder **whether** he can go. | |
| Does he want to go? | Could you tell me **if** he wants to go? | |
| Did he leave? | I would like to know **whether** he left? | |

**1**   Do you have an assignment or test in the next few days? Ask your teacher for more information about it. Change the following direct questions to noun clauses. Be sure to use correct word order. Begin your questions with the following: *Could you tell me . . . ? I would like to know . . . .*

**Example:**   Will there be any more homework this session?

> *I would like to know whether (if) there will be any more homework this quarter.*

1.   Will there be a final test in this class?
2.   Do I have to take a proficiency exam?
3.   Is it necessary to study for the proficiency test?
4.   Have I completed all of the assignments for this class?
5.   Am I going to pass this course?

---

*primordial*   fundamental, primary

6.   Could I talk to you about my progress?

7.   Will we have a class party?

8.   Does anyone want to plan a party?

## B. Clauses with Question Words

| Information Questions | Examples | Notes |
|---|---|---|
| Where is the library?<br><br>How can I find it?<br><br>When does it close? | I would like to know **where the library is.**<br><br>Please tell me **how I can find it.**<br><br>Do you know **when it closes?** | Information questions may also be changed to noun clauses. Question words are used to introduce them. The subject must come *before* the verb in noun clauses. These clauses are often used in polite requests. |

**2**   Imagine that you have to write a term paper for a class. Change the following questions about the assignment to noun clauses. Be sure to correct word order. Begin your new sentences with the following:

- Could you tell me . . . ?
- I would like to know . . .
- I wonder . . .
- I don't know . . .

**Culture Note**

*Questions such as "Could you tell me whether . . . ?" and "Would you please show me how . . . ?" are very polite. If you are not certain how formal or polite to be, you can use these types of questions to avoid offending someone by being too direct.*

**Example:**   When is the paper due?

*Could you tell me when the paper is due?*

1.   How long should the paper be?

2.   How many sources should I use?

3.   Where can I get information on the topic?

4.   Which section of the library should I check?

5.   When could I discuss this with you?

6.   Where can I find a computer lab? I need to do some word processing.

7.   How many drafts do you usually do on your papers?

8.   Who will edit the first draft of my essay?

**3**   The following is an excerpt from an interview with an educational consultant. First read the interview for meaning. Then paraphrase the discussion by completing the sentences that follow. Remember to use reported speech, and try to simplify ideas whenever possible.

*Interviewer:*  What is the greatest problem facing the public schools?

*Educational consultant:*  The greatest problem is class size. The average public school class has 28 students. When class size is too big, teachers can't help students individually.

*Interviewer:*  What's the solution?

*Educational consultant:*  The solution is to develop strategies that help students learn in large groups. Cooperative learning is one of these strategies.

*Interviewer:*  What does it involve?

*Educational consultant:* Cooperative learning involves dividing the class into smaller groups. Teachers' jobs become easier because they deal with the groups instead of individuals. The students learn more because each one in the group has a responsibility. The students learn the material and, at the same time, learn cooperation, an important life skill.

*Interviewer:* How realistic is this solution?

*Educational consultant:* It's very realistic, but it takes time and commitment because teachers and administrators have to be trained in new methods.

**Example:**   The interviewer began by asking what . . .

*The interviewer began by asking what the greatest problem facing the public schools was.*

1.  The educational consultant stated . . .
2.  She explained that the average public school . . . and that . . .
3.  Next, the interviewer asked . . .
4.  The educational consultanst answered that . . .
5.  She said that cooperative learning . . .
6.  The interviewer then asked . . .
7.  The educational consultant responded that . . .
8.  She stated that teachers' jobs . . . and that the students . . .
9.  She added that the students . . .
10. Finally, the interviewer asked . . .
11. The educational consultant said . . .
12. The educational consultant also noted, however, . . .

**4**   Individually, in pairs, or in small groups, combine the following pairs or groups of sentences. Many variations are possible; above all, try to vary your sentence structures and to eliminate unnecessary words.

**Example:**   The greatest puzzle of education is a question.

How can a child learn best?

*The greatest puzzle of education is how a child can learn best.*

How can people learn best?

1.  People everywhere agree on an idea.
    Education is important.
    Few people agree on something.
    How should we provide education?
2.  Does a child learn well in these ways?
    Information is taught by practice.
    Information is taught by repetition.
    Information is taught by memorization.
3.  Does a child learn better in other ways?
    The teacher stimulates the child's curiosity.
    The teacher makes learning fun.
    The teacher makes learning pleasant.

4. Some subjects must be memorized.
   These include the alphabet and numbers.
   These include the rules of spelling.
   These include the multiplication tables.

5. Memorization is a part of education.
   Repetitive drill is a part of education.

6. Does this mean something?
   Can most learning be taught in that way?
   Should most learning be taught in that way?

7. Should learning be fun for the student?
   Is schooling very hard work?
   The student must be forced to do it.

8. Someday we may be able to answer these questions.
   Then we may be able to learn the secret of a truly good education.

## Using What You've Learned

**5**  Reread the quotations on pages 409 and 410. How do these ideas apply to the process of learning a language? Give your ideas and opinions in a brief composition about language learning.

**6**  Find someone outside your class to interview about education. You may want to ask about language learning, or you can look at a different field. You can explore formal learning (in schools and universities, for example), or you can ask about informal learning (through experience).

   First, prepare four to five good questions to ask your interviewee. Tape-record your interview or take notes as the person talks. Later, write a report on the interview. Use reported speech. Finally, share your information with your classmates.

**7**  Read the following quotation from the 20th century British leader Sir Winston Churchill.

   "I am always ready to learn, but I am not always ready to be taught."

Do you agree with Winston Churchill? Write a short paragraph reacting to the quotation. You may want to reflect on your own education. You can use some of the following expressions:

   *I agree / disagree with Churchill because* . . .
   *I think that* . . .
   *I remember once when* . . .
   *When I was* . . .
   *As a result* . . .
   *If I hadn't* . . .
   *Nevertheless* . . .
   *On the other hand* . . .

**8** Organize a debate on the merits of education versus experience. One team will argue in favor of formal education and the other team in favor of experience. If you want, you can focus the debate on the process of language learning: can you really learn a language in a classroom? Without a class and a teacher, do people have enough discipline to learn a language well?

**9** Imagine that you have the opportunity to interview today's world leaders. In small groups, prepare a list of at least ten questions. Use the following expressions in your questions: *We would like to know . . . We would like to ask you . . . Could you please explain to us . . . ? We don't understand . . . Could you tell us . . . ?* Then take turns role-playing world leaders. The rest of the class will ask questions to the "leaders."

---

| PART 3 | # Clause to Phrase Reduction |

---

## Setting the Context

**Prereading Questions** Do you believe that world peace is possible? Or do you believe that there will always be war?

---

### Thoughts on War and Peace

The French statesman George Clemenceau once said, "I don't know whether war is an interlude during peace, or peace is an interlude during war." Given the political changes of the past decades, perhaps we can create a very long interlude of peace. Perhaps,   **5** we can even create a lasting peace. The question is not whether to try, but rather how to achieve it.

---

**Discussing Ideas.** What is your opinion of the quote from Clemenceau? Do war and peace necessarily alternate, or can one exist without the other?

## A. Reduction of Commands

Commands can be reduced to infinitive phrases in reported speech. The infinitive expresses the same meaning as *should* + infinitive. The verbs *advise, beg, command, direct, encourage, order, urge,* and *warn* follow the same pattern as *tell* in infinitive phrases. The indirect object must be used.

| | Reported Speech with Noun Clauses | Reduction to Infinitive Phrases |
|---|---|---|
| **Quotations with Commands**<br>She said "Come early."<br>She told us, "Come early." | She said **that we should come** early.<br>She told us **that we should come** early. | She said **to come** early.<br>She told us **to come** early.<br>She advised (urged) us **to come** early. |

**1** The military is an institution that uses many commands. Change the following commands first to noun clauses and then to infinitive phrases. Remember to add modal auxiliaries and nouns or pronouns when necessary.

**Example:**   The sergeant said, "Stand up."
*The sergeant said that we should stand up.*
*The sergeant said to stand up.*

1. The officer ordered, "March."
2. The officer said, "Do not talk."
3. The commander said, "Halt, soldier."
4. The major advised, "Do not relax."
5. The soldier begged, "Give us some water."
6. The officer warned, "Be quiet."
7. The sergeant commanded, "Salute the general."
8. The general said, "Stand at ease, soldiers."
9. My platoon leader shouted, "Attention."
10. The drill sergeant yelled, "Double time, G.I.s!"

## B. Reduction of Requests for Action and for Permission

Requests with *Will you* . . . , *Can you* . . . , *Would you* . . . , and *Could you* . . . can be reduced to infinitive phrases. The indirect object *must* be used with the infinitive phrase. Requests with *May I* . . . , *Could I* . . . , and *Can I* . . . can also be reduced to infinitive phrases, but no indirect object is used.

| | Reported Speech with Noun Clauses | Reduction to Infinitive Phrases |
|---|---|---|
| **Quotations with Request for Action**<br>She asked (us). "Will you come early?"<br>She asked (us), "Could you help me?" | She asked (us) **if we would come** early.<br>She asked (us) **whether we could help** her. | She said **to come** early.<br>She asked us **to help** her. |
| **Quotations with Request for Permission**<br>She asked (me), "Could I speak to John?" | She asked (me) **if she could speak** to John. | She asked **to speak** to John. |

**2**   First, change the quotations to reported speech using noun clauses. Then reduce the noun clauses to infinitive phrases. Remember to add nouns or pronouns when necessary.

**Example:**   She asked, "Could I help you?"
*She asked if she could help me.*
*She asked to help me.*

1. She asked, "Could you tell me the time?"
2. He asked, "May I use your phone?"
3. They asked their lawyer, "Would you please read this?"
4. The little boy asked his mother, "Can I go to Martin's house?"
5. The police officer asked, "May I see your driver's license?"
6. I asked, "Could you give me some change?"
7. The teacher asked the class, "Can anyone tell me the answer to number five?"
8. The waiter asked the customer, "Wouldn't you like to see the dessert menu?"

## C. Reduction of Embedded Questions

Yes / no questions with modal auxiliaries can be reduced to infinitive phrases. *Whether (or not)* is always used with an infinitive form. Information questions (with *how, what, when,* and *where*) may also be reduced. With both types of questions, the speaker and the subject of the question *must* be the same person(s). Indirect objects are not necessary with either type of reduced question.

|  | **Reported Speech with Noun Clauses** | **Reduction to Infinitive Phrases** |
|---|---|---|
| **Quotations with Yes/No Questions**<br>We asked (her), "Should we leave now?"<br>We asked (her), "Should we come at six or at seven?" | We asked (her) **if we should leave then.**<br>We asked (her) **whether we should come** at six or at seven. | We asked (her) **whether (or not) to leave then.**<br>We asked (her) **whether to come** at six or at seven. |
| **Quotations with Information Questions**<br>We asked (her), "How can we get to your house?"<br>We asked (her), "Where should we park?" | We asked (her) **how we could get** to her house.<br>We asked (her) **where we should park.** | We asked (her) **how to get** to her house.<br>We asked (her) **where to park.** |

**3**   First, change the quotations to reported speech using noun clauses. Then reduce the noun clauses to infinitive phrases.

**Example:**   He asked, "Where can I park nearby?"
*He asked where he could park nearby.*
*He asked where to park nearby.*

1. She asked, "What can I do about that?"
2. He wondered, "Where should I get off the bus?"

3. They asked, "Should we buy that house?"
4. I wondered, "Should I call him?"
5. They asked the police officer, "How do we get to the library from here?"
6. We asked, "When should we leave for the play?"
7. You asked me, "Should I buy a new book?"
8. They asked us, "Whose car can we borrow?"

**4**  Following are classroom requests and commands. First, change each quotation to reported speech using noun clauses. Then reduce the noun clauses to infinitive phrases.

**Example:**   Our teacher warned us, "Do all the homework."
*Our teacher warned us that we should do all the homework.*
*Our teacher warned us to do all the homework.*

1. Our teacher reminded us, "Study for the test!"
2. He told us, "Review the entire chapter."
3. He said, "Go over the information several times."
4. John asked the teacher, "Would you repeat the assignment, please?"
5. Mary asked the teacher, "Could you explain noun clauses again?"
6. Nancy asked the teacher, "How much time should I spend reviewing?"
7. The teacher said, "Don't spend more than two hours."
8. Harry asked, "When should I come for the test?"
9. Susan asked, "What should I bring?"
10. She asked, "May I use a dictionary?"
11. The teacher told her, "Don't bring a dictionary."
12. The teacher added, "Don't worry too much!"

**5**  What are some other typical classroom commands, questions, and answers? Write at least three. After your teacher has checked your paper, exchange it with another classmate. Change your classmate's sentences first to reported speech and then to infinitive phrases.

**6**  **Review.**   First read the following passage for meaning. Then complete it by adding appropriate connecting words. Choose from the following: *although, and, as, because, because of, despite, how many, that, when, where.*

### Our Planet

_Although_ it's often hard to remember, the world _____ we live in is only a frag-
  1                                                          2

ment in history and in the universe. And _____ our different countries and
                                            3

languages, we are *all* part of this same small fragment of life.

Sometimes it takes an extraordinary event or point of view to remember

_____ there is a larger picture beyond our world. For astronaut Russell
  4

Schweikert, this came in 1969 _____ he looked at the earth from space in the
5

Apollo IX Lunar Module. Said Schweikert, "_____ you go around it (the earth) in
6

an hour and a half, you begin to recognize _____ your identity is with that *whole*
7

thing. And that makes a change.

   "You look down there, _____ you can't imagine _____ borders and
8                                9

boundaries you cross, again and again and again, _____ you don't even see
10

them. There you are—hundreds of people killing each other _____ some imagi-
11

nary line _____ you're not even aware of _____ you can't see it. From
12                                    13

_____ you see it (the earth from a spacecraft), the thing is a whole, _____
14                                                 15

it's so beautiful. You wish _____ you could take one (person) in each hand and
16

say, 'Look at it from this perspective. What's important?'

   "You realize _____ on that small spot, that little blue and white thing, is
17

everything _____ means anything to you. All of history and music and poetry
18

and art and birth and love: tears, joy, games. All of it on that little spot out there

_____ you can cover with your thumb."
19

## Using What You've Learned

**7**    Only a few months before his death in 1963, John F. Kennedy talked about our world
during a commencement address at American University. Kennedy said:

> We can help make the world safe for diversity. For, in the final analysis, our most
> basic common link is that we all inhabit this small planet. We all breathe the same
> air. We all cherish our children's future. And we are all mortal.

In a discussion with your classmates or in a brief composition, describe some of the
bonds that you now share with others because of your English studies. What have you
learned about other people and other cultures? How has this affected you?

**8**    Individually, in small groups, or as a class, use the following guidelines to help you
write short poems. You may choose your own topic or select from the suggestions that
follow.

**Possible Topics**
1.  Write a poem about a classmate.
2.  Write a poem about English (grammar, composition, and so on).
3.  Write about an emotion or idea: love, friendship, homesickness, curiosity.
4.  Write about a favorite place.
5.  Write about your home area or country.

**Guidelines**

You need not follow these strictly.

*Line 1:* Write a sentence of three to five words about your topic.
*Line 2:* Take a noun from line 1 and describe it.
*Line 3:* Add movement to the idea in line 2.
*Line 4:* Pick a word in line 3 and compare it to something *(X is like . . . ).*
*Line 5:* Take the idea in line 4 and describe it or add more action.
*Line 6:* Take the idea in line 5 and compare it to something *(X is . . . ).*
*Line 7:* Make the idea in line 6 either very big or very small.
*Line 8:* Describe the idea in line 7.
*Lines 9 to 10:* Make a final statement (your opinion, and so on).

**A Smaller World**

We came from so many places,
Gentle, crowded, warm, noisy, icy places,
Excited travelers, nervous and naive,
Like newborns entering a new world.
Babbling and blundering our way to English,
Like babies learning to talk.
Mountains of words, ideas, customs to climb,
A struggle for understanding.
Yet our world has become smaller
Because we have known each other.

CLASS POEM WRITTEN BY STUDENTS FROM MEXICO,
BRAZIL, JAPAN, COLOMBIA, KUWAIT, HONDURAS,
SWITZERLAND, AND INDONESIA

The earth rising above the moon's horizon.

# Video Activities: An Endangered Species

**Before You Watch.**   Answer the following questions in small groups.

1.   What are kangaroos and where are they found?
2.   How do kangaroos move?
     a.  They run.                         c.  They swim.
     b.  They fly.                          d.  They jump.
3.   Have you ever seen a kangaroo in a tree?

**Watch.**   Answer these questions in small groups.

1.   What kind of animal is this video about?
2.   How is this animal different from a normal kangaroo?
3.   What helps this animal climb trees?
     a.  large teeth                      c.  strong legs
     b.  muscular tail                   d.  curved claws
4.   Where is this animal found?
5.   Scientists believe that there are _____ tree kangaroos left.
     a.  many                 b.  no                    c.  few
6.   What are the two threats to this animal's survival?
     a.  other kangaroos            c.  hunting by people
     b.  loss of habitat               d.  disease

**Watch Again.**

1.   What adjectives describe tree kangaroos?
     a.  dangerous                     d.  happy
     b.  shy                               e.  reclusive
     c.  friendly
2.   Dr. Betts studies how these animals _____, _____, and _____.
     a.  eat                               c.  live
     b.  reproduce                      d.  behave
3.   People hunt tree kangaroos for their _____.
     a.  meat                             c.  claws
     b.  skins                            d.  tails
4.   How many new species of tree kangaroos have been found in the past
     decade? _____

**After You Watch.**   Change these statements to reported speech.

1.   Dr. Betts says, "I have spent many years studying tree kangaroos."
2.   The biologist said, "If we don't try to help these animals, in a few years,
     there won't be any more."
3.   An anti-conservationist said, "It is more important to save people than
     animals."
4.   The biologist said, "Two new species have been discovered in the past
     decade."

## Focus on Testing

### Use of Noun Clauses

Noun clauses are frequently tested on standardized English proficiency exams. Review these commonly tested structures and check your understanding by completing the sample items below.

**Remember that . . .**

- In reported speech, you must be consistent in changes in verb tenses, modal auxiliaries, pronouns, and adverbials.
- In questions used as noun clauses, the subject comes before the verb.
- You *tell someone something,* but you *say something to someone.*

**Part 1:**   Circle the correct completion for the following.

**Example:**   I don't know _____ unhappy with his work schedule.
    a.  why is John
    b.  why does John
    (c.)  why John is
    d.  is John

1. The instructor _____ that the test would cover the last four chapters of the book.
    a.  said the class
    b.  told
    c.  told to the class
    d.  said to the class

2. Our new neighbors wanted to know _____.
    a.  where the nearest store had been
    b.  where the nearest store was
    c.  where was the nearest store
    d.  where is the nearest store

3. We were wondering how _____ to the concert on time.
    a.  could we get
    b.  are we going to get
    c.  we could get
    d.  can we get

4. Lisa asked _____ with the project.
    a.  to Tom to help her
    b.  Tom if he help her
    c.  Tom to help her
    d.  Tom whether he would help to her

**Part 2:**   Circle the letter below the underlined word(s) containing an error.

**Example:**   Overseas travelers frequently experience culture shock whether
           A                                                B

        or not have they already done a good deal of traveling.
              Ⓒ                     D

1.   Could you please tell me how many countries are there in the United Nations
                 A B                 C

    at this time?
        D

2.   Educators often debate whether or not is rote memorization a valuable way
             A          B     C

    of learning.
       D

3.   Margaret Mead, the noted anthropologist, once told that humanity's greatest
             A   B                     C

    attributes are ingenuity, imagination, and faith.
         D

4.   Scientists have long puzzled over the idea of how do many animals
             A       B            C

    communicate with precision.
          D

---

## PART 4    Review: Chapters 9 to 12

**1   Review.**   Complete the following sentences with appropriate past tense forms—active or passive voice—of the verbs in parentheses.

1.   A form of writing _was developed_ by the Sumerians during the fourth century
                  (develop)

    B.C.E.

2.   The Egyptian pyramids _____ over 4000 years ago.
                       (build)

3.   By about 100 B.C.E., the Chinese _____ an Imperial University,
                            (build)

    _____ irrigation methods and water clocks, and _____
    (develop)                                      (invent)

    sundials and seismographs.

4.   By about 300 C.E., the Mayans _____ the "Long Count," a complex
                        (use)

    calendar that _____ extremely accurate. The Mayans _____ a
              (be)                          (develop / also)

    complex arithmetic and _____ the first humans to use a symbol for zero.
                     (be)

5.  In 1456, Johannes Gutenberg and his associates _____ the first book,
    (print)

    the Latin Bible, which _____ of 643 leaves of paper.
    (compose)

6.  Around 1590, William Shakespeare _____ in London and _____
    (arrive)                              (begin)

    writing his first plays, the three parts of *Henry VI.*

7.  During the 1770s, James Watt _____ the steam engine, which
    (develop)

    _____ the beginning of the Industrial Revolution.
    (signal)

8.  Not long before his death in 1827, Ludwig van Beethoven _____ his
    (compose)

    Ninth Symphony, which _____ the first symphony to use singers and a
    (be)

    chorus. At that time, Beethoven _____ completely deaf.
    (become / already)

9.  The daguerreotype photography process _____ in 1837 by Louis
    (invent)

    Daguerre. While Daguerre _____ his process, William Talbot
    (perfect)

    _____ the process of making negatives. In 1839, it _____
    (develop)                                                      (become)

    possible to make multiple copies of a picture.

10. In 1872, Yellowstone National Park _____. It _____ the first of
    (found)                              (be)

    its kind in the world and _____ an example for countries everywhere
    (set)

    to follow.

11. Orville and Wilbur Wright _____ the first sustained flight of a pow-
    (make)

    ered aircraft in 1903. Before then, Otto Lilienthal _____ many
    (make / already)

    flights in gliders.

12. The special theory of relativity _____ by Einstein in 1905.
    (publish)

13. Alexander Fleming _____ the life-saving properties of penicillin in
    (discover)

    1928.

14. On July 21, 1969, Neil Armstrong _____ the first human to walk on
    (become)

    the surface of the moon. Numerous satellites _____ before then, and
    (launch)

    astronauts _____ the moon, but no one _____ the surface
    (orbit)                                          (touch / ever)

    until that day.

**2   Review.**  Complete the following passage with appropriate present and future forms—active or passive voice—of the verbs in parentheses.

### The State of our Earth

How ___is___ our earth ___doing___ these days? Many critics _____ that we
      1 (be)                  2 (do)                                           3 (say)

_____ a disaster of horrible proportions. Others _____ that while we
    4 (approach/fast)                                              5 (claim)

_____ by very serious problems, numerous healthy signs _____. What
    6 (face)                                                          7 (exist)

_____ some of the worst crises that _____ us?
8 (be)                                  9 (face)

■  All three major sources of food—ocean fisheries, rangelands, and croplands—

    _____ in trouble. Much of our existing land _____ or _____.
       10 (be)                                              11 (overgraze)        12 (overfarm)

■  World per capita grain production _____, yet worldwide demand for it
                                          13 (fall)

    _____, in large part because of the demand for beef. Seven pounds
       14 (increase)

    of grain _____ to add one pound to a steer.
              15 (need)

■  Of all 9600 species of birds, 6500 _____ in decline, and 1000 of these
                                          16 (be)

    _____ by extinction.
       17 (threaten)

■  Sixty to 70 percent of the coral reef systems in Southeast Asia _____
                                                                        18 (degrade)

    from dynamite fishing, coral mining, and coastal development.

■  Hundreds of acres of tropical rainforest _____ each day. What _____
                                                19 (cut)                      20 (be)

    some of the positive signs? Consider the following:

■  Child mortality _____ worldwide.
                      21 (drop/currently)

■  Production of CFCs, which _____ holes in the ozone layer, _____.
                               22 (create)                            23 (decrease)

■  Recycled paper _____ in over 60 percent of the U.S. paper output.
                     24 (use)

■  Use of wind power _____, especially in Europe.
                        25 (rise/rapidly)

■  The world _____ three times more bicycles than cars.
                26 (produce)

■  In the United States, the number of commuters who _____ to work
                                                         27 (bicycle)

    _____ during the last seven to eight years. (It's now over four million.)
    28 (double)

■ New genetic techniques _____ it possible to create high-yield, drought-
29 (make / soon)

and insect-resistant plants of all types.

■ Robots _____ humans in a variety of jobs that _____ dan-
30 (replace / now)                              31 (be / traditionally)

gerous or hazardous to health.

■ Computer networks _____ over 30 million people worldwide, and in
32 (link / currently)

theory, through the use of fiber optics, one-half of the world _____ able to
33 (be / someday)

talk directly with the other half!

**3**   **Review.**   Complete the following passage with appropriate active or passive forms of
the verbs in parentheses. In some cases, you will need to add modal auxiliaries. Some
items may have more than one correct answer.

### Life on Earth

Life on earth _developed_ because the conditions _____ suitable for it. If the
1 (develop)                                    2 (be)

earth _____ smaller or colder, for example, life _____ different forms. If the
3 (be)                                    4 (have)

conditions _____ suitable, no living organisms _____ on earth at all.
5 (not be)                                  6 (develop)

The simplest living creatures _____ of a single living unit, the cell. More
7 (consist)

complex creatures _____ up of hundreds and even millions of cells. However, all
8 (make)

living organisms _____ certain characteristics. These _____ reproduction,
9 (share)                                    10 (include)

response, growth, and use of energy. Plants and animals _____ different only in
11 (be)

the way that the basic activities of life _____ out by each organism.
12 (carry)

Of all the creatures alive on earth, humans _____ the greatest impact. The
13 (have)

impact of humans _____ because we _____ able to think. The power to
14 (come / often)           15 (be)

think _____ us ways both to create and to destroy.
16 (give)

In the past, humans _____ less impact, especially on the environment.
17 (have)

Because early humans _____ from place to place, their movement _____
18 (move)                                    19 (give)

nature a chance to recover. For example, even though humans _____ trees,
20 (cut)

forests _____ to their former size after the humans _____ on.
21 (return / soon)                    22 (move)

Today, nature _____ a chance to recover. Our demands on the earth
                    23 (give / seldom)

_____ steadily. All human activity _____ to require more and more land
24 (increase)                                25 (seem)

and more and more resources. Humans _____ this earth with millions of other
                                        26 (share)

animals and plants, yet we _____ without ever thinking about our impact
                            27 (act / often)

on our world.


**4**    **Review.**    Complete the following passage with *a, an, the,* or *X* to indicate that no article is necessary.


### The Mass Movement of Peoples

Across ____*the*____ globe, _____ people are moving to _____ degree
        1                    2                            3

never before seen in _____ history of _____ world. Today, at least
                      4                      5

_____ 100 million people live outside of _____ country where they were
6                                               7

born. This includes approximately 30 million who have moved to _____ America
                                                                8

or _____ Western Europe since _____ 1980. In fact, _____ 1980s
    9                                10                          11

were _____ years of _____ incredible movement and _____ change
      12                    13                                  14

_____ worldwide.
15

_____ largest migrations of _____ people have not been from
16                                 17

_____ country to _____ country, however. Most migration has been from
18                      19

_____ rural to _____ urban areas. Each year 20 million to 30 million people
20                    21

move from _____ countryside to _____ urban areas.
            22                          23

In _____ past, most migrants were _____ men. Today, however,
    24                                    25

almost _____ half are _____ women or _____ girls, looking for
        26                    27                  28

_____ work and _____ ways to send _____ money back _____
29                    30                        31                      32

home.

Adapted from "Focus on Change," *U.S. News and World Report*

**5**   **Review.**   Choose the correct forms of the words in parentheses. An *X* indicates that no word is necessary. The first one is done as an example.

## Living Together on a Small Planet

The environment is (*X*/(the)) world (that/who) all living things share. It is what is—air,
1                          2

fire, wind, water, life, and sometimes (the/*X*) culture. The environment consists of all
3

the things that act and (is/are) acted upon. Living creatures (is/are) born into the
4                                      5

environment and (are/were) part of it too. Yet there is (no/none) creature (who/whom)
6                              7                    8

perceives all of what is and what happens. A dog perceives things (that/what) we
9

can't, and we perceive and understand (much/many) things beyond (its/it's) world.
10                          11

For a dog, a book isn't much different from a stick, (while/on the other hand) for us,
12

one stick is pretty much like every other stick. There is no world (that/who) is experi-
13

enced (by/from) all living creatures. (Despite/Although) we all live in the same
14                    15

environment, we create many worlds.

We actually know very (little/few) of the world, even of what (does surround/
16                                      17

surrounds) us every day. It is worth (to take/taking) the time (to think/thinking) of the
18                          19

variety of ways in (that/which) the environment could be structured and (to discover/
20                                          21

discovering) how (*X*/do) different living things actually structure it. We are all collec-
22

tions of atoms, specks in (*X*/the) universe, just the right size in our own worlds, giants
23

to fleas, midgets to whales. Our view of the world is only one of (many/much). It
24

enriches (our/us) understanding of ourselves to move away from familiar worlds and
25

attempt to understand the experience of others . . . . The respect for life we can

(gain/to gain) from these efforts (might/might have) in some small way help us work
26                          27

toward (preserving/to preserve) the world we share.
28

Adapted from Judith and Herbert Kohl, *The View from the Oak*

**6**   **Review.**   Work in pairs. Each pair chooses a set of charts: 1A and 1B, 2A and 2B, or 3A and 3B. Take turns asking and answering questions in order to complete the charts. Do not look at each other's charts. After you have completed your charts, work with another pair with different charts. Take turns telling some of the information you learned from the charts.

| The State of the Earth Chart 1A: Selected Countries of the World | | | | | |
|---|---|---|---|---|---|
| **Country** | | Czech Republic | Egypt | | |
| **Capital** | Santiago | | | Libreville | Seoul |
| **Population (1998)** | 14.8 million | | | 1.2 million | |
| **Per capita GDP\* (1997)** | | $5240 | | | $10,550 |
| **Primary products** | | machinery, oil products, iron and steel, wheat, sugar beets, potatoes, rye, corn | textiles, chemicals, petrochemicals, food processing, cotton, rice, beans, fruit, grains | | electronics, ships, textiles, clothing, motor vehicles, rice, barley, vegetables, wheat |
| **Literacy rate** | 92% | | | 70% | |

\**GDP*   gross domestic product

| The State of the Earth Chart 1B: Selected Countries of the World | | | | | |
|---|---|---|---|---|---|
| **Country** | Chile | | | Gabon | South Korea |
| **Capital** | | Prague | Cairo | | |
| **Population (1998)** | | 10.2 million | 65.7 million | | 46.1 million |
| **Per capita GDP\* (1997)** | $4820 | | $1200 | $4120 | |
| **Primary products** | fishing, wood products, iron, steel, grain, onions, beans, potatoes | | | oil products, cocoa, coffee, rice, peanuts, palm products, cassava, bananas | |
| **Literacy rate** | | 99% | 44% | | 96% |

\**GDP*   gross domestic product

| The State of the Earth<br>Chart 2A: Endangered Species | | | | |
|---|---|---|---|---|
| **Common name** | blue whale | giant panda | | | tiger |
| **Location** | polar seas | | Japan | Indonesia | |
| **Description** | | a bearlike mammal, a member of the raccoon family, growing 4–5 feet tall and weighing up to 250 pounds | one of the oldest and largest on earth, a magnificent long-necked marsh bird up to 5 feet tall | | |
| **Diet** | | | | herbivorous, browsing on low shrubs and trees in grasslands | carnivorous, eating birds, deer, cattle, and reptiles |
| **Cause of endangerment** | overhunting | loss of habitat | hunting, loss of habitat | | |
| **Current status** | | | fully protected today, its population is slowly increasing, 33% of which is in zoos | currently protected, although only about 50 remain and are still threatened by poachers | |

| The State of the Earth<br>Chart 2B: Endangered Species | | | | |
|---|---|---|---|---|
| **Common name** | | | Japanese crane | Javanese rhinoceros | |
| **Location** | | China | | | Asia |
| **Description** | largest animal, up to 90 feet in length and 125 tons in weight | | | massive horned and hoofed mammal weighing up to 7000 pounds (3.5 tons) | large, powerful, nonclimbing striped cat up to 650 pounds in weight and 10–13 feet in length |
| **Diet** | krill (a small shrimp-like saltwater animal) | vegetarian (preferring bamboo) although they may eat fish or small rodents | omnivorous, eating wild fruit, seeds, water plants, insects, frogs, and reptiles | | |
| **Cause of endangerment** | | | | hunting | loss of habitat, trophy hunting |
| **Current status** | currently protected, although possibly too late | currently protected in Sichuan, China, where fewer than 1000 remain | | | currently protected in India, where the tiger population is increasing slowly |

### The State of the Earth
### Chart 3A: International Organizations

| Organization | | International Bank for Reconstruction and Development (The World Bank) | International Red Cross | United Nations Children's Fund (UNICEF) | |
|---|---|---|---|---|---|
| **Headquarters** | Rome, Italy | | | New York, New York, U.S.A. | Geneva, Switzerland |
| **Year founded** | | | 1863 | | 1948 |
| **Purpose** | to increase production from farms, forests, and fisheries; improve distribution and nutrition in rural areas | to provide loans and technical assistance for economic development projects in developing countries | | | to collect and share information in medical and scientific areas; to promote international standards for drugs and vaccines |

### The State of the Earth
### Chart 3B: International Organizations

| Organization | Food and Agricultural Organizaiton (FAO) | | | | World Health Organization |
|---|---|---|---|---|---|
| **Headquarters** | | Washington, D.C., U.S.A. | Geneva, Switzerland | | |
| **Year founded** | 1943 | 1944 | | 1946 | |
| **Purpose** | | | to lessen human suffering through disaster relief and neutral aid to war victims | to give aid and development assistance to programs for children and mothers in developing countries | |

## Focus on Testing

*Review of Problem Areas: Chapters 9 to 12*

A variety of problem areas are included in this test. Check your understanding by completing the sample items that follow.

**Part 1:**   Circle the correct completion for the following.

**Example:**   John said that when he _____ satisfied with his work, he would submit the project.

a.   will be

b.   is

c.   would be

d.   was

1.  The doctor urged _____ a vacation.
    a.  her patient take
    b.  her patient taking
    c.  to take
    d.  her patient to take

2.  Could you tell me how long _____ to get there by bus?
    a.  it should take
    b.  should it take
    c.  does it take
    d.  it should have take

3.  If she had known the consequences, she _____ that.
    a.  probably would not do
    b.  would not do probably
    c.  would probably not have done
    d.  would not have probably done

4.  _____ problems with the computer, we weren't able to complete the report on time.
    a.  Because
    b.  Due to
    c.  Although
    d.  Since

5.  It was _____ that I fell asleep before the end.
    a.  so boring movie
    b.  such boring movie
    c.  such boring a movie
    d.  such a boring movie

**Part 2:**   Circle the letter below the underlined word(s) containing an error.

**Example:**   Many <u>individuals</u> experience culture shock <u>whether or not they</u>
                             A                                                          B
<u>fluently speak</u> the language of the country <u>where do they live.</u>
      C                                                            (D)

1.  Winston Churchill <u>says</u> that <u>although</u> he <u>was always</u> ready to learn, he
                              A                 B                    C
<u>was not</u> always ready to be taught.
      D

2.  The Great Pyramid in Egypt, <u>that</u> has stood for over four <u>thousand</u> years,
                                         A                                          B
<u>was built</u> without use of <u>the wheel.</u>
      C                              D

3.  Worldwide demand for grain <u>has increased</u> <u>dramatically</u>, in large part
                                            A                    B
<u>because</u> the demand for <u>more</u> beef production.
      C                            D

4.  If inventors <u>such as</u> James Watt <u>didn't develop</u> engines, the Industrial
                       A                             B
Revolution <u>could</u> never <u>have occurred.</u>
                  C                   D

5.  Flash floods have <u>so</u> tremendous <u>carrying</u> power <u>that</u> <u>even</u> a small flood can
                           A                      B              C      D
move rocks the size of cars.

# Appendices

# Appendix 1

## Irregular Verbs

| Simple Form | Past | Past Participle |
|---|---|---|
| arise | arose | arisen |
| awake | awoke / awaked | awaked / awoken |
| be | was / were | been |
| bear | bore | borne / born |
| beat | beat | beat |
| become | became | become |
| begin | began | begun |
| bend | bent | bent |
| bet | bet | bet |
| bite | bit | bitten |
| bleed | bled | bled |
| blow | blew | blown |
| break | broke | broken |
| breed | bred | bred |
| bring | brought | brought |
| broadcast | broadcast | broadcast |
| build | built | built |
| burst | burst | burst |
| buy | bought | bought |
| cast | cast | cast |
| catch | caught | caught |
| choose | chose | chosen |
| cling | clung | clung |
| come | came | come |
| cost | cost | cost |
| creep | crept | crept |
| cut | cut | cut |
| deal | dealt | dealt |
| dig | dug | dug |
| do | did | done |
| draw | drew | drawn |
| drink | drank | drunk |
| drive | drove | driven |
| eat | ate | eaten |
| fall | fell | fallen |
| feed | fed | fed |
| feel | felt | felt |
| fight | fought | fought |
| find | found | found |

| Simple Form | Past | Past Participle |
|---|---|---|
| flee | fled | fled |
| fly | flew | flown |
| forbid | forbade | forbidden |
| forget | forgot | forgotten |
| forsake | forsook | forsaken |
| freeze | froze | frozen |
| get | got | got / gotten |
| give | gave | given |
| go | went | gone |
| grind | ground | ground |
| grow | grew | grown |
| hang | hung / hanged | hung / hanged |
| have | had | had |
| hear | heard | heard |
| hide | hid | hidden |
| hit | hit | hit |
| hold | held | held |
| hurt | hurt | hurt |
| keep | kept | kept |
| know | knew | known |
| lay | laid | laid |
| lead | led | led |
| leap | leapt | leapt |
| leave | left | left |
| lend | lent | lent |
| let | let | let |
| lie | lay | lain |
| light | lit / lighted | lit / lighted |
| lose | lost | lost |
| make | made | made |
| mean | meant | meant |
| meet | met | met |
| overcome | overcame | overcome |
| pay | paid | paid |
| prove | proved | proved / proven* |
| put | put | put |
| quit | quit | quit |
| read | read | read |
| ride | rode | ridden |
| ring | rang | rung |
| rise | rose | risen |
| run | ran | run |
| say | said | said |
| see | saw | seen |

| Simple Form | Past | Past Participle |
| --- | --- | --- |
| seek | sought | sought |
| sell | sold | sold |
| send | sent | sent |
| set | set | set |
| shake | shook | shaken |
| shoot | shot | shot |
| show | showed | showed / shown* |
| shut | shut | shut |
| sing | sang | sung |
| sink | sank | sunk |
| sit | sat | sat |
| sleep | slept | slept |
| slide | slid | slid |
| slit | slit | slit |
| speak | spoke | spoken |
| spend | spent | spent |
| spin | spun | spun |
| split | split | split |
| spread | spread | spread |
| spring | sprang | sprung |
| stand | stood | stood |
| steal | stole | stolen |
| stick | stuck | stuck |
| sting | stung | stung |
| strike | struck | struck / stricken* |
| strive | strove | striven |
| swear | swore | sworn |
| sweep | swept | swept |
| swim | swam | swum |
| swing | swung | swung |
| take | took | taken |
| teach | taught | taught |
| tear | tore | torn |
| tell | told | told |
| think | thought | thought |
| throw | threw | thrown |
| thrust | thrust | thrust |
| understand | understood | understood |
| upset | upset | upset |
| wake | woke / waked | woken / waked |
| wear | wore | worn |
| weave | wove | woven |
| wind | wound | wound |
| withdraw | withdrew | withdrawn |
| write | wrote | written |

*These participles are most often used with the passive voice.

# Appendix 2

## Spelling Rules and Irregular Noun Plurals

### *Spelling Rules for* -s, -ed, -er, -est, *and* -ing *Endings*

This chart summarizes the basic spelling rules for endings with verbs, nouns, adjectives, and adverbs.

| Rule | Word | -S | -Ed | -Er | -Est | -Ing |
|---|---|---|---|---|---|---|
| For most words, simply add *-s, -ed, -er, -est,* or *-ing* without making any other changes. | clean<br>cool | cleans<br>cools | cleaned<br>cooled | cleaner<br>cooler | cleanest<br>coolest | cleaning<br>cooling |

Spelling changes occur with the following.

| Rule | Word | -S | -Ed | -Er | -Est | -Ing |
|---|---|---|---|---|---|---|
| For words ending in a consonant *+y,* change the *y* to *i* before adding *-s, -ed, -er,* or *-est.*<br><br><br><br><br>Do *not* change or drop the *y* before adding *-ing.* | carry<br>happy<br>lonely<br>study<br>worry | carries<br><br><br>studies<br>worries | carried<br><br><br>studied<br>worried | carrier<br>happier<br>lonelier<br><br>worrier | happiest<br>loneliest | <br><br><br><br><br>carrying<br>studying<br>worrying |
| For most words ending in *e,* drop the *e* before adding *-ed, -er, -est,* or *-ing.*<br><br><br><br>*Exceptions:* | dance<br>late<br>nice<br>save<br>write<br>agree<br>canoe | | danced<br><br><br>saved | dancer<br>later<br>nicer<br>saver<br>writer | latest<br>nicest | dancing<br><br><br>saving<br>writing<br>agreeing<br>canoeing |
| For many words ending in one vowel and one consonant, double the final consonant before adding *-ed, -er, -est,* or *-ing.* These include one syllable words and words with stress on the final syllable. | begin<br>hot<br>mad<br>plan<br>occur<br>refer<br>run<br>shop<br>win | | <br><br><br>planned<br>occurred<br>referred<br><br>shopped | beginner<br>hotter<br>madder<br>planner<br><br><br>runner<br>shopper<br>winner | hottest<br>maddest | beginning<br><br><br>planning<br>occurring<br>referring<br>running<br>shopping<br>winning |

| Rule | Word | -S | -Ed | -Er | -Est | -Ing |
|---|---|---|---|---|---|---|
| In words ending in one vowel and one consonant, do *not* double the final consonant if the last syllable is not stressed.<br><br>*Exceptions:* including words ending in *w*, *x*, or *y* | enter<br>happen<br>open<br>travel<br>visit<br>bus<br>fix<br>play<br>sew | buses | entered<br>happened<br>opened<br>traveled<br>visited<br>bused<br>fixed<br>played<br>sewed | opener<br>traveler<br><br><br>fixer<br>player<br>sewer | | entering<br>happening<br>opening<br>traveling<br>visiting<br>busing<br>fixing<br>playing<br>sewing |
| For most words ending in *f* or *lf*, change the *f* to *v* and add *-es*.<br><br>*Exceptions:* | half<br>loaf<br>shelf<br>belief<br>chief<br>proof<br>roof<br>safe | halves<br>loaves<br>shelves<br>beliefs<br>chiefs<br>proofs<br>roofs<br>safes | halved<br><br>shelved | shelver | | halving<br><br>shelving |
| For words ending in *ch*, *sh*, *s*, *x*, *z*, and sometimes *o*, and *-es*.<br><br><br><br><br><br><br><br>*Exceptions:* | church<br>wash<br>class<br>fix<br>quiz<br>tomato<br>zero<br>dynamo<br>ghetto<br>monarch<br>piano<br>portfolio<br>radio<br>studio | churches<br>washes<br>classes<br>fixes<br>quizzes<br>tomatoes<br>zeroes<br>dynamos<br>ghettos<br>monarchs<br>pianos<br>portfolios<br>radios<br>studios | | | | |

## Irregular Noun Plurals

| | | | | | | | |
|---|---|---|---|---|---|---|---|
| person | people | foot | feet | deer | deer | series | series |
| child | children | tooth | teeth | fish | fish | species | species |
| man | men | | | goose | geese | | |
| woman | women | | | ox | oxen | | |

# Appendix 3

## *The* with Proper Nouns

| With *the* | | Without *the* | |
|---|---|---|---|
| *The* is used when the class of noun (continent, country, etc.) comes before the name: *the* + class + *of* + name. | the continent of Asia<br>the United States of America<br>the U.S.A. | *The* is not used with names of planets, continents, countries, states, provinces, cities, and streets. | Mars<br>Africa<br>Antarctica<br>Russia<br>Ohio<br>Quebec<br>Austin<br>State Street |
| *The* is used with most names of regions. | the West<br>the Midwest<br>the equator | | |
| *Exceptions:* | New England<br>southern (northern, etc.) | *Exceptions:* | (the) earth<br>the world<br>the Netherlands |
| *The* is used with plural islands, lakes, and mountains. | the Hawaiian Islands<br>the Great Lakes<br>the Alps | *The* is not used with singular islands, lakes, and mountains. | Oahu<br>Fiji<br>Lake Superior<br>Mt. Whitney |
| *The* is used with oceans, seas, rivers, canals, deserts, jungles, forests, and bridges.* | the Pacific Ocean<br>the Persian Gulf<br>the Mississippi River<br>the Suez Canal<br>the Sahara Desert<br>the Black Forest<br>the Golden Gate Bridge | *Exceptions:* | the Isle of Wight<br>the Matterhorn (and other mountains with German names that are used in English) |
| *The* is generally used when the word *college, university,* or *school* comes before the name: *the* + ... + *of* + name. | the University of California<br>the Rhode Island School of Design | *The* is not used when the name of a college or university comes before the word *college* or *university*. | Boston University<br>Amherst College |
| | | *Exception:* | the Sorbonne |
| *The* is used with adjectives of nationality and other adjectives that function as nouns. | the Germans<br>the Japanese<br>the rich<br>the poor<br>the strong | *The* is not used with names of languages.<br>Note: *The* is used with the word *language: the German language.* | German<br>Japanese |
| *The* is used in dates when the number comes before the month. | the twenty-eighth of March | *The* is not used in dates when the month begins the phrase. | March 28 |
| *The* is used with decades, centuries, and eras. | the 1990s<br>the 1800s<br>the Dark Ages | *The* is not used with specific years. | 1951<br>1890 |
| *The* is used with names of museums and libraries. | the Museum of Modern Art<br>the Chicago Public Library | | |

*The class name is often omitted with well-known oceans, deserts, and rivers: *the Atlantic, the Nile.*

# Appendix 4

## Formation of Statements and Questions

*The Simple Present and Past Tenses and Have as a Main Verb**

| | Question Word | Auxiliary Verb | Subject | Auxiliary Verb (and Negative) | Main Verb | Auxiliary Verb | Pronoun |
|---|---|---|---|---|---|---|---|
| **Affirmative Statements** | | | You (I, We, They) | | study. | | |
| | | | Ted (He, She, It) | | studies. | | |
| | | | She (We, They, etc.) | | studied. | | |
| **Negative Statements** | | | You | don't (didn't) | study. | | |
| | | | Ted | doesn't (didn't) | study. | | |
| **Tag Questions** | | | You | | study, | don't | you? |
| | | | You | don't | study, | do | you? |
| | | | Ted | | studies, | doesn't | he? |
| | | | Ted | doesn't | study, | does | he? |
| **Yes/No Questions** | | Do(n't) | you | | study? | | |
| | | Does(n't) | Ted | | study? | | |
| | | Did(n't) | she | | study? | | |
| **Short Responses** | | Yes, | I | do (did). | | | |
| | | No, | I | don't (didn't). | | | |
| | | Yes, | he | does (did). | | | |
| | | No, | he | doesn't (didn't). | | | |
| **Information Questions** | Where | do | you | | study? | | |
| | When | does | Ted | | study? | | |
| | Who | | | | studied? | | |

*Have as a main verb forms statements and questions in the same way as other simple present and past tense verbs.

## The Continuous and Perfect Tenses, the Modal Auxiliaries, and Be as a Main Verb*

| | Question Word | Auxiliary Verb | Subject | Auxiliary Verb (and Negative) | Main Verb | Auxiliary Verb | Pronoun |
|---|---|---|---|---|---|---|---|
| **Affirmative and Negative Statements** | | | Ted | is (was) (not) | studying. | | |
| | | | Ted | should (may, etc.) (not) | study. | | |
| | | | Ted | has (had) (not) | studied. | | |
| **Tag Questions** | | | Ted | is | studying, | isn't | he? |
| | | | Ted | isn't | studying, | is | he? |
| | | | Ted | should | study, | shouldn't | he? |
| | | | Ted | shouldn't | study, | should | he? |
| | | | Ted | has | studied, | hasn't | he? |
| | | | Ted | hasn't | studied, | has | he? |
| **Yes/No Questions** | | Is(n't) | Ted | | studying? | | |
| | | Should(n't) | Ted | | study? | | |
| | | Has(n't) | Ted | | studied? | | |
| **Short Responses** | | Yes, | he is. | No, he isn't. | | | |
| | | Yes, | he should. | No, he shouldn't. | | | |
| | | Yes, | he has. | No, he hasn't. | | | |
| **Information Questions** | Where | is | Ted | | studying? | | |
| | What | should | Ted | | study? | | |
| | How long | has | Ted | | studied? | | |
| | Who | | | is | studying? | | |

*Be as a main verb forms statements and questions in the same way as the auxiliary be does.

# Appendix 5

## Modal Auxiliaries and Related Structures
*Present / Future Time Frame*

| Modal Auxiliary | Function | Examples |
|---|---|---|
| can | ability | **Can** you touch your toes without bending your knees? |
| | informal request | **Can** you teach me to swim? |
| could | request | **Could** I make an appointment with Dr. Horiuchi? |
| | possibility | Perhaps Noriko **could** take you to the dentist. |
| may | request | **May** I leave now? |
| | permission | Yes, you **may.** |
| | possibility | Sulaiman **may** be sick. |
| might | possibility | He **might** have the flu. |
| must | probability | He **must** be at the doctor's because he isn't at home. |
| | need | You **must** take this medicine on an empty stomach. |
| must not | strong need not to do something | You **must not** drive while you are taking this medicine. |
| ought to | advice | She **ought to** get more rest. |
| | expectation | The doctor **ought to** be here soon. |
| shall | request | **Shall** I get a bandage? |
| | intention | We **shall** probably go to the hospital later today. |
| should | advice | He **should** give up smoking. |
| | expectation | The swelling **should** go down in a few hours. |
| will | intention | I **will** get more exercise from now on! |
| would | request | **Would** you get me a bandage, please? |
| | | **Would** you mind getting me a bandage? |
| | preference | **Would** you like soda pop? |
| | | I **would rather** have juice than soda pop. |
| be able to | ability | **Are** you **able to** swim three miles? |
| had better | advice | You **had better** not swim so soon after lunch. |
| have to (have got to) | need | I **have to (have got to)** lose weight. |
| don't / doesn't have to | lack of need | We **don't have to** get X rays. |

| Modal Auxiliary | Function | Examples |
|---|---|---|
| could | ability | I **could** not swim until last year. |
| could have | possibility | I **could have** taken lessons sooner. |
| may have | possibility | They **may** already **have** gone to the hospital. |
| might have | possibility | Juan **might have** injured his back when he fell. |
| must have | probability | He **must have** been in a lot of pain. |
| ought to have | advice not taken | He **ought to have** been more careful. |
| | expectation | The doctor **ought to have** called us by now. |
| should have | advice not taken | **Should** we **have** waited for help? |
| | expectation | Someone **should have** arrived by now. |
| would | habits | When I was younger, I **would** always faint at the sight of blood. |
| would have | preference | I **would have** liked to visit her. |
| | | She **would rather** not **have** visited the hospital. |
| | intention not completed | Under other circumstances, **would** you **have** had that operation? |
| be able to | ability | Nadia was **able to** run two miles. |
| didn't have to | lack of need | We **didn't have to** practice on Monday because of the rain. |
| had to | need | We **had to** practice twice as long yesterday because we missed practice on Monday. |
| used to | habits | We **used to** eat a lot of sugar, but we don't anymore. |

# Appendix 6

## Summary of Gerunds and Infinitives
### *Verbs Often Followed by Gerunds*

| | | | |
|---|---|---|---|
| admit | She **admitted** stealing the money. | dislike | He really **dislikes** getting up early. |
| anticipate | We **anticipate** arriving late. | dread | She **dreads** going to the dentist. |
| appreciate | I really **appreciated** getting your card. | enjoy | We always **enjoy** traveling. |
| avoid | She **avoids** stepping on cracks—a superstition. | escape | We narrowly **escaped** hitting the other car. |
| | | finish | Have you **finished** writing that paper? |
| be worth | I am sure it **is worth** waiting. | forgive | I can **forgive** his cheating, but I can't forgive his lying. |
| can't help | He **can't help** getting upset about that. | | |
| consider | Have you **considered** moving? | imagine | Can you **imagine** living in Bogotá? |
| delay | They **delayed** starting the game because of the rain. | involve | This job **involves** meeting a lot of people. |
| | | keep (on) | **Keep on** working until I tell you to stop. |
| deny | He **denied** speeding. | mention | Did she **mention** quitting her job? |

| | | | |
|---|---|---|---|
| **miss** | I **miss** hearing your voice. | **risk** | She **risked** losing all her money in that deal. |
| **postpone** | Will they **postpone** calling a meeting? | **spend (time)** | Do you **spend** much **time** doing your homework? |
| **practice** | A good tennis player has to **practice** serving. | **suggest** | They **suggested** having a picnic. |
| **recommend** | I **recommend** taking some aspirin. | **tolerate** | I can't **tolerate** listening to rock music. |
| **regret** | I **regret** saying that. | **understand** | Do you **understand** his not calling? |

## Verbs Often Followed by Infinitives

| | | | |
|---|---|---|---|
| **afford** | We can't **afford** to go. | **intend** | I **intend** to stop there for several days. |
| **agree** | They **agreed** to help. | **know how** | Do you **know how** to play squash. |
| **appear** | She **appeared** to be calm. | **learn** | She is **learning** to play tennis. |
| **be** | We **were** to do the homework in Chapter 3. | **manage** | Somehow he **managed** to finished the race. |
| **be able** | **Were** you **able** to finish the work? | **offer** | They **offered** to help us. |
| **be supposed** | You **were supposed** to do it yesterday. | **plan** | We **planned** to leave earlier |
| **care** | I don't **care** to go. | **prepare** | They **prepared** to get on board the plane. |
| **decide** | He **decided** to stay. | **pretend** | He **pretended** not to notice us. |
| **deserve** | She **deserves** to get a high grade. | **refuse** | I **refuse** to get up at 5:00 A.M.! |
| **fail** | They **failed** to make the announcement. | **seem** | He **seems** to be upset. |
| **forget** | I **forgot** to buy eggs. | **tend** | She **tends** to forget things. |
| **happen** | Did he **happen** to stop by? | **threaten** | The employee **threatened** to quit. |
| **have** | I **have** to leave. | **volunteer** | Several people **volunteered** to help us. |
| **hesitate** | Don't **hesitate** to call! | **wait** | She **waited** for the letter carrier to come. |
| **hope** | We **hope** to visit Rome next spring. | **wish** | We **wished** to go, but we couldn't. |

## Subject + verb + (optional noun or pronoun) + infinitive

| | | | |
|---|---|---|---|
| **ask** | We **asked** to come. We **asked** them to come. | **promise** | She **promised** to help. She **promised** her mother to help. |
| **beg** | He **begged** to go. He **begged** us to go. | **want** | They **want** to leave. They **want** us to leave. |
| **dare** | I **dare** to go. I **dared** him to go. | **would like** | He **would like** to stay. He **would like** you to stay. |
| **expect** | I **expect** to finish soon. I **expect** them to finish soon. | **use** | They **used** to live there. (habitual past) They **used** a hammer to fix the table. (method) |
| **need** | I **need** to go. I **need** you to go. | | |

## Subject + verb + noun or pronoun + infinitive

| | | | |
|---|---|---|---|
| **advise*** | The doctor **advised** me to rest. | **order** | I **am ordering** you to stop! |
| **allow*** | He won't **allow** you to swim. | **permit*** | Will they **permit** us to camp here? |
| **cause*** | The accident **caused** me to faint. | **persuade** | Perhaps we can **persuade** them to let us go. |
| **convince** | She **convinced** us to try again. | **remind** | Did you **remind** her to buy milk? |
| **encourage*** | I **encourage** you to study languages. | **require** | The school **required** us to wear uniforms. |
| **force** | The hijacker **forced** them to land the plane. | **teach*** | He **taught** me to play tennis. |
| **get** | He **got** them to pay ransom. | **tell** | I **told** him not to come. |
| **hire** | We **hired** you to do the job. | **urge** | We **urge** you to change your mind. |
| **invite** | They **invited** us to come. | **warn** | I **am warning** you to stop! |

* These verbs are followed by gerunds if no noun or pronoun object is used after the main verb.

## Verb + gerund or infinitive (same meaning)

| | | | |
|---|---|---|---|
| **begin** | She **began** to work (working) on the project. | **hate** | He **hates** to play (playing) golf. |
| **can't bear** | I **can't bear** to see (seeing) her work so much. | **like** | I **like** to play (playing) tennis. |
| | | **love** | Mary **loves** to read (reading) novels. |
| **can't stand** | She **can't stand** to stay (staying) alone at night. | **neglect** | We **neglected** to tell (telling) her about that. |
| | | **prefer** | I **prefer** to go (going) alone. |
| **continue** | They'll **continue** to practice (practicing) several days more. | **start** | We **started** to worry (worrying) about the situation. |

## Verb + gerund or infinitive (different meanings)

| | | | |
|---|---|---|---|
| **mean** | I **meant** to finish the project sooner. This **means** delaying the project. | **remember** | Did you **remember** to tell her? I **remember** telling her about it, but she forgot. |
| **quit (stop)** | He **quit (stopped)** to take a long break. We **quit (stopped)** taking breaks in order to leave work earlier. | **try** | We **tried** to call you, but the phone was out of order. I **tried** calling, and then I decided to write you a note. |

# Index